THE SUPREME
VEGETARIAN COOKBOOK

Rose Elliot is Britain's foremost vegetarian cookery writer and her books have won her popular acclaim in all parts of the English-speaking world. Her first book, *Simply Delicious*, published in 1967, was widely praised in the press and more books followed including *Not Just a Load of Old Lentils*, *Vegetarian Dishes of the World*, *Gourmet Vegetarian Cooking* and her all-time best seller, *The Bean Book*. *Rose Elliot's Vegetarian Mother and Baby Book* arose from her personal experience as mother of three daughters, and her interest in nutrition generally led to *Your Very Good Health*. Recently, Rose has published a number of books, including *The Zodiac Cookbook*, *Vegetarian Slimming* and *Kitchen Pharmacy*.

Rose has been in the vanguard of the revolution in our eating habits in recent years, as more and more people consume less meat and take greater interest in healthy eating. She frequently contributes to national magazines, gives cookery demonstrations and broadcasts on radio and television. She lives with her husband, Robert, and youngest daughter, Claire, in Hampshire. Rose is also a professional astrologer and, with her husband, runs a computer-based astrological service which provides high quality personality profiles, forecasts and compatibility charts. (For more details, please send SAE to Rose Elliot, PO Box 16, Eastleigh SO5 6BH.)

Other books by Rose Elliot

The Bean Book
Beanfeast
Cheap and Easy
Gourmet Vegetarian Cooking
The New Simply Delicious
Not Just a Load of Old Lentils
Rose Elliot's Book of Beans and Lentils
Rose Elliot's Book of Breads
Rose Elliot's Book of Cakes
Rose Elliot's Book of Fruits
Rose Elliot's Book of Pasta
Rose Elliot's Book of Salads
Rose Elliot's Book of Savoury Flans and Pies
Rose Elliot's Book of Vegetables
Rose Elliot's Mother and Baby Book
Vegetarian Dishes of the World
Your Very Good Health
Complete Vegetarian Cookbook
The Green Age Diet

Rose Elliot

THE SUPREME VEGETARIAN COOKBOOK

Fontana
An Imprint of HarperCollins*Publishers*

Fontana
An Imprint of HarperCollins*Publishers*
77–85 Fulham Palace Road,
Hammersmith, London W6 8JB

Published by Fontana 1990
3 5 7 9 8 6 4

First published as *Rose Elliot's Vegetarian Cookery* by
Collins 1988

Copyright © text Rose Elliot 1988
Copyright © photographs Collins 1988

The Author asserts the moral right to
be identified as the author of this work

ISBN 0 00 637573 1

Set in Palatino

Printed in Great Britain by
HarperCollinsManufacturing Glasgow

Acknowledgements

I would like to express my warmest appreciation to all the people who helped to create the first edition of the book. To my agent at that time, Vivienne Schuster, and to Joan Clibbon and Robin Wood of Collins, for giving me the opportunity to write it and for their care and support throughout the project. A very special 'thank you' to my text editor, Helen Dore, for sharing completely my aspirations for the book and helping me to realize them, and for generously sharing many delicious recipe ideas; to Barbara Dixon, my editor, for her hours of hard work on the manuscript and for checking many elusive details; to Janet James, Art Director, and to Nick Carman for his superb photographs and for making the photographic sessions such a delight (and a special thank you to Nick's assistant, Edward Allwright); to the home economists, Judy Bugg and Janice Murfitt, for making the food look and taste so good; and my grateful thanks to D. MacLean of Dornock Farm, Crieff, for his help and information for the potatoes section of the book; to my daughters Margaret and Claire for help with recipe testing and to my husband Robert and daughter Katy for understanding and support throughout the project.

In addition, I would like to thank all those who have been involved in creating this paperback version of the original colour book. My special thanks to Kelly Davis for her enthusiasm, good ideas and very thoughtful editing; also to other members of the editorial and design team, Juliet Van Oss, Vera Brice, Sarah Smith and Maureen Kearney.

Contents

Ingredients

Recipes

Menu Ideas

Special Menus

Notes on Measurements

Both metric and Imperial measurements are given throughout this book. As long as you keep to one set of measurements or the other in a recipe you should have no problems.

With liquids, I have used fluid ounces as the Imperial equivalent to millilitres, taking 300 ml/10 fl oz as a ½-pint measure, 400 ml/15 fl oz as ¾-pint measure and 600 ml/20 fl oz as 1 pint. Measure liquids with a plastic measuring jug marked in millilitres, pints and fluid ounces.

The eggs used are free-range and always standard, size 3.

MEASUREMENT EQUIVALENTS			
Metric	*Imperial*	*Metric*	*Imperial*
Grammes (g)	Ounces (oz)	Millilitres (ml)	Fluid Ounces (fl oz)
15	½	25	1
25	1	50	2
40	1½	75	3
50	2	125	4
65	2½	150	5 (¼ pt)
75	3	175	6
100	4 (¼ lb)	200	7
150	5	225	8
175	6	250	9
200	7	300	10 (½ pt)
225	8 (½ lb)	325	11
250	9	350	12
300	10	375	13
325	11	450	15 (¾ pt)
350	12 (¾ lb)	475	16
375	13	500	17
400	14	600	20 (1 pt)
425	15		
450	16 (1 lb)		

Note for Australian/New Zealand users

I should like to take this opportunity to say how pleased I am that this book will be available in Australia and New Zealand, and to extend a warm welcome to all readers in those countries. I believe that you will be able to obtain most of the ingredients without difficulty, and I do hope that you will enjoy the recipes. I think that you should find the measurements straightforward, but please note that British standard tablespoons and teaspoons, 15 ml and 5 ml respectively, have been used in the recipes, and are level unless otherwise stated. The Australian/NZ tablespoon holds 20 ml. A teaspoon is standard to all three countries.

OVEN TEMPERATURE CHART

The oven temperatures given throughout this book are for a conventional oven. Fan assisted (circofan or circotherm) ovens generally require a reduction in temperature and cooking time, and you should refer to the oven handbook.

Temperature	Centigrade (C)	Fahrenheit (F)	Gas Mark
	70	150	–
	80	175	–
	100	200	–
Very cool	110	225	¼
	120	250	½
	140	275	1
Cool	150	300	2
Warm	170	325	3
Moderate	180	350	4
Fairly hot	190	375	5
	200	400	6
Hot	220	425	7
	230	450	8
Very hot	250	500	9

MEASUREMENT EQUIVALENTS FOR BAKING TINS

mm	in.
3	⅛
5	¼

cm	in.
1	½
2	¾
2·5	1
3	1½
5	2
6	2½
8	3
9	3½
10	4
13	5
15	6
18	7
20	8
22	8½
23	9
24	9½
25	10
28	11
30	12
32	12½
33	13
35	14
37·5	15
40	16

Introduction

This book has grown out of over twenty years of cooking vegetarian food, and originating, testing and also demonstrating vegetarian recipes. During that time I have had the delight of seeing the great increase in interest in this style of cooking, with a dramatic and continuing swing towards vegetarianism, and many people becoming 'demi-veg', if not changing completely.

I like to think that vegetarian cookery has now become a cuisine in its own right. That cuisine embraces non-meat and non-fish dishes from all over the world, as well as wholefood, macrobiotic and its own idiosyncratic recipes. It happily embraces ingredients as different as tofu and wholewheat pasta, tempeh and rice noodles, Indian spices and sea vegetables, pulses and exotic fruits. The only qualification is that fish and other animals are not used. The result is a lively, colourful, eclectic mix which I hope I have represented here.

One of the delights of being involved with cookery is that it is a living art; novel ingredients, new recipes, a dash of herbs here, a sprinkling of spice there, an unfamiliar ingredient, spark off fresh ideas, inspire creativity . . . Ideas are constantly changing and evolving, as are our shopping and eating habits.

In writing this book, my aim has been to provide the information, recipes and techniques needed in vegetarian cookery, both for those who are new to it, and for more experienced cooks who want to try something different. For those strict vegetarians, vegans, I have also included many recipes and these are marked with a V, together with vegan versions of standard recipes where possible. There is every reason for vegan food to be as exciting and delicious as vegetarian food.

The initial inspiration for the book was, for me, as is so often the case for cooks, the marketplace. Week after week, as I did my shopping, I noticed the increasing range of wonderful, often weird and wonderful, ingredients, particularly fruit, vegetables, nuts, beans, herbs and spices.

These were a godsend to vegetarian cookery, rooted as it is so deeply in the raw ingredients, and dependent on herbs and spices for flavouring. What was needed was information on identifying them, storing, preparing and cooking them . . . And so the Ingredients section of this book was born. This led on naturally to the Recipe section, with more detailed ways of using the ingredients.

Although I hope this book will be used as a reference book, I decided to include many of the comments, tips and techniques near the appropriate recipe, rather than in a separate chapter. This way they have relevance and immediacy, and too much formality is avoided. I do hope you will find the arrangement good to use.

The book begins with information on the nutritional side of vegetarian and vegan cookery, and how to plan meals which are well-balanced, healthy and nourishing, as well as pleasant to eat. This theme of meal-planning is continued both in the Menu Ideas and in the Special Menus. I hope you'll enjoy them, and, indeed, the whole book.

Nutrition

In vegetarian eating, meat, fish and poultry are replaced by fresh-tasting meals based on vegetables and herbs, grains and pasta, dried beans and lentils, fresh fruits and nuts, with or without dairy produce. Many people are enjoying the benefits of eating like this some of the time, while continuing to eat meat and fish occasionally: these are the demi-vegetarians. Others are switching completely to vegetarianism, and some are going still further, excluding all dairy produce, and becoming vegans. Any of these ways of eating can supply all the nutrients needed for vibrant good health. In fact many people find their health improves when they become vegetarians. The key lies in planning meals based on a good variety of fresh, unprocessed foods.

EATING FOR HEALTH

Studies of people in different parts of the world have shown that those who eat mainly unrefined foods, high in fibre, low in sugar and fat, do not tend to succumb to illnesses like high blood pressure, heart disease, diverticulitis, cancer of the bowel and diabetes. Experts now agree that a healthy diet is one which is high in fibre and low in fat, sugar and salt. This was the kind of food which was commonly eaten in Britain before industrialization and mass food production. Contrary to popular opinion, meat was not eaten in large quantities by the majority of the population for whom cereals and vegetables were staples. Vegetarian eating, with its emphasis on cereals, pulses and vegetables, is not therefore as far removed from what our forebears ate as is sometimes thought, and is naturally high-fibre, low-fat and low-sugar.

Protein

Part of every body cell, protein is essential for healthy growth and repair of cells, for reproduction and protection against infection. Daily requirements are, however, small and there is no problem in getting enough protein on a vegetarian or vegan diet. The main sources of protein for vegetarians are:

☐ *Dairy* cheese, milk and milk products such as yogurt; eggs

☐ *Nuts and seeds* such as almonds, cashew nuts, hazelnuts, brazil nuts, walnuts, pine nuts, pecan nuts and peanuts; sunflower seeds, sesame seeds and pumpkin seeds

☐ *Pulses* dried peas, beans and lentils, including soya beans and products

☐ *Cereals and their products* such as rice, oatmeal, wholewheat flour, pasta

Complementary Proteins

Protein consists of about twenty-two parts, called amino-acids. Eight of these are specially important, because they cannot be manufactured by the body. These are called the essential amino-acids. Some foods, such as eggs and oatmeal, contain these in nearly the right proportions for the body to use straightaway. Other foods, particularly dried beans and lentils and most cereals, do not have them in such convenient proportions. But this doesn't matter, because during digestion the amino-acids from all the foods eaten at the same meal get mixed up and the body puts them together again in the right proportions. So even if a protein doesn't contain exactly the right amino-acid balance, the chances are that the shortfall will be supplied by something else eaten at the same meal — such as potato, a green vegetable, or milk in a cup of tea or coffee.

Proteins from the four groups listed above complement each other so you can make more protein available to yourself by eating foods from two or more of the groups at the same meal, such as lentil soup with a wholewheat roll. This is not difficult, but even if you don't mix proteins like this, you are not likely to go short of protein unless you are living on a near-starvation diet.

Carbohydrate

Carbohydrates are used in the body for energy. They are found in starches and sugars which are present in grains, flour and products made from these, such as bread, biscuits and cakes; and in sugar, honey, jams and preserves. Potatoes are also a good source, while most vegetables (especially pulses), milk and nuts contain small amounts. Many carbohydrates, in their natural, unrefined state, also contain fibre. This means that the body can draw the sugar out of the fibre gradually, as it passes through the digestive tract, resulting in a steady stream of energy.

THE SUGAR QUESTION

Refined sugar is an energy food — but that is all it is. It does not supply fibre, to regulate the pace at which the body absorbs it, neither does it contain any vitamins or minerals. It is 'empty calories'. Real barbados sugar — the sticky, molasses type — does contain some minerals, vitamins and trace elements. Honey does not contain fibre, but its sugar is mainly in a form which is slowly absorbed by the body. All forms of sweetening, honey included, are best used with discretion. Make sure that any sugar you eat is through positive choice, such as the occasional favourite pudding, rather than through unquestioned habit, such as sprinkling it unthinkingly into tea or coffee or over breakfast cereal. The majority of the recipes in this book are low in sugar, but some 'sweet indulgences' are included for the occasional treat, which in my opinion does no harm at all — indeed, is to be recommended, so you don't get too rigid and fanatical — if you eat healthily most of the time.

Fat Facts

Fats and oils have been an essential ingredient throughout history — the Egyptians even extracted oil from radishes. There are two sources of fat: animals and plants. The only animal fats used in a vegetarian diet are those found in egg yolks or milk or its products such as cream, butter and cheese. The rest of the fats are of plant origin and include a range of oils and products made from these, namely margarine and hard vegetable fats. Fats can be saturated, unsaturated or polyunsaturated, depending on their chemical structure.

Saturated fats are the ones which are solid at room temperature. Chemically, all their 'bonds' have been filled with hydrogen atoms. Most animal fats are saturated and are thought more likely to raise the level of fats in the blood. Unsaturated fats are thick, but not solid, at room temperature. These fats have room for a few more hydrogen atoms. Unsaturated fats are thought to have a neutral effect on the level of fat in the blood: they do not lower it, but neither do they raise it. Olive oil is an example of an unsaturated fat, and countries where this is the main fat used, such as Italy and Spain, have a much lower incidence of heart disease than countries where saturated fats are used.

Polyunsaturated fats are completely liquid at room temperature. These could take many more hydrogen atoms. Many vegetable oils, including safflower, sunflower, corn and soya, are polyunsaturated and thought to help in lowering the amount of fat in the blood. Polyunsaturated fats can be made more solid, and similar to, but not chemically the same as, saturated fats, by filling up the spare bonds with hydrogen. This process is called hydrogenation and is used in the manufacture of margarines and hard vegetable fats. However, fats which have been hardened in this way may be more harmful to the body than ones which are naturally saturated.

The unsaturated fats are generally considered to be healthiest, although this is a complicated issue, and there are many experts (and I agree with them) who consider that the naturalness of butter makes it preferable to margarine which is a processed food. However, most authorities agree that the important thing is to reduce our total fat intake. Although a small amount of fat is needed for health, most people in developed countries eat too much fat and of the type which the body does not require. Much of this may be in the form of 'hidden fat' in foods like pies, crisps, biscuits, chocolate and cakes. Some foods, such as milk, can be confusing, because although the percentage of fat is low, they are eaten in relatively large quantities, and the fat intake increases. The kind of fat which the body does need is found in cold-pressed unsaturated oils, sunflower seeds and margarines marked 'linoleic-cis'. Apart from these, I think the important thing is to be aware of the amount of fat you're eating and to reduce it where you'll miss it least. Cereal and whole-grain dishes, pasta, pulses, fruit and vegetables are all low in fat, and including generous quantities of these in your meals will automatically reduce the amount of fat you eat.

FIBRE

Fibre is found only in fruit and vegetable products; it is the wood, cellulose and gums which make up their structure. Dairy produce does not contain fibre, nor do meat and fish, although they have a chewy texture. Fibre is needed to enable the digestive system to function effectively and is therefore essential for good health. A typical vegetarian diet is naturally high in fibre. Good sources are peas and beans (both dried and fresh); most vegetables, especially cabbage, carrots, jacket potatoes, spinach and sweetcorn; oats and other whole-grain cereals, including products made from them such as wholewheat bread; dried fruits, especially apricots; fresh fruits, especially apples, bananas, black-berries and raspberries. Try to include at least one good source of fibre at every meal.

Minerals and Trace Elements

Iron

Iron is essential for making red blood cells, and a lack of iron in the diet can lead to anaemia. This is one of the nutrients which needs watching although a properly balanced vegetarian diet can provide quite enough. Iron is found in all pulses, especially lentils and soya beans; in whole grains and their products such as wholewheat bread and pasta; nuts and seeds, especially pistachios, pumpkin and sesame seeds; dark green leafy veget-ables and dried fruits, of which apricots and prunes (also prune juice) are particularly good sources. Seaweeds are also rich sources, as are brewer's yeast, molasses, wheatgerm and egg yolk.

Zinc

An important trace element, zinc is essential for healthy growth and healing, for sexual maturity and reproduction and the digestion of protein and carbohydrate. A shortage of zinc often manifests as white flecks on the fingernails, and sometimes in skin problems. There also seems to be evidence of a link between a shortage of zinc and the 'slimmers'' diseases anorexia nervosa and bulimia. Whole grains appear to be good sources of zinc, as do pulses, but these all contain a substance called phytic acid which can bind the zinc so that we cannot absorb it all. It is not known to what extent this happens, and there is evidence that the body quickly adapts to the phytic acid when whole grains are eaten regularly. Also, when bread is made with yeast, the proving process appears to inhibit the phytic acid. Adding some vitamin c to the dough also helps. The best sources of zinc for vegetarians and vegans are wheatgerm, oatmeal, peanuts and brewer's yeast, and, for those eating dairy produce, cheese and skimmed milk. Dried figs are a good source, as are nuts and seeds (especially sesame seeds and pumpkin seeds), sweetcorn and peas. Small but useful amounts are found in most green and yellow fruit and vegetables, such as spinach, asparagus and mango.

Calcium

Calcium is essential for the healthy formation of bones and teeth, and for normal functioning of bones, nerves, muscles and heart. The best sources are cheese, milk and milk products. Other good sources are pulses, especially soya beans and flour; eggs; dried fruit, especially figs; almonds, sesame seeds and spread (tahini), sunflower seeds; most dark green vegetables, especially watercress and broccoli; brewer's yeast, carob and molasses. Seaweeds, especially hiziki, arame and wakame, are particularly rich and Japanese bancha twig tea, from Japanese stores and some health shops, is another useful source. In areas where the water is hard, some calcium is absorbed from this. White bread, biscuits and cakes, and brown (but not whole-wheat) bread supply useful amounts because the flour is fortified with calcium. Wholewheat flour and bread contains a small amount of calcium but it is not known how well the body can absorb it because of the phytic acid also present.

A balanced vegetarian diet, including some cheese and milk, is unlikely to be short of calcium. Vegans, or vegetarians eating very little dairy produce, need to include plenty of the calcium-rich non-dairy sources mentioned above.

Magnesium

Magnesium is needed for many important roles in the body, including the metabolism of carbohydrates. It is found in a wide range of foods, and is not damaged by heat, though it is soluble, so may be lost if the water in which vegetables have been cooked is thrown away. A deficiency of this mineral alone is rare, except as a result of disease or where there is general malnutrition. The best sources are nuts and seeds, whole grains and products made from them, dried fruits, pulses (especially soya beans), brewer's yeast, fresh fruit and vegetables.

Iodine

This is a vital trace element, essential for the healthy functioning of the thyroid gland. The most reliable sources of iodine are seaweed and iodized sea salt. Sea salt contains iodine but it disappears during storage. Kelp tablets are a useful source, too.

THE SALT QUESTION

We all need some sodium, the main ingredient of table salt, but because of the amount of salt added during processing, cooking and at the table, most of us have two or three times more than is considered healthy. Too much salt can encourage high blood pressure, which, in turn, can make us more vulnerable to heart attacks and strokes. Eating natural high-fibre foods, such as fresh vegetables, pulses and cereals, while using salt sparingly, helps protect against these problems. Personally I like to use sea salt in small quantities rather than one of the salt substitutes or potassium-based salts. Using fresh herbs, spices and lemon juice as seasonings also helps to reduce the need for salt. It is surprising how quickly you get used to the flavour of less salty food.

Vitamins

Vitamin A

Vitamin A is needed for healthy skin, eyesight, hair, nails and mucous membranes, and for resistance to infection. It is found in dairy produce, eggs and margarine, and in all dark green and some yellow vegetables, as carotene, a substance which the body can convert into vitamin A. Carrots are a particularly rich source of carotene, as are apricots (fresh, canned and dried). Prunes, cantaloupe melons, red peppers, spinach, parsley and watercress are also good sources. A normal vegetarian diet, with its emphasis on fresh fruit and vegetables, is unlikely to be deficient in vitamin A.

B Vitamins

The B vitamins are important for the metabolism of other foods, the healthy working of the nervous system, the production of red blood cells and many other vital functions. They are found in whole-grain cereals and products made from them such as wholewheat bread and pasta. Wheatgerm, brewer's yeast and yeast extracts are other excellent sources of B vitamins, as are nuts and seeds, eggs, dried and fresh peas and beans, leafy green vegetables, potatoes, avocados, dried and fresh fruits.

The best sources of B_1, thiamin, are dried and fresh peas and beans, especially soya beans and flour, wheatgerm, oranges, dried fruit, sunflower seeds and brazil nuts.

Milk is a major source of vitamin B_2, riboflavin, so vegans and vegetarians who are not eating much dairy produce need to make frequent use of other foods which are rich in this vitamin: leafy green vegetables, mushrooms, soya beans and flour, nori (p. 119), almonds, prunes and fresh dates.

Levels of B_3, nicotinic acid, also need attention by both vegetarians and vegans; this is found in the foods mentioned above, but one of the richest sources of all is mushrooms. Dried peaches, damsons, sesame seeds and sunflower seeds are also particularly good.

An adequate supply of B_6, pyridoxine, is important when preparing for pregnancy, and studies have found it can also help alleviate pre-menstrual tension. So there's every excuse for eating avocados, as these are a particularly good source, as are bananas, currants, raisins and sultanas, sunflower seeds and soya beans and flour.

Folic acid is another vital B vitamin, especially during pregnancy. In addition to the sources mentioned above, leafy green vegetables are rich in this vitamin, especially endive and lettuce; also avocados, oranges, almonds and walnuts. Up to 50 per cent of folic acid is destroyed by heat, so there is obviously an advantage in eating these foods raw. B_{12} is found in dairy produce and eggs, yeast extracts, fermented foods, alfalfa sprouts and seaweeds. Some soya milks are also fortified with this vitamin. A B_{12} supplement may be advisable for vegetarians who are not eating much dairy produce and for vegans, unless they are eating good quantities of the foods mentioned above.

Vitamin C

Vitamin C protects against infection, speeds healing and the growth and repair of tissues and is needed for the absorption of iron. It is found in a wide range of fruit and vegetables and getting sufficient vitamin C is not usually a problem for vegetarians. Particularly good sources are leafy green vegetables, tomatoes, peppers, potatoes, blackcurrants, kiwi fruit, strawberries, pawpaw, cantaloupe melons and oranges.

Vitamin D

Vitamin D is necessary for the absorption of calcium, which is needed for strong and healthy bones and teeth. It is not damaged by heat, but is found only in a quite restricted group of foods. The richest sources are margarine, fortified dried, skimmed and evaporated milk, eggs and fortified breakfast cereals. If you are using soya milk, it is a good idea to find one which contains vitamin D: read the label. Seaweeds are the only vegetable source of vitamin D (p. 117).

In white-skinned people, vitamin D is also formed by the action of sunlight on skin, but this does not happen in dark-skinned people, so they can become deficient in this vitamin if they are not getting enough in their diet. Vitamin D supplements are available and some experts recommend these for everyone, particularly children and old people (who are not getting out into the sun very often). Vitamin D is toxic in large doses, so if you take a supplement, do not exceed the recommended dose, and check first whether any multi-vitamin you may be taking contains any vitamin D.

VITAMIN SUPPLEMENTS: TO TAKE, OR NOT TO TAKE?

Opinion is divided between those who say vitamin supplements are a necessary protection in these days of pollution and artificial fertilizers, and those who say that taking concentrated doses of nutrients is unnatural and alien to a pure way of eating. And no one knows how well vitamin supplements are actually assimilated by the body.

Personally I don't take any, although I think that in certain cases they can be useful; if for some reason there is difficulty in eating healthy foods in the quantity needed to give enough vitamins and minerals, for instance with faddy children, older people, after illness or during periods of rapid growth.

A vitamin D supplement is recommended for young children and older people who do not get much sun. Yeast tablets are useful if you find it difficult to eat plenty of the B vitamin foods, but you really have to take them by the handful to make any impact. And B_{12} is a good idea for vegans and vegetarians who are not eating much dairy produce. I have a great deal of faith in the ability of a healthy body to adapt to the foods it is given (provided that these are natural and unprocessed) and to utilize the nutrients available. I also believe that if you're eating a healthy diet, with plenty of variety, your body will let you know if it is lacking anything vital, by making you fancy certain foods which have the nutrients that you need at that time. So do listen to your body.

Vitamin E

Vitamin E is needed for the elasticity of tissues, for general vitality and healing, and for the healthy functioning of the heart and arteries. It may also increase fertility and help to avoid high blood pressure.

Vitamin E is found in a wide range of foods and deficiency in this vitamin is rare, especially in a vegetarian diet, which generally contains plentiful amounts. Heat does not damage it significantly, but processing and prolonged storage can. The best sources are cold-pressed corn oil, wheatgerm, nuts and seeds (especially almonds, hazelnuts, peanuts and peanut butter), avocados, blackberries and sweet potatoes. Also valuable are eggs, all whole grains, pulses and leafy green vegetables.

Vitamin K

Vitamin K is needed for the metabolism of proteins and for the clotting of blood. It is made by the intestinal bacteria and is also found in leafy green vegetables, cauliflower, tomatoes, egg yolk, peas and beans, potatoes, carrots, seaweeds and alfalfa. It is not thought to be damaged by cooking processes. A vegetarian diet supplies as much of this vitamin as is required, especially if it includes a daily serving of leafy green vegetables.

Planning Vegetarian Meals

When you're changing to vegetarian eating, or trying out some vegetarian meals, it's probably easiest to think of the meal you'd normally eat and then swap the meat or fish with a vegetarian main course: nut or lentil burgers instead of beef burgers; steamed vegetable pudding instead of steak and kidney pudding; savoury nut or lentil loaf instead of meat loaf. Once you've planned the main course, the vegetables and a sauce if needed can be chosen to go with it.

Vegetarian eating can follow the conventional daily pattern of breakfast, one light and one more substantial meal; or it can be based on several light snack meals, or whatever schedule suits you. I do think that for anyone interested in healthy eating, whether they're a meat eater or a vegetarian, it's helpful to think of the fat content of the day's — or even the week's — eating as a whole, balancing a high-fat meal, such as a cheese flan, with a low-fat meal, such as a mixed salad dressed with lemon juice, or a platter of steamed vegetables with chopped fresh herbs. I personally find breakfast an easy meal to make fatless — fresh fruit and weak tea without milk is my favourite — and this allows scope for the rest of the day. Other low-fat breakfasts would be a whole-grain cereal with skimmed or semi-skimmed milk (or soya milk) or wholewheat toast with honey. (See p. 529 for a typical day's healthy vegetarian menu ideas.)

Vegetarianism in Pregnancy

Ideally, preparation for pregnancy should begin several months before conception, and not only for the prospective mother, but for the father too, as the diet of both determines the health of the baby. During this time of preparation it's a good idea to rely on some form of contraception other than the pill, as this is known to affect the body's ability to metabolize vitamins B_6, B_2, B_{12} and folic acid, as well as zinc and iron. Make sure that your diet contains plentiful sources of these vitamins (see above) and consider taking supplements of vitamins D and B_{12} if your diet is low in dairy produce. Eat plenty of the foods rich in vitamin E and include sea vegetables or seaweed-based jelling agents whenever you can (see p. 15) for iodine and other trace minerals, or take kelp tablets two or three times a week. It's also advisable to cut out or reduce the amount of alcohol you drink, and to stop smoking.

Nutritional requirements increase dramatically during pregnancy and lactation. Extra iron, folic acid and other B vitamins, and vitamins A, C, D, and E are needed, as well as about 50 per cent more calcium than normal. You can meet this by having an extra serving of cheese or yogurt, or by taking an extra 450 ml/ 15 fl oz skimmed milk or calcium-fortified soya milk. Or you could step up the amount of non-dairy sources of calcium in your diet, such as broccoli, kale, dried figs, almonds, sesame seeds, soya beans and flour, arame and hiziki. A couple of glasses a day of the creamy almond milk on p. 51 is another delicious way to take extra calcium as well as plentiful B vitamins, iron and other minerals.

If you don't mind brewer's yeast, a convenient way to boost your intake of the important B vitamins is to take 15 ml/ 1 tablespoon brewer's yeast each day. Sprinkle this over your breakfast cereal or stir it into some fruit juice. This will also supply the additional thiamin, riboflavin, nicotinic acid, B_6 and folic acid needed during both pregnancy and lactation, together with some useful iron, zinc and a little calcium and magnesium too, while providing only 46 calories.

A well-balanced vegetarian diet is probably naturally rich enough in vitamins A, C and E to cover the additional requirements for these during pregnancy. However, you could make doubly sure by having a piece of melon, an extra orange or half cup of orange juice, a large banana or an extra serving of green vegetables each day, to supply vitamins A and C, and by using cold-pressed corn oil, for vitamin E, in salad dressings.

HIGH-VITALITY FOODS

There are certain foods which are particularly rich in a number of nutrients, and worth including in your meals as often as possible. These are:

☐ Pulses *especially soya beans, soya sprouts, soya flour*
☐ Whole grains *especially oatmeal and millet; wholewheat flour and bread; pasta; wheatgerm*
☐ Nuts *especially pistachios, almonds, brazil nuts, hazelnuts and walnuts*
☐ Seeds *sunflower, pumpkin, and sesame seeds and spread*
☐ Fresh fruits *especially apples, bananas, oranges, dates, blackberries, strawberries, cantaloupe melon, kiwi, mango, pawpaw*
☐ Dried fruits *including dried peaches*
☐ Vegetables *especially fresh peas, beans, sweetcorn; mushrooms, avocados, alfalfa sprouts; potatoes, tomatoes, carrots, red pepper and sweet potatoes*
☐ Dark green leafy vegetables *especially broccoli and other brassicas; endive*
☐ Seaweeds *especially hiziki and nori*
☐ Brewer's yeast and yeast extract
☐ Milk and cheese

Vegetarian Babies

For the first six months of life, breast milk supplies all the nutrients a baby needs and ideally solid food should not be introduced before then. It can be given, with care, when the baby is four months old, if he no longer seems satisfied with breast milk, but certainly not before then. The reason for avoiding the early introduction of solid foods is that because the baby's digestive system is immature an allergic reaction is more likely; also the baby needs the closeness and emotional satisfaction which breast-feeding gives.

Start to introduce the baby to solid food by giving half a teaspoon of a fruit or vegetable purée, either before or after one of the main feeds of the day: lunchtime is often most convenient. Either cooked or raw fruit and vegetables can be used; mashed avocado pear, ripe banana, ripe peach or mango; very finely grated raw apple, pear or carrot; or cooked and puréed carrot or mashed potato. These first spoonfuls are really to get the baby used to the texture of solid food; breast milk will still be his main source of nourishment, and he also still needs this for the emotional satisfaction which comes from sucking.

Once the baby is happy with these small quantities of solid food, you can gradually increase the amount so that after a fortnight or so he is having perhaps two tablespoons at a time. Babies of over six months can also have a little bread mashed into the food; remove the crusts and use either a 100 per cent wholewheat bread, or, if this proves to be too laxative (as it can for some babies) try an 81–85 per cent bread, perhaps with added wheatgerm.

Gradually, as the baby takes more solid food, he won't need so much milk, so that when he is about 8 months he will naturally give up one feed completely. Then you can add extra protein ingredients to the basic fruit and vegetable purées to enrich them. Try adding: mashed cooked beans, mashed drained tofu, cooked and puréed lentils, tahini, peanut butter, low-sodium yeast extract, finely grated nuts and seeds, wheatgerm, brewer's yeast, cottage cheese, low-fat white cheeses such as quark, 'live' natural yogurt and hard cheese.

You can gradually increase the quantities that you give to the baby for this meal of solids, and if you like you can give a savoury course, of, say, puréed lentils or mashed cooked vegetables with some protein added, as suggested above, followed by a 'pudding' course of finely grated fresh fruit, yogurt or egg custard. Once the baby gets used to the texture of solid food, you will probably be able to mash, rather than purée, his foods.

Solid foods can be introduced before or after the other main feeds of the day in the same way, so that gradually these, too, can be dropped. When the baby is about 9 months the bedtime feed may be the only one left. Let the baby go on enjoying this for as long as possible; it is important for the bonding with you and the emotional satisfaction which sucking gives. The baby will give it up spontaneously when he is ready, sometimes this happens by the time he is around a year old, but often babies need to continue for longer. My daughter Claire had just managed to give it up by her second birthday!

'Finger foods', such as fingers of bread, rusks, raw apple or carrot, can be given from about 9 months, and can be helpful if the baby is teething. Never leave a baby alone with these foods and be ready to hook them out with your little finger or to turn the baby upside down and smack him gently in the small of his back if he starts to choke.

Soon you will find that the baby can eat a little of what you as a family are eating. Make sure that this is not too highly seasoned, either with salt or spices, which put too much strain on the baby's kidneys. It may be possible to take a little out for the baby before adding these to the mixture. Other things to avoid are foods which contain preservatives, colouring or other additives, and foods which are high in fat, such as pastry and deep-fried foods. Watch, too, the level of fibre; as a vegetarian diet is naturally high in this, make sure that he has, in addition, some sources of concentrated protein such as egg, cheese, peanut butter or tahini, powdered nuts, yogurt or brewer's yeast.

Vegetarian Children

A well-planned vegetarian diet can supply all the nutrients growing children need. Deficiencies would show up as stunted growth, listlessness, poor appetite, lack of energy, slow healing of cuts and wounds, cracks and sores around the mouth, and mouth ulcers. As long as they are healthy, full of energy and growing well, they are almost certainly getting the nourishment they need. It is, however, important that you watch their diet carefully and make sure it is rich in all the essential nutrients.

Few parents manage to get through the child-rearing process

without worrying about their child's diet at some point. One of my daughters was so faddy that I sometimes wondered how she managed to keep going, but we came through this phase and she's bright, happy and healthy. I did get her to take vitamin tablets, and I think that a vitamin tablet, including vitamins B12 and D, is a good idea, for the parents' peace of mind as much as the children's nourishment! In my opinion it's best to let them have the foods that they will eat — provided these are reasonably healthy — rather than trying to make them eat what you think they ought to be eating. There are several good sources of most nutrients, so if they balk at one it's usually possible to find an alternative.

Try to include in their diet as many of the high-vitality foods as you can, keep everything as fresh and unprocessed as possible. Keep a strict eye on the amount of sugar and fat they are eating and make sure there are plenty of wholesome snack foods, such as fruit, wholewheat bread, nuts and dried fruit available, as well as crudités, cubes of cheese and favourite yogurts, to keep them off the sweets and crisps. Encourage them to drink water or unsweetened fruit juice diluted with water or soda water instead of sweetened canned or bottled drinks. If you have the time, presentation of the food does help; I have found that my youngest daughter, Claire, always eats her food better if I take the time to arrange it attractively on the plate or to bake a mini-savoury in a ramekin dish. She loves a supper platter — small amounts of all her favourite foods arranged on a plate — cubes of cheese, thin slices of apple, some dates stuffed with almonds, a few crisp lettuce leaves, some carrot sticks. Sometimes I've arranged a salad or an open sandwich in the shape of a face, with grated carrot hair, tomato mouth and so on. If you go to this trouble, you have to take care not to over-react if your lovingly arranged offering is rejected, though in my experience it isn't usually. (See p. 543 for some menu ideas for children's favourites.)

Vegetarian Teenagers

As with younger children, it's most helpful to concentrate on the foods that are liked, rather than to get into a situation of conflict. Some teenagers may wish to experience eating meat and 'junk foods' if they have always had wholesome vegetarian food at home. If they're into junk foods, try and get them to take some kind of vitamin supplement, and have readily available any natural snacks, such as apples, nuts, wholewheat bread or cake, that they will eat. The less intense the emotional atmosphere, the more quickly they will be able to discover what they as individuals really want to eat and make their own responsible decisions.

During this period of rapid growth teenagers, especially boys, may have a big appetite; plenty of wholewheat bread, pasta, rice and potatoes will fill them up, while giving good nourishment. Include as many of the high-vitality foods as possible; soya is a particularly good food if they'll eat it, perhaps in the form of tofu, well-sprinkled with a good-quality, naturally fermented soy sauce. Wholewheat peanut butter or tahini sandwiches, perhaps with sprouted soya beans, or pitta breads packed with red kidney beans, salad and any other ingredients they particularly like, are quick snacks which I've known to be popular with this age group, as are vegetarian burgers (pp. 313 and 346-7), or bought Vegeburgers, served with a good supply of burger buns and perhaps some baked beans.

At the opposite end of the scale, slimming is another issue which frequently arises with teenagers, especially with girls. This can be healthily achieved on a vegetarian diet (see below). Include as many iron-rich foods as possible in the diet of teenagers, especially girls. Zinc is also important and shortage of this mineral has been linked with the eating disorders anorexia nervosa and bulimia. Including plentiful amounts of the zinc-rich foods (which are also good sources of iron), such as peanuts, sweetcorn and cheese, makes sound sense.

Slimming on a Vegetarian Diet

The key to successful slimming lies in finding a diet which suits your life-style and which can become a permanent way of eating once you're slim, to prevent the endless fluctuation of weight and constant dieting that leads nowhere. I've known people to have dramatic weight losses when they turned vegetarian. The combination of the additive-free foods and the high fibre just seemed to do the trick for them.

If you base meals on whole grains and pulses, eat more fresh fruit and vegetables and reduce fat and sugar, it is difficult not to lose weight. You could eat exactly the meals suggested in the *Typical day of healthy vegetarian eating* (p. 529), using skimmed milk if you have the muesli or only a scraping of butter on the toast; use yeast extract, mustard or skimmed milk soft cheese to spread the bread for sandwiches, if you have these for lunch, or, if you're making the soup, use the minimum of fat. Top the salad with yogurt or a mixture of yogurt and mayonnaise. Prepare the evening meal with the minimum of fat, and have a large portion of leafy salad with it, dressed with lemon juice. Many of the main courses in this book can be used by slimmers (see p. 542 for some which are particularly suitable).

A method of slimming I like is based on the principle of keeping fruit separate from other foods, and not mixing protein foods with carbohydrates. Eat only fruit until noon, and after you have eaten fruit allow an hour to elapse before eating any other foods. For lunch eat fruit (if you want to lose weight fast), or have a large salad, with some bread or a potato if you like. Soup can be included in this meal, or you could have a salad sandwich, but no protein. The evening meal can be built around either protein or carbohydrate, but not both. Fruit can be eaten three hours after other foods.

Older Vegetarians

Unless we are very active, our calorie requirements decrease as we get older. However, our need for nutrients remains as high as ever and it is important to look for foods which provide concentrated sources of these whilst not contributing too many calories. Protein is needed for growth and repair of tissues; vitamins A and C for resistance to infection and general vitality; vitamin D for healthy bones; vitamin E, which has sometimes been called the youth vitamin, for flexibility of joints and tissues, and vitamin B for the nervous system and to combat the effects of stress.

Sometimes it is difficult to eat large enough portions of foods to get the optimum nourishment, and so taking a multi-vitamin pill often makes sense for older vegetarians. It's also helpful to look for foods which are concentrated sources of nutrients, such as nuts and nut butters, cheese, eggs, soya flour, tofu, skimmed milk powder, tahini, brewer's yeast, yeast extract and wheatgerm. Milk is a useful food because it is both easy to eat (or drink) and rich in valuable nutrients, especially calcium and riboflavin. Milk can be fortified further by whisking some dried skimmed milk powder into it. Salads can be difficult to eat, and if you find this to be a problem, fruit and vegetable juices can be useful, but make sure you're getting enough fibre, with foods such as wholewheat bread, soups, baked beans and jacket potatoes.

If you're cooking for one, and have a small deep-freeze, it can be most helpful to make up the full amount of a recipe, divide it into four portions and freeze three of them for later. Many vegetarian dishes freeze well (see p. 35), and if you have a microwave oven as well, this is ideal when you're heating up food for one or two people, see p. 37.

Again, if you're cooking for just one or two people it helps to plan meals for several days at a time. You can often cook extra rice, potatoes, pasta or sauce, for instance, and use them a day or two later, with the addition of some fresh and different ingredients, to create another meal.

Soups make a particularly soothing food and are easy to make. A lentil soup is very nourishing and can be made as thick or thin as you wish. If you serve it with some wholewheat bread and some fresh fruit or vegetable juice, or a little salad, you have a meal which should certainly help to keep you brimming with vitality.

Kitchen Equipment

Equipment needed for vegetarian cookery is modest and likely to be found in most kitchens. Top of the list comes a really good, sharp knife, an essential for any cook. I like traditional Sabatier knives; be sure to get the real thing. There are some cheap substitutes around and these are not satisfactory. The most useful all-purpose size is a knife with a 13 cm/5 inch blade, but a small paring knife is handy, too. You will also need a steel with which to keep them sharp. As well as a good Sabatier knife, I find it useful to have a stainless steel knife with a serrated blade, for cutting delicate fruits like peaches, mangoes and avocados, which can take on a metallic taste when cut with a steel knife.

A good, strong chopping board is another essential. Make sure it is at least 2·5 cm/1 inch thick and measures not less than 40 × 30 cm/16 × 12 inches. This can also double as a pastry board.

It's necessary to have some means of grinding nuts and seeds. You can use a small hand-mill, an electric coffee mill or a liquidizer, but perhaps the best buy for this is a food processor, because it can also be used for so many other jobs. If you're buying a new one, it's worth buying the largest you can.

A pestle and mortar is useful for crushing whole spices. A heavy ceramic one, with a good-sized bowl, is more practical than a wooden one which lacks the weight and tends to absorb and retain flavours.

When choosing saucepans and baking tins, buy the best you can afford because you certainly get what you pay for here. Good ones will last a lifetime and be a joy to use; cheap ones are a source of frustration. I like heavy-gauge stainless steel saucepans; aluminium is not recommended by natural health experts because it is thought that the traces of aluminium absorbed by the food can be detrimental. Cast-iron equipment is pleasant both to look at and to use; the disadvantage is the weight of it, especially when full.

For general frying, a frying pan with a top measurement of 27·5 cm/10¾ inches is best, and for pancakes a shallow frying pan with curved edges, measuring 20 cm/8 inches across. If you make omelettes often it's a good idea to have a frying pan specially for them, although this is a counsel of perfection which I have never managed to achieve. The right size is 13–15 cm/5–6 inches across.

A pressure-cooker saves time and fuel; I find it especially useful for making soups and stews quickly. A stainless steel one is the best from the health point of view, and should last for years.

If you like making stir-fries, a wok is a useful piece of equipment. One with a stand can be used on either gas or electricity, and the most useful size is 35 cm/14 inches in diameter. A wok with wooden handles is easiest to use.

Some of the best baking tins are the ones with a non-stick coating, although I find that they still need lining and greasing in the usual way. Again, look for strong, heavy tins; this applies especially to baking sheets, as cheap, thin ones soon buckle. A spring-clip type is useful for cheesecakes.

When it comes to choosing casserole dishes, the most useful ones are perhaps those which can withstand extremes of temperature, so that you can take them out of the fridge or freezer and put them straight into the oven. Not in this category, but reasonable to buy and attractive and pleasant to use, are French glazed pottery casserole dishes which you can buy in different sizes and lovely muted colours. I also find those round white ceramic pizza plates, measuring 30 cm/12 inches across, very useful for various dishes.

Other useful and time-saving pieces of equipment are a good sturdy metal colander, for draining pasta and vegetables; a sieve with metal mesh and also a nylon one, or a tamis, for sieving delicate fruits and vegetables; a box grater which you can stand on a chopping board and which has a variety of blades of different sizes; some really sharp kitchen scissors; a set of measuring spoons and a 600-ml/1-pint or

1-litre/1¾-pint measuring jug made of glass or translucent plastic, marked in millilitres, pints and fluid ounces.

Non-essential tools include a nylon piping bag with a large plain nozzle and a medium-sized shell nozzle; a melon baller, and an orange zester.

Using the Freezer

The freezer is as much of a boon in vegetarian cookery as it is in conventional cookery and can be used to save both time and money. It is perhaps particularly useful to vegetarians because our main dishes have to be made from scratch. So making a double quantity and freezing half, or freezing some of the components of favourite dishes, such as tomato sauce, pancakes, breadcrumbs for stuffings and toppings, ready-grated cheese and cooked pulses, is really worthwhile. It is also useful to have a supply of favourite commercial frozen foods.

FOODS WHICH FREEZE

- ☐ *Fresh fruit and vegetables*
- ☐ *Cooked pulses*
- ☐ *Dairy produce with a fat content above 40 per cent*
- ☐ *Soups, savoury bakes and pastries, sauces*
- ☐ *Cakes, biscuits and breads*

FOODS WHICH DO NOT FREEZE

- ☐ *Leafy salad vegetables such as lettuce, also raw tomatoes*
- ☐ *Hardboiled eggs, raw eggs in their shells — store raw egg yolk and white separately to prevent the yolk toughening*
- ☐ *Dairy products with fat content below 40 per cent*
- ☐ *Food strongly flavoured with garlic or celery, as garlic may develop 'off' flavours and celery intensifies*
- ☐ *Dishes containing cooked potato, which toughens, although mashed potato is satisfactory*

Freezer Standbys

Commercial frozen foods
Frozen foods which I find particularly useful are orange juice, frozen peas, particularly petits pois and mangetouts;

baby haricot beans, sweetcorn, corn on the cob and asparagus. Frozen raspberries and cream are useful for a spur-of-the-moment special menu.

Home-made dishes

The majority of vegetarian dishes freeze well; either make up a double quantity, and freeze one, or have a cooking session to stock up the deep freeze.

Soups, casseroles and stews freeze well, but don't use garlic or celery to flavour soups and savouries. Freeze in a container which allows enough room for expansion. Allow plenty of time for thawing: 6–8 hours for a quantity to serve 4–6 people. Most vegetable and pulse dishes freeze successfully; Red Cabbage Casserole (p. 268) and Ratatouille (p. 278), for instance; also Red Kidney Bean Stew (p. 308) and Lentils and Mushrooms au Gratin (p. 308).

Both savoury and sweet pies and pastries freeze well; I think they are best frozen uncooked; do not make any holes in the top — add these just before cooking. Mushroom Pâté en Croûte (p. 401) is a useful dish to freeze for a special occasion.

Burgers and croquettes freeze exceptionally well. They are best open-frozen. To open-freeze, place on a tray or baking sheet, freeze until solid, then pack. Spicy Lentil Burgers (p. 313), Peanut Burgers (p. 346), Cheese and Parsley Fritters (p. 326) and Felafel (p. 311) are all worth freezing, as are Nut Balls in Tomato Sauce (p. 355).

Spinach Lasagne (p. 378) and Gnocchi alla Romana (p. 341) (frozen before baking) are particularly useful and successful. Nut and lentil roasts are superb cooked until three-quarters done, then cooled and frozen. To use, thaw, then cook for about 30 minutes. Of the puddings, cheesecakes, ices, sorbets, pies and tarts (as mentioned) freeze well, as do cakes, biscuits, scones and breads. Both scones and breads are good par-cooked before being frozen, then thawed and cooked before eating.

Ingredients

It's very helpful and time-saving to have some much-used

ingredients in the freezer, as well as sauces and other things which are needed for making up dishes.

Stock can be frozen in 300 ml/10 fl oz quantities. Any leftover lemon juice can be poured into ice cube containers and frozen.

There are many uses for spare egg yolks and egg whites. Stir a pinch of sugar or salt into each egg yolk (depending on whether you want to use it for sweet or savoury dishes) to stabilize it. Then freeze yolks and whites separately in ice cube containers.

Basic much-used sauces such as Fresh Tomato (p. 253), Italian Tomato (p. 254), and any others that you particularly like and use often such as Sauce Soubise (p. 258), Béchamel Sauce (p. 261), and Cheese Sauce (p. 261), are also handy to have in the freezer.

Cooked pulses (p. 57) can be packed in 350 g/12 oz portions and frozen, as can cooked crepes. Interleave each crepe with greaseproof paper before freezing so that you can take them out individually as needed.

Pastry flan cases can be baked blind (p. 396) and then frozen. They are handy for filling with vegetables in a creamy sauce or a light egg custard mixture for quick meals.

Chopped parsley, fresh breadcrumbs and grated cheese can all be frozen in polythene bags. Grate up any additional cheese and just add it to the bag.

Secrets of Successful Freezing

Freeze food which is good quality; if it is hot, cool quickly, package carefully, freeze as rapidly as possible.

Pack foods carefully to protect them and to prevent strongly flavoured foods from tainting others.

Allow room for liquid products to expand.

When sealing polythene bags, make sure that as much air as possible has been extracted.

Label each package with as much information as possible, include contents, date frozen and servings.

Freezing Vegetables

For best results, vegetables need to be blanched before freezing. Prepare the vegetables in the usual way. Bring a large saucepan of water to the boil. Put 450 g/1 lb prepared vegetables into a wire basket and plunge this into the boiling water. When the water comes back to the boil start timing the vegetables: 2−3 minutes for leafy vegetables, peas and beans, broccoli, small cauliflower florets, small carrots, Brussels sprouts, courgettes; 7−10 minutes for corn on the cob, depending on size. Remove from the water immediately and put the vegetables under a cold running tap until they are cooled through. Drain well, then package and freeze immediately. To freeze fresh herbs, see p. 167.

Freezing Fruit

Perfect fruit can be frozen raw, or it can be sprinkled with sugar or covered with a syrup made by heating 350 g/12 oz sugar in 600 ml/1 pint water until the sugar has dissolved, then cooling. Less perfect fruit can be stewed in the normal way (p. 123), sweetened with sugar to taste, then frozen; ripe, soft fruits such as strawberries, mangoes and peaches can be puréed raw, sweetened, and frozen. A little lemon juice can be added to prevent the fruit from discolouring. Fruit for making jam or marmalade can be kept in the freezer until you are ready to use it.

Using the Microwave

Another time-saving piece of equipment, the microwave oven can be used to speed preparation of dishes and also to defrost and quickly re-heat prepared dishes. The dishes suggested for freezing can be reheated successfully in the microwave oven if they are frozen in microwave-proof containers.

Microwave Power

The power of microwave ovens ranges from 500–700 watt outputs. Many have a variety of settings, ranging from 'warm' 100 watts and 'defrost' 230 watts, to 'full power' 600–700 watts. Personally I do not think there is any advantage in having numerous settings; I find 'defrost' and 'full power' are the only ones needed. I do think, however, that there is a great advantage in having an oven which combines microwave with a conventional oven and grill. These are more expensive to buy, but give excellent results, combining speedy microwave cooking with traditional browning and crisping.

Microwave Containers

Choose shallow dishes, preferably round or oval in shape, made from pottery or heatproof glass: dishes sold as suitable for dishwashers are usually suitable for the microwave too. Do not use dishes made of metal or with metallic decorations, and avoid covering food with foil, as these can damage the magnetron.

It has been recommended by the Ministry of Agriculture, Fisheries and Food in the UK that clingfilm should not be used in microwave cooking, as it has been found that some of the plasticiser di-2-ethyhexledipate (DEHA) used to soften clingfilm can migrate into the food during cooking. I suggest that you use a plate or lid to cover food in the microwave.

Cooking in the Microwave

Arrange the food around the edges of the dish, with the thickest part of the food towards the outside of the dish; do not pile the food up. Some foods need stirring during cooking time; this helps even distribution of heat. Many dishes need to be allowed to stand (usually for about 5 minutes) after microwaving, to give the heat time to penetrate the food fully. The more food in the microwave oven, the longer the cooking time. When cooking savoury dishes or vegetables, the food cooks more quickly if it is covered; a dinner plate is good for this, and it gets warmed through at the same time, ready to serve the food on.

Vegetables do not cook any more quickly in a microwave oven than by conventional boiling or steaming, but they keep their colour well and the goodness and flavour are conserved because of the small amount of water used. They cook best if cut into fairly small pieces, placed on a large plate and sprinkled with water, allowing about 3 tablespoons water for 450 g/1 lb vegetables.

Pulses can be cooked in a microwave, and although you do not save much time by doing them in this way, they do cook well. Soak the pulses as usual, if necessary (p. 57), then put them into a shallow container. Add boiling water to cover them by about 1 cm/½ inch. Red kidney beans should be soaked and then boiled hard for 10 minutes before you put them into the microwave. Split red lentils and green or brown lentils do not need soaking; just cover them generously with water and cook split red lentils for 10 minutes, and the other types for 20 minutes, in each case followed by 10 minutes' standing. It's a good idea to stir the lentils two or three times during the cooking time. Soaked black-eyed beans, cannellini beans or haricot beans take 20–30 minutes, followed by 10 minutes' standing; soaked chick peas take 30–40 minutes, plus 10 minutes standing. Red kidney beans, black beans and butter beans, all pre-soaked, and red kidney beans boiled hard for 10 minutes as described, take 45–50 minutes, with 15 minutes' standing time after that.

Pasta and rice can be cooked in the microwave, although little time is saved. To cook spaghetti, macaroni or similar pasta shapes, put 225 g/8 oz pasta into a suitable dish and add 600 ml/1 pint boiling water and 1 tablespoon oil. Cook, uncovered, for 12—17 minutes, until *al dente*. For 225 g/8 oz lasagne, use 1 litre/1¾ pints boiling water and 1 tablespoon oil, cook for 10—12 minutes and allow to stand for 2 minutes.

To cook rice, put 225 g/8 oz rice into a deep dish with 600 ml/1 pint boiling water and a knob of butter or vegan margarine; cover and microwave for 12—17 minutes for white long grain rice, 20—25 minutes for brown rice, in both cases followed by 5 minutes' standing.

If you are using the microwave to heat ready-made 'cook-chill' or frozen dishes, special care is needed to make sure that the food is thoroughly defrosted and cooked. Some microwave ovens have caused concern because they have failed to maintain a temperature high enough to destroy possible bacteria. It is important to follow the manufacturer's instructions carefully. These may include placing the dish on a rack if appropriate and turning the food dish around frequently. If in any doubt, do contact the manufacturer for further information.

Entertaining and Wine

Creating food which will give pleasure to others, and then enjoying it with them, is, to me, what cooking is all about, and, in this spirit, even a simple meal becomes a celebration. A perfectly planned dinner party can be a delight; but sometimes an impromptu meal, which you've cooked on the spur of the moment while chatting in the kitchen, and washed down with a bottle of *vin ordinaire*, can be even more pleasurable. The kind of meal and the degree of formality with which it is served depend very much on personal taste and the circumstances such as the people involved, the occasion, the venue and the time available.

At the back of this book I have given menu suggestions for different occasions, and there are many more possibilities. The most important thing is to choose food which you like and make well; if you have particular favourites, don't feel shy about repeating them − your friends are probably looking forward to eating them again − at least, I know that's how I feel about my friends' specialities. Choose dishes which will not give you anxiety, then you will be able to enjoy your own dinner party too. A cold first course or pudding − or both − which can be prepared in advance to leave you free to cope with the main course eases the strain. So does serving a simple vegetable accompaniment with the main course, such as French beans or a green salad.

Entertaining has become much more fun now that so many exciting ingredients are available in the shops. Using exotic fruits and vegetables provides a good conversation piece, too. Experiment with a new recipe or ingredients before trying them out on your friends and you will then be able to serve any dish with confidence.

I think everyone feels some degree of nervousness when entertaining others to a meal; will the food be all right, will they like it, have you overlooked something, or made some obvious mistake in the planning? There are various points to look out for, to make sure that everything is as perfect as possible (see the check-list). Then, having prepared everything as carefully as you can, my advice is to relax and enjoy yourself!

CHECK-LIST FOR PLANNING
A BALANCED MEAL

In planning your meal, check that you have:

☐ Contrasting colours within each course and within the meal as a whole; avoid starting with beetroot soup, for instance, and ending with a compote of red fruits

☐ A variety of different dishes; avoid more than one course based on fruit, pastry, nuts, or any other ingredient

☐ Contrast of textures: crisp crunchy nut roast with a smooth carrot purée, for instance; a creamy soup followed by a crisp main course, such as asparagus in phyllo pastry

☐ A good balance of flavours; avoid, for instance, starting with mint-flavoured soup and ending with mint ice cream

☐ Food of different shapes: don't have a loaf-shaped terrine followed by a loaf-shaped nut roast followed by a chocolate roulade. Plan a balance of round and square, and of dishes which are presented in individual portions and those which are served at the table

Food Presentation

Keep garnishing light, fresh and relevant to the dish. Generally I like to echo one of the ingredients in the dish, rather than introduce something new, unless it is witty or relevant in some way. Good food speaks for itself and does not need much garnishing. Instead of garnishing a main course such as lentil burgers or a nut loaf with slices of tomato or lemon, which do nothing for anybody, it can be nicer to serve it with a fresh, light salad, such as tomato and basil salad, which gives colour to the meal and tastes good as well.

Chopped fresh herbs, the same type as used in the dish, can be sprinkled over as a garnish. It's nice to have a herb garden with a good variety of herbs so you always have a plentiful supply, but supermarkets now sell little packs of most fresh herbs.

Wicker baskets and trays, and wooden bowls, are most useful

for presenting food attractively. A large round wicker tray, lined with leaves, makes an excellent base for crudités and a dip, and also for carrying a steaming hot casserole of food from the oven to the table, acting as a tray and place-mat in one. Small wicker or wooden bowls, perhaps lined with a coloured paper napkin, make attractive containers not only for warm rolls, but also for 'finger salads', especially for children.

Or try using hollowed-out fruit and vegetables as containers for food. Lemons, red, green and yellow peppers, marrows or cucumbers, for example, can all be used imaginatively and give more colour to the meal. Fruits such as pineapples, oranges, grapefruit and melons also make good containers for fruit salad mixtures, ice creams or sorbets, and will add that extra flavour to the food.

Arrange food in clumps of colour, rather than mixing up colours. A pyramid shape is often a most attractive way to present individual items such as Stuffed Vine Leaves (p. 215), Profiteroles (p. 474) or fresh fruit.

Little extras make all the difference: crudités or fruit arranged on fresh (edible) leaves or on crushed ice; ice in a jug of water; a bunch of flowers, simply arranged, on the table, and candles, which immediately give a romantic glow and cover up flaws in the decor and surroundings (which you may be acutely aware of, but which your friends probably won't even notice). An ice bucket will keep white wine chilled throughout the meal. If you can have matching or harmonizing colours in the table linen, napkins, candles and flowers, this, too, will contribute to the overall atmosphere.

Wine

Wine adds to the pleasure of any meal and gives it a celebratory feeling, while experiencing a meal with food and wines perfectly matched, to enhance each other, is perhaps one of life's greatest pleasures. The way to achieve this is really through experimentation — trying a dish with different wines to see what they do to each other. Try drinking up the last of your main course wine with the pudding, and you'll know what I mean; the sweetness makes a pleasant wine taste overly sharp. Yet that wine would probably taste excellent with a mellow cheese like mild Cheddar or Fontina (a very good reason for serving the cheese before the pudding whenever possible). Equally, a sweet, honeyed dessert wine would marry well with the pudding course.

When choosing more than one wine for a meal, it's common sense to start with the younger or less good wine; move from a young, light wine to a medium-bodied wine with some depth, and end with a full-bodied dessert wine. Choosing wine is now much easier and more interesting since some wine shops have introduced a numbering system, grading each wine from 1 to 10 – the dryest being no. 1 and the sweetest no. 10. As a general rule, serve white wine before red, the exception being sweet white dessert wines, which end the meal.

The aim when matching wine with food is to get a balance between the two: light dishes with light wines; sharp, lemon-flavoured dishes, such as a first course, for instance, with a sharp, pointed wine, like a Sauvignon. Mellow, even slightly sweet foods, such as most vegetables, need a more rounded wine, like a Chardonnay or Chenin Blanc; while dishes with many flavours, or a robust, almost 'meaty' taste, need a firm, strong wine which will hold its own beside them, but at the same time is not so good as to be spoilt by the flavourings of the dish: youngish fruity red wines with medium body are ideal.

Some foods do not flatter any wine. Sharply flavoured vinaigrette is an example of this, and it may be better to use a little wine with the olive oil to dress the salad. Strong flavourings of lemon juice, powerful herbs and spices (such as fennel or rosemary, for instance, and curry flavours), artichokes, Brie and Camembert cheese (which make the wine taste strange) and mayonnaise and cream sauces (which coat the palate) are other examples of foods that inhibit the appreciation of a good wine.

Wines with Vegetarian Food

The choice of wine to serve with a special meal begins with the aperitif, which, ideally, should be one which will awaken the palate and prepare it for the meal to follow. My favourite aperitifs to serve (apart from Champagne, the ultimate aperitif, incomparable for putting everyone in a celebratory mood before a special meal!) are light, dry to medium white wines, such as a

Chenin Blanc, a dry Vouvray or Muscat, or a Sylvaner or Riesling. A dryish Vermouth, such as Chambery, served with plenty of sparkling Perrier or Badoit water and a sliver of lemon is another favourite. Wine connoisseurs say that the best nibble to serve with drinks before a meal is plain biscuits, like water biscuits or other unsweetened cocktail biscuits, though I also like juicy salty black olives.

Many vegetable-based vegetarian dishes are flattered by light-bodied, fruity and not too dry white wines, particularly if the dish also contains nuts, which have a slight sweetness to them. A wine made from the Chenin Blanc grape, such as a dry Vouvray, Anjou or, one of the most pleasant, with an excellent balance of acidity and honeyed fruitiness, a Savennières, is ideal. The Savennières is particularly successful where there are a number of divergent vegetable flavours. An alternative would be an Australian Fumé Blanc.

Chardonnay-based wines also, with their softness and almost appley flavour, work well with nut and vegetable main courses: a Macon, Pouilly Vinzelles or Pouilly Fuissé, for instance, or a White Burgundy or Chablis from Australia; or perhaps an oaky Californian Chardonnay or Australian Wyndham Estate Oak Cask.

Alternatively, light-bodied, young, fruity red wines, perhaps served slightly chilled, can be delightful with these types of main course; wines such as a Saumur Champigny, Côtes-du-Rhône, Gamay de Touraine, St Aubin or Beaujolais-Villages. A Brouilly, deliciously round and fruity in flavour, would be another possibility. From Australia, suggestions include Rosemount Beaujolais, Wyndham Estate Beaujolais, Merlot or Chardonnay.

For something fuller-bodied, to support strong herby flavourings, or to go with something like a special nut loaf, a Châteauneuf-du-Pape or a Syrah-based wine from the Northern Rhône, such as a Cornas, St-Joseph, Côte Rotie or Crozes Hermitage; or a red from the Loire, such as a Chinon Bourgeuil or St Nicolas de Bourgeuil, with their raspberry-scented bouquet, or a Fleurie. Californian red wines are generally full-bodied and of reliable quality. Among the wines from Australia that have been recommended to me are Wynns Coonawarra Red from South Australia, a Cabernet Sauvignon, Penfolds Bin 389 or a Wolf Blas Yellow Label Shiraz.

For pasta dishes with an Italian orientation, such as Lasagne (p. 378) and Tagliatelle Verde with Lentil Sauce (p. 374) or Fusille Colbuco with Aubergine and Wine Sauce (p. 377), an Italian red wine would be appropriate: a Chianti Classico, Barolo or Barbaresco; or a Côte Rotie from France, or a Cabernet Sauvignon from France or elsewhere.

When it comes to choosing wines for the pudding course, the same principles apply. Sharp-flavoured fruit salads and compotes do not go well with wine, although if they include a flavouring of a fruit liqueur, such as Cointreau, that, well-chilled, can be a good partner for them. Ice creams generally are not good with wine, either, because they numb the palate, though I have enjoyed a good sweet German dessert wine with home-made raspberry ice cream. The wine needs to be sweeter than the dessert so that it does not taste sour when drunk with it.

Hot fruit soufflés, such as Hot Black Cherry Soufflé (p. 430) are complemented by a good sweet wine — as good a quality as you can afford, a German Beerenauslese, Auslese, Sauternes, Barsac or Montbazillac; or, from Australia, a Brown Bros Orange Muscat. One of these sweet wines also complements Pashka (p. 428), Apricot and Orange Fool (p. 418) and compote of dried fruit (p. 149), in the latter case especially if it is marinated in a little of the sweet wine — a Sauternes would be especially good. A chilled sweet wine or toning eau-de-vie or liqueur can work with a sorbet; ice-cold Poire Williams eau-de-vie with Pear Sorbet (p. 420) for instance, or, with Champagne Sorbet (p. 422) — Champagne!

Ingredients

Good cooking begins with good ingredients, and the aim of this section is to provide a guide both to choosing and getting the best from well-loved basics, and identifying and using some of the more unfamiliar and exotic ingredients. So there are fruits ranging from apples to rambutans; vegetables from potatoes to doody; and pulses from familiar haricot beans to black chick peas and urd; plus a worldwide selection of nuts and grains. The sections on mushrooms and truffles, sea vegetables, and cheeses offer further delicacies, and then there's a glorious profusion of pasta, ranging from tiny stelline and convighi piccole to the larger tortellini, cappaletti and ravioli . . . all comprising a feast of vegetarian delights.

Nuts and Seeds

One of our earliest foods, nuts and seeds feature in traditional recipes throughout the world. Many nuts and seeds, such as walnuts, hazelnuts and sesame seeds, are a useful source of oil. They can also be made into butters, such as peanut butter, or ground into flour. Most nuts and seeds are an excellent source of nutrients, especially protein, iron, calcium and b vitamins. Nutrients vary from nut to nut, and by eating a mixture, you can be sure of getting a balanced range in your diet.

Choosing and storing

Nuts are at their most delicious when eaten straight from the shell. Because of their high oil content, they go rancid quickly once shelled, so buy them in small quantities from a shop with a quick turnover, and, if possible, keep them in the fridge or freezer; otherwise store nuts in an airtight jar or tin, and use them up quickly.

Preparation and cooking

Shelled nuts can be used whole, chopped, flaked or ground. The flavour of some, such as hazelnuts and peanuts, is improved by roasting and this also enables the outer skin to be removed. To roast, place the nuts in a single layer on a baking sheet and bake at 180c/350f/Gas Mark 4 for about 20 minutes, until the skins rub off easily and the nuts underneath are golden-brown. Cool, then rub off the skins in a clean cloth (or leave the skins on if you prefer).

The best way to chop nuts is to place them on a sturdy board and chop with a sharp knife, holding the point down and moving the knife round in a semi-circle. To flake nuts such as almonds and brazil nuts, hold the nut down firmly on a board and slice thinly across with a knife. Nuts can be ground in a food processor, blender, electric coffee grinder or food mill, finely (consistency of ground almonds), medium (like medium-ground coffee) or coarsely (about the texture of rolled oats). Coarsely chopped nuts can be bought as MIXED CHOPPED NUTS.

Nuts can be used in sweet and savoury dishes and as a nibble. They can be made into milks, creams, butters, dips and soups; used as a thickener in sauces and casseroles, added to risottos, pilafs, stuffed vegetable mixtures and salads; as a topping for puddings, gratins, cakes and breads. In vegetarian cookery they can form the principal ingredient of many delicious savouries, including burgers, pâtés, pies and loaves.

MAKING NUT MILKS

You can make some delicious milks from nuts, far superior in flavour, I think, to cow's milk. All you do is whizz up a few cashew nuts or freshly blanched almonds with some water in a liquidizer or blender. You can make the mixture thick, like cream, or thin and delicate. I find 25 g/1 oz blanched almonds (about 30 nuts) to a tumbler of water makes a good consistency for drinking. You can drink as it is, or strain it.

For a fruit and nut drink, which makes a reviving and sustaining lunch or evening meal when you don't feel like eating anything else, try whizzing up a peeled banana or a few strawberries or raspberries with the almonds and water. This is especially good — like a thick milk shake — when made with a fruit which you've popped into the freezer for a few hours beforehand.

ALMOND *Prunus dulcis*

Native to the Mediterranean, almonds are particularly rich in protein, iron, calcium and vitamin B_2. There are two types, sweet and bitter. Bitter almonds are small and contain prussic acid. They are never eaten raw but are made into essence and liqueurs.

Sweet almonds can be bought in the shell, SHELLED, and with the skins removed as whole BLANCHED, FLAKED, NIBBED and GROUND almonds. For best results, buy almonds in the skin and blanch them at home. Put the almonds into a small saucepan, cover with cold water and boil for 2 minutes. Drain and pop the almonds out of their skins by squeezing them.

Almonds are perhaps best known world-wide for their use in sweets and in baking. They are blanched, roasted and salted for serving as nibbles and are delicious in main savoury dishes. Almonds can also be made into a particularly good milk (p. 51).

BRAZIL NUT *Bertholletia excelsa*
Brazil nuts are rich in fat, protein, the B vitamin thiamin and magnesium. They have a creamy texture and a delicate flavour which makes them excellent for eating raw in mueslis and salads or as a stuffing for dates. Although not used widely in traditional cookery, they can be made into tasty vegetarian loaves, crumbles and burgers, as well as making a good addition to a fruit cake. Using Brazil nuts helps save the rainforests.

CASHEW NUT *Anacardium occidentale*
Cashew nuts should be white and plump with a slightly sweet, bland flavour. They can be bought whole, both raw and roasted, halved or in pieces, which is cheapest. They are useful in vegetarian cookery for both sweet and savoury dishes. They can be made into a creamy and delicate milk and topping (above).

CHESTNUT *Castanea sativa*
The sweet chestnut has been cultivated for thousands of years in Southern Europe where it is widely used in sweet and savoury dishes. It contains more starch and less oil and protein than other nuts, although it is rich in B vitamins. Choose chestnuts which are firm with bright, shiny skins.

Chestnuts can be made into soups, added to casseroles, such as Red Cabbage Casserole (p. 268), or pies, used to make a traditional vegetarian Christmas roast (p. 348), or to stuff cabbage leaves, or to be served with Brussels sprouts. Puréed and sweetened, chestnuts also form the basis of some delicious puddings.

DRIED CHESTNUTS are time-saving, although their texture is less floury than that of fresh chestnuts. Dried chestnuts should be soaked and cooked like pulses (p. 57) and can then be used to replace fresh chestnuts in recipes, allowing 1 part dried chestnuts to 3 parts fresh chestnuts. Canned whole chestnuts and chestnut purée (available either plain or sweetened) are useful store cupboard standbys, while chestnuts preserved whole in sugar or syrup as MARRONS GLACÉS make a sweet treat or garnish.

CHINESE WATER CHESTNUT *Eleocharis tuberosa*

This is not actually a nut but a tuber which is cultivated in China, Japan and the East Indies. It is used sliced as a vegetable and outside Asia is usually bought canned. It has a crisp texture.

COCONUT *Cocos nucifera*

Coconuts grow throughout South-East Asia and feature in many tropical dishes. They can be bought whole and you should be able to hear the liquid inside when you shake them. Make sure that the 'eyes' look dry, with no smell of rancidity or mould. To open a coconut, pierce two of the eyes with a skewer and drain out the liquid over a jug. Then hold the coconut horizontally in both hands and bang it down on a stone or concrete surface to break it in half. Cut the flesh away from the shell using a sharp knife, and grate or chop the flesh as required. The liquid is delicately flavoured and makes a refreshing, nutritious drink or flavouring for spiced vegetables.

Coconut flesh can be eaten fresh as a snack or in salads, fruit and vegetable mixtures. It can also be bought DRIED, CREAMED, DESICCATED or in FLAKES or STRANDS. Keep these in the fridge or freezer, or store them in an airtight jar and use them up quickly. Desiccated coconut can be added to cakes, biscuits and Crunchy Granola (p. 359), or reconstituted as coconut milk.

HAZELNUT *Corylus avellana, C. maxima, C. colura*

Cultivated hazelnuts are derived from the cob, which grows wild in Britain, the filbert, which grows in Southern Europe, and the Turkish hazel which grows in the Middle East. The COB NUT (Kentish Cob), which is grown in Kent, is not really a cob but a filbert, and in Spain hazelnuts are known as Barcelona nuts. It is difficult to tell these types apart, once harvested. They can be bought in the shell, shelled but untreated, and whole but skinned.

Hazelnuts are mainly used in baking and confectionery and are a useful nut in vegetarian cookery, being the lowest in fat, a good source of vitamin E and a tasty addition to stuffings, burgers and loaves.

MACADAMIA NUT/QUEENSLAND NUT *Macadamia ternifolia*
A delectable nut, with a melting texture, native to Australia but
now also grown in the Southern USA, South Africa, the Caribbean, Mediterranean and Hawaii, the Macadamia is usually sold
roasted and lightly salted. It is expensive and so probably best
served simply, as a nibble with drinks, or in a salad, where its
flavour and creamy texture can be appreciated.

PEANUT/GROUND NUT/MONKEY NUT *Arachis hypogaea*
One of the best sources of protein, iron and niacin in the
vegetarian diet, peanuts can be bought in the shell, shelled but
raw, roasted unskinned and skinned. They can also be roasted
and skinned at home, as described above. Salted and roasted
and dry-roasted peanuts are also available, and of course
PEANUT BUTTER (without additives), either crunchy or smooth.

Peanuts also make an excellent thick sauce for serving with
salads or lightly cooked vegetables: reduce roasted peanuts to a
purée in a blender or food processor with chilli pepper, garlic
and fresh coriander to taste, and enough milk, coconut milk or
stock to make a thick sauce.

PECAN NUT *Carya illinoensis*
These relatives of the walnut can be bought shelled or unshelled
and are generally used as a dessert nut and in sweet dishes such
as Pecan Pie. In the USA they are also sometimes used as a
turkey stuffing and in vegetarian cooking they provide a useful
flavouring and delicious mealy texture which is good in salads
and hot nut savoury dishes.

PINE NUT/INDIAN NUT *Pinus pinea*
The most protein-rich of the nuts, pine nuts are always bought
shelled and have a fresh, creamy appearance and delicate 'pine'
flavour. They can be used as they are or lightly roasted in a
moderate oven or under the grill. They are added to omelettes in
the pine-clad Landes area of France, but they are more extensively used in Spanish, Italian and Middle Eastern cooking, in
pilafs, Stuffed Vine Leaves (p. 215) and Pesto (p. 257), the classic
Genoese sauce for pasta. Pine nuts make an excellent garnish for
many fruit or vegetable dishes and they can also be made into
delicately flavoured nut savouries (p. 353).

Pistachio nut *Pistacia vera*

Native to Asia but now grown in many other countries, pistachio nuts can be bought in the shell or shelled. They can be eaten as a nibble or as a bright garnish for both sweet and savoury dishes. They are rich in iron.

Tiger nut/Chufa nut *Cyperus esculentus sativus*

This dried rhizome, which grows in the Mediterranean, has a sweet, almond-like flavour. It can be eaten raw, as a nibble, or made into a creamy milk (p. 51). (It is not generally available in Aus./NZ.)

Walnut *Juglans regia*

Walnuts can be bought in the shell, or shelled, as halves or pieces. Buy fresh walnuts, as older ones can become bitter. Their strong flavour is useful in savoury nut dishes, perhaps combined with other milder nuts, such as cashews. Walnuts are good in salads, with pasta, and in many sweet dishes such as walnut cake or walnut biscuits.

Alfalfa seeds *Medicago sativa*

Sprinkle alfalfa seeds over bread before baking, or sprout them as on p. 57 and add to salads. Sprouted alfalfa seeds are rich in nutrients including protein, vitamin c and b vitamins.

Poppy seeds *Papaver somniferum*

Sprinkled over breads, salads or pasta, or added to cakes or savoury dishes, poppy seeds (which vary in colour from grey-blue to cream) give a pleasant, nutty flavour. In India they are ground and used to thicken curries.

Pumpkin seeds *Cucurbita pepo*

Rich in nutrients, particularly protein, iron and zinc, pumpkin seeds can be bought either salted or unsalted and used whole in savoury rice and vegetable dishes and mueslis, sprouted (p. 57) for salads and stir-fries, or ground and added to burgers and savoury loaves.

Sesame seeds/Benne seeds *Sesamum indicum*

Rich in B_3, iron, protein and zinc, sesame seeds are usually white but may be brown, red or black, depending on the variety. They are delicious when lightly roasted and can be added to sweet and savoury crumble toppings, sprinkled over breads, or ground with salt (p. 183). Sesame seeds can also be used in the form of a sticky beige or brown cream, called TAHINI. This is widely used in Middle Eastern cookery, in dips such as Hummus (p. 217) which make delicious additions to vegetarian cuisine. Sesame seeds are also made into the Middle Eastern sweetmeat, halva.

SUNFLOWER SEEDS *Helianthus annuus*
These can be bought whole, salted or unsalted, and added to stuffings, salads and savoury bakes, or ground like nuts. Their flavour is improved by roasting lightly. Sunflower seeds can also be sprouted (p. 57). They are a natural source of many nutrients, notably B_1, B_6 and potassium.

Pulses

A staple food throughout the world for thousands of years, pulses are the dried seeds of pod-bearing plants of the Leguminosae family. They are rich in protein, iron, calcium and B vitamins. They are high in fibre but contain virtually no fat, making them the nutritionists' dream food! The word pulse is linked to the Latin word *puls*, porridge, and the Greek *poltos*, poultice. Pulses are an economical food and when well cooked can be delicious.

Choosing and storing
Pulses will keep for many years, but they become drier and harder with time. So buy small quantities of bright, shiny pulses with no hint of dust, damp or mould. Keep them in an airtight container.

Sprouting

Most whole pulses, with the exception of red kidney beans, can be sprouted, and make a delicious, crunchy and highly nutritious addition to salads and stir-fries.

To sprout pulses, put 2 heaped tablespoons of your chosen variety into a jar − a large empty coffee jar is ideal. Cover pulses with cold water and leave overnight. Next day fix a piece of gauze over the top, securing with an elastic band. Pour the soaking water out through the gauze then, again without removing the gauze, fill the jar with cold water, shake, and pour it out. Leave the jar on its side for 2−4 days until the pulses have sprouted, repeating the rinsing at least twice a day. Once sprouted, the pulses can be stored in a polythene bag in the fridge.

Preparation and cooking

Preparation of pulses is simple and involves washing, soaking (some types do not need this) and cooking in plenty of cold water until tender. If you find pulses indigestible − their one disadvantage for some people − careful preparation, as described here, followed by thorough cooking, can help, as can boiling the pulses in an uncovered pan.

SOAKING AND COOKING TIMES FOR PULSES

Pulses can be cooked until they are just tender,
al dente, or soft, as preferred

All lentils, mung beans and black-eyed beans; split peas	cook without soaking for 25–40 minutes, until tender
Flageolet beans	soak as described, cook for 30–60 minutes
Other beans, including chick peas	soak as described, cook for 1–1½ hours
Soya beans	soak as described, cook for 1½–3 hours

1 Washing

Swish the pulses around in a bowl of cold water then drain in a colander. If you're using brown lentils, look out for little lumps of dirt and stones.

2 Soaking

Put the pulses into a deep bowl and cover them with their depth again in water. Leave to soak for about 6–8 hours or overnight. Then drain and rinse again.

Alternatively, put the washed pulses into a roomy saucepan, cover them with water as before and boil for 2 minutes. Then remove from the heat, cover and leave to stand for 1 hour. (This is equivalent to the long, cold soak.) Drain and rinse the beans and cook as follows.

3 Cooking

Tip the pulses into a large saucepan, cover them with their depth again in cold water and bring to the boil. Red kidney beans need to be boiled hard for 10 minutes, to destroy any enzymes which can cause stomach upsets. This isn't necessary for other beans. Then turn the heat down and simmer the pulses, without a lid, until tender (see chart below). Sometimes pulses are added to a casserole or made into a soup after soaking but before cooking; just allow them to simmer until tender. It is best to season pulses after they are cooked, to avoid any possibility of the salt toughening the outside and preventing the inside from cooking properly.

If you are short of time, canned pulses, available in considerable variety, are an excellent buy.

ADZUKI BEAN *Phaseolus angularis*

These seeds of a bushy plant native to China are a popular ingredient in Chinese and Japanese cookery. Quick-cooking, with a pleasant, slightly sweet flavour, adzuki beans can be used instead of lentils in any recipe for soups, salads, bakes or burgers. They can also be sprouted (p. 57).

BLACK BEAN *Phaseolus vulgaris*

These tasty beans are used to make American black bean soup, and, with rice, to make the Spanish dish, Moors and Christians. Good in vegetable casseroles, as a moist and tasty filling for Vegetarian Moussaka (p. 317), or in mixed bean salads, they have a delicious mealy texture.

Black-eyed bean/cow pea *Vigna unguiculata*

These pretty little beans, native to Africa and often popular with children, have a slightly nutty flavour and are particularly useful because they cook in about 40 minutes, without soaking. Use them in stews, soups, salads and casseroles.

Borlotti bean *Phaseolus vulgaris*

Borlotti beans, also known as 'rose coco' beans, are the most popular dried beans in Italy. They can be used in the same ways as any of the kidney bean family and make a pretty addition to a mixed bean salad.

Broad bean *Vicia faba*

More familiar in their fresh or frozen state, dried broad beans are pale or mid-brown in colour and have quite a strong, earthy flavour. They are widely used in the Middle East and Italy. I find their tough skin a disadvantage, but if well chopped in a food processor and blended with olive oil, garlic, lemon and parsley, they make a good dip.

Butter bean/Lima bean *Phaseolus lunatus or P. limensis*

Known as the lima bean in the USA, this bean is native to South America and is grown extensively in Madagascar. It is a flat, kidney-shaped, tasty bean with a mealy texture which absorbs other flavours well.

A quick way of serving butter beans is in cream with mushrooms: fry 225 g/8 oz sliced button mushrooms in 25 g/1 oz butter or vegan margarine for 3–4 minutes, then add the drained contents of a 425-g/15-oz can of butter beans and heat gently with 300 ml/10 fl oz single cream and 2 tablespoons lemon juice. Season, then serve sprinkled with paprika pepper and chopped parsley.

Cannellini bean *Phaseolus vulgaris*

These large creamy white beans combine well with pasta and make a fragrant salad when mixed with a fresh herb vinaigrette. If you want to adapt chicken or fish recipes to vegetarian cooking, cannellini beans make a good replacement, as do any of the white beans.

CHICK PEA *Cicer arietinum*

Chick peas are available whole, including a BLACK variety, split, ground into FLOUR and also canned, and have a particularly savoury flavour. Their cooking time is rather variable, ranging from 30 minutes to 3 hours, depending on the type. Chick peas are delicious cooked and then sautéed in garlic butter, or combined with mayonnaise and lightly cooked vegetables, including some artichoke hearts (fresh or canned) to make the Provençal salad, Aigroissade. Chick peas are included in many traditional recipes, including Felafel (p. 311), and Hummus (p. 217) from the Middle East and Couscous from North Africa (p. 369).

FLAGEOLET BEAN *Phaseolus vulgaris*

Popular in France, their fresh colour and flavour makes these immature haricot beans particularly suitable for serving as a vegetable (just boil and serve with butter and freshly ground black pepper) or as a salad.

They are also good in a creamy sauce with mushrooms, as described for butter beans (above).

FUL MEDAMES *Lathyrus sativus*

Although popular in the Middle East, I find ful medames one of the less useful beans because of their tough skin. But like broad beans (see above) they can be made into a good dip, using a food processor. Ful medames are not generally available in Aus./NZ.

HARICOT BEAN *Phaseolus vulgaris*

A useful all-purpose bean which absorbs other flavours well, this is popular in Britain as baked beans. In France haricot beans are used to make the popular and filling Cassoulet and Pistou (p. 206). In the USA haricot beans are also used to make another traditional dish, Boston Baked Beans. To make these, simmer 225 g/8 oz haricot beans as described above until almost tender, then drain and add to 1 quantity Italian Tomato Sauce, made as described on p. 254 but not boiled after the tomatoes have been added. Stir in 1–2 tablespoons real barbados sugar, then bake at 160c/325f/Gas Mark 3 for 2–3 hours, until the sauce is rich and thick and has been well absorbed by the beans. Stir from time to time. Serve with hot crusty bread.

Lentil *Lens esculenta*

There are several types of lentil. The most common is the little brown lentil which is very tasty and remains whole when cooked. However, it needs careful checking and washing first to remove small pieces of grit. The dark greenish-grey Puy lentil is considered by some to have the best flavour and is popular in France. Then there is the larger whole green (sometimes called continental) lentil which has a savoury flavour and does not break up during cooking. Finally, there is the split orange lentil, often used in soups. Lentils can be cooked without soaking, although soaking speeds the cooking time. Lentils are used in the Mediterranean and Middle East to make soups, stews, bakes, sauces for pasta (p. 374) and salads (p. 236), and in India, where they are made into spicy dals (p. 312). They make a good replacement for minced meat in recipes such as Shepherd's Pie (p. 314) and Spicy Lentil Burgers (p. 313). Whole lentils can also be sprouted (p. 57), when they become juicy with a slightly spicy flavour.

Mung bean *Phaseolus aureus*

Mung beans are small, round and usually green, although there are some black and yellow varieties. They can also be bought skinned and halved to reveal their golden colour. Whole mung beans make a good salad, dressed with a tangy, lemon vinaigrette. These are the beans which are made into beansprouts (p. 57). As sprouts they are juicy and good in stir-fries and salads.

Dried pea *Pisum sativum*

Most familiar in the UK in the form of sweet-tasting mushy peas, dried peas can also be used in soups and stews. They are known as BLUE BOILERS in Aus./NZ and soup peas in the USA.

Pigeon pea *Cajanus cajan*

Pigeon peas are widely used in African, Caribbean and Indian dishes, but in my opinion are not as tasty or useful as some of the other pulses, such as chick peas.

Pinto bean *Phaseolus vulgaris*

Also called gunga pea and toor dal, pinto beans are popular in India and the Caribbean. They can be used like red kidney beans and are good in casseroles and to add colour to mixed bean salads such as those on p. 236.

RED KIDNEY BEAN *Phaseolus vulgaris*

One of the most useful pulses, widely used in South American and Caribbean cooking, red kidney beans are available both dried and canned. They should always be boiled hard for 10 minutes before using. They are used to make the Mexican dish of Refried Beans, in which the cooked beans are fried like a large potato cake; a delicious West Indian stew where they are cooked with carrots, onions, garlic and thyme, with a knob of coconut cream added at the end, to thicken and enrich, and a tasty vegetarian version of Chilli con Carne (p. 310).

SOYA BEAN *Glycine max*

Soya beans are very nutritious and have a strong flavour but need powerful flavourings, such as curry, tomato and garlic, to make them taste good. I think they're nicest when sprouted (p. 57), and added to sandwiches, stir-fries and salads.

Try a vitality salad of crunchy soya sprouts, alfalfa sprouts, shredded lettuce, chopped tomatoes, grated raw beetroot and carrot, layered into a bowl and topped with mayonnaise.

Many products, such as miso, soy sauce, tempeh, milk (p. 416) and tofu (p. 157) are made from soya beans and described in other sections of this book.

SOYA FLOUR is high in protein and low in starch so it cannot be used to make a normal white sauce, although it can be stirred into savoury sauces and gravies to add bulk and nutrients. It is also sometimes added to flour as a dough improver, in the proportion 8 parts flour to 1 part soya flour.

SPLIT PEAS, YELLOW AND GREEN *Pisum sativum*

The split and skinned version of yellow or green dried peas cook quickly without soaking and can be made into a good purée for serving with vegetables. Alternatively the two colours may be combined and cooked until just tender, then mixed with a lemon or mint vinaigrette to make an attractive salad. Pease Pudding (p. 309) is a cheap and filling traditional British dish.

URD BEAN *Phaseolus mungo*

(Not generally available in Aus./NZ.) The split and skinned version of this black bean, about half the size of a pea, is best cooked without soaking. Urd dal is used to make dosas, the crisp pancakes of Southern India, and also poppadums.

Grains

The seeds of cultivated grasses, grains are the world's most important staple food. They are important in the vegetarian diet, where they are recognized as protein foods and often mixed with other complementary proteins, such as seeds, nuts, pulses and dairy products, to make maximum use of their protein (p. 14). As well as protein and carbohydrate, grains are a valuable source of iron, zinc, calcium and B vitamins, and, in their natural, unrefined state, are also rich in fibre.

Choosing and storing

Grains will keep in their natural unmilled form for a year or so, but they do deteriorate and ideally should be bought fresh and used up within 6 months. Cracked and flaked grains, and flours will keep for 3–6 months. Oats – with the exception of rolled oats, where heat has destroyed the enzymes – do not keep well because of their high oil content. Buy in small quantities and use within a few weeks. Oatmeal should smell and taste sweet with no rancid smell or bitterness. Wheatgerm, especially if it is the best unstabilized type, which is free from additives, deteriorates rapidly; keep it in the fridge and use it up within 3–4 weeks. Keep other grains and flours in airtight containers in a cool, dry place.

Preparation and cooking

Wholewheat, oat, barley and rye grains are soaked and cooked like pulses; they can then be tossed in a dressing or mixed with vegetables to make burgers, roasts or stews. Flaked grains, like jumbo oats, and also kibbled wheat, make a pleasantly chewy addition to muesli mix and home-made breads; jumbo oats can be mixed half and half with rolled oats for extra chewy flapjacks.

COOKING PERFECT RICE

There are two methods of cooking rice and each has its devotees. I find both work equally well; it's really a question of which of the methods you find works best for you.

The only rice which needs washing first is basmati, which should be put into a sieve and rinsed under the cold tap until the water runs clear.

Immersion method
Half fill a large saucepan with water, bring to the boil and add 1 teaspoon salt. Throw in the rice, allowing 50 g/2 oz per person if the rice is to be served as an accompaniment, or up to 100 g/4 oz per person if the rice is the main dish, without much else. Simmer, uncovered, until a grain is tender when you bite it. For timings, see table (p. 67). Drain the rice into a colander and rinse it under the hot tap to remove any starch. Then tip it back into the saucepan and dry the rice off over a low heat for about 5 minutes, stirring it several times with a fork to prevent sticking. Or put the rice into a shallow ovenproof dish and place, uncovered, in a cool oven (170c/325f/Gas Mark 3) for about 10 minutes until it is dry.

Absorption method
For this you need to measure both the rice and the water, and it's handy to use the same container — a large mug, or a 300 ml/10 fl oz measure. Put one measure of rice into a saucepan, add two measures of water and a little salt. Bring to the boil, then cover and turn the heat down as low as possible. Leave the rice undisturbed until it's tender and all the water has been absorbed (see table for timings). Then stir gently with a fork. Or, after it has come to the boil, the rice can be cooked in a cool oven (as above).

BARLEY *Hordeum vulgare*

Barley is available in the form of whole grains, called POT (or WHOLE) BARLEY, as PEARL BARLEY, which is more refined (and, I find, more useful) and as FLAKES and FLOUR. Pearl barley, which contains more fibre than brown rice, is often added to soups and stews, to thicken and enrich, and makes a cheap and tasty homely casserole (p. 368). Pot barley can be cooked to make pilafs or salads.

BUCKWHEAT *Fagopyrum esculentum*

These triangular-shaped seeds are gluten-free and a natural source of rutin, which naturopaths use to treat varicose veins and high blood pressure. Buckwheat can be bought as grains,

ROASTED or UNROASTED, and FLOUR. Roasted buckwheat is the most useful for cooking, and the basis of the Russian dish, kasha. It can be served instead of rice with vegetable dishes and goes well with strongly flavoured winter mixtures. To cook buckwheat, put it into a saucepan with double its volume in water and simmer for about 10 minutes, until the grains are just tender and all the water absorbed. Add butter or vegan margarine and salt and pepper, and perhaps some crushed garlic.

BUCKWHEAT FLOUR is used to make blinis (Russian pancakes). Try making pancakes as described on p. 447 using a half and half mixture of buckwheat and wheat flour and serving with unsalted butter, Black Olive Pâté (p. 383) and soured cream.

BULGUR WHEAT

Sometimes called burghul, cracked wheat or pourgouri, bulgur wheat is easy to prepare and delicious in pilafs with vegetables, nuts, raisins and pulses, and with lots of chopped fresh parsley and mint in the popular Middle Eastern salad, Tabbouleh (p. 239). To prepare bulgur wheat, put the grains into a bowl, allowing 50–100 g/2–4 oz per person, cover with plenty of cold water and leave to soak for about 30 minutes. Then drain and put into a saucepan containing a tablespoon of olive oil, or perhaps an onion or other vegetables such as chopped red pepper and mushrooms, which have been fried in the oil for about 10 minutes, season with salt and freshly ground black pepper and stir over a gentle heat for about 5 minutes, until the wheat is hot. Or put the wheat into an oiled casserole, cover and bake for 15–20 minutes in a moderate oven (180c/350f/Gas Mark 4) until the wheat is hot.

CORN *Zea mays*

Corn is available as whole grains – fun for 'popping' – and as COARSE or FINE FLOUR or MAIZE MEAL; also hulled as HOMINY GRITS (not generally available in Aus./NZ), used to make porridge, puddings and breads. Although it is eaten as a staple food in Italy and South America, corn is not ideal for this because of its deficiency in niacin. The flour made from corn is made into spoonbread in the USA, polenta in Italy and mamaliga in Rumania. The gluten-free maize meal milled from corn is used to make tortillas and tacos in Mexico.

Couscous

Available as PLAIN or WHOLEWHEAT, this is made by processing semolina into tiny pellets and is another easy grain to prepare: just spread the couscous out on a large plate and sprinkle it with salted water, allowing 600 ml/1 pint water and ½ teaspoon salt to 450 g/1 lb couscous (which is enough to serve 4–5 people). Rub your fingers between the grains to help keep them separate, then leave them for 15–20 minutes, to absorb the water. Put the couscous into a steamer saucepan, metal colander or large metal sieve set over a pan of boiling water, or of spicy stew, as on p. 369, for about 15 minutes, or until heated through.

Millet *Panicum miliaceum*

Millet contains more protein and iron than any other grain. It can be bought in the form of GRAINS, FLAKES and FLOUR, and is gluten-free. The grains can be made into tasty pilafs (p. 367) and burgers, and the flakes can be cooked to make a creamy porridge – particularly useful for those on gluten-free diets.

Oats *Avena sativa*

Oats contain more of the B vitamin biotin and more fat than wheat; they are also gluten-free and are one of the best sources of soluble fibre (p. 17). As such they have been found to be valuable in lowering blood cholesterol. In experiments Dr James Anderson of the University of Kentucky found that hyper-cholesterolemic men who supplemented their diet with oat bran reduced harmful cholesterol levels by 20 per cent. Dr Anderson also frequently found that the amount of soluble fibre needed to control cholesterol levels was equivalent to a bowl of porridge in the morning, with rolled oats, perhaps in the form of muffins or oatcakes, included in two other meals during the day. Oats are available as whole GRAINS, called 'whole oat groats', milled to fine, medium or coarse (or 'pinmeal') meal, for making Porridge and Oatcakes (p. 482); as OAT FLAKES, or 'JUMBO OATS', ROLLED OATS, and various precooked 'instant' versions. But even traditional porridge, made from oatmeal, is quick to make. To serve 2 people, bring 600 ml/1 pint water and 1 teaspoon salt to the boil, then gradually whisk in 50 g/2 oz medium oatmeal. Simmer gently for 25–30 minutes, stirring from time to time.

For Super-quick Porridge, made from rolled oats, to serve 2, put 50 g/2 oz rolled oats into a saucepan with 300 ml/10 fl oz water and ½ teaspoon salt. Stir over a moderate heat for about 2 minutes, until thickened. If the porridge is too thick, stir in more water.

Oats are the basis of muesli mixes, and a simple muesli base can be made by mixing 225 g/8 oz rolled oats with 100 g/4 oz each of raisins and nuts. Other whole grains and dried fruits and nuts can be added to taste.

RICE *Oryza sativa*

Although there are many varieties of rice, these can be divided into two basic types: LONG-GRAIN, where the grain is four or five times as long as it is wide, and SHORT-/MEDIUM-GRAIN, where the grain is short and rounded. In long-grain types, which include AMERICAN LONG-GRAIN RICE and BASMATI RICE, with slim pointed grains and a particularly aromatic flavour, the grains are more separate when cooked, so these are most suitable for pilafs and rice salads, where you want a 'fluffy'

COOKING TIMES FOR RICE
Times in minutes

Rice	Immersion method	Absorption method top of stove	Absorption method Oven (180°C/350°F/Gas Mark 4)
white Basmati	10–12	15	25
brown Basmati	12–15	20	30
white long-grain/ Patna	15	15	35–40
brown long-grain	35	45	50
Italian arborio	15	15	35–40
Japanese glutinous	15	15–25	35–40
wild rice	35–40	40	50

texture. The round and medium grains break up more as they cook and cling together. This type includes ITALIAN RICE (ARBORIO), PUDDING (or PEARL) RICE, and SWEET BROWN RICE which is popular in macrobiotic cookery and good as an accompaniment to Japanese dishes.

The test of perfect long-grain rice is for all the grains to be separate when you pick up a small handful of the cooked rice. This does not apply to rice for serving with Chinese or Japanese meals. For these, a more glutinous type of rice should be used, so that it clings together when cooked, making it easy to eat with chopsticks.

Many varieties of rice can be bought in a 'BROWN' version, that is, with just the inedible outer husk removed, or 'POLISHED' so that they are completely white (and less nutritious). BROWN RICE FLAKES, GROUND RICE and BROWN RICE FLOUR (useful for gluten-free baking) are also available.

To make traditional British Rice Pudding, put 25 g/1 oz short-grain pudding rice into a shallow buttered ovenproof dish. Stir in 600 ml/1 pint milk and 2 tablespoons soft light brown sugar. Add a vanilla pod or a few drops of real vanilla extract and dot the top with a little butter. Bake for 2½−3 hours at 170c/325f/Gas Mark 3, stirring in the skin after about 30 minutes, and again about an hour later.

RYE *Secale cereale*

Rye is available in the form of whole GRAINS, FLAKES, FLOUR (white and wholemeal) and kibbled grains for topping loaves. Rye lacks gluten so is usually mixed with wheat flour. It is widely used to make dark heavy breads (such as pumpernickel) and crispbreads in Germany and Scandinavia. Rye is also used to make whiskey in America.

SEMOLINA

Semolina, a flour made from the hard part of durum wheat, is the basic ingredient for the very tasty Italian dish, Gnocchi alla Romana (p. 341) and can also be made into one of the most popular vegetarian dishes, Cheese and Parsley Fritters (p. 326) which are a variation of gnocchi. Semolina is used to make delectable sweet puddings in India and the Middle East, and can be added to cakes and biscuits.

Wholewheat *Triticum vulgare, compactum, durum*

Wheat is available in a number of forms, including WHOLE GRAINS, KIBBLED WHEAT (good in muesli mixes and on top of loaves), WHEAT FLAKES, and flours consisting of various percentages of grain (WHOLEWHEAT FLOUR, 85 per cent and 100 per cent, and WHITE FLOUR, including UNBLEACHED which contains fewer additives than bleached). The parts of the wheat, the nutritious GERM and high-fibre BRAN, removed during the milling of white flour, are also available. The 100 per cent wholewheat flour is milled from whole grain, and contains no additives (except raising agents) in the UK; 85 per cent may be 100 per cent wholewheat with some bran removed, or white flour with some germ and bran put back.

Wheat flour is classified as 'strong' or 'soft' depending on its gluten content. Gluten is the protein-rich substance which becomes springy and stretchy when water and heat are applied. Flour made from gluten-rich, hard wheat is generally considered best for making bread and for puff and flaky pastries because it produces a strong, springy dough, although soft wheat produces a better-flavoured bread and is fine for making the one-rise Grant Loaf (p. 492). Soft flour produces light cakes and biscuits with a melting texture.

Wild rice *Zizania aquatica*

Particularly high in protein, and with a distinctive, slightly smoky flavour, wild rice gives a luxurious touch to a special meal. The long black grains can be cooked on their own, using the absorption method described for brown rice, or with brown rice, replacing some of the rice with the same quantity of chewy, nutty-tasting wild rice (p. 67).

Pasta

Pasta means dough in Italian and is the collective name for all types of spaghetti, macaroni, ravioli, vermicelli and so on. Although there is a tradition of pasta making and eating in other parts of the world such as

China, Spain, Greece and Israel, the Italians are undoubtedly the world leaders and have developed hundreds of different pasta shapes. Both white and wholewheat pasta are good sources of fibre (wholewheat more so) and contain useful amounts of protein, iron and B vitamins.

Pasta may be white or wholewheat, depending on the type of flour used to make it; it can be dyed a variety of colours with vegetable purées and comes in numerous shapes and sizes. Terminology can be confusing, because often the same shape is known by several different names, and in Italy these frequently vary from province to province! Pasta can be bought dried or, increasingly, fresh. Dry pasta may contain eggs — if it does it will say *all'uovo* on the packet; fresh pasta always does. Fresh stuffed pastas, such as ravioli and cappaletti, are increasingly to be found with vegetarian fillings, such as spinach and ricotta.

Quick and easy, cheap and delicious, pasta is welcoming, filling and warming. It can be made into many appetizing vegetarian dishes.

Choosing and storing

Good-quality dried pasta should feel hard and silky-smooth and when cooked should have a deliciously wheaty flavour. Store in a cool, dry place. Fresh pasta should smell fresh and look bright and slightly shiny. Store in the refrigerator and use within 24 hours if possible.

How to make pasta

Pasta is easy to make at home and worth doing if you eat a fair amount of it and enjoy cooking. You can roll the pasta out by hand, but better results are obtained by using a pasta machine. The hand-operated ones, consisting of rollers turned by a handle, are perfectly adequate for making family-sized amounts of pasta, or, for large quantities, electric machines are available.

To make 350 g/12 oz pasta – enough for 4 people – put 200 g/7 oz plain strong flour into a bowl with ½ teaspoon salt. Gradually add 2 beaten eggs, to make a pliable dough. Set the rollers of your pasta machine to their widest position. Take a piece of pasta dough about the size of an egg, flatten it roughly with your hands, then feed it through the rollers. Fold the piece of dough in three, then feed it through again. Repeat this process six or seven times, until the dough is smooth and silky, then lay it on one side and repeat the process with the rest of the dough, keeping the pieces in the right order. Next, tighten the rollers a notch and put the pieces of dough through again, once only this time, and without folding. Repeat three times, tightening the rollers a notch each time. Cut the pieces of pasta in half if they become too long to handle, and support them as they come through the machine so that they don't fall in folds and stick together.

If you want to make lasagne, cannelloni or ravioli, feed the pasta through the machine again with the rollers on the tightest setting but one. The pasta can then be cut to the required size and used straight away in savoury bakes, without further drying or cooking.

For ravioli, spread half the pieces of pasta out on a flat surface and put small mounds of a savoury mixture (such as 225 g/8 oz curd cheese mixed with 75 g/3 oz grated Cheddar cheese and 25 g/1 oz grated Parmesan cheese) on the pasta about 3 cm/1½ inches apart. Brush around each mound with beaten egg, then cover with the rest of the pasta, pressing down around the edges and trying to exclude as much air as possible. Cut between the mounds with a pastry wheel. Put the ravioli on a lightly floured surface and leave to dry for 30 minutes. Then put the ravioli into a large pan of boiling water and cook for 4–6 minutes. Drain well, put into a hot serving dish and cover with hot tomato sauce.

To make tagliatelle, pass the pieces of pasta through one of the cutting rollers, then spread them out on a clean, lightly-floured cloth, or drape over a piece of dowelling, and leave to dry for about 1 hour. Then cook the pasta as described opposite, allowing 2–3 minutes only.

Preparation and Cooking

Fresh or dried pasta needs no preparation before cooking.

Allow 100−175 g/4−6 oz fresh or dried pasta per person for a main course, less if serving as a first course. For every 100 g/4 oz pasta you will need 1·2 litres (2 pints) water. Bring the water to the boil in a large saucepan. Salt can be added to the water, allowing ½−1 teaspoon for every 100 g/4 oz, but I prefer to add some crunchy flakes of sea salt to the cooked and drained pasta. When the water is boiling vigorously, add the pasta all at once.

To add long straight pasta, such as spaghetti, hold the pasta in your hand like a bunch of flowers, put the ends in the water so that it's standing up, then as the ends soften, gradually bend them, pushing more of the dry pasta into the water. When all the pasta is under water, give it a quick stir, then leave it to boil, half-covered, until tender. This will vary from type to type; smaller types cook more quickly, and fresh pasta is ready in about 5 minutes. The packet will give a guide, but check it before the time is up, as cooking time can vary from batch to batch and even be affected by the weather!

To test whether the pasta is done, bite a piece; it should be tender but still slightly firm, so you can feel it on your teeth, or *al dente* as the Italians say. When this stage is reached, remove from the heat and drain the pasta immediately. The easiest way to do this is to stand a metal colander in the sink and tip the pasta straight into it. Give the colander a shake to make sure the water has been dislodged from the pasta, then tip it back into the still-hot pan.

Return to the heat with some olive oil or a knob of butter, a good grinding of black pepper and some sea salt if you didn't add this to the water. Turn the pasta gently with a fork or spoon, so that all of it is coated with butter or oil. Serve immediately on a well-warmed serving dish or individual plates.

Dry lasagne can be cooked as described, then drained and draped over the sides of the colander and saucepan, to prevent it from sticking together, ready for layering into a casserole with a tasty filling and sauce. Or it can be added to the casserole in its dry form. In this case make the filling and sauces with extra liquid for the pasta to absorb during cooking.

Fresh lasagne does not need cooking first, and, again, you should allow extra liquid because it will expand during cooking.

COOKING TIMES FOR PASTA	
very thin pasta, small shapes	5–9 minutes
larger shapes, long tubes	10–20 minutes
fresh pasta	2–3 minutes

Serving pasta

The many varieties of pasta now available provide all sorts of serving possibilities.

The smallest, thinnest types, such as CONVIGHI PICCOLE, tiny bow-shaped FARFALLINE and VERMICELLI, are good to add to soups or lightly fried vegetables as in Pasta Primavera (p. 372), while the ridged tube pastas, such as RIGATONI, PENNE, PIPE and the shell-like CONCHIGLIE RIGATE, all hold sauces very well. Rigatoni is also very good combined with aubergines in Aubergine and Pasta Charlotte (p. 381) or with olives in Pasta with Black Olives (p. 382).

LASAGNE and MACARONI are used with sauces in baked dishes (p. 378 and p. 380), and many of the smaller pastas, tiny tube-shaped MEZZE CANNEONI or WHEATEAR WHOLEWHEAT SHAPES, for example, can also be used in bakes such as Wholewheat Pasta and Mushroom Bake (p. 373).

LUMACHE, the 'snail' shapes, make good containers for fillings such as ricotta cheese with garlic and fresh herbs, served with tomato sauce.

The large pasta tubes such as CANNELLONI and RIGATONI can be stuffed, with chopped mixed vegetables or just one vegetable such as spinach, and baked in a sauce in the same way as lasagne.

The smaller shapes, such as TORTELLINI, RAVIOLI and CAPPEL-LETTI, can also be stuffed – cheese and nuts are good – and can be cooked in stock or water, or in a tomato sauce. Fresh tortellini and ravioli are now frequently available with vegetarian fillings such as spinach and ricotta cheese.

Long pastas, SPAGHETTI, SPAGHETTINI, LINGUINE, TAGLIA-TELLE and FETTUCELLE, are delicious served very simply with just olive oil, garlic and black pepper; or with butter or cream, freshly ground black pepper, some chopped fresh herbs and a

QUICK SERVING IDEAS FOR PASTA

Pasta with Fresh Herbs

Add 1–2 tablespoons chopped fresh herbs to the cooked pasta with the butter or olive oil. Tarragon and basil are delicious.

Pasta with Cream

Stir a little double cream into the hot cooked pasta, allowing 2 tablespoons per person.

Pasta with Poppy Seeds

Add a good sprinkling of poppy seeds to hot, buttery pasta; they add a nutty flavour and crunchy texture.

Pasta with Nuts

Chopped walnuts go beautifully with hot cooked pasta. They're nicest if you buy them in the shell and crack a few while the pasta cooks. Chop roughly and add to the drained and buttered pasta. A little cream mixed in as well makes this extra good.

Pasta with Beans and Black Olives

While the pasta is cooking, heat through a can of cannellini beans in another saucepan. Drain both the beans and the pasta and mix together with a little crushed garlic, 1–2 tablespoons olive oil and a few whole black olives.

Pasta with Chick Peas

Add hot cooked and drained chick peas, crushed garlic and a little olive oil to hot drained pasta for a favourite Italian mixture.

Pasta with Croûtons

While the pasta is cooking, cut a slice of wholewheat bread per person, remove the crusts, and cut the bread into 5-mm/¼-inch squares. Fry the bread croûtons in olive oil until crisp and golden-brown all over. Drain on kitchen paper. Add the croûtons to each serving of hot pasta.

Pasta with Onions

Start this when you put the water for the pasta on to boil, to give the onions time to cook until they're really soft and slightly caramelized. Allow ½–1 large onion per person, peeled and sliced. Heat a knob of butter or vegan margarine in a saucepan or frying pan, add the onion and fry for 10 minutes, then add a sprinkling of salt, pepper and sugar, and continue to fry for a further 5–10 minutes, until the onion is golden-brown but not burnt. Stir the hot, cooked onion into the cooked and drained pasta.

Pasta with Fresh Tomato Sauce

Serve hot spaghetti or pasta spirals with Fresh Tomato Sauce (p. 253); snip plenty of fresh basil on top. Some diced Brie can be mixed with the pasta, to melt deliciously in the heat of the sauce.

Pasta with Avocado

Add a small ripe avocado, peeled and chopped, to the hot cooked pasta after draining.

Sweet Pasta

For a sweet pasta dish, popular in Italy, cook pasta until tender – a bit softer than the usual *al dente*, drain and add (for 350 g/ 12 oz pasta, which gives 4 servings) 3 tablespoons sugar, 40 g/1½ oz butter and 75 g/3 oz good quality plain chocolate, melted. Mix well and serve immediately.

grating of Parmesan cheese. They can also be dressed in numerous sauces; a lentil mixture is a good one to use (p. 374), as is an aubergine and tomato sauce (p. 376). Tagliatelle with Gorgonzola and Walnuts (p. 371) makes a delicious dish for a supper party, while linguine mixed with vegetables and cheese (p. 378) couldn't be simpler for a quick lunch.

Many pastas are now available coloured with vegetable dyes — spinach (*verde*) or tomato, for example. These coloured pastas can make a dish very attractive when served with an appropriately coloured sauce. Children especially enjoy the COLOURED RIGATONI or corkscrew-shaped FUSILLI with a mushroom sauce (p. 259).

There are many varieties of EGG NOODLES available and they are best known for their use in Chinese dishes. They are often sold fresh, coiled in circles or, when dried, in square 'cakes'. They can be used for noodle soups, or stir-fried with vegetable mixtures after they have been boiled.

RICE NOODLES are sold as long strands and are also called rice sticks. TRANSPARENT, or cellophane, RICE NOODLES are lighter in colour. They are both used in soups and stir-fries or can be deep-fried.

Leaf Vegetables

Crisp and refreshing, leaf vegetables whet the appetite and cleanse the palate. Some have been used for centuries — mustard and cress was enjoyed by the Greeks and Romans. Today there is a wide range to choose from and making salads is a particular pleasure. Several of the leaf vegetables, such as watercress, lettuce and spinach, make excellent soups. Leaf vegetables contain vitamin A, calcium, iron, fibre and chlorophyll, which, when eaten raw, protects the body against disease.

Choosing and storing

These vegetables need to be bought as fresh as possible; they should be crisp and slightly damp-looking, with no sign of withering or dryness. They are best used as soon as possible but, if bought really fresh, they will keep in the salad compartment of the fridge for two or three days.

Preparation and cooking

These vegetables, especially lettuce, are often sprayed with fungicide, so they need thorough but gentle washing in plenty of cold water. Many leaf vegetables are tasty when cooked and also make excellent soups. Remove any coarse or damaged leaves and tough stems. Tear, rather than cut, delicate leafy vegetables such as lettuce, and if they are going to be eaten raw, dry them carefully in a salad spinner or with a soft absorbent cloth.

GREEN SALAD INGREDIENTS

- ☐ Lettuce (all kinds)
- ☐ Curly endive
- ☐ Chicory
- ☐ Watercress
- ☐ Lamb's lettuce (corn salad/mâche)
- ☐ Tender spinach leaves
- ☐ Sorrel, rocket and tender nasturtium leaves (they're pungent, so just a few will be sufficient)
- ☐ Spring onions, raw onion rings
- ☐ Celery, cucumber, fennel, green pepper, avocado pear (thinly sliced)
- ☐ Fresh herbs
- ☐ Dandelion leaves (pick these carefully from a place unpolluted by dogs, cars or agricultural sprays, taking the tender leaves from near the centre and washing them very thoroughly)
- ☐ Chopped walnuts or hazelnuts

CRESS/MUSTARD AND CRESS *Lepidium sativum* and *sinapis alba*
The cress widely available in the shops is not the traditional mixture of mustard and cress but often salad rape. This has a mild flavour which particularly appeals to children. All kinds of mustard and cress make a pleasant addition to a salad bowl and are useful for garnishing.

ENDIVE/BATAVIA/ESCAROLE *Cichorium endivia crispum*
There are two main types of endive, curly-leaved and broad-leaved. They all have a refreshing, slightly bitter flavour and make an attractive contrast with other salad ingredients. Endive is particularly rich in folic acid (see p. 23).

FEUILLE DE CHÊNE *Lactuca sativa*
Also called OAK LEAF LETTUCE because of the shape of its leaves, this attractive lettuce has a slightly bitter flavour. It makes an excellent addition to a green salad and can also be used on its own. It is particularly good with a walnut dressing and Chèvre cheese (p. 226).

GOOD KING HENRY *Chenopodium Bonus-Henricus*
Also called GOOSEFOOT, this is a perennial herb which used to be cultivated and then went out of fashion. It has small, pointed leaves growing either side of a central stem bearing small flowers like those of sorrel.
  Both the leaves and the flowers can be eaten. It tastes very similar to spinach and is prepared in the same way.

LAMB'S LETTUCE/CORN SALAD/MÂCHE *Valerianella locusta*
The leaves of a small hardy plant which grows wild, lamb's lettuce has a delicate flavour and makes a useful addition to salads, particularly in winter.

LANDCRESS *Barbarea verna*
This plant looks and tastes rather like watercress, with a similarly pungent flavour, but, as the name implies, it grows on land. It is a useful salad vegetable, and, like watercress, can also be made into soup.

LETTUCE *Lactuca sativa*
Lettuce is an ancient cultivated crop and is probably the number

one salad basic. It can be served on its own or mixed with other ingredients; shredded, it makes a good filling for sandwiches or base for other salad ingredients, and large leaves can be rolled around tasty fillings to make an interesting nibble or snack. Firm lettuce hearts can be braised in the same way as fennel (p. 271); outer leaves can be made into an excellent soup (p. 196), or used to impart flavour to peas cooked à la Française (p. 272).

There are many different types of lettuce, some of the main ones being:

CABBAGE HEAD
These are round or flat in shape, and can be subdivided into crisp lettuces, such as ICEBERG, and the soft-leaf or BUTTERHEAD varieties.

COS
Tall, well-flavoured lettuces, this group includes COS, DENSITY, and, perhaps the best-flavoured lettuce of all, the hearty 'LITTLE GEM' lettuce. Cos lettuce also has a good flavour and the smaller leaves make good edible scoops for dips.

SALAD BOWL
In this type the leaves do not form a solid heart and the leaves can be picked off individually if required while the plant is growing in the garden. They are usually particularly tender and there are some red, bronze or variegated types available.

RADICCIO *Cichorium intybus*
This red-leaved variety of endive has a slightly bitter flavour; it makes a colourful addition to a leafy salad and is a very attractive garnish.

ROCKET *Eruca sativa*
Sometimes classed as a herb, rocket has a hot, almost spicy flavour and a few sprigs make an excellent addition to a green salad.

SORREL *Rumex acetosa*
A few sorrel leaves give interest to a green salad, and a little sorrel cooked with spinach adds a sharp, almost lemony flavour. Puréed sorrel makes a good accompaniment to a nut roast, cutting the richness, and it also makes a refreshing soup.

Sorrel used in a Wilted Leaf Salad makes a delicious variation on Green Salad. Put a mixture of green salad ingredients into a bowl, using interesting varieties such as sorrel, rocket, dandelion leaves and spinach. Fry some small cubes of wholewheat bread in butter or olive oil, to make crisp croûtons. Then, just before you want to serve the salad, pour the croûtons and their cooking fat over the salad ingredients, mix quickly and serve at once. Until the eighteenth century sorrel was popular pounded with sugar and vinegar into a green sauce and it is still sometimes served like this in parts of Yorkshire.

Cooked sorrel should not be taken in large quantities too often because of the high level of oxalic acid it contains.

SPINACH *Spinaca oleracea* and SWISS CHARD *Beta vulgaris*, var. *Cicla*

These are delicious dark green leafy plants which can be shredded raw and added to salads, cooked and served simply as a vegetable accompaniment, or made into substantial main course dishes. The central stem of Swiss chard is particularly good and can be shredded and cooked in a little water for a few minutes before adding the green leaves, or it can be removed, cut into lengths and cooked and served separately.

COOKING PERFECT SPINACH

Allow 900 g/2 lb spinach for 4 people. Wash the spinach well by plunging it into a large bowl of water two or three times, until the water is clear. Remove any tough stems; either discard these, or chop them and add to 1 cm/½ inch boiling water in a large saucepan. Boil for 2 minutes, then put the spinach in on top. If you are not using the stems, put the spinach straight into the pan, without any water − the water still clinging to the spinach from the washing will be enough. Push the spinach down into the pan as it cooks. A fish slice is good for this if you hold it so that you can chop down with the slice part. Half cover the pan with a lid and cook for about 7 minutes, chopping the spinach with the fish slice from time to time. Drain the spinach well in a colander, using the back of a spoon to squeeze out the water. Then return it to the still-hot pan and chop it a bit more with the fish slice if necessary; or turn the spinach out on to a board and chop it quickly with a knife. Add a knob of butter or vegan margarine, a good seasoning of sea salt, freshly ground black pepper and perhaps a touch of grated nutmeg. Spinach absorbs a lot of butter, it's up to you how much to use.

SEA SPINACH, which can be found growing wild around the coast, is a wild form of spinach beet. It can be collected and used just like spinach and has an excellent, naturally salty flavour. NEW ZEALAND SPINACH (*Tetragonia expansa*) is another green leafy vegetable which is not related to spinach botanically but is similar and prepared in the same way.

Spinach is particularly rich in vitamin A, iron and calcium but, like sorrel, contains oxalic acid, which inhibits the body's ability to absorb some minerals. It's therefore best not to eat cooked spinach more than twice a week, although some natural health experts believe that the oxalic acid in raw spinach does not have the same binding effect.

Spinach is available fresh, frozen — a useful alternative to fresh — and canned, which in my opinion is not worth eating.

In Aus./NZ, if English spinach is unavailable, silver beet makes a good substitute.

VINE LEAF *Vitis vinifera*
Vine leaves are much used as edible wrappings for foods in vine-growing countries; dolmades, or vine leaves filled with a rice stuffing, are perhaps the best-known example. They have a delicious, slightly lemony flavour.

Fresh young vine leaves, when available, need to be blanched in boiling water for a few minutes, to soften them, before being rolled up round a savoury stuffing (p. 215). Vine leaves which have been canned or packed in brine need thorough rinsing in warm water, to wash off the salt, before use.

WATERCRESS *Nasturtium officinale*
With its hot, pungent flavour and dark green colour, watercress is useful in salads, soups and sauces, and can also be added to stir-fries (p. 268). Although watercress used to be gathered from the wild, it is now specially cultivated, and eating wild watercress is not recommended because of possible contamination.

Watercress should be well washed and will keep in a polythene bag in the salad compartment of the fridge for 2–3 days.

A tangy, bright green Watercress Sauce tastes and looks wonderful with vegetable mousses and terrines, or a white nut roast. To serve 4, fry a small onion, peeled and finely chopped, in 15 g/½ oz butter or vegan margarine for 10 minutes, until soft but not browned. Add 75 ml/3 fl oz dry white wine and 1 tablespoon white wine vinegar and boil until reduced and syrupy. Meanwhile chop 2 bunches of watercress, then add two-thirds of this to the reduced onion mixture, with 600 ml/ 1 pint Light Vegetable Stock (p. 194). Bubble over a high heat until reduced to about one-third. Add the remaining watercress and purée in a blender or food processor. Stir in 4 tablespoons double or non-dairy cream and reheat gently without boiling. Season to taste with salt and pepper and stir in 15 g/½ oz butter or vegan margarine.

Brassicas

Brassicas come in a variety of shapes and sizes, from tiny Brussels sprouts to big, family-sized cabbages; from knobbly kohlrabi to beautiful purple broccoli. They range in colour from palest greenish-white to deep burgundy red, and they span the seasons. They provide useful quantities of a range of vitamins A, B and C and iron and calcium. They also contain enzymes which are protective and curative when the vegetables are eaten raw.

A real kitchen basic, the brassicas provide useful all-year-round material for soups, salads and main courses, as well as being, if well cooked, second to none as an accompanying vegetable.

Choosing and storing

Select bright, fresh leaves, with no sign of wilting or damp, brownish patches. If there is a heart, as with cauliflower, cabbage and Brussels sprouts, look for one that is firm and tightly packed. Keep in a cool place. Brassicas are best used as soon as possible, although I find that even the more delicate varieties like broccoli, spring greens and cauliflower will keep well if stored in the fridge for several days.

Preparation and cooking

Wash the vegetables in cold water to which some kitchen salt has been added — this acts as a natural disinfectant. Remove hard stems and any tough outer leaves. The way brassicas are cooked makes all the difference to their palatability — and it's so easy. These are the keys to success:

☐ Cut the leaves up as small as possible so that they cook quickly.

☐ Put them into just enough fast-boiling water to prevent the greens from sticking: about 1 cm/½ inch.

☐ Cover the pan so that the vegetables above the water will cook in the steam.

☐ Cook them until they're only just tender — often as little as 4 minutes, or even less for delicate varieties such as pak-choi or Chinese leaves.

☐ Drain them well and add any seasonings and extra ingredients you like. Personally I like to add some crunchy flakes of sea salt, a grinding of black pepper and, unless the vegetable is going to be served with a dish which is high in fat, a little unsalted butter. For other suggestions, see p. 85.

BROCCOLI and CALABRESE *Brassica oleracea*
Sometimes described as 'poor man's asparagus', this is one of the most nutritious vegetables. Voted the top by a panel of nutritionists in the USA, it contains large amounts of vitamin A, folic acid and calcium, and is a particularly valuable vegetable for vegans.

When preparing broccoli, remove the toughest part of the stems. Then, unless it is very tender, pare the stems down a little so that they will cook in the same length of time as the more delicate heads. Or remove the stems, cut them into julienne strips (p. 272) and cook them in the water for 1–2 minutes before you put in the heads.

Broccoli is good stir-fried, too, which brings out its vivid green colour. Combined with ginger and almonds, it makes a good accompanying vegetable dish. To make this, wash 700 g/

1½ lb broccoli, cut the broccoli heads in small pieces and prepare the stems as described above. Peel and finely grate a small piece of fresh ginger root. Heat 2 tablespoons olive oil in a large saucepan or wok, add the broccoli, ginger, a little salt and freshly grated black pepper. Stir-fry for 3 minutes until the broccoli has heated through and softened a little. Sprinkle with 25 g/1 oz flaked almonds and serve at once.

Broccoli tastes good served simply, with melted butter, or tossed in vinaigrette, cooled and served as a salad. It is luscious with Hollandaise Sauce (p. 262) or with cream and toasted almonds, for a special occasion; or with Fresh Tomato Sauce (p. 253). Broccoli makes a good filling for a flan (p. 388) and goes well with other vegetables in a braise (p. 269).

BRUSSELS SPROUTS *Brassica oleracea*

Tiny, firm Brussels sprouts are best; they take longer to prepare, but are worth it. Most people cut a cross about 5 mm/¼ inch into the stalk end of sprouts. Personally I prefer to cut them in halves (or even quarters, if they are big) before cooking, a trick I learnt from my mother. This way they cook more quickly and I think they taste better and look more attractive, with their yellow centre showing.

In any case, Brussels sprouts only need the minimum of cooking – 2–4 minutes – in a very little water; take them off the heat before you think they are done, because they will go on cooking in their own heat after draining.

Brussels sprouts are excellent lightly cooked and served simply; or with cream and grated nutmeg, for a special occasion. Cooked chestnuts – fresh or drained whole canned ones – are a pleasant (and in Aus./NZ traditional) Christmas accompaniment to Brussels sprouts. Young and tender, finely shredded Brussels sprouts make a good salad when combined with raisins and chopped apple, or with grated carrots and chopped dates.

When they are past their best, they can be made into a delicate, pale green purée. To make this, wash and trim 700 g/ 1½ lb Brussels sprouts and cook them in boiling, salted water for about 10 minutes, or until they are tender. Drain them thoroughly, then purée in a blender or food processor. Put the purée back into the saucepan, add 15 g/½ oz butter, and beat in up to 150 ml/5 fl oz single cream until the mixture is soft. Season with salt, freshly ground black pepper and grated nutmeg, then reheat gently and serve.

CABBAGE *Brassica oleracea*

One variety of cabbage or another is available all year round. Early in the year, SPRING GREENS, cut up small and lightly cooked, make a good accompanying vegetable with a clean, refreshing flavour. JANUARY KING, another excellent early cabbage, can be cooked in a similar way, or, if it has a firm heart, makes a particularly good salad when finely shredded and mixed with lemon juice and olive oil, or vinaigrette. ROUND-HEAD CABBAGE is available throughout the year, useful as an accompanying vegetable or shredded to make salads such as Coleslaw (p. 242) or Technicolour Cabbage Salad (p. 345).

WHITE SALAD CABBAGE, a firm variety, good for grating and shredding, is also excellent for salads.

RED CABBAGE is good cooked gently and slowly with onions and butter in a casserole (p. 268) and served as an accompanying vegetable, or, with some cooked chestnuts and perhaps a dash of red wine added, as a main course with jacket potatoes and soured cream. Red cabbage also looks particularly attractive shredded or grated in salads.

SAVOY CABBAGE is attractive as an accompanying vegetable or main course, hollowed out and filled with stuffing. The individual crenellated leaves can also be wrapped round a savoury filling, such as mashed cooked chestnuts and fried onion, or cooked rice with nuts and chopped herbs, packed into a shallow ovenproof dish, covered with a little well-flavoured stock or a sauce (such as Italian Tomato [p. 254] or Savoury Coconut [p. 266]) and baked for about 30 minutes in a moderate oven.

Chopped cooked cabbage is one of the main ingredients of the Russian savoury pastry, Koulibiac. For an easy version of this, mix together 900 g/2 lb finely chopped cooked cabbage, 1 large fried onion, 225 g/8 oz sliced and fried mushrooms, 2 chopped hardboiled eggs, 4 tablespoons chopped parsley, the grated rind and juice of ½ lemon, and plenty of salt and freshly ground black pepper. Cover with puff pastry as described on p. 399, bake in a hot oven, 220c/425F/Gas Mark 7, for 40 minutes and serve with a Soured Cream and Herb Dressing (p. 233).

CREATIVE CABBAGE

Try these serving ideas for hot, lightly cooked cabbage:

☐ Garlic butter

☐ Crushed juniper or coriander seeds

☐ Chopped fresh parsley, coriander or dill

☐ Soured cream, caraway seeds and a sprinkling of paprika

☐ Apple purée and a pinch of cloves

☐ Caraway seeds and melted butter

☐ Chopped fried onion

☐ Chopped spring onions or chives

☐ Skinned (p. 108), chopped tomato and some chopped basil, or Fresh Tomato Sauce (p. 253)

☐ Grated fresh ginger

☐ Grated nutmeg

CAULIFLOWER/GREEN CAULIFLOWER *Brassica oleracea*
Cauliflower has a delicious flavour so long as it is not over-cooked. I think it is best to break the cauliflower into florets and cut these as necessary so that they are all about the same size. Then cook as described above, for only 4–5 minutes, until the cauliflower is just tender but still has some firmness, then drain. Cooked like this, cauliflower hardly needs any accompaniments, though some grated nutmeg, a little grated cheese or a Fresh Tomato Sauce (p. 253) go well with it. One of the tastiest ways to cook cauliflower is in the Indian style, with spices (p. 274).

To make Cauliflower Cheese, a classic vegetarian dish, mix lightly cooked cauliflower florets with a well-seasoned Cheese Sauce (p. 261), sprinkle with breadcrumbs, dot with a little butter and bake or grill until heated through and crisp on top.

Raw cauliflower florets are particularly good for scooping up dips.

CHINESE LEAVES/CABBAGE *Brassica pekinensis*
Chinese leaves are crisp yet juicy and tender. Shredded, they make a good addition to a leafy salad, or they can be the main ingredient.

A refreshing salad in which they are combined with bean-sprouts in a sweet and sour dressing can be made as follows. Soak 175 g/6 oz fresh beansprouts in cold water while you prepare the other ingredients. Combine 1 tablespoon clear honey, 3 tablespoons sesame oil or olive oil, 2 tablespoons soy sauce and freshly ground black pepper in a large bowl. Add 2·5 cm/1 inch peeled and finely grated fresh ginger root and mix well. Then add 350 g/12 oz shredded Chinese leaves and 2 coarsely grated carrots and turn them in the dressing. Drain the beansprouts, place in the bowl and mix well.

The best way to serve them as a cooked vegetable is to shred them, then stir-fry for 2–3 minutes, until heated through. Chopped onion, crushed garlic, grated fresh ginger, grated lemon rind and chopped fresh herbs are good flavourings for Chinese leaves, or stir-fry in sesame oil and serve with a dash of soy sauce and a sprinkling of toasted sesame seeds.

KALE *Brassica oleracea*

Kale is a non-hearting type of cabbage. It should be washed well, as soil and grit tend to lodge between the stems. Kale is particularly rich in calcium and B vitamins and used to be an important winter vegetable in Britain, though many people find its flavour rather strong. It can be good to eat if it is picked or bought when young, shredded (with any tough stems removed) and cooked until tender, then well drained and served with butter and freshly ground black pepper, or with a creamy sauce, perhaps flavoured with a dash of nutmeg.

KOHLRABI *Brassica oleracea*

The leaves of kohlrabi can be cooked like kale. The root resembles a cabbage-flavoured turnip; it can be diced or cut into strips and boiled until tender. Kohlrabi is good in a julienne of root vegetables (p. 272), providing an interesting contrast of colour and flavour.

PAK-CHOI/MUSTARD GREENS *Brassica chinensis*

This variety of Chinese cabbage has a crisp, juicy central stem and pleasantly flavoured leaves; it cooks quickly and is popular in oriental cookery. Prepare and cook it as described for Chinese leaves, above. FLOWERING PAK-CHOI can be cooked in the same way, and also looks pretty in salads and as a garnish. Chinese sauerkraut is made from pak-choi and is available from Chinese shops, as is DRIED PAK-CHOI, which needs to be soaked and can then be added to soups and stews.

Pods and Seeds

Many pods and seeds have a dual role, one when they are young and fresh, as here, and another after they have been dried. So broad beans, French beans, peas and sweetcorn will also be found in their dried form under Pulses and Grains (pp. 56 and 63). Lightly cooked, these vegetables add colour, texture and valuable fibre to meals. Pod and seed vegetables are rich in nutrients, often containing much more protein than most fresh vegetables, and also useful amounts of vitamins A, C and B.

Choosing and storing

Look for small, crisp pods, bright and fresh-looking. Peas, beans and okra are all best when the pods are small. Sweetcorn needs to be young and tender too; pull back the leaves and look for pale yellow, shiny grains. These vegetables will keep in a cool place for a day or so, or in the fridge for 2–3 days, but they are all at their best when eaten as soon as possible after picking.

Preparation and cooking

See under individual varieties.

BROAD BEAN *Vicia faba*

Broad beans can be prepared in two ways. When they are young and tender, and the pods not much bigger than French beans, they are excellent cooked in the pod; just top and tail, then cut into even-sized lengths and cook in a little fast-boiling water until just tender. Drain and serve with chopped parsley and butter or a creamy sauce.

Later, when the pods become too tough to eat, remove the beans from the pod and cook in boiling water until tender. If the skins of the beans are tough, and you have the time, the beans can be popped out of their skins, revealing the bright green beans inside.

Older broad beans can be made into a good soup. Whizzed in a blender or food processor with olive oil and lemon juice, they also make an excellent pale green dip, good served as a first course on top of large flat mushrooms which have been fried in olive oil then cooled, or in a salad, with lettuce and grated carrot.

FRENCH BEAN *Phaseolus vulgaris*
One of the most delicious vegetables, many varieties have been produced including the short, plump BOBBY BEAN. Just top and tail and remove any strings from the side, if present (the beans are nicest if they're young enough to have no strings).

The beans can be cooked whole or cut into shorter lengths. Cook in a minimum amount of boiling water (1 cm/½ inch) in a covered pan until just tender (*al dente*). Cooking time will depend on the thickness of the beans: very slender ones take only about 2 minutes, others up to 10 minutes. Drain and serve simply, as they are, or with a little butter and freshly ground black pepper. A squeeze of lemon juice and some toasted almonds are an excellent addition.

Hot French beans mixed with a vinaigrette dressing and chopped fresh herbs, then cooled, make a good first course or salad, or they can be mixed with other vegetables to make Vegetarian Salade Niçoise (p. 251).

MANGETOUTS/SNOW PEAS *Pisum saccaratum*
This variety of pea (also known as the sugar pea or Chinese pea) has a deliciously sweet flavour and, if properly cooked, crunchy texture. The tender pod contains immature peas and is eaten whole. To prepare them, choose young, crisp pods, top and tail, then cook in a little boiling water for 1–2 minutes, just to heat through and soften slightly. Drain and serve immediately. Or add them to stir-fries (p. 299). Raw mangetouts make good scoops for dips.

OKRA *Hibiscus esculentus*
Also known as 'ladies' fingers' and gumbo, okra is popular in the Caribbean, India and the Middle East. It has an intriguing mucilaginous texture and delicate flavour. Choose small, firm pods and cut off the stalk end. It is delicious prepared as on p. 277 and makes a good addition to vegetable stews, curries and spiced rice dishes.

Pea *Pisum sativum*

Unless you grow your own peas, it is difficult to find fresh peas which taste as good as frozen ones, which are cropped at their peak and frozen within hours of picking. However, cooked fresh peas are a treat if they are young and tender. Simply pop the peas out of the pods and cook in a little boiling water until just tender — about 4 minutes. PETITS POIS, a small, tender, sweet variety, take less time — 1–2 minutes. Drain and serve with chopped mint and a little butter. They make a colourful addition to many vegetable and rice dishes.

Runner bean *Phaseolus coccineus*

Also called stick beans, because of the way the plants grow up sticks, runner beans originated in South America. They are the most popular green bean in Britain. If you're growing them, do pick them before they get too long; they're delicious when young and tender. Top and tail the beans, and if there are strings, remove these by slicing thinly down each side. Runner beans are usually cut into thin diagonal slices. Cook and serve as for French beans, or prepare in the Greek style and serve warm (p. 277). If you have a glut of runner beans, try making some into chutney or piccalilli.

Sweetcorn *Zea mays*

Sweetcorn has a pleasantly sweet flavour, cheering golden colour and chewy texture. Ideally sweetcorn needs to be picked just before cooking, because once it has been cut, the sugar in the kernels starts to turn into starch, making them tough. When buying fresh sweetcorn pull back the leaves and look for pale yellow, shiny grains. To prepare, strip off the leaves and silky threads, then trim off the stalk end. Cook the sweetcorn in a large saucepan of unsalted water for 3–5 minutes. It is done when a kernel pulls away easily from the cob. Serve with butter and sea salt. If you need the kernels for a recipe, just cut down the cob and they will come away.

Corn on the cob makes a pleasant first course or snack for people with good teeth who don't mind getting messy as they eat. The kernels add a bright dash of colour to salads and vegetable mixtures, and are also good made into fritters (p. 356). Sweetcorn kernels are available fresh, frozen and canned, though canned sweetcorn usually tastes over-sweet because of added sugar.

MINIATURE SWEETCORN, the immature cobs, can be bought fresh, frozen or canned and are pretty in salads and vegetable mixtures, especially stir-fries.

Shoot Vegetables

This group includes some of the most delectable vegetables, such as asparagus, artichokes, chicory, bamboo shoots and palm hearts, which are wonderful for special occasion cookery, or for using in small quantities to add interest to simple dishes. Alongside these are cheaper basics such as celery and fennel which, with their clean, refreshing flavours and crisp texture, are good either cooked or raw. They all only contain small amounts of vitamins and minerals.

Choosing and storing
Choose firm, crisp-looking specimens. With asparagus, avoid any which looks limp or has wet or dry wrinkled ends. Keep in the salad compartment of the fridge, or in a cool place.

Preparation and cooking
See under individual varieties.

ASPARAGUS *Asparagus officinalis*
There are three basic types of asparagus, green, white and purple, and experts disagree as to which has the best flavour. Thin spears of green asparagus, called sprue, are a good buy, particularly for inclusion in dishes like Individual Asparagus Tartlets (p. 390), Pine Nut Roulade with Asparagus Hollandaise filling (p. 353), or Asparagus Soup (p. 197).

Allow about 225 g/8 oz asparagus per person. Wash the asparagus carefully, especially around the tips, which can contain grit. Then bend each stem until it snaps — it will break at the point on the stem where it becomes tough and woody. Using a sharp knife or potato peeler, shave right down the stem, from just below the tip to the base, going deeper into the stem as you go down.

Unless you have a special asparagus pan, the best way to cook it is either in a steamer, or to tie it in a bunch and stand this in a saucepan containing 2·5 cm/1 inch boiling water. Arrange a dome of foil over the top, to cover the asparagus tips. Either way, cook for about 10–15 minutes, until just tender. Serve hot with melted butter or Hollandaise Sauce (p. 262), or cold with Vinaigrette (p. 229), or as part of a made-up dish.

Frozen asparagus is useful when fresh is unobtainable, and is best steamed for about 7 minutes; and canned asparagus, while not having the same flavour or texture as fresh, can be used for garnishing or in Asparagus Rolls (p. 504).

Bamboo shoot *Bambusa vulgaris*

Even in China and Japan canned bamboo shoots are often used in preference to fresh ones because of their convenience. They also maintain their crispness well, drained and added to stir-fries, or cold in a salad.

Celery *Apium graveolens*

Celery (green-stemmed or white-stemmed) gives a specially delicious flavour to vegetable casseroles and makes an excellent soup. Break the celery head into individual sticks, trim as necessary, then scrub well under cold water.

Celery can be braised as described on p. 270, or chopped and added raw to salad mixtures. The tender stems are good for serving with dips or for topping with cream cheese or savoury spreads as canapes. Crisp celery sticks are excellent with cheese, especially Stilton.

Chicory/endive/witloof *Cichorium intybus*

Crisp and slightly bitter-tasting, chicory makes a pleasant addition to a leafy green salad and is also good braised. Allow about 1 head per person if you're serving the chicory in a salad, 2 heads for a cooked dish. Remove any damaged outer leaves.

Trim the base, then insert the point of a knife into it and remove the core, which can be bitter. Wash well under cold water, but do not leave chicory soaking in water as this can increase the bitterness. Cook as described for celery on p. 91, or use raw in a salad.

FENNEL *Foeniculum vulgare*

This celery-like shoot with its delicate, feathery leaves and slight aniseed flavour can be used either cooked or raw. Allow 1 small fennel per person, or a larger one between 2. Trim and wash, then halve, quarter or slice.

To cook, braise as described on p. 271, or add to Spring Vegetable Braise (p. 269) or to casseroles. Steam and serve with Italian Tomato Sauce (p. 254), or cover with cream and a sprinkling of grated cheese and bake until golden-brown. Sliced or chopped fennel is refreshing with grated carrot in a salad (p. 242), in a green salad, mixed with diced cucumber, or replacing the celery in Waldorf Salad (p. 250).

GLOBE ARTICHOKE *Cynara scolymus*

These giant thistles have an intriguing, subtle flavour and are excellent served either hot or cold. Very tender young artichokes can be trimmed, added to a casserole of summer vegetables and cooked gently for 20–30 minutes, until tender.

For most artichokes, however, more preparation is needed. Break off the stalk, removing with it any stringy pieces from the sides. Using a sharp knife or kitchen scissors, snip the points off the scales, then prise them apart until the soft leaves in the centre and the hairy choke are revealed. Scrape the choke out firmly with a teaspoon, then rinse under cold water. Sprinkle the inside of the artichoke with lemon juice, and leave it soaking in acidulated water until you're ready to cook.

Bring a large non-aluminium saucepan of water to the boil, put in the artichokes and cook for 30–40 minutes, until a leaf can be pulled away easily. A tablespoon of lemon juice or white wine vinegar can be added to the water. Drain thoroughly and serve hot, with melted butter and lemon juice, or Hollandaise Sauce (p. 262); or cold, with Vinaigrette (p. 229). It's best not to keep cooked artichokes for more than 24 hours, as they can develop a toxin which can cause stomach upsets.

To prepare just the bottoms or *fonds*, remove the stem and choke as described, to reveal the heart, then cut off all the leaves just above the base, and finally trim round the base. Cook in boiling water until tender. The artichoke bottoms may be topped with a creamy sauce or vegetable mixture, or served cold with a tasty dip spooned on top.

Artichoke hearts are available in cans and make a useful addition to the store cupboard, for use in vegetable salads, casseroles and risottos.

PALM HEART *Sabal palmetto*
Delicately flavoured fresh palm hearts are usually boiled until just tender and eaten hot with melted butter or cold with Mayonnaise (p. 231) or Vinaigrette (p. 229). Canned palm hearts can be served similarly; try slicing them and mixing with diced avocado or sliced button mushrooms and a vinaigrette dressing.

Bulb Vegetables

Valuable in vegetarian cooking for adding flavour, bulb vegetables contain useful though not outstanding amounts of minerals and vitamins (but very little vitamin A). Their main value healthwise lies in their natural antibiotic powers and the way in which, if eaten over a period of time, onions and garlic in particular (both raw and cooked) help lower cholesterol and protect against fatty deposits in blood vessels. Both leeks and shallots have a sweet taste, less pungent than that of onion.

Choosing and storing
Bulb vegetables should look bright and crisp; the bulbs should be firm. Avoid any onions which are sprouting, damp-looking, soft or which smell musty. Leeks and spring onions are best stored in a cool place, preferably the fridge, and used within a day or two. Onions will keep for at least a week if stored in a cool, dry place.

Preparation and cooking
See under individual varieties

Leek *Allium porrum*
Delicately flavoured with a slightly sweet taste, leeks are good both raw and cooked. They need careful washing as they may contain grit. First cut off the roots and trim the green leaves to within about 2·5 cm/1 inch of the top of the white part. Make a slit right down one side of the leek from top to bottom and wash it under the cold tap, gently parting the layers and rinsing between each while keeping the shape of the leek intact. Then keep whole or cut into shorter lengths, or shred into fine rings for serving raw in a salad.

Alternatively, if you want a perfectly whole leek, cut a cross shape about 2·5 cm/1 inch deep in the root end and place the leek's root end down in a deep jug of water for 30—60 minutes. After this any grit will show up as dark patches and you can make a small incision at this point and rinse the grit away under the cold tap.

Leeks are good added to vegetable casseroles and curries, or cooked and served hot as an accompanying vegetable, either whole, sliced or puréed. I think the best way to cook leeks is to steam them or cook them in 2·5 cm/1 inch of water in a covered pan for about 10 minutes, until tender. They can also be cooked until tender in olive oil or butter, or sautéed lightly, then braised in red wine or stock. I very much like cooked leeks served cold as a first course, tossed in a little well-flavoured vinaigrette while still hot, then served with a sprinkling of chopped parsley.

For a more elaborate yet easily prepared presentation, make a leek terrine by packing the cooked and drained leeks, cut to fit, into a 450-g/1-lb loaf tin. Press down firmly, cover with several layers of kitchen paper and weight down. Chill for several hours, then pop the terrine into the freezer for 1 hour before serving, so that it is firm enough to cut easily. Slice and pour vinaigrette over before serving.

Onion *Allium cepa*
There are many varieties of onion, ranging in colour from white and yellow to attractive shades of purple and red, and in size from minute bulbs to large Spanish ones weighing around

1 lb/450 g or more. Onions also vary a good deal in strength; some types are mild and sweet, while others are extremely pungent. Even individual varieties can change as the season goes on, changing from mild to strong, or vice versa.

To prepare onions, cut off the root and stalk end, then strip off the outer skins. Wash the onions, then chop or slice as required. If you don't need to use the onions immediately, it's best not to leave them soaking in water; either sauté them in a little oil or butter, or wrap them in clingfilm.

Onions are included in many vegetarian roasts, burgers and savouries as a flavouring. They are also useful sliced raw in salads, for making a delectable flan (p. 386) and for soup. Large onions can be baked whole in their skins then split open and served with butter, sea salt and freshly ground black pepper as an accompaniment, or stuffed with a nut and breadcrumb mixture and baked to make a warming winter main course.

PICKLING ONIONS are good used whole as well as for making into pickles. They can be fiddly to peel, but if you top and tail them, then cover with boiling water and leave for 5 minutes, you should be able to skin them easily.

Here is a quick method of making Pickled Onions which gives an excellent result but is best made in small quantities as the onions do not keep for more than about 4 months. Put skinned pickling onions into jars and sprinkle them with pickling spice between the layers, allowing 1 rounded tablespoon spice to a large jar. Then fill the jars with malt vinegar, making sure that the onions are completely covered. Cover with airtight, vinegar-proof lids and store in a cool, dry, dark place for at least 8 weeks before eating with cheese.

SPRING ONIONS (commonly called shallots in Australia) make an attractive garnish and addition to salads or crudités, and are excellent added to a stir-fry or other lightly cooked mixed vegetable dishes. SHALLOTS (*Allium ascalonicum*) are a variety of onion which produces clusters of bulbs. They may be round or oval in shape and can be used wherever a delicate onion flavour is needed. Shallots are also excellent for pickling; they can be peeled as described for pickling onions.

The strength of PURPLE or RED ONIONS can vary; some are quite mild, but this is not always the case.

Mild-flavoured SPANISH ONIONS are ideal for slicing and adding to salads as well as for cooking, and are excellent baked with a tasty stuffing. To make stuffed onions for 4 people, rinse (but don't peel) 4 large Spanish onions. Put them into a large saucepan of water and simmer for about 20 minutes until they are tender but not cooked right through. Drain and cool, then remove the root ends and cut the onions in half horizontally. Scoop out the centre of each half, making a cavity for stuffing and leaving three or four layers of onion. Arrange the onion halves in a greased, shallow, ovenproof dish. Set the oven to 180c/350f/Gas Mark 4.

The onions can be stuffed with a Herb Stuffing (p. 357), one of the nut roast mixtures (pp. 345, 351, 352), or with an unusual sweet-and-sour mixture. To make this, first chop the onion you scooped out, then crush four macaroons and add to the onion, along with 75 g/3 oz wholewheat breadcrumbs, ¼ teaspoon each ground cinnamon, cloves and nutmeg, 2 beaten eggs, 50 g/2 oz grated Parmesan cheese and 25–50 g/1–2 oz sultanas. Season, then pile the mixture into the onion cavities, dot with butter and bake, uncovered, for 30 minutes. A sharply flavoured cheese sauce goes well with these.

Root Vegetables

Nourishing, warming and filling, root vegetables have long been a winter mainstay because of their excellent keeping qualities and value for money. Radishes, carrots and beetroot add colour to meals, while parsnips and turnips are delicious roasted. They contain useful quantities of iron, calcium, protein and B vitamins, and carrots are one of the richest sources of vitamin A. Root vegetables absorb flavours well and can be made into tasty soups, stews and casseroles or used in salads.

Choosing and storing
Look for bright, firm root vegetables, with no signs of wrinkling.

Store in a cool, dry place; more delicate roots, such as radishes, keep best in the fridge and I like to store carrots there, too, if there's room.

Preparation and cooking

Radishes and tender young carrots, turnips and beetroots only need scrubbing; older ones need scraping. Celeriac, turnips, swedes, parsnips and older beetroot, if used raw, need peeling quite thickly. Cut into evensized pieces, place in a saucepan, cover with cold water and bring to the boil, then simmer gently until tender. Drain, saving the cooking water for a well-flavoured and nutritious stock, and add seasoning, butter or vegan margarine, chopped herbs and perhaps a squeeze of lemon juice. Salsify, scorzonera and beetroot are cooked in the same way (beetroot may require 1–2 hours, depending on size, although a pressure cooker speeds the process) until tender, when the skins will slip off quite easily.

Beetroot *Beta vulgaris*
Beetroot is usually red, although white and golden varieties are also grown. When preparing beetroot for cooking, if the leaves are still attached, break these off about 18 cm/6 inches from the root and do not cut or pierce the skins, or the colour may seep out during cooking. The leaves can also be cooked and taste like spinach. Cooked beetroot can be served in salads, dressed with vinaigrette, or mixed with other ingredients such as apple and celery in a dressing of horseradish, soured cream, yogurt or mayonnaise. In Russia and Poland it is made into Borsch and served with buckwheat (p. 64) – good, cheap, filling food! For a lighter version of Beetroot Soup, see p. 209. Young cooked beetroots are good served with butter, black pepper and a little orange juice and grated rind. Beetroot can also be eaten raw: peel, grate and mix with an equal quantity of grated apple and some raisins, or sliced onion rings and vinaigrette for a very healthy salad which is said to help break up fat deposits in the body.

Burdock *Arctium lappa*
A tough root vegetable with a distinctive flavour which is an acquired taste but popular in macrobiotic cooking. It should be

scrubbed, sliced thinly and boiled for 30–40 minutes until tender, or can be added to vegetable stews.

Carrot *Daucus carota*

One of the most versatile and nutritious vegetables. Delicious either raw or cooked, carrots are useful in salads, soups, stews and casseroles, for serving with dips and even for making into cakes (p. 460). Baby carrots can be cooked whole, while larger ones can be cut into rounds or julienne strips (p. 272), finely or coarsely grated, shaved lengthways into ribbons with a potato peeler or 'turned'. Simply cooked, as a side vegetable, carrots are good with a flavouring of chopped parsley, caraway or anise; or they can be glazed (p. 271).

Celeriac *Apium graveolens*, var. *rapaceum*

This delicious celery-flavoured bulbous root is good both raw and cooked. To serve it raw, cut into fine julienne strips or grate coarsely, then mix with a well-flavoured vinaigrette (p. 229). If liked, celeriac can be blanched for 1 minute in boiling water, then refreshed under cold water to soften slightly before adding the dressing. Cooked celeriac mixed with an equal quantity of potato makes a delicately-flavoured purée.

Daikon/mooli *Raphanus sativus*

Daikon has a slightly hot taste, like a cross between a turnip and a radish. It can be sliced and added to root vegetable mixtures or stir-fries, diced or shredded and combined with salad ingredients, and it can also be used to make a particularly attractive garnish, see Japanese Flower Salad (p. 246).

Horseradish *Armoracia rusticana*

See p. 178.

Parsnip *Pastinaca sativa*

Parsnips are distinctively flavoured and sweet-tasting. They can be roasted like potatoes, cooked and mashed or puréed, added to a julienne of mixed root vegetables (p. 272), made into a winter soup or added to casseroles and stews.

Radish *Raphanus sativus*

There are numerous varieties of radish; they can be the size of marbles or grapefruit, round or long, and range in colour from white to red and black. Thinly sliced pink radishes make a colourful and pungent addition to salads — try adding them to cooked, cooled sweetcorn, along with some chopped spring onion. Radishes with their green leaves still attached if possible make a good addition to a crudités selection, and radish flowers are easy to make for garnishing.

SCORZONERA *Scorzonera hispanica* and SALSIFY *Tragopogon porrifolius*

Cooked and served hot with cream and Parmesan, or cold mixed with vinaigrette or mayonnaise, these delicately flavoured vegetables make a good first course. Or they can be dipped in batter or egg and breadcrumbs and fried until crisp, then served with lemon wedges. Frozen and canned salsify is available.

SWEDE and RUTABAGA *Brassica napus*

Called turnips in Scotland and the USA, swedes and rutabagas are larger than turnips. They have a sweetish flavour but they also absorb other flavours well and are good in casseroles, diced as part of a macedoine of root vegetables or mashed with carrots or potatoes. 'Mashed Neaps' are traditionally served with haggis at Burns Night suppers in Scotland. Raw, swedes make a good salad, coarsely grated and mixed with mayonnaise and chopped dates.

TURNIP *Brassica rapa*

Turnips vary in shape and size. Their skins may be white, green or ringed with purple and their flesh is usually white, juicy and pungent. They can be served in any of the ways described for swede, and baby turnips can be glazed with butter and sugar (p. 272). The tops, eaten like spinach, make an extremely nutritious, strongly flavoured, vegetable.

Tubers

Tuber vegetables (botanically, roots swollen with the plant's winter food supplies) include potatoes (which exceed the world's wheat crop in volume and value), sweet potatoes and yams, which are important throughout the tropics, and delicately flavoured Jerusalem artichokes. As tubers are usually eaten in quite large quantities, they can be an important source of nutrients, including iron, protein and vitamin c and can be made into some particularly economical and delicious dishes.

Choosing and storing

Look for firm tubers with no wrinkles or damp patches. Choose firm, even-sized, dry-skinned potatoes (pre-washed potatoes do not keep as well as unwashed ones). When choosing Jerusalem artichokes, look for ones without too many knobbly bits — it makes peeling easier! Store in a cool, dry, dark place.

Preparation and cooking

See under individual varieties.

JERUSALEM ARTICHOKE *Helianthus tuberosus*
These can be peeled either before or after cooking. If you peel before, you will need to cut off the smaller knobbles along with the peel. Put the peeled artichokes straight into cold water with a dash of lemon juice added, to help preserve their colour. Alternatively, give them a quick wash, then boil them and slip off their skins, using a small sharp knife, after cooking.

Jerusalem artichokes have a distinctive flavour reminiscent of globe artichokes (hence the 'artichoke' in the name), but not as delicate. They are good mashed to a creamy purée, served cold in a vinaigrette or hot with butter and chopped parsley. They also make a soothing winter soup (p. 192) and go well with Fresh Tomato Sauce. To assemble the dish, first prepare the Fresh

Tomato Sauce (p. 253). While it is cooking, peel 700 g/1½ lb Jerusalem artichokes as above and cut into evensized pieces. Put in a saucepan with 15 g/½ oz butter, 4 tablespoons water and salt. Cover and cook over a gentle heat for about 20 minutes until just tender. Drain the artichokes, pour the Fresh Tomato Sauce over them and serve.

Potato *Solanum tuberosum*

Nutritious staple vegetables, rich in vitamin c and potassium, and containing useful amounts of particularly good quality protein, potatoes are made into some of the most delicious and economical dishes throughout the world.

They are sometimes loosely divided into 'waxy' types, which are moist, even slightly translucent after cooking, and those which have a dry, fluffy texture, known as 'floury'. Generally speaking, waxy potatoes are best for salads and for frying, because they stay firm, and floury potatoes are best for mashing, boiling and baking in their jackets.

There are, however, many varieties which are good all-rounders. New potatoes, or young potatoes dug early in the season, such as ITALIAN NEW POTATOES and CYPRUS NEW POTATOES, are best when they are from varieties grown specially for this purpose. They are waxy, tender and excellent for boiling and salads, but not for baking, roasting or chipping.

The colour of potato flesh varies from white through to gold. Until a few years ago the yellow-flesh varieties were not popular in Great Britain; however, they have gained in favour, particularly because of the way they remain intact after cooking.

New varieties of potato are continually being developed. Some, such as DIANA, make a brief appearance and then fade out; others survive to become well-loved favourites. These include WILJA, which is particularly good for boiling and has pale yellow flesh; MARIS PIPER, the most popular white potato in the UK today and a good all-rounder; KING EDWARD, which has made a comeback on account of its popularity with housewives; DÉSIRÉE, the most widely grown red potato in the UK and another excellent all-rounder; MARIS BARD, which has average cooking qualities and needs plenty of flavouring to enliven it; ESTIMA, a Dutch variety, which has grown in popularity; and RECORD, also Dutch, and with very yellow flesh, but a superb potato for making into crisps and indeed for boiling and roasting.

The demand for varieties of potato also varies from area to area. The RUSSET BURBANK, also known as the IDAHO BAKER, is well-known and loved in the USA but virtually unknown in Britain, except to nostalgic expatriates who have been experimenting with the possibility of growing it here. Another type, ARRAN VICTORY, is liked in Scotland and Ireland, but not in England, on account of its blue skin. This potato was bred to celebrate the victory of the 1914–18 war and has very white floury flesh.

Potatoes in Australia are not marketed under variety names, e.g. Désirée, although several varieties are grown. Ask your greengrocer if you are seeking a specific type.

Varieties which are popular with show judges such as the purple-eyed CATRIONA are not always so well-favoured by customers. MARIS PEER, VANESSA (bred from the popular Désirée) and ULSTER SCEPTRE, which have been favoured in the past, are now being replaced by varieties such as ROMANA (also bred from Désirée and with similar qualities). CARA, which was developed in the Republic of Ireland as Oakpark Beauty, and has pink eyes like a King Edward, is growing in popularity and is being widely grown in Cyprus and Egypt.

New potatoes are good just scrubbed and boiled in their skins until tender, then served hot with butter and chopped herbs, or mixed with vinaigrette and served cold. More mature potatoes can be scrubbed and boiled or baked in their jackets, or peeled before use.

Baked Potatoes, cooked so that their skins are crisp (p. 283), and served with butter, soured cream or a variety of toppings (p. 283), accompanied by a salad, are one of my favourite quick and easy meals. Bircher Potatoes are also popular with children: scrub medium potatoes, cut them in half lengthways and place them cut side down on an oiled baking sheet. Bake in a hot oven, 220c/425F/Gas Mark 7, for about 45 minutes, until the tops are soft and the underneath golden-brown and crisp.

Another delicious way with potatoes is to cut well-scrubbed medium ones into 3 mm/⅛ inch slices and arrange overlapping like roof tiles on an oiled baking sheet. Brush the potatoes with olive oil, sprinkle with chopped thyme or rosemary and a little crushed garlic, and bake in a hot oven, 220c/425F/Gas Mark 7, until golden-brown and crisp.

MAKING PERFECT ROAST POTATOES AND CHIPS

Roast potatoes

Set the oven to 230c/450F/Gas Mark 8. Peel even-sized potatoes, allowing about 700 g/1½ lb for 4 people, and cut them into halves or quarters. Parboil the potatoes for 5 minutes.

Meanwhile, pour into a roasting tin just enough oil to cover the base. Don't make it more than 3 mm/⅛ inch deep. Heat the oil in the oven.

Drain the potatoes. Make sure that the potatoes and the oil are both piping hot; a good way of doing this is to put the roasting tin over the gas flame or hotplate while you put the hot potatoes into it, but stand back as the oil will sizzle and splutter.

Turn the potatoes in the oil, then put the tin back into the oven and bake the potatoes for 45–60 minutes, until they are golden and crisp, turning them over after about 30 minutes.

If they are ready before you are, turn the heat of the oven down to 170c/325F/Gas Mark 3, but don't cover the potatoes or they will soften. Drain them well on kitchen paper before serving.

Potato chips

There are two ways of making crisp potato chips. One is to fry the chips in oil heated to 190c/375F until they are soft but not browned, then remove them from the oil and reheat it to 195c/390F and give the chips a final quick dip to brown and crisp them. The other way is to fry them steadily in the oil until they get past the soft stage and become crisp and brown.

Personally I use the first method if I am cooking a large number of chips, because I can get them all partially cooked and then give them their final quick frying in batches just before they're needed; and I use the second method when I'm just making a small quantity which can be cooked in one batch.

Cut potatoes into chips about 1 cm/½ inch wide and 1 cm/½ inch thick and rinse in cold water, then thoroughly dry before frying. After cooking, drain well on crumpled kitchen paper.

Désirée, Maris Piper, King Edward or Majestic are the best potato varieties for chips.

Potatoes mashed until very light and creamy, with hot milk, or cream for special occasions, butter or vegan margarine and a good seasoning of salt and freshly ground black pepper, are one of my favourite accompaniments. Mashed potatoes can be used as a topping for vegetarian shepherd's pie, and any left over can be fried to make crisp potato cakes, a good quick snack for children, especially with some grated nuts added. I start off most soups by frying an onion and one or two potatoes together in butter, then adding the other vegetables: the potato thickens the soup and gives it body. I find children like a plain potato soup, without other vegetables except for a flavouring of onion, whizzed to a smooth creamy purée.

Every national cuisine has its own range of potato dishes: delicious Spiced Potatoes from India (p. 275); Hashed Browns from the USA (p. 285); Rösti from Switzerland (p. 282) and Gratin Dauphinois from France (p. 284), to mention just a few.

Potatoes are available fresh or frozen in the form of the ubiquitous chip, canned and in various dried and powdered forms.

Potato flour makes a lighter, healthier thickening for sauces than flour and butter, and it is also good for making clear fruit soups, such as the Chilled Raspberry or Black Cherry soups on pp. 208-9.

SWEET POTATO *Ipomeoa batatas*

A member of the convolvulus family, the sweet potato has sweet, mealy flesh. There are two main types, one with yellow flesh and a dryish texture, and the other with particularly sweet white flesh and a more watery texture. The skins vary in colour and may be white, red or purple. Sweet potatoes can be quite large and it is usually possible to buy a piece.

They can be boiled, roasted, fried or mashed and are enhanced by a sprinkling of sweet spice: cinnamon, nutmeg, ground cloves or allspice. Sweet potatoes are also delicious baked like jacket potatoes and served with butter. In the USA, they are boiled and then candied and served as a traditional accompaniment with the Thanksgiving dinner. Perhaps the nicest way to serve them (but not the most slimming!) is glazed with butter and brown sugar; simply parboil them, then put them into a shallow casserole, dot with butter, and sprinkle with brown sugar. Bake in a fairly hot oven for about 40 minutes until they're golden brown and glazed. Or follow the recipe for Glazed Carrots on p. 271. Cooked in either of these ways they make an excellent accompaniment to an almond nut roast for a special autumn meal.

YAM *Dioscorea rotundata, D. cayenensis*

The yam is a staple food, widely consumed in West Africa and the Caribbean. Yams have brown, woody skins, and their flesh is moist and sweet. They come in a variety of shapes and sizes and are usually cooked in the same way as sweet potatoes. They can be made into casseroles or boiled and served with spicy vegetable mixtures. They absorb other flavours well.

They can also be used instead of ordinary potatoes in potato salad. Peel the yams and quarter them. Boil for about 15 minutes until tender, drain and cool, then dice them. Continue as for any of the other Potato Salad recipes on p. 284.

Yams are also good peeled, sliced and fried like sauté potatoes.

Fruit Vegetables

Originally from tropical or sub-tropical countries, fruit vegetables offer vibrant colours, succulent textures and intense — sometimes hot — flavours. They are also very nutritious. Avocados are outstandingly so, being rich in protein, vitamin E and B$_6$ (particularly good for women); while raw sweet peppers are high in vitamin C, green peppers containing twice, and red peppers, four times, the amount in oranges. Fruit vegetables are available all year round but are plentiful in summer.

Choosing and storing

Aubergines, sweet peppers and tomatoes should be bright and firm, with no signs of withering or discoloured patches. They vary a good deal in shape and size, so look for ones which are suitable for your purpose; choose squarish peppers, for instance, and medium-sized aubergines, if you plan to stuff them. Store in a cool place — the salad compartment of the fridge is ideal. When choosing an avocado, either choose one which will yield all over to gentle pressure, or buy a hard one and allow up to a week for it to ripen at room temperature. Ripe avocados will keep for 1–2 days in the fridge.

Preparation and cooking

See under individual varieties.

AUBERGINE/EGG PLANT *Solanum melongena*, var. *esculentum*

Aubergines are usually degorged before cooking, to draw out any bitter juices: cut into cubes or slices, then sprinkle with salt and place in a colander for 30 minutes, before rinsing under cold water and drying in kitchen paper ready for use. I must admit I do not always bother to do this and have never come across a bitter aubergine, but degorging does also prevent the aubergine from absorbing too much oil if it is fried.

Aubergines are usually cooked with the skin on, though this can be removed with a potato peeler if you prefer for dishes like Parmigiana (p. 304). Cut aubergines into rounds, short lengths, or cubes or dice. Aubergines for stuffing should be cut in half lengthways, and the cut sides scored diagonally in both directions, without piercing the skin. Salt can then be pressed into the cuts and the aubergines left to degorge for 30 minutes. The flesh will then have softened and can be scooped out with a small knife and a teaspoon.

Aubergines are excellent stuffed (p. 287), in stews and casseroles, such as Middle Eastern Chick Pea Stew (p. 315), and in dips (p. 219). I also like them peeled and cut into strips, then dipped into a light batter, deep-fried and served with lemon slices and Soured Cream and Herb Dressing (p. 233) as a main or first course.

AVOCADO *Persea americana*

Avocados range in colour from green with yellow or reddish flecks to almost black, and may be round or pear-shaped. It's best to use a stainless steel knife to cut them as a steel one can leave a metallic taste. Cut the avocado in half lengthways, then hold one side in each hand and twist in opposite directions to separate them, and remove the stone. With their delicate, buttery flesh, avocados are delicious halved and served simply with a good vinaigrette, or stuffed and served either hot or cold. They can be added to salads (p. 244), made into delicious flans (p. 390), or blended into a creamy dip (p. 218) or chilled soup (p. 210).

Avocado flesh discolours after an hour or so, though coating it with lemon juice will help prevent this. If you need to keep a dip for longer, bury the avocado stone in it (remove it before you serve the dip!) and cover with clingfilm: this will preserve the colour. One half of an avocado will also keep its colour if you leave the stone in it, cover with clingfilm and keep in the fridge overnight. Undeveloped baby avocados, without stones, are available too; they are attractive sliced into rings as a garnish or in salads.

CHILLI PEPPER *Capsicum annuum*

Chillis can be green, yellow or red. They vary in hotness and a general guide is the smaller the chilli, the hotter. ANCHO CHILLIS are quite sweet and only fairly hot; KENYAN CHILLIS are quite hot and are delicious fried in oil and sprinkled with salt, as a first course. Really HOT CHILLIS need careful handling. One is ample in a dish for 4–6 people. If the recipe requires the chilli to be chopped, cut it and remove the seeds under running water. Be careful not to touch your eyes or skin, as chilli juice can cause irritation, and wash your hands well afterwards. Dried red chillis are used in making chutneys and pickles.

SWEET PEPPER/CAPSICUM *Capsicum annuum*

Peppers start off green, then become yellow or red as they ripen; very dark, almost black, peppers are also available, as well as creamy coloured ones for pickling. With their bright colours and fresh flavour, sweet peppers are useful both raw, in salads, as part of a crudités selection, and as a garnish, and cooked, in casseroles, stir-fries and vegetable mixtures. Cored and de-seeded peppers make a perfect container for a stuffing. To prepare peppers, cut a thin slice off the stalk end. Remove the seeds, rinsing out any stray ones under the cold tap. Use the peppers as they are, for stuffing, or cut into rings, strips, diamond shapes or dice.

If you want to remove the outer skin, and end up with a semi-cooked pepper, which is good in salads, put the whole peppers under a hot grill and turn them from time to time until the skin is charred, blistered and rubs off easily. Rinse off the skin and also the seeds under the cold tap. Dried peppers can be a good flavouring for casseroles.

TOMATO *Lycopersicon esculentum*

There are many varieties of tomato, ranging in size from the baby CHERRY TOMATO (attractive in salads or hollowed out and stuffed with a dip) to the large BEEFSTEAK variety (ideal for stuffing or slicing in salads). PLUM (or EGG) TOMATOES, which are much grown around the Mediterranean, have a particularly intense, sweet flavour and make excellent sauces and salads.

Tomatoes can be used with or without their skin, depending on the recipe and how tender the tomato is. To skin tomatoes, cover with boiling water and leave for 1 minute, then drain and cover with cold water. Use a small sharp knife and your fingers to peel off the skin.

Sometimes recipes suggest de-seeding tomatoes, but I very rarely do this as so much of the tomato is wasted and the jelly around the seeds is a valuable form of soluble fibre.

To make tomato salad to serve 4 people, slice 700 g/1½ lb tomatoes, put into a shallow dish and sprinkle with 1–2 tablespoons olive oil and salt, freshly ground black pepper and chopped basil to taste. A little sliced raw onion can also be added.

Cucumbers and Squashes

The name squash originates from the Red Indian, *askoot-asquash*, and is the name given to the members of a very varied family of fruiting vegetables which includes pumpkins, gourds, marrows, courgettes and cucumbers. One of the most ancient vegetable families of the world, squashes are not particularly nutritious, although the yellow-fleshed varieties contain useful amounts of vitamin A and some fibre.

Cucumbers

CUCUMBER *Cucumis sativus*
One of the first vegetables to be cultivated by man, and one of the most refreshing, cucumbers were a great favourite with the Roman Emperor Tiberius, who demanded a constant supply,

even in winter. Various types of cucumber are available including RIDGED (with a delicious, slightly lemony flavour) and BABY (used for pickling).

Choosing and storing

Cucumbers should be firm and tender with a bright shiny skin. They need to be stored in a cool place, preferably the fridge, and used within a few days.

Preparation and using

The skin should be scrubbed well before use, or if the cucumbers have been waxed, as in the USA, it should be removed. The cucumber can then be grated, sliced or diced for use in salads: it is particularly good in a sweet and sour dressing using a little vinegar, fresh dill and white mustard seeds, or prepared in the Middle Eastern manner, with yogurt or soured cream and chopped mint (p. 250). Cucumber can also be used as a garnish, formed into cones to hold a savoury filling for a cocktail nibble, or cut into sticks for serving with a savoury dip.

Chilled Cucumber and Yogurt Soup (p. 210) makes a delightful start to a summer meal and, perhaps surprisingly, cucumber also makes one of the most delectable cooked vegetables, gently sautéed in butter with some fennel or dill seeds and a bay leaf, in a covered pan, until the flesh is golden and almost translucent.

Cucumber can also be stuffed and baked; try cutting a good plump cucumber into 20-cm/4-inch lengths, removing the skin, scooping out the seeds and filling the cavity with a mixture of finely chopped walnuts, onions, tomatoes and garlic. Bake in a well-buttered casserole, with a lid, for about 45 minutes in a moderate oven, and serve with Soured Cream and Herb Dressing (p. 233).

Dill pickled cucumbers are widely available and make a piquant addition to salads and sandwiches. Small fresh cucumbers are sometimes available for making your own pickles (p. 517).

Squashes

Squashes come in varied colours, shapes and sizes, but they can be roughly divided into summer and winter types. Summer squashes have soft skins — they are said to be too old to eat if you cannot pierce the skin with your fingernail — and watery flesh, while winter squashes have hard skins and firmer, more mealy flesh. It was this hard, protective skin developed by the winter squashes which made them such useful vegetables to store for the winter in the days before refrigerators.

Choosing and storing

The more delicate summer squashes should be firm and tender, with a smooth, shiny skin. They need to be stored in a cool place, preferably the fridge, and used within a few days. The more robust winter type should be shiny and hard, with no blemishes. As a rough guide, allow 450 g/1 lb summer squash, or 900 g/2 lb winter squash, for 4 people.

Preparation and cooking

See under individual varieties.

Courgette/Zucchini *Cucurbita pepo*

These baby marrows, which can be green or gold, reach their peak of perfection when they are no more than 10−15 cm/4−5 inches long. At this point they are tender, with flesh which almost melts in your mouth, and only need topping and tailing. They can then be cooked whole, sliced into rounds or matchsticks, or coarsely grated. Some recipes suggest degorging courgettes, as described for aubergines on p. 106, and this can be helpful if you are planning to sauté the courgettes in butter because it makes them less absorbent.

My favourite way of cooking courgettes is to steam them, either in a vegetable steamer or by cooking them in a deep, covered saucepan containing only 1 cm/½ inch of water, so that most of the courgettes are above the water, cooking in the steam. As soon as the courgettes are just tender − 2−4 minutes − drain them and add coarse sea salt, freshly ground black pepper, fresh chopped herbs − parsley, mint, tarragon or basil − and a little butter. Or serve the cooked courgettes with a Fresh Tomato

Sauce (p. 253). Courgettes can also be cooked in butter or oil, in a covered pan, over a low heat: this gives a luscious result, but I find it rather too rich and fatty unless they are served with something very plain.

Courgettes are excellent cooked with onions, garlic, peppers, aubergine and tomatoes, in Ratatouille (p. 278). And Provençal Courgette and Tomato Gratin makes a delicious light supper or lunch dish. Grated courgettes (1 kg/2¼ lb for 4 people) are fried lightly in butter, then layered in a shallow ovenproof dish with Fresh Tomato Sauce (p. 253) and sprinkled with breadcrumbs mixed with grated cheese. They are then baked in a moderate oven for 30–40 minutes.

For another excellent Provençal dish, Rice and Courgette Gratin, cook 250 g/8 oz brown rice. Fry a large onion and 4 diced courgettes in 2 tablespoons of oil until tender, then add to the rice with 50 g/2 oz grated cheese, an egg and seasoning. Spoon into a gratin dish, sprinkle with grated cheese and bake at 180c/350f/Gas Mark 4 for 45 minutes.

Larger courgettes make a good base for tasty stuffings, and courgettes always make a pleasant addition to vegetable pilafs and casseroles. They are best added towards the end of cooking time so that they do not overcook.

If you are able to obtain them, COURGETTE FLOWERS make a delicious treat dipped in a light batter and deep-fried, or filled with one of the nut roast mixtures (pp. 348-352) and baked.

MARROW *Cucurbita pepo*

Marrows and larger types of summer squash are nicest when the skin is tender enough to eat; they can then be cut into small dice. If the seeds are very tender, these can be cooked along with the flesh; if not, they should be scooped out. Marrow can be cooked as described for courgettes (the butter/oil method suits marrows especially well, giving a tender, translucent, golden result). A finely chopped shallot or some grated fresh ginger or crushed garlic can be included for extra flavour. Marrow cooked in this way is good served with a crunchy topping of roasted cashew nuts. Béchamel Sauce (p. 261) with chopped herbs complements plainly cooked marrow — steamed until just tender — well.

Marrows with the seeds removed make excellent containers for stuffing, either hollowed out from one end, or halved lengthways, or cut crossways into sections and stood on end. A marrow which has been allowed to mature on the vine can be made into a spicy chutney or that traditional old British favourite, marrow and ginger jam. Warwickshire cottages used to decorate such marrows with streamers, suspend them from the rafters in the autumn and keep them until Christmas!

Small, individual-size summer squash such as the delectable little PATTYPANS should be boiled in their skins until tender; the top can then be sliced off, a little butter and seasoning added, and the flesh scooped out with a spoon. The CHINESE WINTER MELON and the DOODY or WHITE PUMPKIN (not generally available in Aus./NZ) can be prepared like marrow, but it may be necessary to remove the skin unless this is tender.

SPAGHETTI SQUASH *Cucurbita pepo*

This has fibrous flesh which looks like spaghetti (but tastes like marrow) when cooked. Halve or quarter without peeling, then boil until the flesh is tender and can be scraped out. Toss the flesh in a little butter or olive oil and season well before serving.

PUMPKIN *Cucurbita pepo*

A pumpkin probably looks more exciting than it tastes, with its rounded shape and golden-orange skin and flesh. Pumpkin can, however, be made into an excellent smooth and creamy soup that is delicious eaten with hot garlic bread on a chilly autumn day. It is of course a traditional ingredient in USA Thanksgiving celebrations in the form of spicy Pumpkin Pie (p. 434), and one of Australia's most popular vegetables. Pumpkin can be served as a vegetable, and I like it best layered in a shallow gratin dish with garlic butter, topped with crumbs and baked in the oven, or cooked with some grated fresh ginger and garlic, then puréed. TURBAN, BUTTERNUT and ACORN SQUASH, HOKIDO PUMPKIN, HUBBARD, GOLDEN NUGGET or ONION SQUASH, and BUTTERCUP (or YELLOW BUTTON) SQUASH can all be prepared in a similar way. (Neither Turban squash nor Hokido pumpkin are generally available in Aus./NZ.)

SNAKE GOURD *Tricosantes cucumerina*

This unusual-looking, green squash is native to South-East Asia and Australia, and although sometimes grown in USA and Europe it is not easy to come by. It is much used in Indian vegetarian cookery and has a firm texture and an excellent flavour. It has a white down on the skin, which can be removed by rubbing the gourd all over with coarse salt. It is then cooked without peeling, and is delicious in lightly spiced vegetable dishes and curries. The snake gourd is sometimes confused with the BOTTLE GOURD, a much tougher squash, which is pointed at both ends.

COOKING AND SERVING IDEAS FOR WINTER SQUASHES

☐ Winter squashes make an excellent purée; steam until tender, then whizz to a cream in a blender or food processor. Season with salt, pepper and garlic. Good with a crisp hazelnut roast or burgers.

☐ For a richer version, stew the diced squash gently in butter with a sliced onion, some garlic and grated ginger, until tender, then purée in a blender or food processor.

☐ Winter squashes, and pumpkin in particular, make an excellent soup, creamy and golden. Allow 1 kg/2¼ lb pumpkin to make a soup for 6 people. Remove the skin and seeds; dice the flesh. Fry 2 large onions in 25 g/1 oz butter for 10 minutes, then add the pumpkin and 2 crushed garlic cloves and fry for a further 5 minutes. Add 1 litre/2¼ pints water and simmer for about 20 minutes, then reduce to a purée in a blender or food processor and add 150 ml/5 fl oz single cream and seasoning to taste. Delicious sprinkled with chopped parsley or crunchy croûtons.

☐ All the winter squashes absorb flavours well and are enhanced by the flavour of garlic and warming spices: ginger, curry powder, allspice, chilli, cinnamon, cardamom.

☐ Pumpkin, or any winter squash, is excellent baked in a casserole. Allow 450 g/1 lb pumpkin (weighed with the skin and seeds) per person, peel and cut into 1-cm/½-inch dice. Toss in seasoned flour, add a generous sprinkling of chopped parsley and crushed garlic, then pack into a well-greased casserole, dot with butter or oil and bake in a cool oven (170c/325f/Gas Mark 3) for 2–2½ hours, until the top is crisp and brown and the pumpkin underneath is tender.

☐ For an unusual pudding, try pumpkin in orange-flavoured syrup. For 4 people, peel and slice 1·5 kg/3½ lb pumpkin, then cook very gently, for about 10 minutes, in a syrup made from 300 ml/10 fl oz water, 100 g/4 oz sugar and the grated rind of 1 orange. Serve chilled.

Mushrooms and Truffles

Wild mushrooms have long been used to add interest and nourishment to meals. Mushrooms, whether wild or cultivated, are among the most useful flavouring ingredients in vegetarian cookery, as well as being filling and substantial if cooked in quantity. Mushrooms are also interesting nutritionally, being unusually rich in vitamins B2 and B3 (which vegetarians need to be sure of including in their diet).

Choosing and storing

Wild mushrooms can be found in woods and fields if you're lucky or know where to look; or they can sometimes be bought from specialist greengrocers and markets, but the supply is usually erratic: grab them when you see — or can afford — them! If buying cultivated mushrooms, avoid any that are brownish-looking. Choose mushrooms which smell fragrant and look fresh, almost with a slight bloom on them. Use quickly; they do not keep well, although they can be stored in the fridge for 24–36 hours.

Preparation and cooking

Wild mushrooms should be carefully washed — personally I like to wash cultivated mushrooms, too — and any tough bits should be cut out. Field mushrooms should have the top layer of skin removed.

Most mushrooms are best sliced as necessary and then cooked simply by frying lightly in butter, for about 5 minutes, until cooked through. If mushrooms exude a great deal of liquid during the frying process, you can either pour this off and save it as a flavouring for a soup or sauce, or thicken it by adding a small quantity of cornflour mixed with water. Or — the best way, I think — continue to cook the mushrooms over a high heat until all the liquid has disappeared and you are left with very tasty, tender mushrooms: this may take 20–30 minutes. They are also delicious stuffed, in pâtés, flans and raw in salads.

For Mushrooms in Cream, prepare as described above, allowing 900 g/2 lb mushrooms for 4 people. Fry in 25 g/1 oz butter over a high heat for 20–30 minutes, until all the liquid has disappeared, then add 150 ml/5 fl oz double cream and season with salt, freshly ground black pepper, a squeeze of lemon juice and a grating of nutmeg.

BLACK TRUFFLE *Tuber melansporum* and WHITE TRUFFLE *T. magnatum*

Wildly expensive, black truffles (found in the Périgord region of France) are chopped and added to dishes as a flavouring. White truffles are cut into fine slivers, while raw, over the top of dishes to give them an exquisite fragrance. Canned truffles do not have the aroma and flavour of fresh ones.

CEP *Boletus edulis*

Ceps have tubes under their caps instead of the more usual gills. Ceps are delicious cooked as described above and are also excellent added to casseroles. Italian dried mushrooms, FUNGHI PORCINI, are ceps. They are expensive to buy, but just a few mixed with cultivated mushrooms, or added to a vegetable casserole, give a pronounced flavour. Just rinse, then use as required.

CHANTERELLE or GIROLLE *Cantharellus cibarius*

The trumpet-shaped chanterelle has the colour and aroma of apricots. It is delicious cooked as described above or added to casseroles. It has a slightly peppery flavour and remains chewy however long it is cooked.

CHINESE STRAW MUSHROOM *Volvariella volvacea*

Chinese straw mushrooms, available in bottles, make a tasty addition to vegetable stir-fries.

CULTIVATED MUSHROOMS *Agaricus bisporus*

These are available at various stages of development. First come the little tight white delicately flavoured BUTTON MUSHROOMS, which are excellent in creamy sauces (p. 259), sliced in salads (pp. 237, 244), or for using whole in Marinated Mushrooms. The next stage is MEDIUM-SIZED MUSHROOMS and the more strongly flavoured SMALL OPEN MUSHROOMS. These, too, are useful for most purposes, particularly for making into fritters or adding to batter for a mushroomy vegetarian version of toad in the hole, while LARGE FLAT OPEN MUSHROOMS are ideal for stuffing, and for grilling or frying. CHAMPIGNON MARRON (with a brownish skin) and CHAMPIGNON DE PARIS are other cultivated mushrooms.

FIELD MUSHROOM *Agaricus campestris*

These have a wonderful rich mushroomy flavour, much more intense than that of cultivated mushrooms. Delicious fried and served as they are, or made into duxelles, a concentrated mixture of finely chopped mushrooms fried with a finely chopped onion for about 30 minutes, uncovered, until they become a thick purée.

MOREL *Morchella esculenta* and *M. vulgaris*

This tasty mushroom tends to harbour grit and sometimes insects in its honeycomb cap, so it is best to cut it up first, then wash it in salted water. Fry morels and use in any of the ways suggested above. Dried morels are well worth buying (when you're feeling rich). Soak them in hot water for 30 minutes, then strain, reserving the soaking water for use in cooking. Wash them well, then chop and add to casseroles, soups and sauces for a deliciously intense mushroom flavour.

OYSTER MUSHROOM *Pleurotus ostreatus*

Oyster mushrooms grow on tree clumps and are available both fresh and bottled. With their firm texture these make a useful addition to casseroles — use them like cultivated mushrooms.

PLEUROTTE *Pleurotus ostreatus*

This attractive delicately flavoured mushroom can be prepared in a similar way to chanterelles.

SHIITAKE *Lentinus edodes*

These Chinese and Japanese fungi need to be gathered and eaten when young, or they become tough. Fresh shiitake can be sliced, fried and added to rice dishes, stews and stir-fries; soak the dried ones in boiling water for 30 minutes then drain and chop. Add the soaking water to the dish or keep as stock.

Woodear or Cloudear *Auricularia polytricha*
Rather tough mushrooms, used in Chinese recipes. Soak in
boiling water for 30 minutes, to gain a gelatinous texture, before
use.

Sea Vegetables

Seaweeds, or sea vegetables, as they are more
appetizingly called, have been an important
food for people all over the world since
ancient times, many types being cultivated
and used. In some poor coastal areas they
were eaten as a survival food, but in Japan
they are an important part of the national
cuisine, and many types are cultivated. Seaweeds are high in nutrients, including protein, iron, calcium, potassium, sodium,
iodine and are also one of the rare non-
animal sources of vitamin B_{12}.

Choosing and storing

Seaweeds can be bought dried from health shops and wholefood
shops, as well as shops stocking Japanese ingredients. Keep
them in an airtight container in a cool, dry place.

Sea vegetables may not be generally available in Aus./NZ due
to import restrictions.

Preparation and using

Most seaweeds (with the exception of nori, see below) need
soaking before use. Put the seaweed into a bowl, starting with a
small amount, say 15 g/½ oz, if this is the first time you've used
it, cover with boiling water and leave for 20 minutes, then drain.
The soaking water, which contains useful nutrients, can be used
in the recipe or discarded if it is too salty and strongly flavoured.
Then put the seaweed into a saucepan, cover with fresh cold
water (which can be flavoured with grated fresh ginger or

tamari) and simmer gently until tender — generally 20–30 minutes. Alternatively, the seaweed can be added to a vegetable stew or casserole at this point. The cooked seaweed can be added to other cooked vegetables, or cooled and mixed with fresh vegetables and a dressing to make a salad.

Seaweed is naturally gelatinous and some types, notably carageen and AGAR AGAR, can be used to make vegetarian jellies and moulds (see Carageen below).

ARAME *Eisenia bicyclis*

Arame is cut into long thin strips after harvesting. It is a good seaweed to start with if you're unfamiliar with sea vegetables. Arame has a slightly sweet flavour; it is pleasant in salads, such as Radish, Cucumber and Arame Salad (p. 245), and in vegetable side dishes. It needs only 5 minutes' soaking followed by 20 minutes' cooking before use.

CARAGEEN *Chondrus crispus*

This pale-coloured branching seaweed can be cooked and served in vegetable dishes or salads. I think it is more useful as a jelling agent, producing a light, delicately flavoured jelly, or blancmange — my mother often made this when I was a child and I loved its curious, delicate flavour. To make Carageen Mould, soak 7 g/¼ oz carageen in warm water for 10 minutes, then drain and put into a saucepan with 900 ml/1½ pints milk and a vanilla pod and simmer for 20 minutes. Strain through a fine sieve, pressing the carageen to extract all the jelly. Add 4 tablespoons clear honey or sugar and an egg yolk; finally fold in the whisked egg white. Pour into moulds to set. This can be made with soya milk and without the egg for a vegan version.

DULSE *Rhodymenia palmata*

Reddish-purple in colour, dulse never gets very soft even if you cook it for 40–50 minutes. It isn't to everyone's taste, though it's a seaweed I particularly like, finely shredded raw (after soaking) and added to a soup, salad or rice dish.

HIZIKI *Hiziki fusiforme*

Sold coarsely shredded, hiziki has a sweet, delicate flavour rather like that of arame (see above). Hiziki is an outstanding source of iron and calcium, just 15 g/½ oz supplying nearly half

IDEAS FOR USING SEA VEGETABLES

☐ Toast nori and crumble over any salad, stir-fry or creamy dip, for a tangy, salty flavour.

☐ Soak and shred kombu, flavour with chilli powder, crushed garlic, chopped spring onion, vinegar, sugar, salt and pepper. Serve as a side-dish with Japanese-style sweet-vinegared rice (p. 361) and stir-fried vegetables.

☐ Soak and shred wakame, mix with diced cucumber, sliced radishes, sugar, vinegar, salt and pepper. Leave for 1–2 hours (or longer) to marinate; serve sprinkled with sesame seeds, as a side-dish with Japanese-style rice.

☐ For an interesting nibble or side-dish, add soaked and diced wakame to beaten egg; fry on both sides to make a kind of pancake. Cut into pieces. Sprinkle with a few sesame seeds if liked; dip into soy sauce to eat.

the recommended daily requirement for an adult. I think it is most delicious added to salads or rice and vegetable mixtures or stir-fried vegetable side dishes.

KOMBU *Laminaria japonica*

Most often used to flavour stocks, and an essential ingredient of the Japanese stock, dashi, kombu is a strongly flavoured sea vegetable which comes in thick black strips: one strip will flavour 600 ml/1 pint water.

LAVER *Porphyra umbilicalis*

Prepare fresh laver as described above, cooking for 50–60 minutes. Laver can also be bought ready-cooked and canned; it looks like a thick green purée. A purée of laver is mixed with oatmeal to make the Welsh delicacy, laver bread. In my opinion, you have to be either Welsh or a real seaweed devotee to enjoy either laver or laver bread.

NORI *Porphyra tenera*

This is the most popular sea vegetable, and my own favourite. It is made into sheets in Japan by pressing the seaweed out by hand after drying. Another good one to try if you're not familiar with seaweeds, nori is prepared differently from the others. Take a sheet of nori and hold it close to a hotplate or gas flame for a minute or so, moving it slightly until it is toasted and crisp all over. It can then be used to wrap up tasty savoury ingredients to make sushi (p. 213), or you can scrunch it up in your fingers and sprinkle it over the top of salads, soups, stir-fries or vegetable soups.

WAKAME *Undaria pinnatifida*

Wakame is a mild-flavoured, useful, all-purpose seaweed. After soaking (see above), open up the leaves, cut out the central spine and cook the wakame as described above. Wakame is used to make the classic Miso Soup (p. 201), and is also useful for flavouring soups and stews and adding to salads and vegetable side dishes. For a tangy rice salad, add soaked and shredded wakame to cooked brown rice. Season with salt, pepper, sugar and vinegar, then add shredded fresh vegetables. Garnish with sesame seeds.

Apples, Pears and Grapes

Apples, pears and table grapes have been cultivated and enjoyed for centuries. Delicious and refreshing, they are available all year round. They contain a range of useful vitamins and minerals, and apples and pears are rich in particularly valuable fibre. There are many varieties of these fruits, although with apples and pears, in recent years, there has been a tendency to concentrate on a few outstanding ones.

APPLE *Malus pumila*

Choosing and storing

One of the basics of the store cupboard, one variety or another of apple is available all the year round. Choose bright, firm, sweet-smelling apples with no wrinkles or bruises. They are best stored in a cool, airy place. Only late season apples will store over winter, and if these are wrapped individually in newspaper and put in boxes or shelves in a cool place they will keep for several months.

Preparation and using

Good eating apples are delightful just as they are, or with cheese, such as a piece of mature Cheddar. They can be sliced and added to fruit salads and compotes, or mixed with vegetables in a savoury salad such as the famous Waldorf (p. 250). If you need to keep raw apple for any length of time, either dip the pieces in a light salt and water mixture, or toss them in lemon or orange juice, to preserve the colour. Grated apple forms the basis of the original Bircher muesli (p. 360). Eating apples can also be used for cooking; in fact I prefer them to the sharper cooking apples for some dishes because their natural sweetness means less sugar is needed. Sliced and peeled COX'S ORANGE PIPPIN apples are delightful stewed with raisins, baked in a pie (p. 439) or made into an open tart: follow the recipe on p. 435 but use lightly poached apple slices instead of red fruit, and glaze with sieved and warmed apricot jam.

Another widely cultivated apple is the YELLOW/GOLDEN DELICIOUS, firm, crisp and, some would say, tasteless, when young, becoming golden and sweeter when more mature. Like Cox's, Golden Delicious apples can be used in piés and flans, and are frequently used for this purpose in France. The GRANNY SMITH apple is another variety which you either like or you don't; it is green in colour and very crisp, with a clean, refreshing flavour. The STARKING apple has a red skin. It is a delicious eating apple, very crisp, with sweet, white flesh. Another popular red-skinned apple is the RED DELICIOUS, a firm, sweet variety developed in the USA. This apple can be eaten raw or baked. The MCINTOSH is another popular all-purpose American variety. This has a slightly sharp flavour, good for eating raw or baking. SPARTAN apples, developed in Denmark, can be used for both cooking and eating and have a custard-like flavour. Other good eating apples are LAXTON FORTUNE, EDWARD VII and ELLISON'S ORANGE, with a flavour not unlike a Cox apple; the brown-skinned EGREMONT RUSSET with its deliciously mellow flavour; CRISPINS, JAMES GRIEVE,

GREENSLEEVES, and JONAGOLD which has a long season, lasting from autumn until the spring.

Cooking apples are best used if a sharp flavour is required; some cooking apples, such as BRAMLEY'S SEEDLINGS, also collapse when cooked, so these are best if you want a soft purée. Large cooking apples are excellent cored, scored round the middle to prevent bursting, stuffed with dried fruit or mincemeat, or honey and chopped nuts, and baked whole for 40–50 minutes in a moderate oven. Or they may be peeled, cored, wrapped in shortcrust pastry and baked to make apple dumplings.

Cooked apple is used as a basis of many excellent puddings: apple crumble and apple meringue, apple fool and apple amber, to mention just a few. I like to make apple purée into ice cream (p. 418), to serve with a Blackberry Coulis (p. 448) or sorbet (p. 420). Cooking apples are also used to make apple sauce, which makes an excellent accompaniment to Savoury Lentil Loaf (p. 318). To make Apple Sauce cook 450 g/1 lb peeled, cored and sliced cooking apples in 25 g/1 oz butter or vegan margarine in a covered pan for about 10 minutes until pulpy. Cooking apples can be used, too, to make herb-flavoured apple jelly, one of the best preserves, and also a sweet and spicy chutney (p. 517).

CRAB APPLES, the original apple, are small, more the size of large cherries than apples as we know them, and very sharp. They range in colour from yellow to red and are mainly useful because they are full of pectin, so they can be made into an excellent ruby-coloured jelly which is delicious for serving with nut roasts (instead of redcurrant or cranberry jelly). They can also be mixed with other wild fruits to make, for very little expense, a delicious sweet/sour Hedgerow Jelly. To make this you need 450 g /1 lb each of crab apples, blackberries and elderberries, and 225 g /8 oz each of sloes, hips, haws and rowan berries. Cook the blackberries and elderberries together in a little water until tender, and, in another pan, cook the rest of the fruits, in water, until tender. Mix the fruit purées, strain. Measure the liquid and return to the pan with 450 g/1 lb sugar for each 600 ml/1 pint, heat gently until the sugar is dissolved, then boil until setting point is reached as described on p. 510.

STEWING FRUIT

Juicy fruits such as apples (also black and red currants, bilberries, blackberries and rhubarb) are best cooked in the minimum of water, or none at all. Put the fruit into a heavy-based saucepan with 2 tablespoons of water to each 450−700 g/ 1−1½ lb fruit. Cover the saucepan and then heat gently until the juices run and the fruit is tender − this will probably take around 10 minutes.

Instead of water, butter can be used for stewing apples, and redcurrant jelly for rhubarb. When the fruit is soft, add sugar or honey to taste. Do not put this in sooner or the outside of the fruits may toughen before the inside is properly cooked.

PEAR *Pyrus communis*

Choosing and storing

There are around 5000 named varieties of pear, but only about 20−30 are widely cultivated. Pears need choosing carefully, because once perfectly ripe they deteriorate very quickly. It is best to buy them slightly under-ripe and keep them at room temperature for a day or two until they are just right, when they should 'give' slightly at the stalk end. Once this stage is reached, they will keep for a day or two in the fridge, but bring them to room temperature before serving, to draw out all the flavour.

A good dessert pear can be really superlative, with a delicate flavour, natural sweetness and melting flesh.

Preparation and using

Pears like this really need no accompaniment, although they do complement a good ripe cheese, such as a Brie, well and make a delicious first course with a Roquefort Dressing (p. 225), or with a cream and yogurt dressing flavoured with tarragon vinegar to give a hint of sharpness (p. 224).

Perfectly ripe pears can be peeled and served in some of the combinations for which cooked pears are traditionally used, such as Poire Belle Hélène, where they are filled with vanilla ice cream and topped with Hot Chocolate Sauce (p. 449).

Perhaps the most delicious dessert pear is the COMICE, delicately flavoured, juicy and very sweet when at its best. The

POACHING FRUIT

This method is best for pears and other firm fruits such as apricots, peaches and plums. First make a sugar syrup. For 450−700 g/ 1−1½ lb fruit you need 300 ml/ 10 fl oz water, or other liquid such as wine, cider or fruit juice, and 75 g/3 oz granulated sugar. Honey can be used instead of sugar but will add its own strong flavour. Put the sugar and water into a heavy-based saucepan and heat gently until dissolved. Then turn up the heat and boil rapidly for 2 minutes. Put in the prepared fruit, bring back to the boil, then simmer gently, half covered, until the fruit feels tender when pierced. It's important to give large fruits like whole or halved peaches or pears time to cook right through to the centre or they may discolour. Allow at least 20−30 minutes for whole pears and 15−20 minutes for the others. Let the fruit cool in the syrup, or remove the fruit with a draining spoon and thicken the syrup by boiling rapidly until reduced in quantity.

yellow-skinned WILLIAMS pear is another popular dessert variety. The CONFERENCE pear has a rather tough brownish-green skin, and this, too, has a delicious flavour, especially when fully ripe, but also cooks well (see above), as does the PACKHAM and indeed many dessert pears, including the LOGIPONT. Poached as described, then drained and chilled, these pears are delicious served with some whipped cream, or in the traditional ways described above. They are also excellent, deeply stained and delicately flavoured, poached in a syrup made with cheap red wine instead of water. In addition cooking pears can be pickled or made into chutney.

It is also possible to buy Asian pears, such as the TIENTSIN YA PEAR and the CHINESE PEAR. These are eaten when they are still firm, and can be used raw, adding a crisp texture to fruit and vegetable salad mixtures, or cooked as described above.

GRAPE *Vitis vinifera*

Choosing and storing

Many varieties of table grape are grown, ranging in colour from white through red, as in the NAPOLEON RED, to deepest purple of which the HOTHOUSE GRAPES are an example. Grapes also vary in sweetness, and the only way to be sure of what you are

IDEAS FOR USING A GLUT OF PEARS OR APPLES

☐ Spiced pears are easy to make and go well with nut or lentil loaves.

☐ Both pears and apples can be made into excellent ice cream, following the recipe on p. 418. These are good served with a toning sauce or sorbet: pear ice cream with pear sorbet; apple ice cream with blackberry sorbet; pear ice cream with chocolate or raspberry sauce; apple ice cream with blackberry or orange sauce.

☐ If you make wine, both pears and apples can be made into good medium-dry white wine.

☐ Make pear or apple jelly or jam, perhaps flavoured with fresh herbs.

☐ Pear or apple sauce goes well with a savoury lentil loaf.

buying is to try one. The green MUSCAT GRAPES are particularly sweet with the characteristic 'MUSCAT' flavour, and SEEDLESS GRAPES, too, are particularly sweet.

Once bought, grapes need to be used quickly, although they will keep for 2—3 days in the refrigerator. Bring them out and allow them enough time to get back to room temperature before serving.

Preparation and using

A bunch of grapes makes a decorative addition to a fruit bowl or cheese board and, like apples and pears, they are excellent all put together in a salad, with watercress and walnuts too. Grapes make an attractive addition to a fresh fruit salad — choose the colour to complement the other fruits — and can also be made into a delicate jelly, with grape juice set with agar agar (p. 427). Black and white grapes, arranged in alternating circles, make an attractive filling for a flan case or topping for a cheesecake. A white nutmeat made from pine nuts or almonds is good served with a garnish of fresh green grapes, while little bunches of seedless grapes are a mother's best friend as lunch-box fillers and replacements for sugary sweets.

Pitted Fruits

This is another group which includes some of the most delectable fruits, many of which delighted the people of China, Greece and Rome thousands of years ago. At the peak of perfection, these fruits all make a fine dessert, served fresh and raw without any adornment. They are also health-giving, containing useful amounts of a range of vitamins and minerals. Peaches and apricots are particularly good sources of vitamin A, while dates are rich in B vitamins (especially B2 and B3, and iron).

Choosing and storing

Superb when perfectly ripe, these fruits are soon past their best, so need buying and storing carefully. As they are soft, pitted fruits are particularly susceptible to damage during transport, so look for sound fruits without bruises. When buying fresh dates make sure that they really are fresh, with no sign of 'sweating' or flaking. If they have a slightly winey flavour, they are off and, while they won't hurt you, they are certainly not at their best. If you need to keep these fruits, store them in a cool place (or the fridge).

Preparation and cooking

Perfect fruits can be served as they are, or the stones can be removed and the fruit sliced and added to a fruit salad. Peaches can be skinned in the same way as tomatoes (p. 108). Under-ripe peaches, apricots and nectarines can be poached in a sugar syrup (p. 125); plums can be stewed (p. 123), baked into pies and made into crumbles.

APRICOT *Prunus armeniaca*
Perfectly ripe apricots make one of the best dessert fruits; they are also pleasant with cream cheese in a salad or as part of a fruit

compote. Less perfect fruits are good poached in vanilla-flavoured syrup and served with thick yogurt or cream, or in a flan or little tartlets. Apricots are used in savoury recipes in the Middle East and go well with chick peas and white beans; an apricot sauce is good served with a savoury nut roast instead of apple sauce, and I also like apricot sauce with Deep-fried Camembert (p. 333) instead of the more usual gooseberry sauce.

Cooked, drained apricots can be topped with an all-in-one cake mixture (p. 456) and a scattering of flaked almonds and baked to make an apricot sponge pudding, and they are included in Danish pastries. They can be pickled or made into jam or chutney. Apricot jam, melted and sieved, makes a useful glaze for fruit dishes and is often used to stick the almond paste on a fruit cake (p. 468). Apricot brandy makes a delicious addition to sweet apricot dishes such as compotes and fools. Apricots are available fresh, dried (p. 147), canned either in syrup or their own juice or made into preserves or chutney (p. 516).

CHERRY *Prunus avium*

Sweet juicy cherries make an easy and refreshing pudding. Ones which are less than perfect, or the sour MORELLO CHERRIES can be poached to make a compote or jelly, or covered with batter to make a clafoutis, so popular in France. In Central Europe cherries are made into chilled soups and they are also excellent made into a tart, or served hot and flambéd with ice cream. The famous Black Forest gâteau, consisting of layers of lightest chocolate sponge, black cherries and cream, with a liberal sprinkling of cherry liqueur, may have been devalued by the popularity of synthetic-tasting versions, but is still a wonderful gâteau when properly made.

Cherry brandy, and Kirsch, an eau-de-vie made from the stones of cherries, are delicious flavourings for any cherry dish, and Kirsch is also traditionally added to Cheese Fondue (p. 325). Cherries are available fresh, frozen, canned and made into preserves: black cherry preserve is one of the most delectable.

DATE/USA GOLDEN DATE *Phoenix dactylifera*

Fresh dates are one of the best sweet-substitutes, either as they are, or with their stones removed and replaced by a freshly cracked brazil nut, a mixture of whipped cream, cream cheese, ground almonds and honey or orange flower water. They are much more succulent than dried dates, and make a good addition to a fresh fruit salad. Or they can be served with thick Greek yogurt with a topping of a clear honey and, for a really superlative pudding, a little double cream.

LYCHEE *Litchi chinensis*
See p. 135.

NECTARINE *Prunus persica*, var. *Nectarina*
Particularly juicy and well-flavoured, nectarines can be used in similar ways to peaches. They are available both fresh and dried.

PEACH *Prunus persica*
Peaches may be white- or yellow-fleshed and free-stone, cling-stone or semi-clingstone. A sweet, ripe, juicy peach is a delight and needs no accompaniment. Not-so-perfect peaches can be skinned (as described for tomatoes, p. 108), sliced and added to fruit salads and compotes, or sliced, covered with sweet white wine and chilled.

Peach Brûlée is also good: put sliced peaches into a shallow heatproof dish, cover with whipped cream and an even layer of brown sugar, chill, then just before serving, grill until the sugar caramelizes.

Ripe peaches can be made into an excellent ice cream using the recipe on p. 417. This is good served with Raspberry Sorbet (made as for Blackberry Sorbet, p. 420) or Raspberry Coulis (p. 448). Spiced Peaches (made as for Orange Slices, p. 519) and Peach Chutney (made as for Sweet Spiced Apricot Chutney, p. 517) are other good ways of using less than perfect specimens. Peaches are available fresh, dried (p. 149) and canned in syrup and in fruit juice.

PLUM/GREENGAGE *Prunus domestica, P. institia*
Like the other fruits in this group, sweet and tender plums and greengages are excellent eaten *au naturel*. VICTORIA are examples of excellent dessert plums, and when at their peak need no accompaniment. Other good dessert varieties are the SANTA ROSA, RED ACE and GOLDEN CAPE plums. Many varieties, like the SWITZEN, BURBANK and PRUNE PLUM, can be eaten raw when ripe or used for cooking, though sour varieties, like the tiny DAMSON (*Prunus institia*) need to be stewed in a sweetened

syrup, perhaps with a touch of cinnamon added (p. 123), made into crumbles (p. 441) or pies (p. 439). Plums are available fresh, dried (in the form of prunes, p. 150) and canned, and also in the form of preserves, crystallized fruits and some liqueurs.

There are also pickled plums, known as UMEBOSHI plums. A popular ingredient in Japanese and macrobiotic cooking, umeboshi plums are pickled for at least two years. During this time they develop lactic acid which makes them a particularly healthy ingredient, cleansing the gut and aiding digestion. They have a sharp, pungent, salty flavour and can be added to dishes − particularly grain dishes − or served alongside.

ↄↄↄ

Berries and Soft Fruits

These luscious fruits are also some of the most nutritious. Blackcurrants contain a useful amount of calcium and are one of the best of all sources of vitamin C, and strawberries, too, are unusually rich in this vitamin. Raspberries, blackberries and all the currants contain high levels of fibre. Rhubarb contains calcium but also oxalic acid, preventing its absorption, so it is inadvisable to eat rhubarb more than twice a week.

Choosing and storing

With the exception of cranberries and rhubarb, these fruits are delicate and need gentle handling. Look for bright fruit that is firm but not hard, with no sign of bruising, wetness or mildew. Check the punnets to see if they are stained with juices, and avoid any that are. Rhubarb should be crisp, bright and the sticks not too large (or they could be tough). Use the fruit as soon as possible; if necessary, keep in a cool place, preferably the fridge. Most of these fruits are available frozen, bottled and canned, as well as fresh.

Preparation and cooking

Many people advise against washing soft fruit, but I prefer to do so, to remove dust and any residues of sprays. Pat them dry on kitchen paper. For further preparation, see under the individual fruits. To cook these fruits, put them into a pan over a gentle heat without water for a few minutes until the juices run. A little sugar or honey can then be added to taste, and rhubarb is good cooked with a few tablespoons of redcurrant jelly. This group of fruit is particularly good for preserving.

BLACKBERRY *Rubus macropetalus*

Pickling wild blackberries is one of the pleasures of late summer. Plump juicy berries make a delicious pie, perhaps combined with apples (p. 439). Blackberries can also be made into one of the best sorbets (p. 420), or an excellent coulis (p. 448).

BLACKCURRANT and REDCURRANT *Ribes nigrum, R. sativum*

Unless they are going to be sieved, currants need to have the stems and flower ends removed. This is easily done with bunches of currants by drawing the prongs of a fork down through the clusters. A few raw currants can be added to a fruit salad or compote, but generally currants are best cooked and can be made into pies, tarts, ice cream and sorbets and the famous Danish red fruit pudding, Rödgröt, where a mixture of red fruits is stewed then puréed, thickened with cornflour, arrowroot or potato flour and allowed to become cool, when it will have a soft, slightly jellied texture.

Summer Pudding is another traditional use for currants; stew them with other red fruits, then dip thin crustless slices of bread into the juices and use to line completely the sides and base of a pudding basin. Fill the basin with the drained fruit, then put more juice-soaked bread on top. Put a plate and a weight on top, then leave for several hours. Turn out of the basin and serve with thick yogurt or cream.

BLUEBERRY *Vaccinium corymbosum*

Related to the bilberry, blackberry or whortleberry, the blueberry is very popular in the USA. Fat, juicy blueberries are delicious served with cream or thick yogurt and a little sugar or honey, or they can be made into pies, crumbles, flans, cheesecake toppings and muffins, or stewed to make a filling for pancakes.

CRANBERRY *Vaccinium macrocarpum*

Perhaps best-known in the form of Cranberry Sauce (p. 260), which, by the way, is as delicious with a white, delicately flavoured Christmas nut roast as it is with turkey. Bright red cranberries can also be made into pies and tarts, but they have an acidic, slightly spicy flavour, and need a lot of sugar to make them palatable.

GOOSEBERRY *Ribes uvacrispa*

A sharply flavoured fruit, gooseberries can be yellow, green or reddish-purple, smooth or hairy. Dessert gooseberries just need topping and tailing before eating. Cooking varieties can be stewed gently with a few tablespoons of water to prevent them sticking to the pan. A few sprigs of elderflowers added to the pan give a delicate muscat flavour. Puréed stewed gooseberries make a good sauce for a brazil nut roast and also for deep-fried Camembert or Brie. Or add to the puréed gooseberries cold custard, yogurt, cream, or a mixture, to make a fool (p. 419). Gooseberries can also be made into excellent pies (p. 440) and crumbles.

LOGANBERRY *Rubus ursinus* var. *loganobaccus*

A natural hybrid between the raspberry and blackberry, first discovered in the garden of Judge J. H. Logan at Santa Cruz in California and named after him. Loganberries have a sharp flavour and can be eaten raw or cooked, in ways similar to blackberries and raspberries. Loganberry ice cream and sorbet are specially good.

RASPBERRY *Rubus idaeus*

Raspberries are wonderful eaten raw, with sugar and cream, or made into ice cream (p. 417), sorbet or a coulis (p. 448). They do not need initial cooking for these, just rubbing through a sieve (nylon, not metal) to purée and remove the pips.

RHUBARB *Rheum rhabarbarum*

Rhubarb has a tart flavour and has to be cooked with sugar before it can be eaten. To prepare rhubarb, cut off the leaves (which are poisonous) and trim the base. Peel off any tough skin, then cut the rhubarb into manageable lengths and cook as described above. Rhubarb is complemented by the flavour of cinnamon, ginger or orange and can be made into a creamy fool, an excellent quick crumble (p. 441), or covered with all-in-one sponge mixture (p. 456) and baked to make squashy Rhubarb Upside Down Cake.

STRAWBERRY *Fragaria x ananassa*

Strawberries are good simply hulled and served with cream and sugar. They also make an attractive addition to a summer fruit salad or a luscious topping for a cheesecake or little tartlets. The French way of serving them with light, heart-shaped moulds of cream cheese, is also as delectable as it is pretty. Less perfect strawberries can be made into jam, ice cream or fools and mousses. Little WILD STRAWBERRIES (*Fragaria vesca*) or ALPINE STRAWBERRIES make a pretty decoration for something delicately coloured like a Champagne Sorbet (p. 422), or addition to a compote of summer fruits.

Tropical and Exotic Fruits

Often vividly coloured and with intriguing flavours, fragrances and textures, tropical and exotic fruits bring a welcome touch of variety and luxury to the vegetarian table. Some are rather expensive, but many are also rich in valuable nutrients: bananas are an excellent source of magnesium and B6; passion fruit of protein, fibre and B1; kiwi fruit and guavas of vitamin C; and mangoes of vitamin A and zinc.

Choosing, storing, preparation and using

See under individual fruits

BANANA *Musa sapientum*

Bananas for exportation are cut when they have reached their full size but are still green, and sometimes they are still slightly green and under-ripe when they reach the shops. Bananas will ripen if left at room temperature for a day or two. As they become riper they become softer and develop brownish spots on the skin; peeled and well-mashed, very ripe bananas are a good early food for babies and can also be made into moist cakes and tea breads (p. 496).

Buy bananas in bunches attached to the stalk, as the skins of loose bananas are easily torn and the flesh will discolour.

In Europe, the USA and Aus., bananas are mainly used in sweet dishes, although they may be served as a side-dish with a curry. They contrast well with other fruits, so are a popular addition to a fruit salad mixture. More luxuriously, bananas can be split lengthways and served with Vanilla Ice Cream (p. 413) and Chocolate Sauce (p. 449), or flambéd with rum, or made into fritters and served with slices of lime — all rich and fattening ideas, these. But bananas can be a slimmer's friend too, because one or two bananas make a complete, filling, easy, transportable and nutritious meal for around 200 calories.

In India, South America and the Caribbean, GREEN BANANAS are used in filling and nutritious savoury dishes. The leaves of the banana plant are also used in Mexico and India, for wrapping food before cooking, as we might use tin foil, with the extra advantage that the banana leaf adds a delicate flavour to the dish. The leaves are used to make disposable plates, too. Bananas are available fresh and dried (see p. 147).

CARAMBOLA or STAR FRUIT *Averrhoa carambola*
The carambola looks better than it tastes, although it does have a delicate fragrance and a juicy texture. Look for plump yellow fruits without blemishes. To use, wash then cut into slices with a sharp, stainless steel knife. The slices will be star-like in shape and make a pretty decoration for a gâteau, cheesecake, sorbet, jelly, or fruit salad.

CUSTARD APPLE *Anonacea squamosa*
Widely used in the tropics, custard apples are ripe when they feel soft to the touch. They have a creamy, custard-like flavour and texture and can be used in compotes or made into fools and ice creams.

Fig *Ficus carica*

The best figs I ever ate were left on our verandah early one morning by the gardener when we were staying in Corfu. We did wonder where he had found them, but they made a fabulous breakfast. There are several types of fig and they vary in colour from golden to red and purple. They need to be completely ripe, when they are fairly soft, but they are highly perishable, so are best used immediately, although they will keep in the fridge for 24–48 hours.

Figs are good to eat at any time of the day, either on their own, or served simply: quartered, for instance, with some cream cheese or thick Greek yogurt and a little clear honey. They are delicious cut almost in half from the pointed end, then almost in half again, gently opened, topped with a little Greek yogurt or whipped cream and served on a Raspberry Coulis (p. 448). In North Africa and other Mediterranean countries, figs are commonly made into a preserve. Figs are available fresh, canned and dried (p. 148).

Guava *Psidium guajava*

In my experience fresh guavas can be rather disappointing, because it's not easy to buy one that is sweet and ripe. If you do, use immediately or keep the guava in the fridge briefly. The juicy flesh can be pink, white or yellow; the whole fruit is edible, although guavas are usually peeled, and can be eaten fresh or stewed. They are frequently made into jellies and preserves. Guavas are available fresh and canned: I think canned guavas are a safer buy than fresh ones, and their pink colour looks good in a fruit salad.

Japonica *Chaenomeles*

These fruits are hard and only suitable for cooking, although they have an exquisite heady fragrance. They are difficult to cut and peel, but only need halving or quartering if you are going to make them into a jelly preserve, the most common way of using them – follow the recipe for Crab Apple Jelly on p. 512. This sweet, scented preserve is good for serving with nut roasts, or for eating on bread.

Kiwi *Actinidia sinensis*

These little furry fruits from New Zealand are ripe when they yield to slight pressure. They keep well, either at room temperature, or in the fridge, and should be peeled thinly with a sharp knife before using. The greatest asset of the kiwi fruit is its stunning bright green flesh and attractive central arrangement of seeds which give it a flower-like appearance when sliced. The traditional use for kiwi fruits is, of course, the Pavlova or fruit meringue (p. 425). Kiwis are extremely high in vitamin c and can be a good way of getting children to take this — try slicing the top off a ripe kiwi fruit and letting them scoop the flesh out with a teaspoon, like eating a boiled egg. Kiwi fruits are available fresh and canned.

LYCHEE *Litchi chinensis* and RAMBUTAN *Nephelium lappaceum*
Ripe lychees are about the size of a small plum with a red knobbly skin which becomes brown and hard; rambutans have spines, reminiscent of a small hedgehog. The skin comes away quite easily if you pull it back with your fingers, like peeling an orange. Inside, the flesh is white, juicy and translucent-looking with a distinctive, scented (and very pleasant) flavour, and there is a large shiny brown stone in the middle.

Available fresh and canned, lychees make a delicious addition to an exotic fruit salad: try a mixture of lychees, ripe segments of orange, with all the skin removed, and slices of kiwi fruit. Canned lychees lack the crisp texture of fresh ones but make a good sorbet or jelly.

MANGO *Mangifera indica*
Choose a mango which feels just soft all over or buy one when it is hard and let it ripen at room temperature for a few days. I think the rounded, greeny-red variety of mangoes are better than the flatter, more oval yellowy ones. The mango has a large stone in the middle, so it is best to slice it down each side of the stone. You can eat the skin, but it is generally peeled off as it is very chewy.

Mango is excellent on its own and I like making it into a compote. For this, put slices of mango into a bowl, then liquidize half a cup of chopped mango with enough water to make a thin purée and pour this over the mango slices. Serve chilled, for a special breakfast or brunch. Or allow half a mango for each person and 'turn' the halves. To do this, place half the mango, cut side up, on a board. Using a sharp knife, make a series of lengthways cuts about 1 cm/½ inch apart, taking care not to pierce the skin. Then cut across at the same intervals, and gently press the skin upwards. The mango should be neatly cubed and still attached to the skin, looking rather like a hedgehog. It is now ready to be served. Mango makes an excellent fool, sorbet or ice cream (p. 418): the flesh does not need cooking before use. Mango also goes well with other sweet fruits in a salad or compote.

PAWPAW *Carica papaya*

Look for a pawpaw which is slightly soft all over — like a good dessert pear or perfectly ripe avocado. Pawpaw can be served for breakfast or as a first course; cut the pawpaw in half, scoop out the seeds from the centre, and serve with a slice of lime: halved pawpaw is eaten with a spoon, like an avocado. Peeled and sliced, pawpaw, with its pink flesh, makes an attractive addition to fruit salads.

PERSIMMON *Diospyrus kaki*

Native to China, this fruit ripens and becomes deep orange on the tree. Persimmons must be very ripe and soft before eating because until then their tannic content makes them unpleasantly acidic. When ripe they are good puréed and made into ice cream, or added to a fruit compote.

PINEAPPLE *Ananas comosus*

Most of the pineapples which are available outside the tropics are poor examples of the fruit, because the sugar which is stored in the stem only enters the fruit when it is ripe, and pineapples for export are picked before this stage. When choosing a pineapple, look for one which has a strong 'pineapple' smell and try pulling out one of the leaves: if it comes out, the pineapple is ripe. To use, cut off the leafy top and peel the pineapple thickly to remove the skin and 'eyes' too. Then slice, removing any hard central core.

Pineapple makes a juicy and refreshing addition to sweet and savoury salads and can be made into ices and sorbets. Baby pineapples are pretty halved right through the leaves with the flesh scooped out, diced, mixed with strawberries and liqueur and then piled back into the skins again. A large pineapple, hollowed out, makes an attractive container for a party fruit salad, or for ice cream or sorbet (made from the scooped-out flesh), with the leafy top replaced for serving. Pineapple is available fresh, dried (p. 150), as juice, canned in syrup or its own juice, in slices, cubes, pieces and 'crush'.

PLANTAIN *Musa paradisiaca*
This starchy banana is widely used in savoury dishes in India, South America and the Caribbean. It is often thinly sliced and fried like potato crisps.

POMEGRANATE *Punica granatum*
The pomegranate is full of seeds surrounded by shiny, jewel-bright pulp which is sweet and very juicy and arranged in irregular compartments divided by tough skin. The seeds can be scraped from the skin with a teaspoon or sharp knife and make an attractive topping for puddings or salads. They are widely used in Persian cookery.

PRICKLY PEAR *Opuntia magacanlaa* and *O. fiscus-indica*
These fruits have prickly skins and you need to wear gloves to handle them. Cut off all the skin, then slice the flesh. Sometimes the flesh is a vivid pink and makes a striking addition to a fruit salad, but it can also be paler and less interesting. The flavour is fairly boring.

PURPLE PASSION FRUIT *Passiflora edulis* and GOLDEN PASSION FRUIT *P. laurifolia*
Buy passion fruits when the leathery skin is wrinkled, as this denotes ripeness. Cut the fruits in half and scoop out the greenish pulp and seeds. This passion fruit pulp makes a delectable addition to a fruit salad, which it permeates with its flavour, or sauce for a sorbet or arranged fruit salad, but is at its most delicious, I think, in a sorbet — one of my very favourites (p. 419).

QUINCE *Cydonia oblonga*
This small hard fruit is golden and fragrant when ripe. Like japonicas, quinces need cooking before use. Peel, quarter and slice them as you would apples, then simmer them in a little water and add sugar to taste. They can be made into compotes, fools and pies and are widely used in Middle Eastern cooking. In

the sixteenth and seventeenth centuries they used to be popular in Britain for making into preserves. Quince jelly has a pleasant and distinctive flavour.

TAMARILLO *Cyphomandra betacea*
The tamarillo can be red or yellow and is related to the kiwi fruit and tomato. When ripe, it feels soft to the touch and can be peeled and sliced and added to fruit salads. The seeds are edible and the fruit has a sweet-sharp flavour.

Melons

Melons, with their high water content, are one of the most refreshing fruits. They belong to the same family as cucumbers, and there are many different types of varying size, flavour and colouring. They can, however, be divided into three basic groups: winter melons, cantaloupe melons and musk or netted melons. Watermelons belong to a different branch of the family and contain useful minerals. Melons with golden flesh (especially cantaloupes) are exceptionally rich in vitamin A.

Choosing and storing

The small, deeply ridged, orange-fleshed cantaloupe melon has given its name to the cantaloupe group of melons. These melons, including the CANTALOUPE (or ROCK MELON) itself and the CHARENTAIS and small greenish-yellow OGEN melons, smell deliciously fragrant when they're ripe, and yield to a little pressure at the stalk end. Netted melons look as if they are covered in white net. GALLIA (not generally available in Aus./NZ) is one of the best. When ripe, these melons give a little when pressed at the stalk end. (In the USA the melon called a cantaloupe is actually a netted melon.) CASABA and HONEYDEW

MELONS (with greenish flesh) are ripe when they will yield to a little pressure at the end opposite the stalk.

Characterized by their smooth, shiny skin and watery, melting flesh, WATERMELONS are usually dark green-skinned with crimson flesh and dark brown seeds, though there are many varieties with other colourings, some with pale seeds or even seedless. It is difficult to tell when a watermelon is just right for eating. One way is to look for a matt-skinned (rather than a shiny) melon, and to rap it with your knuckles: it should sound hollow, like a drum; alternatively, you can usually buy cut melon slices, in which case go for bright red flesh without any white streaks or a pale-looking middle. The seeds should look shiny and hard. Never buy cut melon slices from foreign markets because they may be contaminated.

Fully ripe melons should be used as soon as possible; others can be kept for a few days if stored at room temperature.

Preparation and using

Unless you want to marinate melon flesh in a syrup or flavouring liquid, which is useful for melons which are under-ripe or dull-flavoured, it's best to prepare the melon just before you want to eat it.

Large melons can be cut down from the stalk end into sections; smaller melons can be cut in half at right angles to the stem. With very small ones, such as small Ogens, allow a whole one per person, slice the top off, like a boiled egg, and carefully scoop out all the seeds. The melon flesh can also be served without the skin, scooped out into balls using a melon-baller, or simply remove the skin and cut the melon flesh into small dice.

Melons are very low in calories and are therefore an ideal choice if you are trying to lose weight. There are many different ways of serving melon as a low-calorie starter or dessert (see below).

Watermelon contains less vitamin C than other melons, but is wonderfully refreshing on a hot summer's day. If you are feeding a lot of people, for a summer barbeque, for example, you could buy a small, whole watermelon. Scoop out the flesh and remove the seeds. Mix the chopped flesh with other fruit and serve it in the hollowed-out shell. You can also use the halved

SERVING IDEAS FOR MELON

- [ ] Marinate diced melon and diced peeled cucumber in a mint and honey vinaigrette for a refreshing starter.

- [ ] Scoop out the flesh of halved Ogen melons and mix with small strawberries; pile back into the melon shells for a pretty dessert.

- [ ] Mix balls of bright orange melon flesh (such as Charentais) and pale green melon (such as honeydew or Ogen) for a pretty, simple and low-calorie starter.

- [ ] Marinate the diced flesh of winter melons, sliced kiwi fruit, green grapes and slices of green apple in a ginger sugar syrup (1 tablespoon grated fresh ginger added to 300 ml/10 fl oz sugar syrup) for several hours (or overnight) to make green ginger fruit compote.

- [ ] Cheer up a poorly flavoured melon by topping each portion with some port, ginger wine or chopped stem ginger with a little of the syrup.

- [ ] A whole melon makes a delightful picnic food, cooling and refreshing on a hot day. Take plenty of kitchen paper and a container to put the seeds in.

- [ ] Fill halved Charentais melons with ginger ice cream, top with chopped preserved stem ginger and a little of the syrup.

- [ ] For a pretty and refreshing soup, purée two melons, one with green flesh and the other with orange flesh. Put the mixtures into separate jugs, thin with enough water to make a pouring consistency, and sweeten slightly, if necessary. To serve, hold the jugs at either side of a chilled bowl and pour from them at the same time, to create a two-coloured effect. Garnish with fresh mint.

- [ ] Watermelon mixed with plenty of chopped mint makes a refreshing first course.

- [ ] Try a red fruit salad made from cubes or balls of watermelon, halved and seeded black grapes, sliced figs and strawberries.

- [ ] To make Melon Jelly, put cubes of melon into a large bowl or individual bowls. Bring 600 ml/1 pint fruit juice — grape, apple or orange — to the boil and sprinkle in 2 teaspoons agar agar, whisking well until dissolved. Boil for 1 minute. Cool slightly, pour over melon and leave to set.

and hollowed skins of any of the smaller melons for individual servings filled as suggested below.

Melon is best served chilled, but do not let it get too cold, or the flavour will be dulled. Prepare the melon, then chill it in the fridge for no more than 30 minutes before serving. Or, if the melon has been stored in the fridge, take it out about 30 minutes before you want to serve it, to allow it to 'come to'.

If you have to store cut melon in the fridge, cover it carefully with clingfilm as it easily absorbs the smell and flavour of other foods. Use the melon as quickly as possible as it will soon deteriorate.

Melon seeds are not usually eaten with the melon, although I like eating them, and they are in fact a good food and in some parts of the world are dried and used in cooking or as a nibble.

Citrus Fruit

Valued not only for their juicy flesh, but for the oils they contain which are used for making flavourings and scent, and for citric acid, citrus fruits bring tangy flavours to the kitchen and a sharpness which helps to draw out the taste of other ingredients. They are one of the best sources of vitamin C, and oranges are also rich in B1, vitamin A and folic acid, while the bioflavinoids in the white skin and pith of citrus fruit are thought to be particularly helpful to women with menstrual problems.

Choosing and storing

Citrus fruit should look bright and plump, with no brown patches or shrivelled skin. The fruits, especially grapefruits, should feel heavy, so pick them up before you buy them — it's surprising how they vary.

Preparation and using

Citrus fruits should be scrubbed well if you are going to use the skins, as these are often treated with sprays. Adding a table-spoon of cider vinegar to the washing water is said to help counteract the harmful effect of any chemical residues on the skins.

Left-over citrus juices can be frozen for future use; just put them into ice cube containers, freeze, then transfer to a polythene bag. Slices of lemon, orange and rind also freeze well and can be added straight to drinks, without defrosting. Freeze them until solid on a plate or tray, then put them into a polythene bag or container.

GRAPEFRUIT and PINK GRAPEFRUIT *Citrus x paradisi*

Probably most often served halved as a first course, the skin can be vandyked. To do this, pierce the grapefruit halfway down with a sharp knife, then slice about 1 cm/½ inch up and down in a zigzag pattern all the way round. When you pull the two halves apart, each one will have an attractive serrated edge. The flesh can then be scooped out and mixed with chopped orange segments and mint, for variety. Or the grapefruit can be halved, the segments loosened with a sharp knife and the top sprinkled with brown sugar, then popped under the grill until the sugar has melted and the fruit warmed through. One of my favourite grapefruit dishes is a salad of grapefruit and orange segments, avocado and watercress. Pink grapefruit are particularly sweet and juicy as well as attractive. Canned grapefruit is available, as well as grapefruit juice, natural and sweetened.

JAFFA SWEETIE *Citrus* spp

One of the citrus hybrids (a cross between a grapefruit and a lime) which have recently been developed, this has a sharp, refreshing flavour.

KUMQUAT *Fortunella margarita*

These sharp-tasting miniature oranges are delicious stewed whole in a sugar syrup, or made into a preserve (p. 519), then spooned over home-made Vanilla Ice Cream (p. 413).

LEMON *Citrus limon*

Both the juice and rind of lemons are indispensable in the

kitchen for flavouring; lemon juice brings out the flavour of other foods, and the rind gives a subtle tang. A strip of lemon rind added to a bouquet garni is good in soups and vegetable casseroles. Lemon juice can be used to make salad dressings, and I often use it with fruity olive oil instead of wine vinegar. Lemon juice also helps to preserve the colour of other fruits and vegetables which discolour easily; brush the cut surfaces, or dip them in a cupful of water which has had the juice of ½ lemon added. Lemon is used to flavour cakes and puddings — one of the most delicious is traditional Sussex Pond Pudding, in which a whole lemon is surrounded by a suet crust, then steamed, resulting in a delicious lemony syrup filling. Cut into circles, wedges or tiny pieces, lemon makes one of the most refreshing and attractive garnishes.

The candied peel is best bought in whole pieces: it's expensive, but there's no comparison between this and the chopped variety. Bottled lemon juice is a useful store cupboard item, although not as good as fresh.

To make lemon barley water, old-fashioned but soothing, refreshing and easy to make, put 4 tablespoons pearl barley into a saucepan with 600 ml/1 pint water and the pared rind of half a lemon and bring to the boil. Simmer gently, uncovered, for 20 minutes, then strain and cool. Add the juice of ½ lemon and sugar or honey to taste — about 1 tablespoon. Serve chilled, with ice if liked.

LIME *Citrus aurantifolia*

This very sour small green citrus fruit is a wonderful flavouring ingredient; try it squeezed over exotic fruit or hot sugary pancakes, or in Guacamole (p. 218). It has many uses in sweet dishes, including Key Lime Pie and as a flavouring for ice cream, parfaits and cheesecake.

ORANGE *Citrus sinensis*

There are a number of types of dessert oranges, including NAVEL ORANGES which are deliciously sweet and have the characteristic navel at the flower end; the juicy, slightly sharp-tasting JAFFA (or SHAMOUTI) and the sweet VALENCIA. Oranges are good to eat just as they are, with all the skin and pith removed. The best way to peel an orange is to cut into the top quite deeply, making sure you get right down through the pith. Then bring the knife round in a spiral pattern, working down the orange and cutting the peel and pith away in a continuous strip, as if you were peeling an apple. You may then wish to cut the segments out from between the membranes with a sharp knife. Sprinkled with orange flower water and a little orange blossom honey, and chilled, they make one of the most refreshing desserts which is good served with an almond or cashew nut cream (p. 51), rather than dairy cream. Alternatively the sliced oranges can be sprinkled with crushed caramel for a sweet crunchy topping. Oranges also make an excellent addition to a fresh fruit salad and their juice helps pale fruits, such as apples and pears, to keep their colour. Whole oranges can be simmered in sugar syrup then cooled and served with shreds of the peel, blanched and drained.

Orange peel is included in chopped mixed peel, but the best way to buy it is in whole pieces. Various types of orange juice are available: read the packet or carton to make sure it is real juice you are getting.

BLOOD ORANGES are small oranges shot with red; the juice and a little shredded peel is added to Hollandaise Sauce (p. 262) to make Maltese sauce, traditionally served with asparagus.

POMELO or SHADDOCK *Citrus grandis*
Probably the fruit from which the grapefruit evolved, it has a sour, slightly bitter flavour. (Not generally available in Aus./ NZ.)

SEVILLE ORANGE *Citrus aurantium*
These sour oranges are unsuitable for eating raw but are used in marmalade and to make liqueurs and orange flower water. The grated rind and juice can also be used as a flavouring.

TANGERINE, MANDARINE, MINEOLA, CLEMENTINE, SATSUMA *Citrus reticulata*
These members of the citrus family are all very easily peeled, and their flesh separates readily into segments. Clementines (a cross between the tangerine and the orange) are the smallest, have a good flavour and, like some satsumas, have no pips. They all have a more delicate flavour than oranges. Mandarine segments can be bought canned, either whole or in pieces. De-

MAKING CANDIED PEEL

Candied peel, for use in cakes and puddings, can be made at home using grapefruit, orange or lemon skins. You will need the skins of 6 oranges or lemons, or 4−5 grapefruits, or an equivalent amount of more than one type.

Scrub the fruit thoroughly, halve and remove the pulp, or use the (well-scrubbed) skins of fruits after you have squeezed the juice from them.

Put the skin halves into a saucepan, cover with cold water, bring to the boil and simmer until tender. This takes 1−2 hours, and it's a good idea to change the water 3 times, to remove any trace of bitterness, especially with grapefruits.

Drain the skins thoroughly, reserving the liquid. Make the liquid up to 300 ml/10 fl oz with water if necessary, then pour into a saucepan and add 225 g/ 8 oz sugar. Heat gently until the sugar has dissolved, then bring up to the boil. Add the peel, remove from the heat and leave for 2 days.

Remove the peel from the syrup with a perforated spoon; add another 100 g/4 oz sugar to the syrup, heat gently until dissolved, then add the peel and simmer gently until translucent.

Leave the peel to soak in this syrup for 2 weeks, then remove peel with a perforated spoon and place on a wire rack to drain and dry. Once the peel is dry, it can be stored in an airtight jar.

licious for eating just as they are and a popular way of making sure children get their daily requirement of vitamin c, these are also good in fruit salads. (Mineolas − a hybrid sweet orange − are not generally available in Aus./NZ.)

UGLI *Citrus* spp
A cross between a tangerine and a grapefruit, the ugli is native to the East Indies. It tastes like a superb grapefruit, and can be prepared in the same ways. In fact an ugli can be a better choice than grapefruit if you want sweet, juicy segments for a breakfast compote or salad.

Its lumpy mottled skin peels easily and the flesh can be segmented very quickly. It is very juicy and has few pips. (Not generally available in Aus./NZ.)

Dried Fruit

Fruit has been preserved by drying in the sun for the last 5000 years and when the early settlers travelled to America they took with them supplies of dried apples, nectarines, peaches, apricots, quinces and grapes. Today, dried fruit is still an important ingredient and a concentrated source of nutrients. Dried fruit is high in fibre, rich in B vitamins and minerals, apricots and peaches being notable for their iron content and also for vitamin A, and apricots for calcium, too.

Choosing, storing and preparation

Fruit is either dried in the sun or in dehydration chambers where the moisture is evaporated by hot air. Dried fruit may be treated with sulphur dioxide gas during the drying process to prevent it from becoming too dark in colour. Sulphur dioxide interferes with the body's ability to absorb vitamin B1 and has been linked with digestive upsets and possibly genetic mutations. So look for unsulphured fruits if possible. The effect of the sulphur dioxide can be reduced if you first wash the fruit well in warm water, then cover it with cold water and bring to the boil. Allow the fruit to simmer without a lid for 5 minutes, then drain off the water and rinse the fruit again. It can then be used, or soaked in cold water, or covered with fresh water and simmered gently until tender.

Many fruits are also coated with mineral oil in order to prevent them from sticking together. This, too, is an additive which is not recommended as it can interfere with the body's ability to absorb some minerals. It can be removed by washing the fruit in several changes of warm water, or can be avoided altogether by looking for fruit which has been packaged without oil, or with vegetable oil rather than mineral oil (although I still prefer to wash this off before using the fruit). Drain the rinsed fruit in a colander then spread it out on a tray lined with absorbent kitchen paper and leave it in a warm place overnight to dry off.

When buying dried fruit, check the date stamp on the packets, buy in fairly small quantities and keep the fruit in an airtight jar.

APPLE RINGS
These slightly rubbery, creamy white rings are nearly always treated with sulphur dioxide (hence their pale colour). They can be eaten as they are, or chopped and added to cakes and puddings. They are often included as part of a dried fruit salad mix and make a pleasant addition to fruit compotes.

APRICOTS
Apricots are available whole or in halves or pieces; small dried HUNZA APRICOTS are sold whole, still containing their kernels. If the apricots are orange or yellow in colour, they have probably been treated with sulphur dioxide. Sun-dried ones are a brownish-orange. Dried apricots can be eaten as they are or soaked (and cooked until tender, if liked) and served simply with yogurt or cream, or made into purées, fools (p. 418) and other desserts. Sun-dried Hunza apricots have a particularly good flavour and make a wonderful compote, just soaked and simmered gently until tender if necessary.

Dried apricots can be made into an excellent jam all the year round. To make about 2·3 kg/5 lb, put 450 g/1 lb dried apricots into a bowl, cover with 2·4 litres/4 pints of water and leave to soak overnight. Next day, put the apricots and their water into a preserving pan, add the juice of a lemon and simmer until the apricots are really tender — about 50–60 minutes. Then remove from the heat and add 1·4 kg/3 lb granulated sugar and 50 g/2 oz blanched almonds, roughly chopped. Heat gently until the sugar has dissolved, then boil for about 20–25 minutes, stirring often. Test for a set (p. 510) and when this is reached, remove from the heat and add a knob of butter. Let the mixture cool slightly, then spoon into warm, sterilized jars.

BANANAS
Ordinary DRIED BANANAS, which look like slim (or flattened) dark brown versions of fresh bananas, make a pleasant nibble or addition to home-made dried fruit bars and bonbons. They can be reconstituted by soaking in water, but the texture is rather soggy and not particularly pleasant. Soaked and puréed dried banana could be used to make a tea bread (p. 496) instead of

mashed fresh banana. BANANA CHIPS, slices of banana prepared with a crisp sugar coating, are also available and make a relatively healthy sweet treat which children like.

CURRANTS

These are small sweet grapes which are dried without the addition of sulphur dioxide. A very useful ingredient, currants are used extensively in baking, for instance in currant buns, Eccles cakes, fruit cakes (p. 470) and Christmas pudding (p. 442); they are also often added to savoury pilafs and stuffings in Middle Eastern cookery.

Mixed with almonds and spice, they make sweet crisp biscuits. Sift 100 g/4 oz plain wholewheat flour, ½ teaspoon baking powder and ½ teaspoon allspice into a large bowl. Tip the bran from the sieve into the bowl and add 50 g/2 oz butter, 15 g/½ oz ground almonds, and 50 g/2 oz currants. Mix well, then stir in 1 tablespoon water to make a dough. On a lightly floured board, roll dough out to about 5 mm/¼ inch thick, then stamp into rounds of 5 cm/2 inches. Prick each round, place on floured baking sheets and bake for 10 minutes at 200c/400f/Gas Mark 6.

DATES

Dates make a pleasant sweet treat or nibble, either as they are, or with the stone replaced with an almond or brazil nut, some almond paste or cream cheese.

Dates can be added to cakes and puddings and made into very good biscuits (p. 480). If you're buying cooking dates, check that they're not 'sugar-rolled', an unnecessary treatment in view of the intense sweetness of dates. Pitted dates need looking over before use, because the odd stone or hard stalk end does creep in.

FIGS

Often sold squashed in blocks, figs are high in fibre and generally unsulphured. The white powderiness is natural sugar which has seeped through the skin. They can be eaten as they are, soaked as part of a fruit compote, or made into wholesome sweetmeats and cookies. Steamed fig pudding with rum sauce is a warming winter pudding.

Dried fruit salad

This is a mixture of a number of fruits; usually prunes, apple rings, apricots and perhaps peaches and pears. You can buy it ready-made or make it up yourself from your favourite varieties.

Dried fruit salad mix can be made into an excellent compote. To do this, cover the mixture with boiling water and leave to soak overnight. Allow 350 g−450 g/12 oz−1 lb to serve 4 people. Next day, simmer gently, half-covered, until the fruit is tender and all the liquid reduced to a glossy syrup. Serve hot or chilled. If you are serving it cold, some fresh fruits can be added for contrasting flavour and texture. It's a pleasant dish for serving at breakfast as well as for a pudding. A friend of mine makes an alcoholic version with brandy added, which is excellent, though perhaps not for breakfast.

Pawpaw

This is dried in sugar-dipped chunks. It is perhaps not as healthy as naturally dried fruit, because of the added sugar, but is still a pleasant and relatively healthy sweet treat.

Peaches

Usually sold in halves, dried peaches do not taste particularly like fresh peaches but have their own charm. You can eat them as they are, but I prefer them lightly soaked, or soaked and simmered until tender. They make a pleasant addition to savoury dishes such as pilafs as well as being delicious in cakes, puddings and compotes.

Pears

These may be whole or halved and have usually been treated with sulphur dioxide. They have a delicious, true pear flavour and moist texture. Dried pears can be eaten raw, or soaked and cooked; chopped, they make an unusual and delicious addition to a fruit cake and are one of the ingredients in the famous Swiss Christmas fruit pastry, Birnbrot.

To make Birnbrot, make up a half quantity of dough as described for Quick Rolls on p. 492. While the dough is rising for the first time, make the filling. Chop 225 g/8 oz dried pears and 100 g/4 oz dried stoned prunes and put them into a saucepan with 50 g/2 oz seedless raisins and 300 ml/10 fl oz water. Bring to the boil, then simmer gently until the mixture is thick and dry.

Sieve or purée in a blender or food processor, then add the grated rind and juice of half a lemon, 50 g/2 oz soft brown sugar and a little ground cinnamon and grated nutmeg.

Knead the risen dough, then roll it out to a square about 38 × 38 cm/15 × 15 inches and not more than 6 mm/¼ inch thick. Spread the pear mixture to within about 2·5 cm/1 inch of the edges. Fold the edges over to enclose the filling, then roll it up firmly, like a Swiss roll and put it on to a baking sheet. Prick the roll all over, then cover it with a clean cloth and put it into a warm place for 30 minutes, to rise.

Heat the oven to 180c/350f/Gas Mark 4. Brush the bread all over with beaten egg and bake it in the centre of the oven, for about 35 minutes, until golden brown and crisp. Serve warm. It's an excellent pastry for serving with coffee, or as a pudding after something rich like Fondue.

Pineapple
Crunchy cubes of pineapple preserved in sugar syrup make a delicious addition to rich fruit cake mixtures, tutti frutti ice cream or a platter of bonbons to serve with after-dinner coffee.

Prunes
Prunes (a variety of black-skinned plums) are not usually treated with sulphur dioxide but may have undergone other processes to 'tenderize' them or soften the skins, and they are often coated with mineral oil, so wash them carefully. They are one of those things which you either like or you don't; if you still have unfortunate childhood memories of them, do try them as part of a boozy compote, extra light Christmas pudding or ice cream — you may have a pleasant surprise! Prune mousse is surprisingly good, as is the classic French Prune Tart. Prune juice is available and is extremely rich in iron, one of the best sources, if you're feeling run down.

Raisins
There are many varieties of raisin available. Muscatel raisins are the large purplish-black ones with a delicious muscat flavour. Lighter-coloured Lexia raisins come from Australia; they are sold seeded and are particularly juicy and sweet. The smaller and more common sun-dried 'seedless raisin' does not have as much flavour or moistness but is still useful. Any type of raisin

DRYING FRUIT AND VEGETABLES

Drying fruit and vegetables is one of the most natural and ancient methods of food preservation. It involves drying out the natural moisture present in all fruit and vegetables so that the enzymes which cause decay are inhibited. The drying process can be done in the sun or in an oven. Oven-drying can be done over several days, perhaps in the residual heat of the oven after it has been used for something else. The drying temperature needs to be between 50−70c/120−150f and it is best to leave the oven door ajar to allow moisture to escape.

Fruit and vegetables to be dried in the sun need to be spread out on clean mesh or trellis trays, slats of wood or wire trays. Raise them off the ground and turn the produce over twice a day so that it dries evenly. Cover the produce with clean muslin to keep off flies and dust. Bring the fruit in at night time because the increased moisture in the air then will affect the drying process. Alternatively, fruits and vegetables can be threaded on to string and hung up to dry.

Preserve the colour of fruits such as apples and pears by plunging them into a bowl containing 10 g/¼ oz citric acid to every 1 litre/1¾ pints of water; drain and pat dry, then dry in the oven or in the sun as described.

Vegetables such as mushrooms, onions, garlic and peppers can be dried as they are; others, such as runner or French beans, need blanching for 2 minutes in boiling water before being patted dry with a cloth and then dried as described above.

Store dried fruit and vegetables in an airtight jar or tin. They will keep for a year. Dried fruit can be used as it is; dried vegetables should be soaked for a few hours first, then cooked in the soaking water, or they can be added to stews and casseroles without pre-soaking.

is excellent for eating with nuts as a snack or for adding to mueslis or fruit or vegetable salads. Raisins are also indispensable in baking, for fruit cakes, puddings and cookies.

Sultanas

These are dried seedless white grapes. Some sultanas are treated with sulphur dioxide, others are not: check the packet. They are useful in baking for cakes, Christmas pudding (p. 442) and mince pies (p. 444), as well as in salads, puddings and mueslis.

Dairy and Non-Dairy Ingredients

These foods enrich and fortify vegetarian cooking. Some are concentrated and high in fat so are generally used in small quantities. They include dairy and non-dairy products as well as a range of high protein foods, some of which have been used in countries in the East for thousands of years but are relatively new to the West.

MILK

MILK is a basic ingredient, containing a balanced range of nutrients including protein, calcium, riboflavin and vitamins A, D and B12, and is available in various forms. Most milk is pasteurized, which means it has been heated to 71c/160F for 15 seconds, to destroy bacteria. Milk is available with all the cream remaining, with some removed, or semi- or fully skimmed. DRIED SKIMMED MILK is also available in tins and is useful for adding to drinks and other dishes to increase their nutritional value; I prefer the powder (from health shops and not to be confused with milk powder with added fat) to the granules. Skimmed milk may have been fortified with the fat-soluble vitamins, A, D and E which are lost when the fat is removed. GOAT'S MILK, thought by some experts to be healthier and more digestible than cow's, is also available in both liquid and powdered form.

HOMOGENIZED MILK has been mechanically treated so that the cream does not separate from the milk and rise to the surface, while UHT MILK has been heated to 132c/270F for 1–2 seconds, then rapidly cooled and packed in sterile conditions.

EVAPORATED MILK, a useful store cupboard item, has been homogenized and had half its water removed by evaporation. It is then sterilized and canned. CONDENSED MILK is whole or skimmed milk which has been boiled down to about a third of its original volume and then, usually, sweetened with sugar and canned. It's useful for making fudge (p. 523) and a wonderful ice cream (p. 416), as well as being the binding ingredient in the traditional Bircher Muesli (p. 360). If you boil a can for 4 hours, then cool the can, beat lightly and pour into a crumb-crust or pastry flan case and chill, you have Gypsy Tart. It's also useful for making Toffee Shortcake: boil the contents of a small can of condensed milk with 100 g/4 oz each of sugar and butter and 2 tablespoons golden syrup for 5 minutes, then pour on top of a shortbread baked in a tin (p. 480). When it's cool, spread 175–225 g/6–8 oz melted chocolate on top! Wicked, but delicious.

The milk left over after butter-making, buttermilk is low in fat and has a sour flavour. It is mainly useful in making certain breads and cakes, as in Soda Bread (p. 495), where it helps the bread to rise. The SMETANA sold outside Russia is like a low-fat soured cream and can replace soured cream in recipes. Various brands of SOYA MILK are available. The nutritional content of most is not the same as that of cow's milk although the taste is similar; if the milk is for babies, children or old people, I recommend buying a soya milk which has been fortified with vitamins so that it has the same nutritional value as cow's milk. Check the labels; you may need to go to a health shop. Or you may wish to make your own soya milk (p. 416), but not for tiny babies.

Yogurt

Look for 'live' YOGURT cultured from *lactobacillus bulgaricus*. Avoid those which contain thickeners or which have been pasteurized after culturing. Although the bacterium does not survive in the gut, yogurt is more digestible than milk. Good yogurt should be sweet and thick, not thin and sour. GREEK EWE'S MILK YOGURT, both the normal version and the thicker, strained type, are excellent. If you think you don't like yogurt, try these before finally writing it off! NON-DAIRY SOYA YOGURT, suitable for vegans, is available from health shops, and can also be made at home from soya milk (p. 416).

Yogurt is easy to make at home, in a wide-necked Thermos which will hold 600 ml/1 pint. Bring 600 ml/1 pint milk to the boil, then remove from the heat and leave to stand until you can comfortably dip your little finger into it. Whisk in the skin on the top of the milk together with 4 tablespoons skimmed milk powder or granules and 1 teaspoon real live yogurt. Pour into the scalded Thermos, screw on the lid and leave overnight or for 10–12 hours, until thick and creamy. Store in the refrigerator, where it will thicken further, and save a teaspoonful for starting off your next batch.

You can make yogurt from any kind of milk – 'untreated' gives the creamiest result, but use skimmed milk if you want to reduce the calories. When you leave the mixture to stand, make sure you put the Thermos in a place where it won't get touched, and don't open it for 10 hours or so, because for some reason knocks and rough movements can upset the fermentation process. You may find you need to buy a new tub of real live starter yogurt from time to time, if the finished mixture does not get as thick as usual.

For fruit yogurt, make the yogurt as described. When it is ready, simply add chopped fresh fruit, cooked fruit purée or good-quality jam and sugar or honey to taste. Reduced sugar jams are excellent stirred into yogurt.

For gloriously thick, Greek-style yogurt, line a large sieve or colander with muslin or gauze. Scald the gauze by pouring a kettleful of boiling water through it. Set the sieve or colander over a bowl, pour the yogurt into the sieve or colander and leave to drip overnight.

CREAM

CREAM, a concentration of the fatty part of the milk, comes in various concentrations. HALF CREAM is the lowest in fat, containing around 12 per cent; SINGLE CREAM and SOURED CREAM contain 18 per cent fat (and cannot be whipped), while CANNED CREAM has around 23 per cent. WHIPPING CREAM contains 35 per cent fat, DOUBLE CREAM 48 per cent and CLOTTED CREAM 55 per cent. Obviously, in view of its relatively high fat content cream needs to be used with discretion, but is useful for adding richness to soups and sauces, making a quick sauce for pasta, and in special puddings such as ice cream and parfait. CRÈME FRAÎCHE is a sharp-tasting cream, the flavour somewhere between double cream and soured cream. It goes particularly well with sweet fruits, such as strawberries, and it makes a good alternative to SOURED CREAM (though it is higher in calories) when a dish is going to be cooked, as it doesn't separate. You can make crème fraîche by whipping together equal quantities of double and soured cream, then leaving at room temperature for 24 hours. Refrigerate after this, which will make the cream thicker. Crème fraîche will keep in a covered container in the fridge for 2 weeks. SOYA CREAM, with the consistency of single cream, and various non-dairy whipping creams, including the kosher PAREV, are available and can replace dairy cream in some recipes. (These are usually made from a mixture of vegetable oil, water and flavourings.) All fresh dairy products need to be kept in a cool place, preferably in the fridge, as do canned and packaged milks once opened. Use within 1−3 days.

EGGS

When buying hen's eggs, look for genuine free-range eggs from a reliable, healthy flock, free from the salmonella enteritidis virus. All the recipes in this book assume the use of these eggs. Store in a cool place − not the fridge − for up to 7 days. Always bring eggs to room temperature before use. DUCK'S EGGS (which some say are tastier and more nutritious than hen's eggs) should be well cooked before eating because shells are porous, and ducks are not always choosy about where they lay their eggs!

Tiny QUAIL'S EGGS can be hardboiled (for 4 minutes), then shelled (which needs patience!) and either used whole or sliced for a pretty, luxury garnish to starters, salads and savouries. They look charming set into a clear jelly (made from 300 ml/ 10 fl oz boiling Dark Vegetable Stock (p. 199), with 1 teaspoon agar agar (p. 427) whisked into it and boiled for 1 minute). Add a few sprigs of leafy tarragon and any small lightly cooked vegetables you fancy.

In the UK, eggs are graded by size according to weight. Size 1, for example, is over 70 g/2¾ oz, while size 7, the smallest, is below 45 g/1¾ oz. Size 3, 60−65 g/2¼−2½ oz, is used in most recipes.

FOUR SIMPLE WAYS TO COOK AN EGG

These cooking methods assume that the eggs are clean and healthy, because if you cook eggs lightly, as they should be cooked, you cannot be sure of killing off the salmonella virus. Unless you hardboil, fry, poach or scramble them very thoroughly, the important thing is to get them from a reliable source in the first place.

Boiling an egg

For foolproof boiling, it helps to prick the rounded end of the egg to allow the air to escape and prevent bursting. You can buy a special egg-pricker for this purpose, or pierce the rounded end of the egg with a needle. Then, three-quarters fill a small saucepan with water and bring to the boil. Put the egg into the water and start timing, keeping the water at a steady simmer. Remove the egg with a slotted spoon.

Timings for boiled eggs

These timings are for medium-sized eggs at room temperature:

For a runny yolk	4 minutes
For a slightly runny yolk	6 minutes
For a lightly hardboiled egg	8 minutes
For a dry yolk and set white	10 minutes

When hardboiling an egg, plunge the egg straight into cold water once the time is up; this will prevent over-cooking and the formation of a grey mark between the yolk and white.

Frying an egg

Pour enough oil into a non-stick frying pan to lightly cover the base, then heat it until it sizzles. Break an egg and slip it into the oil. As the egg cooks, spoon over some of the hot oil, to cook the top. As soon as the white in the centre, around the yolk, is set, slip a fish slice under the egg, lift and hold it over the frying pan for a moment or two to drain off excess oil. Put the egg straight on to a warmed plate.

Poaching an egg

Fill a wide, shallow pan, such as a deep frying pan, with water. Add 1 tablespoon vinegar and bring to the boil. Break an egg into a cup, then slip it into the water. Turn up the heat so that the water boils vigorously and the bubbles help draw the white around the yolk, then lower the heat and poach gently until set — 2–3 more minutes. Remove with a slotted spoon, and trim the edges to neaten if you wish.

Scrambling eggs for 2

Beat 4 eggs, and, for perfection, pass through a strainer to remove threads. Season with salt and pepper. Melt 20 g/¾ oz butter in a medium heavy-based saucepan. When it sizzles, add the eggs. Cook over a low heat, stirring. For creamy scrambled eggs, remove from the heat just before the eggs set. They will cook a little more in the heat of the pan. If you want firmer scrambled eggs, cook for a moment or two longer, until no longer runny. But don't overcook: remember they'll go on cooking in their own heat. Serve immediately on warmed plates.

Vegetarian protein foods

Seitan is a chewy, high protein food made from protein-rich wheat gluten. It is available frozen and in cans, jars and vacuum packs; various types of seitan pâté and spreads are also available. (Seitan is not generally available in Aus./NZ.) It is also easy (but rather messy) to make seitan at home by making dough out of a high-gluten flour and water, soaking it under water for 1 hour, then rinsing it under cold water until all the white starch has come out and you're left with an elastic-like, thread-like mass. This is then simmered in seasoned stock to which some tamari (p. 185) has been added. The resulting seitan is a brownish colour because of the tamari. It can be cut into cubes or slices, marinated in more tamari and other tasty ingredients such as garlic and fresh grated ginger, then fried or used to make kebabs. Or it can be grated and used as meat-eaters would use minced meat, for shepherd's pies, burgers and savoury loaves.

Tempeh (made by fermenting cooked soya beans in banana leaves) is another nutritious, high protein food and has anti-biotic properties. It is much liked by some wholefood cooks, but not by me: I find the flavour of soya beans too strong and the texture too stodgy. It needs to be soaked in, or served with, a good strong marinade of crushed garlic, grated ginger and soy sauce, maybe some Dijon mustard, too. It is usually cut into cubes or slices and shallow-fried in oil.

Firm tofu can be treated in any of the ways described for seitan and tempeh; it should be kept covered with water in a bowl in the fridge before use. Soft tofu, in a vacuum pack, can be kept outside the fridge until opened. It can be beaten to a smooth consistency for dips, dressings, flan fillings and fools. Various other types of tofu such as smoked tofu, aromatic dried tofu and dried, deep fried tofu can sometimes be obtained, and make an interesting addition to stir-fries.

You may like to make your own tofu. This is best when made from the super soya milk (p. 416). You also need nigari, a white powder which, when added to the soya milk, makes it separate into curds and whey. You can buy nigari at some health shops. If you cannot get it, Epsom salts can be used, but the result is not as good.

Put 600 ml/1 pint super soya milk (p. 416) into a saucepan and bring to the boil. Dissolve ½ teaspoon nigari (or Epsom salts) in

IDEAS FOR USING TOFU AND VEGETARIAN PROTEIN FOODS

☐ Make vegetarian toad-in-the-hole: set the oven to 220c/425f/Gas Mark 7. Put 2 tablespoons of oil into a 20 × 20 cm/8 × 8 inch roasting tin and heat in the oven until smoking hot. Put 100 g/4 oz plain 85 per cent wholewheat flour into a bowl with ½ teaspoon salt and 2 eggs. Gradually mix in 300 ml/10 fl oz milk, to make a batter. Have ready 225 g/8 oz seitan or tempeh, cut into cubes, or reconstituted textured vegetable protein cubes. Quickly pour the batter into the tin containing the hot oil, add the cubes of seitan, tempeh or vegetable protein and return to the oven. Bake for about 35 minutes, until puffed up and golden brown. Serve with a vegetarian gravy and cooked vegetables.

☐ Thread cubes of firm tofu, seitan, tempeh or textured vegetable protein on to skewers with mushrooms, tomatoes and onions. Marinate in a mixture of 1 tablespoon each of soy sauce, brown sugar, mustard and wine vinegar, then brush with oil and grill to make tasty kebabs.

☐ Whizz tofu with strawberries and honey to make a smooth, dairy-free fruit fool.

☐ Dip slices of firm tofu, tempeh or seitan in flour which has been seasoned and flavoured with a crushed garlic clove, shallow-fry in olive oil until crisp on both sides and serve with wedges of lemon.

☐ Any of these protein foods can be mashed then mixed with fried onion, garlic, herbs and spices, formed into burgers, coated in flour, or egg and breadcrumbs, and fried in oil, or baked on an oiled baking sheet.

☐ Simmer textured vegetable protein in red wine with a bay leaf then drain, reserving the liquid. Fry chopped onion, crushed garlic clove and some button mushrooms in butter or vegan margarine for 10 minutes, then add the protein chunks and stir over the heat until they are heated through. Add a very little flour, to take up any excess fat, then add the reserved cooking liquid and simmer for 10 minutes. Add a small carton of soured cream and cook over a gentle heat until the cream is hot (but don't let it boil). Season and serve.

☐ For a vegetarian-style mixed grill, fry chunks of seitan, textured vegetable protein or tempeh in oil and serve with grilled tomatoes, fried potatoes, onions and mushrooms.

☐ For a tasty dressing, whizz together some tofu with fresh herbs such as basil or coriander, lemon juice and seasoning.

about 4 tablespoons hot water and add to the milk. Leave for 5 minutes for the mixture to curdle. Line a sieve with a piece of muslin, then pour the curdled mixture through, separating the curds from the liquid. The liquid will not be needed. Fold the muslin over to cover the curds and place a weight on top. Leave for at least 1 hour, then remove the curds — which are now tofu — from the muslin and store in cold water in the fridge.

Tofu absorbs flavours well and benefits from being soaked in a marinade before use. Wine, herbs, spices, garlic, oil, citrus rinds and juice, mustard, soy sauce and strongly flavoured stock can all be used.

A stock made by simmering a sea vegetable such as wakame in water, until the water has reduced well, then straining it, makes a very pleasant marinade when you feel like giving tofu a taste of the sea.

TEXTURED VEGETABLE PROTEIN (TVP) is available in various meat flavours as well as natural, and comes in assorted shapes and sizes, including 'chunks' and 'mince'. It is easily rehydrated in hot water according to packet instructions, but has more flavour if left to soak in stock overnight. Many vegetarians find this a useful product when they are making the changeover from meat-eating, or if they have to cook for a meat-eater too. Non-vegetarians can eke out mince and make it healthier by adding or replacing one-third to one-half with reconstituted textured vegetable protein. Reconstituted textured vegetable protein can be added to nut and lentil dishes, such as roasts, savoury loaves, burgers and shepherd's pies, to add bulk, nourishment and flavour. It is useful for this because it adds moisture and also a chewy texture, which can be pleasant and is also particularly valuable in vegetarian cookery where a lot of the ingredients lack this.

Cheese

Cheese was first made by herdsmen as a convenient way to carry milk, and contains all the nutrients present in milk in a more concentrated form. Cheese was made by the

Sumerians 6000 years ago, then by the Ancient Greeks and by the Romans, who brought their cheesemaking skills to the UK. Delicious to eat as it is or to use in cooking, cheese is a very nutritious food, being one of the best vegetarian sources of protein, calcium, vitamins A, B (including B12), D and E, and zinc.

Fresh, unripened cheeses are for eating shortly after they are made. Soft cheeses, which have been matured for a short period of time and so contain less moisture than fresh cheeses, are firmer but still spreadable. Blue cheeses are ripened by the growth of mould from within them, giving them their characteristic sharp, tangy flavour and dappled blue-green appearance. The fat content of these cheeses, which is usually given on the packet or wrapping in the form of a percentage of the whole cheese, varies from very low to high, depending on the type of milk or cream they are made from.

Choosing and storing

All cheese is best bought at its peak and used as soon as possible, within twelve hours, if practicable. This applies especially to unripened and fresh soft cheeses, though semi-hard and hard cheeses will keep for longer.

A cold larder is said to be the best place to store cheese, lightly covered. I keep mine, in small quantities, in a polythene container in the fridge for up to a week. If stored in the fridge, the cheese should be removed and allowed to 'come to' at room temperature for an hour or so before serving.

Hard, semi-hard and fresh soft cheeses which contain over 45 per cent fat, such as full fat and cream cheeses, can be wrapped in polythene and kept for up to 3 months in the deep freeze. Grated Cheddar or Parmesan keeps well in a container in the freezer and can be used from frozen. I grate up left-over pieces of cheese and add them to the container, to save waste and ensure a supply of grated cheese when I need it. Unripened cheese with a high fat content will freeze, but the low-fat ones like cottage cheese, fromage blanc and quark will not.

In order to separate milk into curds and whey, cheesemaking rennet is added to milk in the proportions 1 part rennet to 5000 parts milk. The rennet most commonly used is a digestive juice taken from the stomachs of calves. This means that many cheeses are not totally vegetarian. However, now that vegetarian rennet is available (and, I am told, gives cheesemakers more reliable results than traditional rennet) it is possible to buy vegetarian versions of a number of cheeses, and the range is increasing. However, cheese made with vegetarian rennet is not always labelled as such, so it's well worth making enquiries.

Cooking and using
See under individual sections.

UNRIPENED CHEESES
Delicious to eat just as they are, with vegetable or fruit salads or as fillings for cherry tomatoes, pitted apricot halves or juicy fresh dates; beaten with fresh herbs and garlic, coarsely crushed black peppercorns or paprika pepper as a dip or topping for crisp crackers, or shaped into small balls or corks and coated with crushed roasted nuts as a cocktail nibble.

The low-fat cheeses such as QUARK, FROMAGE BLANC (which has a consistency almost like whipped cream) and SKIMMED SOFT CHEESE are particularly useful as cream substitutes to reduce the fat in traditional dishes such as fools, flan fillings and uncooked cheesecakes. They can be diluted to a creamy consistency with skimmed milk, flavoured with a dash of honey and vanilla, and served with puddings instead of cream. For cooked cheesecake, low-medium fat, tangy-flavoured CURD CHEESE or Italian RICOTTA give just the right moist texture, while ricotta is also excellent with pasta, as a filling for ravioli or layered into a lasagne bake (p. 378).

Lumpy-textured, low-fat cottage cheese or higher-fat cream cheese and rich creamy Boursin are good in salads; cream cheese with pineapple is a classic salad mixture, served on a base of crisp lettuce, with tomato and cress. Boursin makes a particularly pleasant addition to a cheeseboard and is available with different flavourings such as garlic and herbs. Genuine Italian MOZZARELLA, too, is particularly good in salads; with avocado and tomato, in the famous Italian Tricolour Salad, for instance, and it is the best cheese to use as a topping for pizza (p. 327) or Parmigiana (p. 304), because it melts to a delectable soft, creamy consistency and has a very mild flavour. PETIT SUISSE, served as it is, or with fresh or poached fruit, makes a pleasant and easy pudding course.

SOFT CHEESE

You can make your own curd cheese from milk which has turned sour, or from milk which you have soured yourself by adding lemon juice and boiling for 10–15 minutes, using 2 tablespoons lemon juice to 1 litre/1¾ pints of milk.

Pour the soured milk through a metal sieve or colander lined with a double layer of muslin. Leave the sieve over a bowl until it stops dripping – this should take an hour or so. The residue in the sieve is your curd cheese; add salt and flavourings, such as chopped fresh herbs or crushed garlic, to taste.

SOFT CHEESES

These cheeses make an excellent addition to a cheeseboard, and, like the unripened cheeses, are good in salads; the mixture of cubes of FETA cheese with tomato, cucumber, onions and black olives in a Greek salad is a classic. This fresh soft Greek cheese, made from ewe's milk, has a crumbly texture and a sharp, tangy flavour. Hot BRIE or Deep-fried CAMEMBERT are a favourite first course or light main course (p. 333).

As the rind of this creamy-textured, mild-flavoured French cheese can be eaten, a whole Brie baked in phyllo pastry makes a spectacular (and easy) dish for a supper party. Either stronger-flavoured Camembert or Brie can be mashed with walnuts and cream to make a dip or a filling for open mushrooms which are then baked. CHÈVRE, or goat's cheese, comes in a range of shapes and sizes, and may be mild or strong, creamy or firm. CHÈVRE LEZAY is a mild variety of the larger log-shaped Chèvre; CHÈVRE BOUCHERON is more strongly flavoured. Small logs of Chèvre sliced into little circles just ask to be made into pretty salads. Slices of large Chèvre logs are excellent just melted under the grill; try grilling them on top of tomato slices and serving on a base of crisp lettuce and watercress for supper.

SELECTING A CHEESEBOARD

When choosing cheeses for a cheeseboard, I prefer to concentrate on one or two perfect pieces of cheese, rather than offer a great variety. An excellent, generously sized piece of matured Cheddar, for instance, really needs no accompaniment except some crisp crackers or crusty bread and perhaps some fresh celery. A 'white' cheeseboard made up of just three or four Chèvre cheeses is another favourite of mine, especially if it is served before the pudding and there is some dry white wine to be finished up with the cheese.

Alternatively, try making up a cheeseboard of a complementary pair of cheeses, one soft and creamy, such as Brie or a creamy Chèvre, and one hard or semi-hard — perhaps a red one, like DOUBLE GLOUCESTER or LEICESTER, or, a superb piece of STILTON, or, another of my favourites, WENSLEYDALE.

If you have a large gathering of cheese-lovers at Christmas, it's fun to offer them a whole Stilton, but make sure everyone slices it across and no one wrecks the cheese by pouring port into the middle!

BLUE CHEESES

Blue cheeses, such as STILTON, ROQUEFORT (made from ewe's milk), DANISH BLUE, GORGONZOLA and creamy DOLCELATTE (not generally available in Aus./NZ), are ripened by the growth of green moulds which develop inside them, giving the characteristic flavour and colour. These cheeses are excellent eaten with crispbread or fruit — they have a special affinity with pears. They are also useful in dips, dressings, salads, soups and sauces for pasta because they are one of few very strongly flavoured ingredients in vegetarian cooking.

SEMI-HARD AND HARD CHEESES

Semi-hard and hard cheeses contain less moisture than soft cheeses; they cut easily but do not spread. They have been ripened by the action of enzymes and bacteria within over a period of months. Most can be used either for grating and cooking or as dessert cheese. CHEDDAR, Britain's best-known cheese, is an example of this adaptability. A fine Cheddar is one of the best cheeses to serve for dessert, but is also one of the best cooking cheeses, because it melts well and has a good flavour. Cheddar is available in various strengths, mild as well as strong and well-matured. A piece of mature FARMHOUSE CHEDDAR, some crusty bread and pickled onions (p. 95), washed down with a glass of beer, makes a traditional Ploughman's Lunch. TILSIT (a strongly flavoured cheese made in Germany), GOUDA, the famous Dutch cheeses, and MONTEREY JACK (with its high moisture content and creamy flavour) from the USA, are other cheeses which are particularly good eaten with crusty bread, crisp crackers or salad.

For another quick snack meal, try putting a round slice of PROVOLONE (a smoked Italian cheese) on top of a lightly fried large, open mushroom, or a thick slice of large beefsteak tomato, grilled until the cheese has melted, then serve with salad and French bread.

EDAM, with its red waxy skin, is another popular cheese, particularly with slimmers, because it is lower in fat than many cheeses. I find Edam a good cheese for making fondue, although EMMENTHAL is the classic for this. GRUYÈRE, another nutty-flavoured Swiss cheese which is also made in France, has a smooth, uniform texture containing some holes, much smaller than those in Emmenthal. Gruyère, too, is used for fondue and is a useful cheese for cooking, because of its fine flavour and good melting qualities.

Other cheeses which melt well are CANTAL, the French cheese quite similar to a mild Cheddar, and the slightly smoky-flavoured FONTINA which is used to make, among other things, an Italian version of cheese fondue with eggs and truffles. RACLETTE (not generally available in Aus./NZ) is an interesting cheese with a sweet, mild flavour. It is melted to make a Swiss dish which is eaten with potatoes and accompanied by gherkins.

PARMESAN cheese is an important cheese for cooking because of its strong, sharp flavour. It can be bought ready-grated, but for the best flavour, buy a piece of Parmesan, if possible, and grate it yourself as needed. PECORINO is another excellent hard cheese from Italy, suitable for grating, cooking and eating as it is. One of the most unusual cheeses is GJETOST from Norway. This looks like fudge and has a slightly sweet, floury taste. It can be eaten with bread or made into savouries, starters and desserts.

QUICK SERVING IDEAS FOR CHEESE

Cheese is one of the most useful convenience foods; here are some ideas for using it:

☐ Form low-fat soft cheese into a log shape; roll log in a mixture of sesame seeds and chopped parsley.

☐ Alternatively, roll low-fat soft cheese into balls the size of walnuts and roll in chopped herbs, sesame seeds or ground nuts.

☐ Make raw kebabs: spear cubes of firm cheese on to skewers with wedges of tomato, cubes of cucumber or pineapple, spring onions, radishes, baby button mushrooms, gherkins, stoned olives, or any other fruit or vegetable you fancy. The skewers can be coated with a vinaigrette marinade before serving if you like.

☐ Slice the top off green peppers and scoop out seeds and core, then pack peppers with a mixture of curd cheese and sultanas or chopped spring onion, press down firmly and chill until required, then cut into slices and serve as part of a salad.

☐ Make cheese spread for sandwiches by mixing very finely grated Cheddar or Cheshire cheese with milk to make a soft paste. Flavour with chopped chives or spring onion, curry powder or a pinch of chilli powder.

☐ For a sweet and sour salad with a crunchy texture, mix 350 g/12 oz shredded cabbage with 225 g/8 oz diced cheese and 100 g/4 oz each of chopped dates and roasted peanuts. Dress with natural yogurt.

☐ For Cheese Curry, melt 25 g/1 oz butter in a saucepan and fry a chopped onion for 10 minutes. Then stir in 25 g/1 oz flour and 2–3 teaspoons curry powder. Add 300 ml/10 fl oz water, stirring over the heat until the sauce thickens. Simmer gently for 10 minutes, then add 225 g/8 oz cubed cheese and 25 g/1 oz sultanas. Serve immediately, with hot cooked rice.

Herbs

Herbs have been used for centuries, both for flavouring and for healing. Some, like parsley, which is rich in iron, potassium, calcium and vitamin c, are unusually high in nutrients, others have medicinal and curative properties. Thyme and rosemary (which is an excellent hair tonic) are natural disinfectants; dill is sleep-inducing, fennel is helpful for nursing mothers, mint aids digestion, and sage not only makes a good hair rinse but is said to promote a healthy old age.

Choosing and storing

The best way to experience herbs is freshly picked. Once picked, they should be kept in a jar of water or loosely wrapped in a polythene bag in the fridge for a day or so. Dried herbs lack the aroma of fresh herbs, but are useful when fresh ones are unavailable, and bay leaves actually taste better when dried. Keep dried herbs in small airtight bottles, in a dark place if possible.

Preparation and cooking

Fresh herbs should be lightly washed, then patted dry before use. Handle them gently to preserve their fragrant oils. Then use them whole, or chop them, according to the recipe. To chop herbs, remove any coarse stems, then put the herbs on a board and chop with a sharp knife, holding the point of the blade down with one hand and pivoting the knife from the point in a quarter-circle. Herbs can also be chopped in a food processor; this is excellent for chopping large quantities.

As dried herbs are more strongly flavoured than fresh ones, a smaller quantity is needed: only a quarter to a third of the amount of fresh herbs. Dried herbs can be added to a dish at the beginning of cooking, as can a bouquet garni and the robust fresh herbs such as bay, rosemary, thyme, but the fresh delicate green herbs are better added towards the end of the cooking, to make the most of their flavour and colour.

To make a bouquet garni, tie a sprig of parsley, thyme and a bay leaf together. Sometimes I like to include a strip or two of lemon peel too, for a fresh, citrus flavour. Alternatively, one of the best ways to make a bouquet garni is to slit a trimmed, washed leek down one side, pop the herbs inside the leek and tie it to hold the herbs in place.

Chopped fresh herbs make an excellent flavouring for butter or vegan margarine; just mix finely chopped herbs into soft butter or margarine, together with a few drops of lemon juice, if you like. Keep in the fridge for a day or two; or freeze for several weeks. Add to hot cooked vegetables, use to make herb bread or swirl into hot cooked pasta.

Drying and preserving

Pick herbs for preserving at the height of their season, before they flower, on a sunny day after the dew has dried. Cut them with long stems and hang up in bunches in a cool, dark place to dry naturally. Keep different herbs apart so that the flavours do not merge. When the herbs are completely dry and brittle, store them in dark, airtight containers.

Alternatively, herbs can be deep-frozen. Cut them as described, then blanch them by dipping them briefly into a deep pan of boiling water. Refresh immediately in cold water, pat dry, then freeze on open trays. When frozen, pack in polythene bags. Or chop the herbs, put into ice cube containers, top up with water and freeze. When frozen, transfer to a polythene bag, keeping individual types together.

One of the best ways of preserving the flavour of basil is to chop the leaves, then put them into a jar in layers, sprinkling each layer with salt. Cover with olive oil and keep the jar in the fridge. Although the leaves darken, the flavour remains.

Or make basil-flavoured oil, to bring a summer taste to winter salads. Put several sprigs into a bottle and fill up with olive oil; the oil will be impregnated with the flavour after several weeks. Herb-flavoured vinegars can be made in a similar way.

ANGELICA *Angelica archangelica*
Best known in its crystallized form, angelica has a musky scent and can be used fresh in salads and vegetable dishes.

BASIL *Ocimum basilicum*
Best known as a flavouring for tomatoes and the classic Italian sauce, Pesto (p. 257), basil is good in any salad mixture or chopped over lightly cooked vegetables. It is the flavouring for Pistou soup (p. 206).

BAY *Laurus nobilis*
Bay can be used either dried or fresh. It is usually included in a bouquet garni and gives depth to vegetable casseroles, soups and stews, and to flavour the milk used to make sauces, such as Bread Sauce (p. 262). A bay leaf is an old-fashioned flavouring for rice pudding. Fresh bay leaves make an attractive garnish or base for serving fresh cheeses or sorbet in fresh orange skins.

BORAGE *Borago officinalis*
An unusual herb in that the flowers are used, giving a cucumber flavour and attractive colour to salads and summer punches. Try adding the flowers to ice cubes.

CAMOMILE *Anthemis nobilis*
A popular herb for making into tea, camomile is soothing and sleep-inducing.

CHERVIL *Anthriscus cerefolium*
Chervil has a fresh, delicate flavour and can be used lavishly in salads and over lightly cooked vegetables. As part of the traditional *fines herbes* mixture (along with parsley and chives), it is a delicious flavouring for an omelette.

CHIVES *Allium schoenoprasum*
Very useful wherever you need a subtle onion flavour, chives are also one of the most useful garnishing herbs; just snip them over the top of pale-coloured soups, dips and salads. Chives are a particularly good flavouring for egg and cheese dishes and are added to some cheeses.

COMFREY *Symphytum officinale*
Cucumber-flavoured, like borage, comfrey can be chopped into salads or dipped in batter and fried as a nibble. The leaves have healing properties and the flowers can be used in fruit cups.

Coriander *Coriandrum sativum*

Similar in appearance to flat-leaved parsley, this is the world's most popular herb, with a strange but addictive flavour, widely used in South America, China and Japan, South-East Asia and India, and the Middle East.

Curry plant *Murraya koenigii*

The leaves of this herb smell and taste of curry and are widely used in Indian, Malaysian and Indonesian cooking.

Dill *Anethum graveolens*

Widely used in Scandinavian cuisine, dill is a pretty, feathery herb, attractive as a garnish as well as a flavouring. It goes particularly well with any cucumber dish; I like it chopped into soured cream as a sauce or topping for jacket potatoes; it's also very good in Potato Salad (p. 248).

Fennel *Foeniculum vulgare*

This herb, with its aniseed flavour, helps to cut the oiliness of rich foods; sprinkle it over fried potatoes or aubergines, add a little to nut burgers (p. 346), or mix it with yogurt and serve with a nut roast made from an oily nut, like brazil nuts (p. 352). Fennel is also good in a green salad dressed with fresh lemon and fruity olive oil.

Fenugreek *Trigonella foenum-graecum*

A spicy, rather bitter-tasting herb, popular in Indian cookery.

Feverfew *Chrysanthemum parthenium*

Most useful, as some people have found, as a cure for migraine. Eat a few of the hot, peppery leaves each day in a sandwich.

Hyssop *Hyssopus officinalis*

A warm, aromatic herb which grows wild in Southern Europe and is used in liqueurs such as Chartreuse.

Lemon balm *Melissa officinalis*

Delicately flavoured with lemon, and soothing to the digestion, lemon balm is good in tea and added to fruit cups, or used to flavour a cake by sprinkling on the lining paper before putting in the cake mixture.

LOVAGE *Levisticum officinale*
An unusual but delicious herb, particularly good in a lettuce or cabbage salad, or added to celery soup to intensify the flavour. Lovage has a powerful spicy, lemony celery flavour; a little goes a long way.

SWEET MARJORAM *Origanum marjorana*
A useful herb, related to oregano, which is best added towards the end of cooking time, to preserve its sweet, slightly spicy flavour. Excellent in nut and pulse roasts (pp. 357, 318) and savoury bakes, in stuffings and burgers.

MINT *Mentha*
One of the most important and widely used flavourings, there are many varieties of mint. These include apple mint (used in apple dishes, fruit cups and teas), spearmint (the best all-purpose mint) and ginger mint, among others. Mint is a traditional flavouring for peas and new potatoes and is chopped to make fresh Indian chutneys and Mint Sauce which is good, in a vegetarian meal, as an accompaniment to a lentil roast. To make Mint Sauce, mix 4 tablespoons chopped mint with 1 tablespoon caster sugar, 1 tablespoon boiling water and 2 tablespoons wine vinegar.

OREGANO *Origanum vulgare*
This is one herb which retains its flavour well when dried. It is useful in any dish where you want quite an intense savoury taste, and is widely used in Italian cookery, in sauces to serve with pasta, lasagne bakes, and sprinkled on top of pizza (p. 327). Oregano is also pleasant in a nut or lentil roast or burgers.

PARSLEY *Petroselinum crispum*
The most commonly used herb in European and American cooking, parsley comes in CURLY and FLAT LEAF (or ITALIAN) varieties. Parsley has a fresh, mild flavour, and can be used lavishly, added to sauces and stuffings, sprinkled over cooked vegetables and pasta, included in salads. It is used almost like a vegetable in the Middle Eastern salad, Tabbouleh (p. 239). Parsley stalks make an excellent flavouring; tie them together and add to any soup or casserole. Flat leaf parsley is considered to have a superior flavour to the curly type.

ROSEMARY *Rosmarinus officinalis*
This fragrant herb, with pine and camphor notes, is good in pilafs and nut dishes; as a natural 'skewer' for kebabs and as a flavouring for bread, egg custards and ice creams.

SAGE *Salvia officinalis*
A strongly flavoured herb, traditionally used with onions to make a stuffing (which can be baked between layers of a cashew nut roast or used to fill a marrow). Sage complements split peas and split orange lentils, and is a good flavouring for savoury apple jelly; it is found in cheeses and is a tasty addition to home-made cheese dips. With its camphor-like flavour, sage also makes a pleasant tea.

SALAD BURNET *Poterium sanguisorba*
With a cucumber fragrance when crushed, salad burnet is a popular salad herb in many Southern European countries.

SUMMER and WINTER SAVORY *Satureja hortensis* and *S. Montana*
These peppery herbs go well in any savoury dish, particularly any which include split peas or lentils. Try adding spicy winter savory to lentil soups; chop more delicately flavoured summer savory over tender young broad beans or add to a haricot bean salad.

SWEET CECILY *Myrrhis odorata*
A sprig of sweet cecily added to stewed fruit reduces the need for sugar.

TARRAGON *Artemisia dracunculus*
One of the most important herbs, tarragon comes in two varieties; choose French tarragon rather than Russian, as it has a finer flavour. Tarragon is good in omelettes, or any delicate egg dish. Try adding it to a savoury jelly, delicately flavoured flan filling, omelette or mildly flavoured cheese soufflé. Or add some chopped tarragon to the filling for stuffed eggs, then serve them on a base of fresh tarragon leaves. It's also good chopped into salads, including rice salad, and added to butter for serving with fresh summer vegetables or pasta.

THYME and LEMON THYME *Thymus vulgaris* and *T. serpyllum*
Excellent for adding to any long-cooking casserole or stew, and
one of the components of bouquet garni. Thyme is one of the
herbs which survives the drying process well. It makes a
fragrant addition to almost any savoury mixture.

Spices

Spices are the dried buds, flowers, fruits,
leaves and barks of aromatic plants, mainly
from tropical countries. They have been used
for centuries, highly revered for their rarity
and use in the preservation of food and the
making of medicines and scents. For hundreds of years spices were a precious trading
commodity. Today they are an essential ingredient in good cooking and especially in
vegetarian cooking because of the strong
flavours they provide for so many dishes.

Choosing and storing

Buy spices in small quantities — enough to be able to use it up
within six months — from a shop with a rapid turnover. Keep
the spices in airtight jars. Strictly speaking, they should be kept
away from the light, or stored in dark jars, but I like the
decorative look of them on an open shelf and find I experiment
with them more if I have them in front of me. Prices vary, and
although it's worth spending extra for high-quality spices, make
sure that you're not really paying for fancy packaging. Indian
and Middle Eastern food shops often sell excellent spices, simply
packaged and reasonably priced.

There's no doubt that many spices are best bought whole so
that you can grind them as you need them. This is easy and
practical with some of the spices, such as black and white
peppercorns, which can be kept in separate grinders, and also
whole coriander, which you can grate through a pepper mill,
too. Nutmeg is easy to grate as you need it, either on a special

nutmeg grater (which may have a handy compartment for keeping the pieces of half-grated nutmeg) or on the finest blade of a box grater. Most other spices can be pounded in a mortar with a pestle, or — easier — whizzed to a powder in an electric coffee grinder.

Using

Spices are used to flavour both sweet and savoury dishes, and some can also be added in large quantities to thicken sauces. The basic spices are black peppercorns and fresh nutmeg; others can be added as you need them for individual recipes. One way of getting to know spices is to cook a new spicy recipe every week or so and buy the spices needed for it, then see how they taste added to other dishes, too.

Spices can also be used as flavourings for ice creams, hot and cold milk, and as toppings and garnishes.

ALLSPICE *Pimenta diocia*
The dried berries of an evergreen tree native to the West Indies, allspice can be bought whole or ground and tastes like a mixture of cinnamon, nutmeg and cloves. It is useful in baking, instead of mixed spice (of which it is often an ingredient), or a few whole berries make an interesting addition to stews and casseroles.

ANISEED *Pimpinella anisum*
This fragrant spice is available whole or ground, but is most useful whole, when it can be added to cooked vegetables (it goes particularly well with carrots). Aniseed can also be used in baking, to flavour cakes, pastries and biscuits. It is also a flavouring used in ouzo, Ricard and pastis.

CARAWAY SEEDS *Carum carvi*
The curved seeds of a plant native to Europe and Asia, caraway has a sweet, slightly aniseed flavour and is popular in German and Austrian cookery. It is famous in England for its use in seed cake, which was popular in Victorian times. Caraway can be used to sprinkle on top of bread or savoury pastries, included in coleslaw and sprinkled over cooked cabbage. It is used in goulash and in liptauer cheese, a flavoured cheese dip from Hungary. Some cheeses contain caraway seed, and caraway is

used to make certain liqueurs, such as Kümmel, made in Germany, Denmark and Holland.

CARDAMOM *Elettaria cardamomum*

Cardamom pods can range in colour from white or pale green to almost black (an inferior type). Cardamom is available whole or ground and is a fragrant spice, one of my favourites, with a eucalyptus-like scent. It can be used to flavour spiced vegetable dishes and pilafs, or the small black seeds can be taken out of the pods and crushed. Cardamom also makes a pungent and unusual flavouring for sweet dishes such as the Indian ice cream Kulfi, and the Middle Eastern sweetmeat, Halva.

Ground cardamom is available, but it is better to buy it in the pod and crush the seeds to a powder yourself using a mortar and pestle.

CAYENNE PEPPER *Capsicum annuum*

This powder made from dried small hot red chilli peppers is useful for giving a kick to bland dishes such as an avocado dip or cream cheese dip; it is also good in cheese dishes.

CELERY SEEDS *Apium graveolens*

Used whole or in the form of celery salt, these seeds can be added to any dish requiring a celery flavour: soups, savouries, casseroles, on top of loaves, even in a salad dressing; but use with discretion as too many can taste bitter.

CHILLI *Capsicum annuum*

The dried fruit of a hot and spicy pepper from South America, chilli can be bought whole, flaked or ground. The pungency of ground chilli varies from mild to very hot, depending on the blend. Use in Chilli con Carne Vegetariana (p. 310) and other Mexican dishes; like cayenne pepper, chilli can be used to give a kick to mild dishes.

CHINESE FIVE-SPICE

This slightly aniseed-tasting flavouring is used in Chinese dishes; try adding a pinch to vegetable stir-fries. It is made from equal parts of finely ground fennel, cloves, cinnamon, star-anise and anise.

Cinnamon *Cinnamomum zeylanicum*

Cinnamon can be bought as pieces of dried bark, 'quills' made from the inner bark, and powder. This warm, fragrant flavouring is good in both sweet and savoury dishes. The bark and quills can be used to flavour pilafs and spiced vegetable dishes; the quills are also useful for flavouring poached fruits and fruit compotes. Cinnamon is difficult to grind at home, so it's useful to buy it ready-ground too for adding to cakes and biscuits. A cinnamon stick can be kept in a jar of caster sugar, to flavour it; this sugar, or sugar mixed with cinnamon, is good for cheering up a bland melon; sprinkled on top of hot buttered toast it makes cinnamon toast.

Cloves *Syzygium aromaticum* and *Eugenia aromatica*

Cloves are the dried flower buds of a tall aromatic evergreen of the myrtle family native to South-East Asia. It is useful to have both whole and ground cloves, since cloves are difficult to grind at home, and ground cloves are useful in fruit cakes and in some bean dishes. Whole cloves make a delicious flavouring for apple pie, whole baked onions, bread sauce and cheese fritters.

Cloves also have natural antiseptic and preservative properties, as I discovered for myself when my young daughter had half made a pomander: the half of the orange studded with cloves was still dry and perfectly preserved, while the other side was rotten.

Coriander seeds *Coriandrum sativum*

Coriander seeds have a slight burnt-orange flavour and are available whole and ground. I find it useful to keep both. Coriander complements many vegetable, grain and bean dishes. The whole seeds can be roasted in a dry saucepan then lightly crushed or finely ground before use; or you can keep a pepper mill full of coriander, or it can be bought ready ground.

Ground coriander is used to flavour spicy Pakoras from India. They can be served as a first course or as a side dish. To make pakoras, put 100 g/4 oz chick pea flour into a bowl with 1 teaspoon each salt and grated fresh ginger, ½ teaspoon each chilli powder and ground coriander, ¼ teaspoon turmeric, and enough water to mix to a thin batter — about 200 ml/7 fl oz. Leave the batter to stand for about 30 minutes. Meanwhile, peel and slice into rings 2 large onions. Dip the onion rings into the batter, then fry in deep or shallow fat until crisp — deep fat gives the crisper result. Drain the onion rings on kitchen paper and serve immediately. Other vegetables, such as sliced aubergine and cauliflower florets, can also be used.

As it is mild, coriander is often used in quite large quantities to thicken as well as flavour Indian or Middle Eastern vegetable dishes. Mushrooms or vegetables can be flavoured with coriander to make a delicious first course (p. 228). Coriander is also an essential ingredient of curry powder and garam masala (see below).

CUMIN SEEDS *Cuminum cyminum*
Cumin seeds come from a plant related to the parsley family and have a slightly bitter flavour. The whole seeds are best if roasted in a saucepan before use to mellow the flavour. Along with coriander, cumin is frequently used in curries and spiced vegetable dishes. I find it useful to have both the whole seeds and ground cumin on my kitchen shelf.

CURRY POWDER
A popular flavouring in the West, but not much used in India, curry powder consists of a blend of spices, usually including coriander, turmeric, fenugreek, cumin and chilli. It can be bought in varying strengths from mild to hot. I find it quite useful for perking up some bland mixtures such as the filling for devilled eggs, or to flavour mayonnaise, but not for making curries — for these a mixture of coriander, cumin, fresh ginger, chilli, garlic and other spices gives a much better flavour.

DILL SEEDS *Anethum graveolens*
Probably best known as the flavouring in dill pickled cucumbers, dill seeds have a refreshing, slightly sweet flavour. They are a popular flavouring in Scandinavian cooking, and dill is excellent in any cucumber dish, such as cucumber soups and salads, as well as with cabbage, carrots and any of the root vegetables.

FENNEL SEEDS *Foeniculum vulgare*
These aniseed-flavoured seeds are much used in Indian cookery and when added to pulse dishes are said to counteract any indigestibility, though I have never had any proof of such

effectiveness. They are nice lightly roasted in a dry pan before use.

FENUGREEK *Trigonella foenum-graceum*

Ground fenugreek is an ingredient in curries and Indian dishes, but you do not need much as it has quite a harsh flavour. I think the rectangular, yellowish-brown seeds are best to use, and they should be lightly roasted in a saucepan before use. The seeds can also be sprouted (p. 57) but watch your teeth when you eat them.

GARAM MASALA

Garam masala can be bought ready-blended, although in India cooks make up their own mixture, often to old family recipes. The mixtures usually include roasted and ground coriander, cumin, cloves, cinnamon and black pepper. Add to curries at the end of the cooking, to flavour and thicken.

GARLIC *Allium sativum*

Garlic is indispensable for subtly enhancing the taste of other ingredients or giving its own wonderful flavour to savoury dishes. It can be used in a whole range of savoury dishes, from soups and salads − rub a salad bowl with a cut clove of garlic, for a delicate flavour − to casseroles, bakes, accompaniments such as hot buttery garlic bread and dips and sauces such as the famous aïoli of Provence.

Garlic Potatoes are delicious. Peel and cut potatoes into even-sized chunks and boil for about 15 minutes until just tender. Drain and spread the potatoes in a shallow, ovenproof dish. Crush one or two garlic cloves with some butter and dot over the surface of the potatoes. Season and cook in a fairly hot oven for about 40 minutes, turning the potatoes from time to time to coat them in the garlic butter.

Garlic can be bought fresh, as a paste in a tube, as flakes, powder or as a salt. Fresh garlic is by far the best, and worth the small effort involved in peeling and crushing the individual cloves from the bulb.

A bulb of garlic will keep well for several weeks in a dry kitchen; when I can I like to buy a string of garlic − it looks attractive hanging up in the kitchen and means there's always plenty available. Choose firm bulbs with no sign of powderiness and look for nice big fat ones made up of fat individual cloves — they're so much easier to peel and crush. To crush garlic, either use a good-quality, sturdy garlic press with nice large holes, or crush with the side of a knife on a small board, adding a little salt to help grind it into a paste.

Garlic is a natural antiseptic, excellent for cleansing heavy metals from the body and keeping colds (and, alas, probably one's friends) at bay.

GINGER *Zingiber officinale*

This is the rhizome of a flowering plant which is native to South-East Asia but has been grown in China for thousands of years. It can be bought fresh, dried and ground. FRESH GINGER has a deliciously fresh, citrus-like smell and flavour, along with the characteristic 'hotness', and is used in Chinese, Caribbean and Indian dishes. It transforms a dish of simple root vegetables into a gourmet feast and can give a wonderful lift to a winter compote of dried fruit. DRIED GINGER ROOT is useful when making preserves and chutneys, and POWDERED GINGER is a popular flavouring for cakes (such as gingerbread, Parkin [p. 462] and fruit cakes), biscuits and cookies.

Gingerbread Men are a perennial children's favourite. To make about 12, set the oven to 180c/350f/Gas Mark 4. Melt 25 g/ 1 oz butter or vegan margarine, 40 g/1½ oz barbados sugar, 1 tablespoon black treacle and 2 tablespoons golden syrup gently in a saucepan, then cool until you can put your hand against the saucepan. Sift in 100 g/4 oz fine 100 per cent wholewheat flour and ½ teaspoon each bicarbonate of soda and ground ginger. Mix to a pliable dough. If the dough is too soft to roll, chill in the fridge for about 20 minutes, otherwise roll it out about 5 mm/ ¼ inch thick and cut into gingerbread men shapes. Put the gingerbread men on the baking tray and bake for about 10 minutes, until firm and beginning to darken round the edges. Cool on a wire rack.

Ginger is available preserved in syrup and crystallized, both excellent for adding to ice cream, cakes, fruit salads, and compotes of dried fruits.

HORSERADISH *Armoracia rusticana*

Finely grated horseradish can be added to mayonnaise or cream to make horseradish sauce. Or it can be made into a dressing for sliced tomato salad. To make this, combine in a bowl 125 g/4 oz curd cheese, 2 tablespoons natural yogurt, 2 teaspoons olive oil, ½ teaspoon wine vinegar and 1 teaspoon grated horseradish. Mix until creamy then pour over sliced tomatoes and garnish with chopped fresh herbs. It is hot and pungent and can make your eyes water as you grate it. I think a jar of preserved grated horseradish or, nicer, creamed horseradish is a better bet.

JUNIPER BERRIES *Juniperus communis*
Juniper berries take three years to ripen, so the bushes carry berries at different stages of development. Juniper berries can be used fresh or dried, and a few berries added to casseroles and vegetable dishes give an intriguing flavour. Juniper is used to make gin, and in Germany juniper is added to sauerkraut and preserves.

MACE *Myristica fragrans*
Mace is the lacy covering surrounding the kernel inside the apricot-like fruit of an evergreen tree of the myrtle family. A BLADE of mace is useful for flavouring Béchamel Sauce (p. 261) and delicate soups; while a pinch of GROUND MACE enhances many savoury mixtures and is specially good in delicate nut roasts made from white nuts (p. 357).

MIXED SPICE
This usually consists of four parts each ground nutmeg and cinnamon, two parts ginger and one part ground cloves. The flavour of different makes of mixed spice varies, so it's worth experimenting to find your favourite. A useful flavouring for cakes, biscuits and fruit mixtures such as mincemeat.

MUSTARD SEEDS *Brassica hirta* and *B. nigra*
WHITE, BLACK (the hottest) and BROWN mustard seeds are used in curries and Indian dishes and the white ones make a delicious addition to cucumber and dill salad, cucumber pickle and chutneys. MUSTARD POWDER is a mixture of varieties together with wheat flour and turmeric. A pinch or so brings out the flavour of cheese dishes: it should be blended with cold water for the best flavour. Many types of prepared mustard are available, often with intriguing additions like fresh herbs and green peppercorns. They are interesting to try, but the best

basics to have in the store cupboard, in my opinion, are DIJON MUSTARD, which is delicious in salad dressings, and a whole-grain mustard, especially MOUTARDE DE MEAUX which, as well as being a useful ingredient, is a good accompaniment to many cold savoury dishes.

NUTMEG *Myristica fragrans*
The dried kernel of an apricot-like fruit, nutmeg is available whole and ground and has a slightly sweet aromatic flavour. Traditionally, nutmeg was used for sweet dishes, such as milk puddings, egg custards and custard tarts, while mace was used in savoury dishes. However, nutmeg is equally at home with vegetables such as mushrooms, spinach and cabbage, and in dishes such as onions in cream sauce. The flavour of freshly grated nutmeg is much better than that of ready-ground nutmeg.

PAPRIKA *Capsicum tetragonum*
This sweet mild powder made from a variety of peppers makes a cheering garnish to a plate of creamy-coloured Hummus (p. 217), Cheese and Fresh Herb Dip (p. 214), Guacamole (p. 218) or mashed potato. Paprika is useful for its subtle, peppery taste as well as its colour, and is an essential ingredient in many Hungarian recipes, where it is used to thicken, as well as flavour. The best paprika is Hungarian noble sweet, followed by semi-sweet, rose, strong and commercial, in descending order of quality.

PEPPERCORNS *Piper nigrum*
GREEN PEPPERCORNS (available dried, pickled and sometimes fresh) are included in some special dishes, for their colour as much as their sharp, hot flavour. BLACK PEPPERCORNS have a mellow flavour and, when freshly ground, give an appetizing piquancy to food. WHITE PEPPERCORNS have a sharper, more astringent flavour, which is useful at times, and some cooks prefer to use white pepper for seasoning pale mixtures which would be discoloured by flecks of black pepper. MIGNONETTE is a mixture of white and black peppercorns and is widely used in France. You can make up your own mignonette mixture by putting both white and black peppercorns in a pepper mill. This gives a pleasant flavouring, worth trying. The other flavouring

which is based on either black or white pepper and popular in France (where it can be bought at any supermarket) is Quatre Epices, a mixture of ground peppercorns, cloves, nutmeg and cinnamon – a pleasant mixture to experiment with. PINK PEPPERCORNS (*Schinus molle*), also known as Baie rose and false pepper of America, are the fruits of a small ornamental tree of the cashew family. They can be used to make an attractive garnish because of their pretty colour.

PICKLING SPICE
An essential ingredient in chutneys and pickles, a little pickling spice can also be added to a casserole or ground in a mortar with a pestle and used to add piquancy to a nut roast.

POPPY SEEDS *Papaver somniferum*
Widely used in Indian and Jewish cookery, poppy seeds have a nutty flavour and crunchy texture and make a pleasant addition to curries, hot vegetable dishes and salads, and sprinkled over hot buttery pasta. They are also used as a topping for breads (p. 493) and as an ingredient in the famous Jewish poppy seed cake.

SAFFRON *Crocus sativus*
The world's most expensive spice, saffron has an aromatic flavour and will colour pale ingredients (such as rice) soft yellow. Classically it is used in Paella (p. 364) and in Cornish saffron cake. Buy the dried stamens (rather than 'powdered saffron' which is almost always a dye) and soak a few in a couple of tablespoons of boiling water for 15 minutes before use, then add to the dish, together with the soaking water.

STAR ANISE *Illicium verum*
This star-shaped fruit is a pod which contains shiny golden-brown seeds. It is added whole to casseroles and stir-fries and has a delicate aniseed flavour. It is used particularly in China where it is believed to have a beneficial effect on the digestive system.

TAMARIND *Tamarindus indica*
The dried fruit of the tamarind tree, native to East Africa and known as 'Indian dates' because of its sticky, fibrous appear-

ance, tamarind can be added to curries and Indian dishes to give lemony sharpness. To use, soak a small piece in water until pulpy, then press through a sieve and use the liquid and pulp which comes through.

TURMERIC *Curcuma longa*

Turmeric is a rhizome. It is sometimes available fresh, when it looks rather like fresh ginger, but it is normally bought either whole or ground, when it is bright gold. Ground turmeric is useful for adding flavour and a vivid golden colour to rice and vegetable dishes and is much used in Indian cookery. It is also used in some chutneys and pickles.

A traditional British use for turmeric is in piccalilli, piquant pickle for serving with cold nut or lentil savouries. To make piccalilli, prepare 450 g/1 lb each of pickling onions, cucumber, cauliflower florets and runner beans, cutting them into bite-sized pieces. Put the vegetables into a large dish or on to a plastic tray, sprinkle with 225 g/8 oz kitchen salt and leave for 24 hours. Meanwhile, put 1·2 litres/2 pints white vinegar into a saucepan with 4 dried chillis, 4 cloves, 25 g/1 oz dried ginger, bruised with a rolling pin, and 175 g/6 oz granulated sugar. Heat gently until the sugar has dissolved, then bring to the boil. Remove from the heat, cool and strain. Rinse and drain the vegetables. Put 75 g/3 oz flour into a bowl with 25 g/1 oz mustard powder, 15 g/½ oz turmeric and 2 crushed garlic cloves. Add enough cooled vinegar to make a smooth paste. Bring the rest of the vinegar to the boil, add some of this to the flour mixture and stir, then add the flour mixture to the vinegar in the pan and stir well until thickened. Add the vegetables to the pan. Cook for 5 minutes. Spoon the mixture into warm, sterilized jars. Cover with vinegar-proof tops. Keep for 3 months before using. Makes 2·5–3 kg/5–6 lb.

VANILLA *Vanilla planifolia*

Black, snake-like pods of a climbing orchid native to Central America, vanilla has a sweet, delectable flavour. Vanilla pods are expensive, but they can be used over and over again. Break a vanilla pod in half and bury the pieces in a jar of caster sugar to make a delicate vanilla-flavoured sugar for using in ice cream, delicate fruit dishes and egg custards. Or simmer a whole pod in a sugar syrup or milk which you're going to use to make egg custard. The vanilla pod can later be extracted, rinsed in warm water, patted dry on kitchen paper and left to dry on an airy shelf in the kitchen before storing in an airtight jar. A more extravagant use is to grind the whole vanilla pod up with cashew nuts, carob powder and honey to make rather superior healthy sweet treats (p. 524). Vanilla extract, made by extracting the vanilla flavouring from the pods with alcohol, is available but expensive. Cheaper vanilla essence is made from a synthetic vanillin, made from eugenol, which is found in clove oil.

Other Flavourings

Flavouring is particularly important in vegetarian cookery; there are many ingredients available so there is absolutely no need for the food to be bland or uninteresting. Here are some of the most useful basic flavouring ingredients. Some of them, for instance the soya and yeast extract, and tomato purée, add colour as well as flavour. Although you may find some of these items expensive, they are very concentrated and keep for many months. Build up a stock gradually and enjoy experimenting with the different flavours.

Gomasio

This is a savoury mixture of roasted sesame seeds and salt, much used in Japan. To make gomasio, put 10 parts sesame seeds and 1 part sea salt into a frying pan and heat gently, stirring, for a few minutes, until the sesame seeds smell roasted, turn a darker brown and one or two start to 'pop'. Then remove from the heat and grind to a fairly fine powder in a coffee grinder. Store in an airtight jar. Use in cooking or at the table instead of salt. This is a useful way of reducing salt intake as well as adding a savoury flavour.

MISO

This thick brown paste is made by fermenting soya beans, barley or rice under pressure for up to 2 years, then adding a little salt. Miso is rich in nutrients, including protein and B vitamins. There are various types: light-coloured miso has a more delicate flavour than darker ones, but they all have a deliciously savoury taste and are useful in soups, casseroles, sauces and gravies. Miso should be added at the end of cooking time to conserve the vitamins.

SALTS

Salt, or sodium chloride, has been used as a flavouring and food-preservative since Neolithic times. It is available in various forms.

SEA SALT, sometimes called 'gros sel', is evaporated naturally in bays and enclosures or from salt marshes. It contains traces of minerals, including iodine. Most cooks agree that there is nothing to touch sea salt from the point of view of flavour. Sea salt is available as coarse granules, for use in a grinder, or as fine grains or flakes.

ROCK SALT is mined from the deposits made by ancient seas. It is sold in various degrees of coarseness.

TABLE SALT, BLOCK SALT and KITCHEN SALT are produced from rock salt. Iodine is sometimes added to table salt, to make iodized salt. This is a useful way of adding essential iodine to the diet in parts of the country where it is not present in the soil (and thus in the vegetables). Flavoured salts, such as onion salt, garlic salt and celery salt, are made from table salt with dried and powdered onion, garlic or celery seed added.

SALT SUBSTITUTES

Various substitutes for salt are available, some based on potassium chloride instead of sodium chloride, others consisting of mixtures of herbs and other seasonings. These are certainly worth a try, though none of them are very satisfactory, in my opinion – personally I'd rather use just a little sea salt with other flavourings such as fresh herbs, sea vegetables and lemon juice, than one of the substitutes. If you have a heart condition, or are on a potassium-restricted diet, you should get your doctor's advice before using a potassium-based salt.

Soy sauce
This is a richly flavoured, slightly sweet liquid which has been used in China and Japan for centuries and is useful for adding both flavour and colour to stews, casseroles, sauces and marinades, as well as for flavouring stir-fries, and as a dip for tempura. Choose a naturally fermented soy sauce without added caramel. Tamari has the strongest flavour and the darkest colour; shoyu is lighter; the difference between these in cooking terms can be compared to that between red and white wine, though they can really be used interchangeably in most recipes.

Sugar
Sugar is produced from sugar beet and from sugar cane. Sugar cane contains a rich, sticky sap, which consists of water, molasses and sugar, and this sap goes through a number of refining processes during which the sugar crystals are separated from the molasses. Natural brown sugars, called Light Muscovado, Muscovado and Molasses are the sugars which retain the natural molasses, light brown sugar having the least, and molasses sugar the most. You can tell a genuine brown cane sugar (as compared to refined white sugar with molasses added later) because it should have the name of the country of origin on the packet; this applies to demerara sugar as well as the soft brown sugars.

Syrups
GOLDEN SYRUP is a refined version of molasses (below) but lacking the nutrients. HONEY is the sweetening preferred by natural health experts, though others argue that it is just another form of sugar (but lower in calories); there are many different flavours available. MALT EXTRACT is a syrup obtained from malted cereal grains, especially barley. MAPLE SYRUP is the smoky-tasting sap of maple trees; be sure to buy the genuine article, not 'maple-flavoured syrup'. MIRIN, a sweet brown liquid made from rice, has been used in Japan for centuries. Boil

for 1 minute before using. MOLASSES is the dark, treacly syrup left behind when sugar is refined; rich in iron, calcium and B vitamins. TREACLE is a blend of refined syrup and molasses.

TABASCO

This is a hot flavouring liquid made from the tabasco variety of chilli pepper. It is very useful for perking up all kinds of mixtures from avocado dip to cheese sauce. It is very hot, so you only need a drop or two. Do get the original type: the imitations are not as good.

TOMATO PURÉE

This can be bought in a can, tube or jar, and is useful for adding extra flavouring and natural thickening to tomato dishes or other savoury mixtures which would be complemented by a tomato flavour. Use discreetly, as too much can give rather an acid flavour. I find tomato purée in a tube the most useful, as a little can be used at a time and the rest stored in the fridge where it will keep for several weeks.

YEAST EXTRACT

A sticky dark brown paste made from brewer's yeast, and often fortified by other vitamins (such as B_{12}), yeast extracts are highly nutritious and are useful for giving a savoury flavour to casseroles, sauces, nut roasts and other dishes, and also as a spread for bread. Use with a light touch; add a little at a time.

Oils and Vinegars

Two of the most ancient and basic of ingredients, both oils and vinegars are store-cupboard essentials and come in a number of varieties. Different oils and vinegars each have their own flavour and value, although the healthiest oil for general purposes (including frying) is probably a light, pure olive oil, not a highly flavoured virgin oil, which is best kept for salad dressings where the flavour can be really appreciated. It is interesting to experiment with vinegars and they keep extremely well.

Oils

Oils are extracted from nuts, seeds, pulses and (in the case of olive oil) from fruits by pressing them. This is usually done several times, at first by using pressure alone and later, to extract the maximum oil, by using heat too.

Cold-pressed oil is oil obtained by the early pressings and is the richest in flavour and nutrients (some of which are damaged when heat is used). Other chemicals may also be used in the later pressings and anti-oxidants may be added to increase the keeping qualities.

Cold-pressed oil is the best both for flavour and health. It is more expensive, and should be bought in small quantities (that can be used up within about a month) and kept in the fridge. If the oil goes a bit cloudy or solid, don't worry; it will return to normal if you take it out of the fridge and leave it at room temperature.

Some oils and fats are chemically more stable than others (and therefore better for health) when heated and so are better for cooking. These include butter, clarified butter and ghee, and of the oils, olive and ground nut oil.

Olive oil is perhaps the most delicious oil, made by pressing ripe olives. The oil is extracted by centrifugal force to give pure, pale green-gold 'first pressing', cold-pressed oil. The pulp is then pressed again, under heat, to yield more virgin oil. 'Virgin' on the label means that the oil has not been chemically treated to keep its natural acidity at a safe level. There are several permitted categories of 'virgin' oil: extra virgin must be under 1 per cent acidity; soprano or extra fine virgin can be up to 1·5 per cent acidity; fine virgin can have less than 3 per cent acidity; virgin can have up to 4 per cent acidity. These categories are often grouped into just two: extra virgin, below 1 per cent acidity; and virgin, below 4 per cent acidity.

Many other types of cooking oil are also available.

CORN OIL, made from the kernels of maize, is a bland oil, high in polyunsaturates and suitable for general purposes and for cakes and pastry.

GRAPESEED OIL, made from the seeds of grapes, is a light oil, high in polyunsaturates and with a high flash point, so it is good for deep-frying.

GROUND NUT OIL is another useful all-round oil, fairly low in polyunsaturates but stable when heated, and so a healthy oil for deep-frying.

SAFFLOWER OIL is made from the seeds of the safflower (a relative of the sunflower). This is one of the most nutritious oils, rich in polyunsaturates, and cold-pressed safflower oil can be mixed with olive oil to increase the polyunsaturates. However, safflower oil has rather a strong flavour which limits its uses.

SESAME OIL keeps well and is fairly high in polyunsaturates. Made from roasted sesame seeds, it has a strong, distinctive flavour. It is much used in Chinese and Indian cooking.

SOYA OIL is a good, mild-flavoured oil made from the soya bean and rich in polyunsaturates. It is reasonably priced and useful for all general-purpose cooking, including cakes and pastries.

SUNFLOWER OIL is high in valuable linoleic acid, and in polyunsaturates generally. It has a delicate flavour and is another useful general-purpose oil.

Then there are the more unusual oils made from walnuts and hazelnuts. A delectable oil for use in salad dressings, WALNUT OIL is high in polyunsaturates and has a rich, nutty flavour. HAZELNUT OIL is equally delectable − and expensive! − but both are wonderful for making the occasional extravagant salad dressing, or for tossing freshly cooked pasta in. These oils make lovely presents for keen cooks.

VINEGARS

One of the earliest flavouring ingredients of all, vinegar is made by souring wine, beer or cider and generally contains 4−6 per cent acetic acid.

MALT VINEGAR is dark brown in colour and made from beer. It has a strong flavour which is too harsh for most cooking purposes, though it is good for some chutneys and pickles.

WINE VINEGAR, made from both red and white wine, by the

slow Orléans method, has a delicate flavour and makes a delicious dressing. Look for the word 'Orléans' on the bottle.

RICE VINEGAR is made from rice wine and used widely in the Far East.

CIDER VINEGAR, made from cider, has many health-giving properties associated with it. It can be used for salad dressings and complements fruity mixtures, though I personally do not much like the flavour.

DISTILLED VINEGAR is malt vinegar which has been distilled so it is clear and contains up to 12 per cent acetic acid. It is used for pickling.

Many different kinds of flavoured vinegar can be bought, such as tarragon, raspberry, garlic, chilli, rose and violet. These are fun to experiment with, and you can quite easily make them yourself by adding flavouring ingredients — such as sprigs of tarragon — to a bottle of wine vinegar.

SPICED VINEGAR is used for some chutneys and pickles. Tie 15 g/½ oz each of blade mace, cinnamon stick, allspice and cloves, and a few peppercorns, in a piece of muslin. Put into a saucepan with 2·4 litres/4 pints vinegar and 1 tablespoon salt. Bring to the boil, then cover and simmer for 5 minutes. Strain and use immediately, or cool, bottle and store. For sweet pickles, add sugar to the vinegar, allowing 450 g/1 lb to 600 ml/1 pint, and add a few strips of lemon rind. For pickled pears poach 900 g /2 lb peeled cooking pears (whole if small, halved or quartered if larger) in spiced vinegar with 450 g/1 lb soft brown sugar, for 30–40 minutes. Bottle and keep for 6 weeks before using.

BALSAMIC VINEGAR is a sweet, mellow, rich, dark vinegar which is made by concentrating grape juice over a low heat and then ageing the vinegar in wooden barrels. It is expensive to buy, but makes a delicious salad dressing for a special meal.

Recipes

In choosing recipes for this section, I've aimed for a balance between the essential basics, such as Nut Roast, Lentil Soup, Cheese Flan and Soufflé, to more unusual recipes such as Two-Colour Soup, Roasted Cashew Nut Roulade with Wild Mushroom Filling, and Aubergine and Pasta Charlotte. I have also borne in mind both the dictates of healthy eating and of the palate, which are not by any means always contradictory, as is demonstrated in the majority of the recipes. However, some indulgences have crept in, like Profiteroles and Summer Fruit Meringue, as have some particularly health-conscious recipes, including Sugarless Dundee Cake and Reduced-Sugar Jam. None of the recipes are unduly difficult or time-consuming, and all vegan recipes are marked with a V; I hope you will enjoy both making and eating them.

Soups

Thick, warming and filling, thin and elegant, or ice-cold and refreshing, soup is one of the most versatile dishes. It is also economical and quick and easy to make. Vegetarian soups are flavoured with vegetable stocks, herbs, spices, and, for more intensity, miso (p.201) or yeast extract (p.186). Using home-made stock produces an excellent soup, but if you haven't any don't let this deter you; use ordinary water and season carefully, for a delicate soup which lets the flavour of the vegetables sing out.

$\boxed{V}$ Jerusalem Artichoke Soup with Roasted Pine Nuts

The flavour of the pine nuts goes particularly well with the artichokes, but toasted hazelnuts or flaked almonds are also good.

SERVES 6

2 tablespoons lemon juice
700 g/1½ lb Jerusalem artichokes
1 onion, peeled and chopped
15 g/½ oz butter or vegan margarine
600 ml/1 pint Light Vegetable Stock (p. 194) or water

600 ml/1 pint milk or soya milk
freshly grated nutmeg
salt and freshly ground black pepper
25 g/1 oz pine nuts, toasted under the grill

1 Add the lemon juice to a bowl of cold water. Peel the artichokes, cut them into even-sized pieces and put them into the acidulated water, to prevent them from discolouring.

2 Fry the onion in the butter or vegan margarine in a large saucepan, covered, for 5 minutes, without allowing the onion to brown.

3 Drain the artichokes. Add to the pan, cover again and cook gently for a further 5–10 minutes. Stir from time to time during the cooking, and don't let the vegetables brown.

4 Stir in the stock or water and milk. Cover the pan and leave the soup to simmer for 20–30 minutes, until the artichokes are tender. Test by piercing them with a fork.

5 Purée the soup in a blender or food processor, then sieve for a really velvety texture. Season to taste with nutmeg, salt and pepper. Reheat gently without allowing it to boil.

6 Serve the soup in warmed bowls, each portion sprinkled with a few pine nuts in the centre.

Carrot and Ginger Soup

A delicately flavoured soup with a beautiful colour.

SERVES 4

1 onion, peeled and chopped
15 g/½ oz butter or vegan margarine
700 g/1½ lb carrots, scraped and sliced
1 teaspoon grated fresh ginger
salt and freshly ground black pepper

900 ml/1½ pints Light Vegetable Stock (p. 194) or water
TO GARNISH (OPTIONAL)
4 tablespoons single or non-dairy cream

1 Fry the onion gently in the butter or vegan margarine in a large saucepan, covered, for 5 minutes, without browning, then add the carrots, ginger and a sprinkling of salt. Cover and fry for a further 10 minutes, stir from time to time and do not allow the vegetables to brown.

2 Add the stock or water and bring to the boil, then simmer gently for about 15 minutes, until the carrots are tender. Purée the soup in a blender or food processor, then sieve.

3 Return the soup to the rinsed-out pan, reheat gently and season to taste with salt and pepper. Serve in warmed bowls, each topped with a spoonful of cream, if liked.

LIGHT VEGETABLE STOCK

Some good vegetable stock powders and cubes are available, but if you use these regularly, all your soups tend to have a similar flavour. On the other hand, home-made vegetable stock has a delicate flavour which varies from batch to batch. To make your own Light Vegetable Stock, just put an onion, a couple of garlic cloves, a celery stick, a carrot and a bouquet garni into a saucepan. Cover generously with water and bring to the boil. Simmer half-covered, for about 1 hour, then strain.

Other vegetables and flavourings, such as leeks, thinly pared lemon rind and allspice berries, can be added. Peelings from well-scrubbed potatoes also give a particularly pleasant flavour to vegetable stock.

Variations

CARROT, APPLE AND GINGER SOUP

Make as described, adding 450 g/1 lb peeled, cored and chopped dessert apples with the carrots, increasing the amount of water to 1 litre/1¾ pints and adding 3 tablespoons sherry with the water. Serves 4–6.

CARROT, ORANGE AND CORIANDER SOUP

Add 1 tablespoon coarsely crushed coriander seeds and the thinly pared rind of 1 orange with the carrots. Flavour the puréed and sieved soup to taste with 2–3 tablespoons orange juice. This looks pretty with each portion of soup garnished with a scattering of shreds of pared orange rind.

SPICED PARSNIP SOUP

Use parsnips instead of carrots and add 1 tablespoon curry powder to the onions when you fry them. A swirl of single or non-dairy cream is good on top of this version, and add some crisp croûtons for extra flavour.

SKINNING TOMATOES

Put the tomatoes into a bowl and cover with boiling water. Leave for 1 minute, drain, then slip off the skins with a sharp, pointed knife.

Tomato Soup with Basil

V

Made with fresh tomatoes and basil, this is one of the most delicious soups, wonderful for supper in the cool of a summer evening.

SERVES 4

1 onion, peeled and chopped
15 g/½ oz butter or vegan margarine
350 g/12 oz potatoes, peeled and diced
450 g/1 lb tomatoes, skinned (below) and sliced, or 1 × 400-g/

14-oz can tomatoes
900 ml/1½ pints Light Vegetable Stock (opposite) or water
salt and freshly ground black pepper
TO GARNISH
basil sprigs

1 Fry the onion in the butter or vegan margarine in a large saucepan, covered, for 5 minutes, without browning.
2 Add the potatoes, cover again and cook gently for a further 5–10 minutes, then add the tomatoes and cook for a further 4–5 minutes. Stir from time to time and do not allow the vegetables to brown.
3 Add the stock or water, cover the pan and leave the soup to simmer for 15–20 minutes, until the potatoes are tender.
4 Purée the soup in a blender or food processor and if you want it really smooth, sieve it to remove the tomato seeds – this isn't essential. Reheat the soup gently without boiling.
5 Serve in warmed bowls, garnished with basil sprigs.

Watercress Soup

V

The all-time most popular soup in my family, and very quick and easy to make. I like to add the watercress at the end of cooking, as this gives the soup a better flavour and colour. Most watercress seems to come, stalks removed, in a packet; if you are using a bunch of watercress with stems, separate the stems from the leafy

tops and cook the stems with the potatoes.
Watercress soup, with all its variations, is
excellent served chilled, as well as hot.

SERVES 4

15 g/½ oz butter or vegan
  margarine
1 onion, peeled and chopped
900 ml/1½ pints Light Vegetable
  Stock (p.194) or water
1 bunch or packet of watercress

700 g/1½ lb potatoes, peeled and
  diced
salt and freshly ground black
  pepper
3–4 tablespoons double or non-
  dairy cream, optional

1 Fry the onion in the butter or vegan margarine in a large
saucepan, covered, for 5 minutes, without browning.
2 Add the potatoes, cover again and cook gently for a further
5–10 minutes. Stir from time to time and do not allow the
vegetables to brown.
3 Stir in the stock or water, cover the pan and leave the soup to
simmer for about 20 minutes, until the potatoes are tender.
4 Reserve 4 small watercress sprigs for garnishing if liked, then
liquidize the soup with the rest of the watercress. Season to taste
with salt and pepper, reheat without boiling and serve in
warmed bowls, each topped with a swirl of double or non-dairy
cream and a watercress sprig if liked.

Variations

LETTUCE SOUP
For this delicious summer variation, omit the watercress, and
cook 450 g/1 lb chopped outside lettuce leaves along with the
potatoes. Some fresh chopped mint or parsley stirred in at the
end of cooking is pleasant, and a little single or non-dairy cream
swirled on top is even better.

SPINACH SOUP
Omit the watercress and cook 450 g/1 lb chopped spinach leaves
with the potatoes. Flavour the soup with a little freshly grated
nutmeg.

SORREL SOUP

A sharp, refreshing variation, made by substituting the water-cress for 75 g/3 oz chopped sorrel leaves which are added with the potatoes. Season with plenty of salt, freshly ground black pepper and freshly grated nutmeg. A swirl of single, non-dairy or soured cream on top of each bowl makes this soup extra good.

FRESH HERB SOUP

For this fragrant variation, liquidize the soup with a small bunch of herbs instead of the watercress. Parsley, tarragon or chives are particularly good.

Asparagus Soup

This is a very good way of making full use of all
the asparagus; the tips can be used as a
luxurious garnish, or served at another meal in
a dish such as Asparagus Tartlets (p.390).
Asparagus soup is also very good chilled.

SERVES 6

700 g/1½ lb asparagus, well-washed

2 onions, peeled and chopped

700 g/1½ lb potatoes peeled and diced

1.4 litres/2½ pints Light Vegetable Stock (p.194) or water

25 g/1 oz butter or vegan margarine

150 ml/5 fl oz single or non-dairy cream

salt and freshly ground black pepper

1 Cut the tips from the asparagus, then simmer these in 2·5 cm/1 inch boiling water for about 4 minutes, until tender.

2 Set the asparagus tips aside (in the pan) for garnishing, or drain and keep for another use. Cut the asparagus stalks into even-sized pieces.

3 Fry the onion in the butter or vegan margarine in a large saucepan, covered, for 5 minutes, without browning. Add the asparagus pieces and potatoes and cook gently for a further 5–10 minutes.

4 Stir in the stock or water, cover the pan and leave the soup to simmer for about 30 minutes, until the asparagus pieces are very tender.

5 Liquidize the soup, then sieve. Return to the rinsed-out pan, add the cream, reheat without boiling and season to taste with salt and pepper. Reheat the asparagus tips, if used, then drain. Ladle the soup into warmed bowls and place the asparagus tips on top, dividing them equally between the bowls.

GARNISHES FOR SOUP

☐ Fresh parsley or chives, snipped, on top of a bowl of soup, looks attractive, tastes good and goes well with most soups.

☐ Snip fresh basil over tomato soup, mint over pea soup, dill or fennel over cucumber soup.

☐ A swirl of single or soured cream looks good on a dark soup such as ruby-red beetroot soup, or on carrot and ginger soup, or chilled avocado soup.

☐ A few roughly chopped walnuts or toasted flaked almonds or pine nuts go well with creamy soups such as cauliflower or Jerusalem artichoke.

☐ Wholewheat croûtons add a pleasant crunch to vegetable soup. Make these by frying 6 mm/¼ inch dice of wholewheat bread in a little oil until golden brown and crisp all over; drain on kitchen paper.

☐ Top mushroom soup with a few slices of fried mushroom, and asparagus soup with one or two asparagus tips, cooked at the beginning of the soup-making process and reserved.

Celery and Stilton Soup

SERVES 4–6

1 head celery, tough outer stalks removed
1 onion, peeled and chopped
15 g/½ oz butter

900 ml/1½ pints Light Vegetable Stock (p.194) or water
100 g/4 oz Stilton cheese, grated
salt and freshly ground black pepper

1 Wash and chop the celery. Discard most of the leaves, reserving a few.

2 Fry the onion in the butter in a large saucepan, covered, for 5 minutes, without browning. Add the celery, cover again and cook gently for a further 5–10 minutes. Stir from time to time and do not allow the vegetables to brown.

3 Add the stock or water. Cover the pan and leave the soup to simmer for 30 minutes, until the celery is very tender.

4 Purée the soup, together with the cheese, in a blender or food processor, until smooth. Season to taste, return to the rinsed-out pan and reheat gently.

5 Serve the soup in warmed bowls and snip the reserved celery leaves on top.

Variations

CELERY AND CHESTNUT SOUP

For this vegan version, add 225 g/8 oz fresh peeled chestnuts (p.347) or the drained contents of a 400 g/14 oz can of chestnuts to the onion with the celery. Use 1·2 litres/2 pints liquid for this recipe.

CELERY AND PEAR SOUP WITH TARRAGON

Another vegan version which sounds strange but tastes good. Add 450 g/1 lb pears, peeled, cored and diced, with the celery. Use 1·2 litres/2 pints stock or water. Snip some fresh tarragon on top of the soup before serving.

CAULIFLOWER SOUP WITH CHEDDAR CHEESE

Use a medium–large cauliflower instead of the celery, and grated Cheddar cheese instead of the Stilton. A few chopped walnuts make a pleasant garnish.

DARK VEGETABLE STOCK

Wipe and chop 225 g/8 oz mushrooms, then put them into a saucepan with a sliced onion, a bouquet garni and 1.2 litres/ 2 pints water. Bring to the boil, then cover and simmer gently for 1 hour. Cool, then leave overnight before straining. This makes just under 900 ml/ 1½ pints.

The water which vegetables have been cooked in makes good stock and contains useful nutrients. Strain it into an old jug, cool and keep in the fridge for 2–3 days.

French Onion Soup

This soup is very filling, and makes a good main course, followed by fruit or a light pudding.

SERVES 4–6

900 g/2 lb onions, peeled and
  thinly sliced
2 tablespoons oil
4 teaspoons sugar
salt and freshly ground black
  pepper

1.8 litres/3 pints Dark Vegetable
  Stock (p.199)
2 garlic cloves, crushed
a few drops of lemon juice
TO GARNISH
chopped parsley or chives

1 Fry the onions in the oil in a large saucepan for 10 minutes until soft. Add the sugar and salt and pepper to taste and fry for a further 15–20 minutes, until the onions are a deep golden-brown, but don't let them burn.

2 Add the stock, garlic, and lemon juice. Bring the soup to the boil and let it simmer for about 10 minutes. Check the seasoning and serve in warmed bowls, sprinkled with parsley or chives.

Variations

GOLDEN ONION SOUP

Make as described, adding 3 tablespoons sherry and 2–3 table-spoons Dijon mustard along with the stock.

GARLIC BREAD

Crisp, hot garlic bread goes well with many soups and also with salads, and it's easy to make. Make slices in a French stick 2·5 cm/1 inch apart, cutting almost through so that the slices are still joined at the base. Beat 2-3 crushed garlic cloves into 100 g/4 oz butter or vegan margarine and spread this on both sides of the slices of bread. Push the slices together to re-form the loaf, then wrap it in foil. Place on a baking tray and bake for about 20 minutes at 200 c/400F/Gas Mark 6 for about 20 minutes, until the bread has heated through and the butter melted. Serve immediately.

FRENCH ONION SOUP GRATINÉE

Ladle the soup into a warmed heatproof tureen (or large casserole dish) or individual bowls for this non-vegan version. Top with a slice of French bread for each person sprinkled with about 25 g/1 oz grated cheese per person. Place under a hot grill until the cheese is melted and golden-brown.

Miso Soup with Bean Curd [V]

This Japanese soup is light but sustaining, and has a savoury flavour. It is particularly good as part of a Japanese menu (p.533), perhaps followed by Vegetable Tempura with Dipping Sauce (p.297) and Sweet Vinegared Rice (p.361).

SERVES 4

300 g/10 oz firm bean curd (tofu, p.157)
2 spring onions, trimmed and finely chopped

900 ml/1½ pints Light Vegetable Stock (p.194)
4 tablespoons miso (p.184)
1 teaspoon soy sauce

1 Cut the bean curd into 16 equal cubes and divide between warmed soup bowls. Divide the spring onion between the bowls, too.
2 Heat the stock in a saucepan, then take out a little and blend with the miso, to soften it and give a creamy consistency. Tip this back into the saucepan with the rest of the stock.
3 Bring the soup almost to the boil, but do not let it boil, or valuable enzymes in the miso will be destroyed. Add the soy sauce, then pour the soup into the bowls on top of the bean curd and spring onion. Serve immediately.

Variation

MISO SOUP WITH BEAN CURD AND WAKAME

This is made exactly as described, except that wakame seaweed (p.120) is added to the bowls. Soak 4 pieces of wakame in cold water for 10 minutes, then cut out the spine and any hard pieces and snip the wakame into rough pieces with kitchen scissors. Put into the bowls along with the bean curd and spring onion. Serve the soup immediately.

Leek and Potato Soup

V

This makes a thick soup, a real meal in itself on
a cold day. For a lighter result, add enough
extra stock or water to give the consistency you
want. For real luxury, add an extra spoonful or
two of cream and top with some snipped
chives.

SERVES 4–6

3 leeks, washed and sliced
700 g/1½ lb potatoes, peeled and
   diced
25 g/1 oz butter or vegan
   margarine
1 litre/1¾ pints Light Vegetable
   Stock (p.194) or water

3–4 tablespoons double cream or
   non-dairy cream (optional)
salt and freshly ground black
   pepper
TO GARNISH (OPTIONAL)
chopped parsley

1 Fry the leeks and potatoes very gently in the butter or vegan
margarine in a large saucepan, covered, for 10 minutes, stirring
often.
2 Cook gently, without browning, still covered, for a further 10
minutes, stirring from time to time to prevent vegetables
sticking to the pan.
3 Add the stock or water, stir, then simmer for 5–10 minutes,
until the vegetables are tender.
4 Purée in a blender or food processor, adding the cream if
using. Season to taste with salt and pepper, stir, and serve in
warmed bowls, sprinkled with a little chopped parsley, if used.

Variation

VICHYSSOISE
For this creamy, chilled version of Leek and Potato Soup, purée
the mixture, adding 300 ml/10 fl oz milk or soya milk and
300 ml/10 fl oz single or non-dairy cream. Sieve, then chill the
soup. Season carefully with salt, pepper and grated nutmeg.
Serve in chilled bowls, sprinkled with snipped chives. Serves 8.

MAIN COURSE SOUP

Some soups make warming and satisfying main courses, especially welcome for a winter lunch or Sunday supper round the fire. The thick bean and lentil soups, and those which contain cheese, such as Celery and Stilton (p.198) and Cauliflower and Cheddar (p.199), make a filling meal with just some warm crusty bread or rolls, or (especially with Lentil Soup) Garlic Bread (p.200). I like French Onion Soup (p.200) with a small side salad or some crudités; grated cheese is good on top of Tomato Soup (p.195) or thick Leek and Potato soup, and for a really hearty meal, add tasty wholewheat dumplings (p.207) to Simple Vegetable Soup (p.206).

Golden Lentil Soup

$\boxed{V}$

A satisfying, comforting soup which makes an excellent, cheap, filling main course with crusty wholewheat rolls or garlic bread. If you have a pressure cooker, you can make it in about 10 minutes.

SERVES 4

1 large onion, peeled and chopped
15 g/½ oz butter or vegan margarine
225 g/8 oz split red lentils
1 litre/1¾ pints Light Vegetable Stock (p.194) or water

1–2 teaspoons lemon juice
salt and freshly ground black pepper
TO DECORATE
thin slices of lemon

1 Fry the onion in the butter or vegan margarine in a saucepan or pressure-cooker pan, for 10 minutes, until it is soft but has not browned.

2 Add the lentils and stir for 1–2 minutes, then add the stock or water. Bring to the boil, then half cover the pan and leave the soup to simmer gently for 20 minutes, until the lentils are very tender and pale-coloured. Or cook in a pressure-cooker for 5 minutes.

3 Beat the soup with a spoon to break up the lentils and make it

smoother, or purée in a blender or food processor. Add the lemon juice and salt and pepper to taste. Decorate with lemon slices to serve.

LENTIL SOUP IDEAS

Lentil soup lends itself to experimentation. Here are some ideas:

☐ Fry 1–2 teaspoons curry powder with the onions when making the soup; purée the soup with 25 g/1 oz coconut cream.

☐ Fry an onion and some garlic, and perhaps a teaspoon of ground cumin, in a little butter or vegan margarine and add to the soup after puréeing.

☐ Garnish with plenty of chopped parsley or some croûtons made as described on p.198 and tossed in a little curry powder or crushed garlic.

V

Roasted Hazelnut Soup

SERVES 4

1 onion, peeled and chopped
25 g/1 oz butter or vegan margarine
450 g/1 lb potatoes, peeled and diced
1 garlic clove, crushed
salt and freshly ground black pepper

900 ml/1½ pints Light Vegetable Stock (p.194) or water
90 g/3½ oz roasted, skinned hazelnuts (p.53), finely ground
1 tablespoon lemon juice

TO GARNISH
a few chopped, roasted hazelnuts
chopped chives

1 Fry the onion in the butter or vegan margarine for 5 minutes, until lightly browned, then add the potato, garlic and a little salt and pepper. Cook gently, covered, for a further 5–10 minutes.
2 Add the stock or water, bring to the boil, then leave to simmer gently for 15–20 minutes, until the potatoes and onion are tender. Purée the soup in a blender or food processor and stir in the ground hazelnuts, lemon juice and salt and pepper to taste.
3 Serve the soup in warmed bowls, each topped with a sprinkling of chopped hazelnuts and chives.

Variation

ALMOND SOUP

Use ground almonds instead of hazelnuts.

Corn Chowder

$\boxed{\text{V}}$

This thick and filling soup is most delicious
when made with fresh sweetcorn, cut from the
husk with a sharp knife (one husk will yield
about 100 g/4 oz corn), but frozen sweetcorn
kernels are a very good alternative. The
chowder can be made just with stock or water,
which is my preference, or with half milk (or
soya milk) and water.

SERVES 4

1 onion, peeled and sliced
700 g/1½ lb potatoes, peeled and
   diced
25 g/1 oz butter or vegan
   margarine

salt and freshly ground black
   pepper
900 ml/1½ pints Light Vegetable
   Stock (p.194) or water
350 g/12 oz sweetcorn kernels,
   fresh or frozen

1 Fry the onion and potatoes very gently in the butter or vegan
margarine in a large saucepan, covered, for 10 minutes, stirring
often.

2 Season to taste with salt and pepper, stir, then cook gently,
still covered, for 10 minutes, stirring often. It doesn't matter if
the vegetables brown slightly, but don't let them get too brown.

3 Add the stock or water, stir, then simmer for 5–10 minutes,
until the potatoes are almost tender. Add the sweetcorn and
cook for a further 5 minutes. Check the seasoning and adjust if
necessary.

4 Serve the chowder as it is, in warmed bowls, or purée 1–2
cupfuls in a blender or food processor, then add to the rest of the
chowder. This thickens the liquid and gives a pleasantly creamy
texture.

Pistou

A wonderful, easy-to-make and very filling
vegetable soup from the South of France. Serve
it with crusty bread for a complete main course.
If you're using dried beans, you need to soak
and cook them first. This soup reheats well and
tastes even better the next day.

SERVES 4

1 onion, peeled and chopped
2 tablespoons olive oil
100 g/4 oz haricot beans, soaked
    and cooked, or 1 × 425-g/15-oz
    can cannellini beans, drained
2 carrots, scraped and diced
2 potatoes, peeled and diced
3 leeks or courgettes, washed and
    sliced
1 × 425-g/15-oz can tomatoes

2 garlic cloves, crushed
1–2 tablespoons chopped fresh
    basil or 1 teaspoon dried basil
salt and freshly ground black
    pepper
1 litre/1¾ pints Light Vegetable
    Stock (p.194) or water
50 g/2 oz thin pasta or pasta
    shapes

1 Fry the onion in the oil in a large saucepan for 5 minutes, then
add the drained haricot beans, all the vegetables, the garlic, the
dried basil, if used, and salt and pepper to taste, and cook for a
further 5 minutes.

2 Add the stock or water, cover and simmer for 20–30 minutes,
then add the pasta and cook for a further 10 minutes. If you're
using fresh basil, add this now and check the seasoning. Serve
the soup in warmed bowls.

Variations

VEGETABLE AND LENTIL SOUP

Use continental lentils instead of dried beans. Omit the pasta, or
not, depending on how hearty you want the soup to be.

SIMPLE VEGETABLE SOUP

For this lighter version (which makes a good basis for dumplings, opposite) make as described, but omit the haricot or
cannellini beans and pasta.

DUMPLINGS FOR SOUP

Put 175 g/6 oz plain wholewheat flour into a mixing bowl with 1½ teaspoons baking powder, ½ teaspoon salt and 65 g/2½ oz grated hard butter. Mix well. Dissolve 1 teaspoon yeast extract in 2 tablespoons water and add to the flour mixture, then add more water, just enough to make a soft dough. Form the mixture into 8 dumplings, then drop them into half a panful of gently simmering water and simmer for 20 minutes, until puffed up. Remove with a slotted spoon and serve them in a vegetable soup.

Cream of Mushroom Soup [V]

A few dried Italian mushrooms intensify the flavour of this soup and make it extra good for a special occasion. They are horribly expensive to buy, but they keep well and a few of them go a long way. Soak about 25 g/1 oz in 600 ml/1 pint boiling water for about 30 minutes, then remove and chop the mushrooms and add to the fresh mushrooms. Use the soaking water as part of the water or stock.

SERVES 4

1 onion, peeled and finely chopped
25 g/1 oz butter or vegan margarine
350 g/12 oz mushrooms, washed and finely chopped
1 tablespoon plain flour
600 ml/1 pint Dark Vegetable Stock (p.199) or water
300 ml/10 fl oz milk or soya milk
salt and freshly ground black pepper
freshly grated nutmeg
dash of lemon juice
2–3 perfect button mushrooms, thinly sliced and fried in butter or vegan margarine

1 Fry the onion in the butter or vegan margarine in a large saucepan, covered, for 5 minutes, without browning.
2 Add the mushrooms, cover again and cook gently for a further 5 minutes. Stir in the flour and cook for 1–2 minutes.

3 Stir in the stock or water and the milk, cover the pan and leave the soup to simmer for 15–20 minutes.

4 Check the seasoning, adding grated nutmeg to taste and a dash of lemon juice. Serve in warmed bowls, with a few slices of fried mushroom on top of each.

Chilled Raspberry Soup

Fruit soups, such as this, are popular in Europe and Scandinavia, and make an attractive and refreshing start to a summer meal. For special occasions, all the following chilled soups can be dramatically presented by standing each bowl of soup in an outer bowl of crushed ice.

SERVES 4

750 g/1½ lb fresh or frozen
   raspberries
100 g/4 oz sugar
450 ml/16 fl oz water
6 teaspoons potato flour or
   cornflour

3 tablespoons port
3 tablespoons fresh orange juice

TO GARNISH
4 tablespoons soured or non-dairy
   cream

1 Put the raspberries into a saucepan with the sugar and water. Heat gently until the sugar has dissolved, then cook over a gentle heat for 5–10 minutes, until the raspberries are very soft.

2 Purée the soup in a blender or food processor, then return to the rinsed-out pan and reheat gently.

3 Blend the potato flour or cornflour to a smooth paste with the port and orange juice, then pour the mixture into the soup, stirring all the time. Stir over a gentle heat until thickened, then remove from the heat and allow to cool.

4 Taste and add more sugar if necessary, then pour into a bowl, cover and chill.

5 Serve the soup in chilled bowls, each topped with a swirl of cream.

Variation

CHILLED BLACK CHERRY SOUP

Use 3 × 425-g/15-oz cans black cherries. Remove the stones from the cherries, then put them into a saucepan with their liquid and 50 g/2 oz sugar and bring to the boil. Blend the potato flour or cornflour with the port and orange juice and continue as described.

Iced Beetroot Soup with Dill

Although it's wonderful cold, this soup,
incidentally, is also very good served hot. Use
cooked beetroot without vinegar (see p.97 for
cooking beetroot). Serve with hot Herb and
Onion Bread (p.492).

SERVES 4–6

1 onion, peeled and chopped
1 tablespoon oil
225 g/8 oz potatoes, peeled and diced
450 g/1 lb cooked beetroot, peeled and diced
1·2 litres/2 pints Light Vegetable Stock (p.194) or water

grated rind of ½ lemon
1 tablespoon lemon juice
salt and freshly ground black pepper
TO GARNISH
3 tablespoons single or non-dairy cream
dill sprigs

1 Fry the onion in the oil in a large saucepan, covered, for 5 minutes, without browning. Add the potatoes, cover again and cook gently for a further 5–10 minutes.
2 Add the beetroot and stock or water. Bring to the boil, then cover the pan and leave the soup to simmer for about 20 minutes, until the potatoes are tender.
3 Purée the soup in a blender or food processor, then add the lemon rind and juice, and salt and pepper to taste. Allow to cool, then pour into a bowl, cover and chill until ice-cold.
4 Serve the soup in chilled bowls, each topped with a swirl of cream and a small sprig of dill.

Chilled Avocado Soup

| V |

One of the easiest soups to make, with a
beautiful colour. It's best to make it no more
than 1 hour in advance, in case it discolours.

SERVES 6

2 large ripe avocado pears
1 small onion, peeled and roughly
  chopped
1 garlic clove, crushed
2 tablespoons lemon juice
900 ml/1½ pints Light Vegetable
  Stock (p.194) or water

1 tablespoon red wine vinegar
salt and freshly ground black
  pepper
TO GARNISH (OPTIONAL)
6 tablespoons soured or non-dairy
  cream
1–2 tablespoons snipped chives

1 Halve the avocado pears and remove the stones and skin
(p.106). Cut the flesh into chunks and purée in a blender or food
processor with the onion, garlic, lemon juice and about a third of
the stock or water.
2 Add the rest of the stock or water and blend again until very
smooth.
3 Add the vinegar and season carefully to taste with salt and
pepper, then pour into a bowl and cover. Allow to cool, then
chill.
4 Check the seasoning, then serve in chilled bowls, each topped
with a swirl of soured or non-dairy cream and/or chives, if liked.

Variation

CHILLED CUCUMBER AND YOGURT SOUP

Make as described, using a peeled and cubed cucumber instead
of the avocado and 450 g/16 oz plain live or vegan yogurt and 2–3
tablespoons double or non-dairy cream instead of the stock.
Garnish with chopped fresh mint.

Chilled Two-colour Soup

This stunning vegetable soup is made from
leeks, carrots and potatoes. Make it well in
advance, so it is thoroughly chilled, and pour
into bowls just before serving.

SERVES 8

350 g/12 oz sliced leeks, white part
    only
450 g/1 lb carrots, scraped and
    diced
1 onion, peeled and chopped
350 g/12 oz potato, peeled and
    diced
1·2 litres/2 pints water

50 g/2 oz butter or vegan
    margarine
2 tablespoons double or non-dairy
    cream
salt and freshly ground black
    pepper
TO GARNISH
8 small mint sprigs

1 Put the leeks into one large saucepan and the carrots into
another. Divide the onion, potato and water between the
saucepans, cover and simmer until tender.
2 Purée each mixture separately, adding half the butter or vegan
margarine to each. Add the cream to the leek mixture.
3 Season both mixtures, then put each soup into a separate jug
and chill.
4 To serve, pour the soup into chilled bowls, holding one jug at
each side of the bowl, and pouring from both at the same time,
so that there is one colour in each half of the bowl. Top each
bowl with a mint sprig.

Variation

CHILLED TWO-COLOUR BEETROOT AND POTATO SOUP
For this colourful variation, omit the carrots and use instead
450 g/1 lb cooked, skinned beetroot. Purée the cooked beetroot
as above, then flavour the beetroot mixture with a little lemon
juice. Continue with the other ingredients as above. Chill the
jugs of soup, then serve as above, carefully pouring from each
jug. Decorate each bowl of soup with some fresh dill sprigs just
before serving.

First Course Dishes

*First courses are rewarding to make because
they can be perfect little works of art, with
plenty of scope for imaginative use of colour,
flavourings and garnishes. This chapter contains
a range of possibilities for both first courses and
nibbles. You'll also find recipes in other sections
particularly Salads (pp. 229–252),
Accompanying Vegetables (pp. 267–286), Main
Vegetable Dishes (pp. 287–306), and Pasta (pp.
371–383) which, served in small portions, make
equally tempting first courses. Similarly, many
of the first courses in this section make good
light main courses if served with suitable
accompaniments such as warm bread or rolls.*

Three-colour Layered Omelette

This is easy to make and very effective, either
sliced into bite-sized pieces as a nibble, or into
larger pieces and served with a sauce as a first
course. It can be made in advance.

SERVES 6–8 AS A FIRST COURSE, 12 AS A NIBBLE

1 tomato, skinned (p.108) and
   chopped
1 small red pepper, de-seeded and
   chopped
50 g/2 oz butter

175 g/6 oz mushrooms, wiped and
   finely chopped
225 g/8 oz frozen chopped
   spinach, thawed
6 eggs
salt and freshly ground black
   pepper

1 Fry the tomato and pepper gently in 15 g/½ oz of the butter in
a small saucepan for about 5 minutes, until tender, then purée in
a blender or food processor.
2 Fry the mushrooms in another 15 g/½ oz of the butter for 2–3
minutes, until they are just tender.

3 Squeeze all excess water out of the spinach.

4 Have three bowls ready and break 2 eggs into each. Beat, then add the spinach to one, the mushrooms to another, and the red pepper mixture to the third. Season all three mixtures to taste with salt and pepper.

5 Melt one-third of the remaining butter in a small frying pan (p.35). When it's hot, pour in the spinach-flavoured mixture.

6 Cook until it's set on the bottom, then reduce the heat, cover and cook until the top is set – about 5 minutes.

7 Lift the omelette out with a spatula and put it, moist side uppermost, on to a large plate.

8 Make an omelette with the red pepper mixture in the same way, then turn it out on top of the spinach omelette, moist side down.

9 Repeat the process with the mushroom mixture, then press the layered omelette down lightly all over and leave to cool completely – about 1 hour.

10 Cut the omelette into bite-sized or larger slices as required and place them sideways on a plate to show off the coloured stripes.

Sushi

Creamy-coloured rice with a deep purple wrapping of nori makes piquant, intriguing-looking morsels to have with drinks, or they can be served as part of a Japanese meal. Serve them arranged around the dipping sauce, on a small tray or flat plate.

MAKES ABOUT 20

2 sheets of nori (p.119)
½ quantity Sweet Vinegared Rice (p.361)
100 g/4 oz cooked spinach, fresh or frozen, drained and chopped
1 umeboshi plum (p.129), stone removed, flesh chopped

FOR THE DIP
2 teaspoons Dijon mustard
6 tablespoons shoyu

TO GARNISH
radish flowers

1 Toast the nori sheets on both sides by holding them above a gas flame or electric hot plate until they become crisp.

2 Put one of the nori sheets on a Japanese raffia mat or double layer of kitchen paper and spread with half the rice, taking it to within 1 cm/½ inch of the top of the nori. Place the spinach on top of the rice in a horizontal strip about 1 cm/½ inch from the bottom of the nori.

3 Starting from the bottom, carefully roll up the nori so that the spinach is enclosed and the rice and nori rolled round, like a Swiss roll.

4 Press the roll firmly together and bang each end on the work surface to firm them up. Leave the roll for 20 minutes (or longer) to settle.

5 Using a sharp knife, carefully cut the roll crossways into 1 cm/½ inch slices.

6 Repeat the process with the second piece of nori and the rest of the rice, using the chopped umeboshi plum instead of the spinach.

7 To make the dip, put the mustard into a bowl and gradually blend in the shoyu, to give a smooth consistency. Put the mixture into a small bowl, placed in the centre of a small tray or large plate and arrange the sushi around, alternating the 2 types of filling. Garnish with a radish flower.

Cheese and Fresh Herb Dip

This is a simple dip which is popular with children. We sometimes eat it with crudités for a weekend lunch, with perhaps a vegetable soup as a first course.

SERVES 4

40 g/1½ oz soft butter
150g/5 oz vegetarian Cheddar cheese, grated
6 tablespoons milk
3–4 drops Tabasco sauce
salt and freshly ground black pepper

1 tablespoon chopped fresh herbs, such as chives, chervil or parsley

TO GARNISH
1 chervil sprig

1 Cream the butter, then gradually add the cheese and milk, beating until smooth and soft; or blend in a blender or food processor.

2 Add the Tabasco sauce and salt and pepper to taste. Stir in the chopped fresh herbs and mix well. Transfer the dip to a small bowl, smooth the surface slightly with a fork or the back of a spoon and serve, garnished with chervil.

Stuffed Vine Leaves with Yogurt Dip [V]

These make a light and refreshing first course
or nibble with drinks: serve the vine leaves on
a large plate or in a flat basket, with the yogurt
dip in the middle.

MAKES ABOUT 36

36 fresh vine leaves or a package
   of preserved vine leaves
225 g/8 oz long-grain brown rice
1 large onion, peeled and chopped
2 tablespoons chopped parsley
2 tomatoes, skinned (p. 108) and
   chopped
50 g/2 oz pine nuts
50 g/2 oz raisins
½ teaspoon ground cinnamon or
   allspice

2 garlic cloves, crushed
salt and freshly ground black
   pepper
6 tablespoons olive oil
150 ml/5 fl oz water
juice of 1-2 lemons

TO SERVE
Yogurt and Mint Dressing (p.233)
lemon slices

1 If you're using preserved vine leaves, drain them and rinse under the cold tap, then drain again.

2 For fresh vine leaves, half fill a large saucepan with water and bring it to the boil. Trim the stems off the leaves, then put into the boiling water, cover and simmer for 2 minutes. Drain and refresh under the cold tap and drain again.

3 Half fill a large saucepan with water, add the rice and boil for 10 minutes, then drain and mix with the onion, parsley, tomatoes, pine nuts, raisins, cinnamon or allspice, garlic and salt and pepper to taste.

4 Place a vine leaf on a flat surface, shiny side down. Then place

a heaped teaspoon of the filling close to its base. Fold the lowest pair of leaf sections over the filling, then fold in the middle sections and roll up the leaf. Repeat until you have used all the filling, and arrange the little bundles side by side in a frying pan with a lid. If there are some leaves left over, use them to fill in any gaps.

5 Mix together the oil and water and pour over the vine leaves. Sprinkle a little lemon juice on top.

6 Cook, covered, over a very gentle heat for 2–2½ hours until the rice and leaves are tender. Keep an eye on the water level, and add a little more from time to time if necessary. Cool, then chill.

7 Arrange the stuffed vine leaves on a large plate or in a shallow basket with the bowl of Yogurt and Mint Dressing in the middle to dip the stuffed vine leaves into. Garnish with lemon slices.

Little Asparagus Timbales with Fresh Tomato Sauce

An attractive first course, pretty to look at, easy to make, light yet filling to eat. If you have some Fresh Tomato Sauce in the freezer, the dish can be assembled very quickly.

SERVES 4

200-g/7-oz packet frozen
  asparagus
150 ml/5 fl oz single cream
2 eggs
salt and freshly ground black
  pepper

grated nutmeg
butter for greasing
TO SERVE
1 quantity Fresh Tomato Sauce
  (p.253)

1 Preheat the oven to 170c/325f/Gas Mark 3. Grease four 100-ml/4-fl oz dariole moulds thoroughly with a little butter.

2 Cook the asparagus as described on the packet; drain thoroughly.

3 Remove the four best asparagus tips, cutting them to fit into the base of the dariole moulds. Reserve.

4 Purée the stems, and the rest of the asparagus, with the cream and eggs, in a blender or food processor.

5 Season the purée with salt, freshly ground black pepper and a little grated nutmeg.

6 Pour the asparagus purée into the dariole moulds. Cover the top of each mould with foil.

7 Put the darioles into a roasting tin; pour boiling water into the tin so that it comes halfway up the moulds. Place the tin in the oven.

8 Bake the timbales for about 40 minutes, until they are firm in the centre and a knife comes out clean.

9 While the timbales are cooking, heat the sauce.

10 Slip a knife round the edges of the timbales to loosen, then turn them out on to warmed plates and pour a little of the sauce round. Place one of the reserved asparagus tips on top of each mould. Serve at once.

Hummus

Served with warm wholewheat pitta bread or some crudités, such as raw cauliflower florets, celery, carrot and spring onion, for dipping in the mixture, this delectable creamy dip makes a filling main meal for two.

SERVES 4

225 g/8 oz dried chick peas, soaked and cooked, or 1 × 425-g/15-oz can chick peas
½ garlic clove, crushed
1 tablespoon light sesame cream (tahini)
3 tablespoons olive oil
2 tablespoons lemon juice

salt and freshly ground black pepper

TO GARNISH
olive oil
paprika pepper (optional)
black olives
lemon wedges

1 Drain the chick peas, reserving the liquid. Put the chick peas into a blender or food processor with all the other ingredients and blend until the mixture is smooth.

2 Alternatively, mash the chick peas as smoothly as possible and then beat in the other ingredients to make a smoothish mixture. Add enough of the reserved cooking liquid to give a

light, soft consistency like softly whipped cream.

3 Spoon the hummus on to a plate and level it with a knife so that it is about 1 cm/½ inch deep. Pour a little olive oil over the top, then sprinkle with paprika, if using, and garnish with lemon wedges and olives.

CRUDITÉS

Crudités are popular with most people; served with a piquant dip they make a refreshing and easy-going starter, and are pleasant to have with drinks. Choose really crisp, fresh vegetables in contrasting colours and flavours. Have at least three different types, arranged in little heaps on a leaf-lined plate or tray, or pile them up in a small basket with the dips arranged around the outside. The basic preparation of the vegetables can be done several hours in advance and the vegetables kept in a polythene bag in the salad compartment of the fridge until needed, but it is best to cut vegetables into matchsticks just before you want to serve them.
Some possibilities are:

- ☐ Ruby-red radishes, with the root trimmed but the leaves left on
- ☐ Spring onions, trimmed
- ☐ Matchsticks of scraped carrot
- ☐ Matchsticks of crisp celery
- ☐ Matchsticks of red, green or yellow pepper, or cucumber
- ☐ Sprigs of cauliflower — especially good for scooping up dips
- ☐ Crisp chicory leaves
- ☐ Large juicy black olives
- ☐ Cherry tomatoes
- ☐ Baby button mushrooms

 ## *Guacamole*

The chilli pepper in this smooth green dip gives it quite a kick; leave it out for a less hot version. As well as being a delicious starter or dip for serving with drinks, Guacamole makes an excellent vegan alternative to mayonnaise.

SERVES 6–8 AS A FIRST COURSE

2 ripe avocado pears, halved, peeled and stones removed (p.106)

2 tablespoons lemon or fresh lime juice

1 small onion, peeled

2 tomatoes, skinned (p.108) and de-seeded

1 garlic clove

1 small green chilli pepper, de-
   seeded
a few coriander or parsley sprigs
salt and freshly ground black
   pepper

TO GARNISH
mild paprika pepper (optional)
parsley sprig

1 Mash the avocado with the lemon or lime juice, then finely
chop the rest of the ingredients and add, mixing well.
2 Check the seasoning, then spoon into a small bowl, smooth
the top and sprinkle with paprika, if wished. Garnish with a
parsley sprig.

Variation

AVOCADO CREAM
For this mild, creamy, non-vegan variation, omit the onion,
tomatoes and chilli pepper. Add 225 g/8 oz curd cheese to the
mashed avocado and other ingredients. Mix well until smooth
and light. Garnish with coriander, parsley or chopped chives.

Aubergine Dip   [V]

Aubergines make an excellent dip, moist yet
with body, and there are a number of classic
versions. Here is the simplest of these. Some
crisp Melba Toast (p.221) goes well with this dip.

SERVES 6-8

2 aubergines, total weight about
   450 g/1 lb, washed
4 tablespoons lemon juice
4 tablespoons olive oil
4 tablespoons chopped parsley
1–2 garlic cloves, crushed
salt and freshly ground black
   pepper

TO GARNISH
chopped parsley
lemon wedges (optional)
extra olive oil

TO SERVE
Melba Toast (p.221) or Crudités
   (opposite)

1 Preheat the oven to 200c/400f/Gas Mark 6. Put the aubergines
on a baking sheet and bake for about 40 minutes, until soft.

Remove from the oven and leave until completely cold.

2 Remove the stalks from the aubergines (use a cloth or gloves to avoid getting the little prickles in your hands – they can be extraordinarily difficult to get out).

3 Purée the aubergine in a blender or food processor with the lemon juice, oil, parsley and garlic (or chop the aubergine very finely by hand, then mash and mix in the other ingredients). Season to taste with salt and pepper.

4 Serve the dip on individual plates, garnished with parsley, lemon wedges, if wished, and olive oil. Or spoon it into a small bowl and garnish before serving with Melba Toast.

AUBERGINE DIP IDEAS

Aubergine dip has a delicate flavour which can be intensified in various ways:

☐ Try adding a tablespoon of tahini to the dip before puréeing; garnish with toasted sesame seeds.

☐ For a smoky, 'mock caviar' version, grill the aubergine for 20–30 minutes until charred all over. Scrape off the charred skin, rinse the aubergine, then continue as described in the recipe.

⟦V⟧ *Red Pepper and Almond Dip*

SERVES 6

2 large red peppers, total weight about 300 g/10 oz
4 garlic cloves
50 g/2 oz ground almonds
3 tablespoons oil

salt and freshly ground black pepper
TO GARNISH
extra ground almonds
red pepper strips

1 Put the whole peppers and garlic cloves into a saucepan and half cover with cold water. Bring to the boil, then simmer for 15–20 minutes until very tender. Drain and remove the pepper stems and seeds. Pop the garlic cloves out of their skins.

2 Purée the peppers and garlic in a blender or food processor, together with the ground almonds and oil, to make a smooth cream. Season to taste with salt and pepper. Turn into a small

MELBA TOAST

This thin, crisp toast goes well with many dips. It can be made a few hours in advance and kept in an airtight tin until needed. It's easiest to make using bread from a sliced loaf. Toast the bread on both sides, then with a sharp knife cut horizontally through the bread, making each into two thin slices. Place the bread slices, untoasted side up, on a grill pan and grill until crisp and browned: the edges will curl up. Transfer to a wire rack and leave to cool completely.

bowl and garnish with ground almonds sprinkled around the edge and in 3 lines across the dip, and with red pepper strips placed at one side.

Roquefort Dip

SERVES 4

100 g/4 oz Roquefort cheese
150 ml/5 fl oz soured cream
freshly ground black pepper

TO SERVE
Crudités (p.218)

1 Mash the cheese in a small bowl, then gradually stir in the soured cream. Add a grinding or two of black pepper, to taste.
2 Serve in a small bowl, with fresh crisp Crudités for dipping.

SERVING DIPS

Serve small quantities of 3 or more contrasting dips, say beige-cream Hummus (p.217), Red Pepper and Almond Dip (above), pale green Guacamole (p.218) and golden Cheese and Fresh Herb Dip (p.214), on individual plates, or in bowls on a wicker tray, surrounded by an equally colourful selection of crudités and some big juicy black olives and lemon wedges.

Any of these dips make excellent fillings or toppings for skinned and hollowed-out tomatoes, lightly fried cup mushrooms (with the stalks removed) or artichoke hearts. A selection of quickly made (or bought) dips, together with a couple of different cheeses, a basket of warm, assorted rolls and a simple fresh crisp salad – say lettuce, tomato wedges, cucumber and onion rings – with fresh fruit to follow, and good coffee, makes a delicious spur-of-the-moment lunch.

Mushroom and Herb Terrine

SERVES 6

700 g/1½ lb small firm button
   mushrooms, washed
50 g/2 oz butter or vegan
   margarine
1 tablespoon chopped fresh herbs,
   such as chives, parsley or
   chervil

salt and freshly ground black
   pepper

TO GARNISH
rosemary sprigs
tiny lemon wedges

1　Remove one or two perfect mushrooms and slice; set aside for garnishing. Grate the rest of the mushrooms in a food processor, or finely chop them by hand.

2　Heat the butter or vegan margarine in a large saucepan and quickly fry the reserved sliced mushrooms for about 2 minutes, then remove from the pan and set aside.

3　Fry the rest of the mushrooms over a moderate heat for about 15 minutes, until all the liquid has evaporated. Add the herbs and salt and pepper to taste.

4　Press into an oiled and base-lined 450-g/1-lb loaf tin, cover with greaseproof paper, top with a weight and leave until completely cold. Turn out and slice carefully. Garnish with the reserved mushroom slices, rosemary and lemon wedges.

Avocado on a Raspberry Coulis

A pretty, summery first course which is simple
to make but needs assembling at the last
minute so that the avocados do not discolour.

SERVES 4

1 quantity Raspberry Coulis
   (p.448)
4 tablespoons olive oil
salt and freshly ground black
   pepper
2 ripe avocado pears

2 tablespoons raspberry or wine
   vinegar

TO GARNISH
thyme sprigs
a few pink peppercorns (optional)

1 Make a vinaigrette by mixing together the Raspberry Coulis, vinegar and oil. Season to taste with salt and pepper.

2 Pour a pool of this dressing on to 4 individual serving plates.

3 Halve the avocado pears and carefully remove the skin and stones (see below). Place half an avocado cut-side down on a palette knife, then cut it across into fairly thin slices.

4 Slide the sliced avocado off the palette knife into the centre of the plate on top of the Raspberry Coulis, so that the avocado half keeps its shape.

5 Repeat this process with all the avocado halves. Garnish with thyme sprigs and a scattering of pink peppercorns. Serve immediately.

Variation

AVOCADO ON TWO PEPPER SAUCES

Make two sauces as described on p. 257, using a large green and a large yellow pepper. Add 1 tablespoon olive oil to each, with wine vinegar to taste. Cool, then put the sauces into two jugs. Holding one jug in each hand, pour from them both at once on to the serving plates, to create a 2-colour effect. Arrange each avocado half on the plate where the 2 sauces meet.

HALVING AN AVOCADO

Using a stainless steel knife, cut each avocado lengthways, cutting as far in as the large central stone. Then, holding the avocado in both hands, twist the two cut halves in opposite directions to part them. Ease out the stone using your fingers, or a knife point, and take off the skin with the help of a sharp knife. Sometimes the skin strips off easily, other times you may have to peel it off thinly with the knife.

Pears with Piquant Cream Dressing

The pears for this recipe need to be perfectly
ripe, so that they slice like butter. If they are a
bit on the hard side when you buy them, they
will ripen up if left in a fruit bowl for a day or
two.

SERVES 4

150 ml/5 fl oz whipping or non-
  dairy cream
4 tablespoons plain or vegan
  yogurt
1–2 teaspoons tarragon or wine
  vinegar
a little sugar
salt and freshly ground black
  pepper

2 Comice pears
lemon juice

TO GARNISH
pink peppercorns
6 tarragon sprigs

TO SERVE
tender lettuce leaves

1 Whisk the whipping or non-dairy cream until thick, then add
the yogurt and 1 teaspoon vinegar and whisk again.
2 Add a little sugar, salt and pepper to taste, and the remaining
teaspoon of vinegar if liked.
3 Give the mixture a final whisking, so that it holds its shape.
4 Halve the pears, then carefully remove the cores and peel.
Brush the pears all over with lemon juice.
5 Put a lettuce leaf on each serving plate, then place a pear half
on top, cut-side down. Spoon the piquant cream mixture on top
and garnish each with a few pink peppercorns and a tarragon
sprig. Serve immediately.

Variations

CUCUMBER WITH PIQUANT CREAM

For this delicious version, replace the pear with 1 cucumber,
peeled and thinly sliced. Place the cucumber slices in a colander,
sprinkle with salt and leave for 30 minutes, then rinse and drain
well. Sprinkle with sugar, wine vinegar and salt (if necessary).
Divide the cucumber between the serving plates just before
serving. Top with the cream and garnish.

PEARS WITH ROQUEFORT CREAM

Use the Roquefort Dip mixture (p.221), instead of the piquant cream for an excellent (but non-vegan) version.

Linguine with Tomatoes, Basil and Cream [V]

A delicious and easy first course, excellent
before a main course of summer vegetables.

SERVES 4

225 g/8 oz green linguine
1 bunch spring onions, trimmed
  and chopped
25 g/1 oz butter or vegan
  margarine
450 g/1 lb firm tomatoes, skinned
  (p.108), de-seeded and chopped

150 ml/5 fl oz single or non-dairy
  cream
salt and freshly ground black
  pepper
TO GARNISH
1–2 tablespoons chopped fresh
  basil

1 Cook the linguine in a large saucepan as described on p.72, until *al dente*. Drain the pasta in a colander immediately.
2 Meanwhile fry the spring onion gently in the butter or vegan margarine in a large saucepan for 2–3 minutes, then add the tomatoes and cook for a further 1–2 minutes. Stir in the cream, remove from the heat and keep warm.
3 Add the pasta to the tomato and cream mixture. Season to taste with salt and pepper, then serve in heated deep plates, each portion sprinkled with a little chopped fresh basil.

Salad of Feuille de Chêne, Chèvre Cheese and Walnuts with Walnut Vinaigrette

This is very quick to make and delicious before
a main course of pasta, for a quick supper.

SERVES 4

1 head feuille de chêne
1 medium firm Chèvre cheese,
    about 2·5 cm/1 inch in diameter,
    sliced into circles, or soft goat's
    cheese, cut into cubes

1 quantity Walnut Vinaigrette
    (p.229)
4 tablespoons chopped walnuts
TO GARNISH
lovage sprigs

1 Wash the feuille de chêne and shake, pat or spin dry. Divide
among 4 individual serving plates, tearing the leaves in half if
necessary to fit, and putting a few curly pieces in the centre.
Place the Chèvre cheese circles or goat's cheese cubes on top of
the feuille de chêne.

2 Just before serving drizzle a little of the Walnut Vinaigrette
over the top and sprinkle with the chopped walnuts and garnish
with lovage.

Variation

SALADE TIÈDE

Arrange the feuille de chêne and walnuts on the plates as
described. Just before serving, grill the Chèvre cheese, on a
lightly-oiled baking sheet, until melting, and add to the feuille
de chêne and walnuts. Serve the vinaigrette separately at the
table.

PHYLLO PASTRY

Fresh phyllo pastry can be
bought from Greek or Middle
Eastern shops; frozen phyllo
pastry, which works just as well,
can also be bought from ethnic
shops and many large
supermarkets. Frozen phyllo
usually comes in 400-g/14-oz
packets, containing around 16
sheets pastry. Allow the frozen
phyllo to thaw in its packet in the
fridge for up to 2 days.

Flaky Spinach and Fennel Pastries

Crisp golden triangles of phyllo pastry
enclosing a tasty filling. Serve them with
Soured Cream Dressing (p.233).

MAKES 20

8 sheets phyllo pastry
75 g/3 oz butter or vegan
   margarine, melted

FOR THE FILLING
1 onion, peeled and finely chopped
1 tablespoon olive oil
225 g/8 oz cooked fresh spinach,
   well-drained and chopped, or

frozen spinach, thawed and
squeezed as dry as possible
2 tablespoons chopped parsley
1 teaspoon fennel seed
salt and freshly ground black
   pepper

TO GARNISH
parsley sprigs

1 First make the filling. Fry the onion in the olive oil in a large saucepan until soft but not browned, then add the cooked spinach, chopped parsley and fennel seed. Mix well, then season the mixture to taste with salt and pepper.

2 Preheat the oven to 190c/375f/Gas Mark 5.

3 Unroll the sheets of phyllo pastry and spread them out flat in a pile with a damp cloth over them.

4 Take 1 phyllo pastry sheet, spread it out on a board and brush the top surface all over with the melted butter or vegan margarine. Lay another phyllo pastry sheet on top, and brush with more butter or vegan margarine, then make 4 equally spaced cuts from one short end of the phyllo to the other so that you end up with 5 long strips.

5 Place a teaspoon of the filling about 2·5 cm/1 inch from the top of one of the strips and fold one of the top corners over it, making a triangular shape. Then fold the triangle down from the base, and then at an angle again, and continue in this way until you end up with a neat layered triangle. Place on a baking sheet.

6 Continue with the rest of the phyllo and filling in this way, until they are all used up, then brush the triangles all over with butter or vegan margarine. Bake for about 15 minutes, until the pastry is golden-brown and crisp, and the filling piping hot. Serve immediately, garnished with parsley sprigs.

Marinated Vegetables

V

This fragrantly spiced dish makes an excellent
first course, or it can be served as a light lunch.
Some warm crusty bread goes well with it.

SERVES 6

2 tablespoons olive oil
1 large onion, peeled and chopped
2 large garlic cloves, crushed
1 medium cauliflower, trimmed,
  washed and broken into florets
350 g/12 oz French beans, trimmed
  and cut into 2·5-cm/1-inch
  pieces
225 g/8 oz button mushrooms,
  washed and cut into even-sized
  pieces

1 tablespoon coriander seeds,
  crushed
1-2 tablespoons lemon juice
salt and freshly ground black
  pepper

TO GARNISH
chopped parsley
black olives

1 Heat the oil in a large saucepan, then add the onion and fry
gently for 5 minutes, without browning.
2 Add the garlic, cauliflower and French beans and fry gently
for a further 2–3 minutes, stirring often, then add the
mushrooms and coriander seeds and fry for a further 2 minutes.
3 Remove from the heat, stir in the lemon juice, and salt and
pepper to taste. Cool, then chill. Serve garnished with parsley
and olives.

Variation

MARINATED MUSHROOMS
Make as above, just using 700 g/1½ lb baby button mushrooms.

Salads

*Another versatile category, salads can be as
light and refreshing or as substantial and filling
as you choose; they can be first courses,
accompaniments or, if they are substantial
enough, and perhaps served with bread,
potatoes or rice, the main course itself. They are
particularly healthy and slimming, too, if you
use a light dressing or a richer one in
moderation. This section contains a variety of
salads for different occasions, as well as a
selection of useful and easy dressings. When
making salads, you will get excellent results if
you use the freshest ingredients you can find and
aim for a good contrast in colours, textures and
flavours.*

Vinaigrette [V]

Exact proportions for this basic French dressing
are very flexible. If you use good ingredients
and are generous with the oil and fairly mean
with the vinegar you can't go wrong!

MAKES ABOUT 60 ML/2-3 FL OZ

1 teaspoon salt
2 teaspoons red wine vinegar

freshly ground black pepper
3 tablespoons olive oil

Whisk all the ingredients together until thoroughly blended.

Variations

WALNUT VINAIGRETTE
Make as described, using 3-4 tablespoons walnut oil.

GARLIC VINAIGRETTE

Add a crushed garlic clove to the mixture, blending well.

MUSTARD VINAIGRETTE

Start by mixing 2–3 teaspoons Dijon mustard with the salt and vinegar, then gradually mix in the oil, for this thick and tangy version.

HERB VINAIGRETTE

Add 1–2 teaspoons chopped fresh herbs.

DRESSING TIPS

☐ A quick and easy way to make a vinaigrette-type dressing is to put all the ingredients into a screwtop jar and shake until emulsified. If you only need a little of the dressing, the jar makes a convenient storage container for the fridge. Let the dressing 'come to' at room temperature for 30 minutes or so before use, then give it a shake to re-emulsify the ingredients.

☐ Although you can make dressing in bulk and store in the fridge, it only takes a moment to make, and I think it's better made fresh when you need it. If you are making the salad in a bowl, it saves time and washing up to make the dressing straight into the bowl. If it's a delicate, leafy salad, and you are not planning to serve it straight away, put a pair of crossed salad servers in the bowl, then put the salad in on top. The salad servers will keep the salad above the dressing until you are ready to toss and serve the salad, preventing it from getting soggy.

Avocado Dressing

A delicious vegan dressing for salads. It can be diluted with a little water to make a thinner dressing.

MAKES ABOUT 200 ML/7 FL OZ

1 ripe avocado, halved, peeled and
    stone removed (p.223)
1 tablespoon lemon juice
1 tablespoon white wine vinegar

1 teaspoon Dijon mustard
salt and freshly ground black
    pepper
dash of Tabasco sauce

1 Put the avocado into a blender or food processor with the lemon juice, wine vinegar and Dijon mustard and blend to a smooth cream.

2 Season to taste with salt, pepper, and a drop or two of Tabasco. Taste and add more Tabasco if wished.

Mayonnaise

Home-made mayonnaise is a delicious treat, is not difficult to make and will keep for at least a week in a covered container in the fridge (but it won't freeze).

MAKES ABOUT 225 ML/8 FL OZ

2 large egg yolks	2 teaspoons white wine vinegar
¼ teaspoon salt	2 teaspoons lemon juice
¼ teaspoon mustard powder	200 ml/7 fl oz cold-pressed
2–3 grindings black pepper	sunflower oil

1 Put the egg yolks, salt, mustard, pepper, vinegar and lemon juice into a bowl and whisk lightly until combined.

2 Add the oil, a drop at a time, whisking well after each addition.

3 When you have added about half the oil, the mixture will emulsify and start to look like mayonnaise. At this point you can add the oil a little more quickly, still whisking well.

4 Continue until the mixture is really thick, then taste and adjust the seasoning if necessary.

5 If the mayonnaise seems a bit on the thick side, you can thin it by beating in a teaspoon or two of boiling water.

Variations

BLENDER METHOD

Mayonnaise can be speedily made in a blender or food processor. Put in the egg yolks, seasonings, vinegar and lemon juice and blend for 1 minute. Then gradually add the oil, drop by drop, through the top of the goblet. When you have added about half the oil and the mixture has thickened, you can add the rest more quickly, in a thin stream.

MAYONNAISE WITH GREEN PEPPERCORNS

Add 1 tablespoon drained and rinsed pickled green peppercorns to the finished mayonnaise for a pungent, green-flecked version. Makes an excellent sauce for slices of cold Quick Savoury Nut Loaf (p.351), or Savoury Lentil Loaf (p.318).

AÏOLI

For this very delectable garlic-flavoured mayonnaise, blend 6–8 peeled garlic cloves in the blender or food processor, then proceed exactly as for mayonnaise. Makes a wonderful dip for crudités.

MAYONNAISE WITH GREEN HERBS

Add 2–4 tablespoons finely chopped fresh herbs to the mayonnaise. You can use a mixture of herbs, such as parsley, chives and another herb such as basil, tarragon, coriander or mint. Or use just one herb (and only 2 tablespoons), to complement the dish you're going to serve with the mayonnaise. Fresh coriander mayonnaise goes well with grain and lentil salads, and basil mayonnaise with a tomato-based mixture.

MANGO CHUTNEY MAYONNAISE

A good variation for serving with cold lentil loaf or nut burgers. Stir 2–4 tablespoons mango chutney into the mayonnaise, first chopping up the mango.

⩔ *Cream and Mustard Dressing*

This makes an excellent alternative to
mayonnaise, especially for vegans if non-dairy
cream is used.

MAKES 200 ML/7 FL OZ

1 tablespoon Dijon mustard
2 tablespoons white wine vinegar
150 ml/5 fl oz whipping or non-
dairy cream

salt and freshly ground black
pepper

1 Mix the mustard and vinegar together in a small bowl, then add the whipping or non-dairy cream.
2 Whisk until thick, then season to taste with salt and pepper.

Soured Cream Dressing

MAKES 150 ML/5 FL OZ

150 ml/5 fl oz soured cream   *salt and freshly ground black pepper*

1 Just stir the soured cream and season to taste with salt and pepper, for a simple yet delicious dressing.

Variations

SOURED CREAM AND CHIVE DRESSING

Add 2 tablespoons snipped chives to the soured cream.

SOURED CREAM OR YOGURT AND HERB DRESSING

Add 2 tablespoons chopped fresh green herbs – mint, parsley, tarragon or basil, or a mixture of them all – to the soured cream or yogurt.

VEGAN YOGURT AND MINT DRESSING

Use vegan yogurt instead of soured cream and add 2 tablespoons chopped mint. Mix well.

LOW-CALORIE SALAD DRESSINGS

☐ Sprinkle vegetables with lemon juice or rice vinegar, seasoning and chopped fresh herbs or finely chopped onion.

☐ Use fresh orange juice to dress root vegetable salads: grated carrot and grated raw beetroot are particularly good with orange.

☐ Plain yogurt, or the Yogurt and Herb Dressing above.

☐ Lemon or lime juice makes a good dressing for grated cabbage salad, perked up with herbs, seasoning and perhaps a dash of Dijon mustard.

☐ For a low(er)-calorie mayonnaise, mix mayonnaise (home-made or bought) with an equal (or even double) quantity of plain yogurt.

Sweet Pepper Dressing

This light, translucent dressing is another one which makes an excellent vegan alternative to mayonnaise.

MAKES ABOUT 200 ML/7 FL OZ

1 large red pepper, about 175 g/
   6 oz
50–75 ml/2–3 fl oz olive oil

2 teaspoons wine vinegar or
   raspberry vinegar
salt and freshly ground black
   pepper

1 Put the whole pepper into a saucepan and half cover with water. Bring to the boil, then simmer for 15–20 minutes, until the pepper is very tender. Test by piercing it with a fork.
2 Drain the pepper and remove the stalk and seeds. Purée the pepper in a blender or food processor, then add the oil and blend again. You should have a thickish scarlet emulsion, like a mayonnaise. Gently stir in the vinegar and salt and pepper to taste.

Red Kidney Bean Salad

A bean salad looks colourful and attractive and contrasts well with other salads if you're serving a selection. It is filling and, served simply, with warm rolls or wholewheat pitta bread and a little lettuce or watercress, makes an excellent quick meal.

SERVES 4

225 g/8 oz red kidney beans,
   soaked, cooked and drained
   (p.57), or 2 × 425-g/15-oz cans
   red kidney beans, drained
2 tablespoons finely chopped
   onion

2 tablespoons tomato purée
1 quantity Vinaigrette (p.229)
salt and freshly ground black
   pepper
a pinch of sugar
1 tablespoon chopped parsley

1 Put the red kidney beans into a bowl with the onion. Add the tomato purée and vinaigrette and mix well.

2 Season the beans with salt, pepper and sugar. Mix again, then leave for 2–3 hours for the beans to absorb the flavours. Sprinkle with chopped parsley.

Variations

RED KIDNEY BEAN AND SWEETCORN SALAD

Make the salad as described, adding 100 g/4 oz cooked fresh or frozen sweetcorn kernels, for a pretty colour contrast.

RED KIDNEY BEAN AND WALNUT SALAD

Make the salad as described, using either the basic vinaigrette or the walnut version, and adding 1 large coarsely grated carrot, 2 sliced celery sticks and 100 g/4 oz roughly chopped walnuts.

MULTICOLOUR BEAN SALAD

For this vibrantly coloured version, which is lovely for a party, use a mixture of beans in contrasting colours: red kidney beans, butter beans, cannellini beans, flageolet beans, black beans, black-eyed beans. Cook them separately, until tender, and make the salad as described above, but omit the tomato purée. Garnish with chopped parsley and coriander sprigs.

RED KIDNEY BEAN, HARICOT BEAN AND BLACK OLIVE SALAD

Use 100 g/4 oz red kidney beans and 100 g/4 oz haricot beans, soaked, cooked and drained, or a 425-g/15-oz can of red kidney beans and one of cannellini beans, drained. Omit the tomato purée and add 100 g/4 oz black olives to the mixture.

PULSE SALADS

Pulses – peas, beans and lentils – make excellent salads, filling and full of flavour. Particularly good are all members of the kidney bean family, including of course the red and black varieties; butter beans; continental, brown and puy lentils, and the always-delicious chick peas. A mixture of different colours, shapes and sizes gives a particularly attractive result, great for a buffet party.

Put the dressing on these salads – a vinaigrette is delicious – when the beans are freshly cooked, drained, but still hot. Add flavouring ingredients such as raw onion rings, chopped spring onions fresh chopped herbs, grated fresh ginger, garlic, black olives – the possibilities are wide. Leave to get cold, stirring the salad gently from time to time. The beans will absorb the full flavour of the dressing and any flavouring ingredients, resulting in a moist, shiny salad, full of flavour.

Continental Lentil and Walnut Salad

This makes an excellent winter salad, filling and satisfying.

SERVES 4

225 g/8 oz continental lentils, cooked and drained (p.57)
50 g/2 oz walnuts, chopped
1 garlic clove, crushed
1 bunch spring onions, trimmed and chopped

1 quantity Walnut Vinaigrette (p.229)
salt and freshly ground black pepper
TO GARNISH
1–2 tablespoons chopped parsley

1 Put the lentils into a bowl with the walnuts, garlic, onions and vinaigrette. Mix well, season with salt and pepper, then leave to marinate for several hours.
2 Put the salad into a serving bowl, then chill until needed. Sprinkle the parsley on top just before you serve the salad.

Variations

LENTIL, MUSHROOM AND WALNUT SALAD

Add 175–225 g/6–8 oz very fresh button mushrooms, washed, thinly sliced and sprinkled with 1–2 tablespoons lemon juice, to the mixture.

CONTINENTAL LENTIL, CARROT AND WALNUT SALAD

Add 1–2 coarsely grated carrots to the mixture for a good contrast of colour.

CONTINENTAL LENTIL, WALNUT AND ONION SALAD

Add a mild raw onion, peeled and sliced.

CONTINENTAL LENTIL, WALNUT AND EGG SALAD

For this excellent (but non-vegan) version, make the salad as described, put into a shallow bowl and surround with 2–4 hardboiled eggs cut into wedges.

Rice and Vegetable Salad ⬜V⬜

This is one of my favourite rice salads, and is especially effective if you make it in a ring.

SERVES 6 AS A MAIN COURSE SALAD, 10-12 AS
PART OF A MEAL WITH OTHER SALADS

225 g/8 oz long-grain brown rice
600 ml/1 pint water
1 garlic clove, crushed
1 onion, peeled and chopped
225 g/8 oz aubergine, washed and
    diced
1 small red pepper, de-seeded and
    chopped

2 tablespoons olive oil
1 large tomato, skinned (p.108)
    and chopped
a few drops of Tabasco sauce
salt and freshly ground black
    pepper
TO GARNISH
chopped parsley

1 Cook the rice in a heavy-based saucepan as described on p.64, then drain.

2 Meanwhile, fry the garlic, onion, aubergine and pepper in the oil for 10 minutes. Add the tomato and cook for a further 5 minutes.

3 Add the cooked rice to the vegetable mixture, together with a drop or two of Tabasco and season to taste with salt and pepper.

4 Cool, then sprinkle with parsley before serving.

RICE SALAD IDEAS

Rice salad is easy to make: just add the ingredients to the rice. The more contrast you can get in the ingredients you add, the better.

Choose from chopped raw onion or spring onion, small cubes of cucumber, chopped red or green pepper, sweetcorn kernels, cooked peas, small cubes of cooked carrot or coarsely grated raw carrot, finely chopped celery, raisins or sultanas, finely chopped dried apricots, chopped nuts, chopped skinned tomato, cooked beans, black olives, chopped fresh herbs.

Moisten the mixture with a little vinaigrette dressing or mayonnaise thinned with some milk.

MAKING A ROUND RICE SALAD MOULD

If you haven't a ring mould, make a round rice salad mould instead, using a cake tin or soufflé dish, lined with well-oiled foil. This mould looks pretty if you fry 6-7 small flat open mushrooms in oil and arrange these attractively in the base of the mould, black side down, before putting in the rice. Add the rice gently, to keep the pattern intact.

Any rice salad mixture can be moulded in this way. Make sure your serving plate is large enough, because the salad tends to crumble once it is cut.

To unmould the salad, slip a knife between the rice salad and the sides of the mould to loosen. Invert your serving dish on top of the rice mould. Then turn the mould and the serving dish over together. Give the mould a gentle shake to help the rice to slide out, and lift off the mould.

Variations

RICE SALAD RING

For this attractive moulded version, make the salad as described. Fry 6 flat or button mushrooms and place these gills side down in a 2–2·4 litre/3½–4 pint ring mould. Spoon the rice salad into the mould and press down. Leave until cold, then turn out and garnish with sprigs of watercress and flat or button mushrooms. Fill the centre with watercress, mayonnaise, sliced tomatoes, diced avocado, cold ratatouille, or any colourful mixture of salad ingredients that you fancy, if desired.

1. **Sunday Brunch** (Special Menu p.547)

2. **Spring Dinner Party** (Special Menu p.548)

3. Chilled Two-colour Soup (p.211)

4. Pasta Primavera (p.372)

5. Sushi (p.213) and Three-colour Layered Omelette (p.212)

6. Spinach Roulade with Curd Cheese and Pink Peppercorns
(p.338)

7. Moulded Layered Soufflé (p.336) and Spanish Omelette (p.331)

8. Vegetable Hotpot (p.301) and Spinach Gnocchi (p.305)

9. Multicolour Bean Salad (p.235) and Rice Salad Ring (p.238)

10. Waldorf Salad (p.250) and Greek Salad (p.252)

11. **Summer Celebration** (Special Menu p.549)

12. **Quick and Easy Supper** (Special Menu p.550)

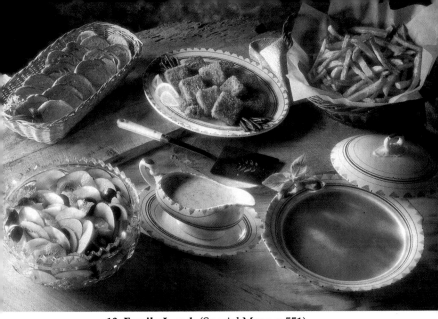

13. **Family Lunch** (Special Menu p.551)

14. **Midsummer Wedding** (Special Menu p.552)

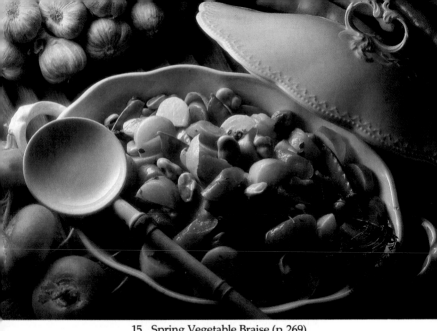

15. Spring Vegetable Braise (p.269)

16. Sweet and Sour
    Vegetable Stir-fry
    with Almonds
    (p.299)

RICE SALAD WITH BEANSPROUTS AND WILD RICE

For this particularly good version, cook 50 g/2 oz wild rice with the long-grain rice, using 750 ml/1¼ pints water. Omit the aubergine and tomato. Fry the onion with the garlic and pepper, then add to the rice, together with 350 g/12 oz beansprouts.

Tabbouleh

This is a Middle Eastern salad based on bulgur wheat. Although it's substantial, the herbs and lemon juice give it a light, refreshing flavour and it's a good hot-weather salad.

SERVES 4-6

225 g/8 oz bulgur wheat
600 ml/1 pint boiling water
4 tablespoons lemon juice
2 tablespoons olive oil
8 tablespoons chopped parsley
8 tablespoons chopped spring onion
a 10-cm/4-inch piece of cucumber, diced
4 tablespoons chopped fresh mint

4 tomatoes, skinned (p.108) and finely chopped
salt and freshly ground black pepper
TO GARNISH
lemon slices
tomato slices
black olives
mint sprig

1 Put the bulgur wheat into a bowl and cover with boiling water; leave for 10–15 minutes, until the water is absorbed.
2 Add the lemon juice, oil, parsley, spring onion, cucumber, mint and tomato. Mix well and season to taste with salt and pepper. Spoon the mixture into a large, shallow serving dish. Garnish the salad with lemon and tomato slices, black olives and mint.

Variations

TABBOULEH RING

To make a moulded ring, like the Rice Salad Ring (above), press the mixture into a 2–2·4-litre/3½–4-pint ring mould, press down firmly, and leave until cold. Then turn out and fill the centre with some watercress, black olives, or thinly sliced tomatoes.

Lumache with Spring Onions, Fennel and Mayonnaise

Served on individual bowls or plates, this salad
makes a light, refreshing first course.

SERVES 4-6

225 g/8 oz lumache (snail-shaped
   pasta)
8 tablespoons Mayonnaise (p.231)
8 tablespoons plain yogurt
1 bunch spring onions, trimmed
   and finely chopped

salt and freshly ground black
   pepper

TO GARNISH
2 tablespoons chopped fennel herb

1 Cook the lumache in a large saucepan as described on p.73,
until *al dente*. Drain immediately.
2 Add the mayonnaise, yogurt, spring onion and salt and
pepper to taste. Mix well and leave to cool completely.
3 Transfer to a serving bowl or individual plates and sprinkle
with the fennel.

Pasta Bow Salad

This is a filling, main course salad, good with
some crusty bread.

SERVES 4

225 g/8 oz pasta bows
1 quantity Vinaigrette (p.229)
1 red pepper, de-seeded and
   chopped
½ cucumber, washed and diced

50 g/2 oz black olives
175 g/6 oz red Leicester or red
   Cheshire cheese, diced
TO GARNISH (OPTIONAL)
½ bunch watercress

1 Cook the pasta in a large saucepan as described on p.72, until
al dente. Drain thoroughly and put into a bowl. Add the
vinaigrette, pepper, cucumber and olives and mix well. Leave
until the pasta is cold, then mix in the red Leicester or red
Cheshire cheese.

2 Put the salad into a serving bowl and garnish with the watercress divided into sprigs, if liked.

Variations

VEGAN PASTA SALAD

Use 1 large scraped, grated carrot and 100 g/4 oz roasted cashew nuts, peanuts or chopped walnuts or pecan nuts instead of the diced cheese.

Chicory, Watercress and Walnut Salad

An example of one of the many varieties of
green salad; this is particularly good with
cheese dishes. Other leafy salad ingredients can
be used as available: endive, laitue frisée,
dandelion and spinach leaves and
lamb's lettuce.

SERVES 4

2 heads chicory, washed
1 bunch watercress, washed

1 quantity Vinaigrette or Walnut
Vinaigrette (p.229)
50 g/2 oz chopped walnuts

1 See that the chicory and watercress leaves do not have any excess water clinging to them. If there's time, wash and dry them in advance and put them into a polythene bag in the salad compartment of the fridge, to chill and crisp.
2 Put the dressing into a salad bowl, cross the salad servers on top, then put in the chicory, watercress and walnuts. Turn the leaves in the dressing at the last minute, just before serving.

Variations

CHICORY, WATERCRESS AND ORANGE SALAD

Make as described, substituting 2 large oranges, peeled and cut into segments, for the walnuts. Hold the oranges over a bowl as you cut them, to catch the juice. Use some of this to make the vinaigrette dressing for the salad, instead of the vinegar.

This is a particularly good accompaniment to hot pulse and

nut dishes; or, topped with a blue cheese dressing, and served with warm wholewheat rolls, it makes a good light lunch or supper dish on its own.

Favourite Coleslaw

This traditional favourite is a useful salad because it can be made ahead of time. It goes particularly well with crisp nut burgers.

SERVES 4

225 g/8 oz white cabbage, finely shredded
100 g/4 oz carrots, scraped and coarsely grated
1 tablespoon chopped chives
1 small green pepper, de-seeded and chopped

2 tablespoons plain yogurt or water
2 tablespoons Mayonnaise (p.231)
salt and freshly ground black pepper
TO GARNISH
chive tassels

1 Put the cabbage, carrot, chives and green pepper into a large bowl. Add the yogurt or water, mayonnaise and salt and pepper to taste. Garnish with chives.

Variation

CARAWAY COLESLAW

Make as described, adding 1 teaspoon caraway seeds, to give the salad a mid-European flavour.

 # Sweet Carrot and Fennel Salad

SERVES 4

2 bulbs fennel
450 g/1 lb carrots, scraped and coarsely grated
½ quantity Vinaigrette (p.229)

salt and freshly ground black pepper
a little sugar
TO GARNISH
fennel leaves

1 Remove any tough outer leaves from the fennel. Cut off and reserve any feathery green leaves. (If you find the flavour of fennel rather strong, plunge the bulbs into boiling water for 2 minutes before slicing.) Slice the fennel and put it into a bowl with the grated carrot.

2 Add the vinaigrette and mix well. Season to taste with salt and pepper, then add a little sugar to taste, if liked. I think this touch of sweetness enhances the flavour of the carrot and fennel pleasantly. Garnish with fennel.

Variation

SWEET CARROT, FENNEL AND RED PEPPER SALAD

Make as described, adding a small, red pepper, de-seeded and chopped, to the ingredients. This is a good salad for serving with a creamy pasta dish.

Scandinavian-style Cucumber Salad

Serve with rich dishes, or as a contrast to
creamy salads in a buffet selection.

SERVES 4–6

1 large cucumber, peeled and sliced	1 tablespoon white mustard seeds
salt	2 tablespoons chopped fresh dill
1 onion, peeled and thinly sliced	freshly ground black pepper
2 tablespoons white wine vinegar	TO GARNISH
1 teaspoon sugar	1–2 dill sprigs

1 Put the cucumber slices into a sieve or colander and sprinkle with salt. Set a weight on top and leave for 30 minutes, to draw out the excess liquid. Then squeeze and pat dry on kitchen paper.

2 Put the cucumber into a bowl and add the onion, vinegar, sugar, mustard seeds, dill and pepper. Stir well.

3 Leave to marinate for at least 2 hours. Garnish with dill before serving.

DRESSING A SALAD

Some salads, such as pulse and grain salads and those made from cooked vegetables and firm vegetables, such as cabbage, are ideal if dressed in advance and left for the flavours to blend. Others, especially delicate leafy mixtures, are best dressed at the last minute, even at the table, just before serving.

For a really good salad, leafy ingredients need to be dried of excess water. This can be done by putting them in a salad shaker or drier, or by patting them gently in a clean, absorbent cloth or kitchen paper. I find a salad drier, consisting of a perforated basket which spins the salad inside a container, so removing the water, most useful. If there is time, wash and dry the leaves, then put them into a polythene bag and chill them in the fridge for 30-60 minutes to crisp.

Avocado and Mushroom Salad

A useful salad for serving with hot pasta or
jacket potatoes, to turn them into a meal –
quick, simple and good.

SERVES 4

2 avocado pears, halved, peeled,
    stones removed (p.106) and
    diced
2 tablespoons lemon juice
450 g/1 lb small white button
    mushrooms, washed and sliced

1 quantity Garlic Vinaigrette
    (p.230)
2 tablespoons snipped chives
salt and freshly ground black
    pepper

1 Put the avocado into a large bowl and sprinkle with the lemon juice. Add the mushrooms, together with the vinaigrette and the chives.

2 Check the seasoning and add more – especially pepper – if needed.

Variations

AVOCADO, LETTUCE AND TOMATO SALAD

Make as described, replacing the mushrooms with a small round lettuce, torn into pieces, and 4 skinned and chopped tomatoes. Mix well with the vinaigrette and the chives.

AVOCADO AND PALM HEART SALAD

Make the salad as described, then drain a 425-g/15-oz can of palm hearts, slice them into thin circles and mix them into the salad.

Technicolour Cabbage Salad

SERVES 4–6

350 g/12 oz white cabbage, finely
    shredded
2 large carrots, scraped and
    coarsely grated
1 medium red pepper, de-seeded
    and chopped

1 onion, peeled and finely chopped
2 tablespoons chopped parsley
50 g/2 oz raisins or black olives
1 quantity Vinaigrette (p.229)
50 g/2 oz roasted peanuts or
    sunflower seeds

1 Put the shredded white cabbage into a bowl with the grated carrots and the chopped pepper, onion and parsley. Stir in the raisins or black olives.
2 Add the vinaigrette and stir well to coat all the ingredients.
3 Add the nuts or sunflower seeds just before serving.

Radish, Cucumber and Arame Salad [V]

Don't be put off by the seaweed – arame – in this recipe. With a sweet and sour dressing, it makes a very good salad, full of nutrients, and looks pretty with the cucumber and radishes. Excellent for serving with Japanese-style rice dishes.

SERVES 4

15 g/½ oz arame
½ cucumber, peeled and diced
1 bunch radishes, trimmed and
    sliced

1 teaspoon sea salt
1 teaspoon sugar
2 tablespoons rice vinegar

1 Rinse the arame under the cold tap, then soak in cold water for 5 minutes. Drain the arame, place in a saucepan, cover with

water, bring to the boil, and simmer gently for 10 minutes. Drain
and leave the arame to cool.
2 Add the cucumber, radishes, sea salt, sugar and rice vinegar to
the cooled arame and mix well to combine all the ingredients.

Variation

RADISH, CUCUMBER AND HIZIKI SEAWEED SALAD

Make this in the same way, using hiziki, another kind of
seaweed, instead of the arame. Prepare the hiziki as described
on p.117.

V

Japanese Flower Salad

This pretty salad makes an excellent
accompaniment to a rich main course such as
Cheese Soufflé (p.334), Cheese Fondue (p.325)
or a creamy flan. Serve Vinaigrette (p.229)
separately. If you have the time to cut the
vegetables as suggested, it adds to the charm of
this salad.

SERVES 4

*1 medium head laitue frissée,
leaves separated, washed and
broken into even-sized pieces*
*1 medium head radiccio, leaves
separated, washed and broken
into even-sized pieces*
12 radishes, cut into roses (below)
*12 cherry tomatoes, skinned
(p.108)*

*2 large carrots, scraped and cut
into 8 chrysanthemums (below)*
*a 10-cm/4-inch piece of daikon
(mooli), scraped and cut into 8
chrysanthemums (below), or 8
cauliflower florets*
*8 spring onions, trimmed and
curled*
a few parsley sprigs

1 On 4 individual plates, or in 4 small shallow baskets lined
with coloured napkins, make a base of mixed laitue frissée and
radiccio.
2 Arrange the radishes, tomatoes, carrot and daikon flowers, or
cauliflower florets, attractively amongst the mixed leaves on the
plates.
3 Garnish with the spring onions and parsley sprigs.

DECORATIVE SALADS

Radish Flowers
Cut a thin petal of skin from the tip of the radish to the stem, and repeat, making 5 petals in all. To make a rose, cut a slice off the root end. Then make 3 small cuts round that before making the petals. Drop the radish flowers into iced water for the petals to open.

Carrot and Daikon Flowers
Cut the carrot or daikon into 2·5-cm/1-inch rectangular blocks. Round off the corners slightly. Hold the block pointing upwards between two chopsticks and cut across first one way then the other, cutting down as far as the chopsticks. Sprinkle salt into the criss-cross cuts and leave for 30 minutes, then rinse. Gently open up the cuts with your fingers to create a chrysanthemum effect.

ROOT SALADS

Root vegetables, carrots, swedes, celeriac and raw beetroot make good, substantial salads. They can be made several hours in advance if convenient, as they will not spoil. The effect can be varied according to how coarsely you grate the roots, and the dressing used. Little heaps of different coloured root vegetables on a base of lettuce, with perhaps a creamy dip or dressing in the centre, and some parsley sprigs or black olives to decorate, make a colourful and vitamin-rich lunch. Or the roots can be served separately, as part of a mixed salad selection. Here are some good combinations:

☐ Grated raw beetroot and apple, dressed with orange juice or Herb Vinaigrette (p.230).
☐ Grated raw beetroot and sliced raw onion rings, with Vinaigrette (p.229).
☐ Grated swede with chopped dates, dressed with a mixture of yogurt and Mayonnaise (p.231)
☐ Celeriac, cut into julienne strips, dressed with Mustard Vinaigrette (p.230) or Soured Cream Dressing (p.233)
☐ Young turnips, coarsely grated, mixed with Vinaigrette (p.229) and raisins or chopped parsley
☐ Coarsely grated raw carrot with apple and celery, dressed with orange juice

Variation

Other vegetables of your choice can be used in this salad, as well as edible flowers, such as nasturtiums and borage. Garnish with parsley sprigs or flowers.

Potato Salad

New potatoes, cooked in their skins, as
described, are specially good for this salad,
though I make it all the year round and find it
works well with old potatoes: the secret is to
undercook them slightly, so that they still have
a bit of bite to them and hold together well.
And if you can get hold of an interesting, well
flavoured variety, they will make this salad
extra good.

SERVES 4

450 g/1 lb small even-sized
  potatoes, scrubbed
3 tablespoons Mayonnaise (p.231)
3 tablespoons plain yogurt or
  soured cream

salt and freshly ground black
  pepper
2 tablespoons snipped chives,
  chopped spring onion or parsley

1 Cook the potatoes in boiling water to cover, until they are just tender when pierced with a knife – about 15 minutes, depending on the size of the potatoes.
2 Drain the potatoes immediately they are done and, if you wish, slip off the skins with a sharp knife. (Usually I prefer to leave the skins on.)
3 Dice the potatoes if necessary and put them into a bowl with the mayonnaise and yogurt or soured cream. It's fine – indeed, best – to do this while they are still hot.
4 Leave to get completely cold, then check the seasoning and serve, sprinkled with the chives, spring onion or parsley.

Variations

PINK POTATO SALAD

Make as described, adding 1–2 tablespoons cooked and diced beetroot to the mixture. This will turn the whole salad a pretty pink, making this a good salad for serving with a pale dish, such as French Onion Flan (p.386)

POTATO SALAD WITH VINAIGRETTE DRESSING

A good vegan version. Use ½–1 quantity of Vinaigrette (p.229) instead of the mayonnaise. A bunch of radishes, trimmed and sliced, or a little chopped red pepper, are good added to this, for extra colour.

Green-Bean Salad with Radiccio

This is a light salad, made from fresh rather than dried beans, and the different shades of green look pretty against the red of the radiccio leaves. This salad goes excellently with Cheese Soufflé (p.334) for a nourishing lunch or supper.

SERVES 4-6

225 g/8 oz frozen broad beans
225 g/8 oz fresh or frozen French beans, trimmed and cut into 2·5-cm/1-inch lengths
½ quantity Vinaigrette (p.229)
salt and freshly ground black pepper

2 tablespoons chopped summer savory or other fresh herbs (such as chives or mint)
1 medium head radiccio, leaves washed and separated

1 Cook the broad and French beans together in a little boiling water for 5–10 minutes, until just tender and still crisp. Drain well.
2 Put the hot beans into a bowl with the vinaigrette, salt, pepper and herbs. Mix well, then leave until cool.
3 Just before serving, add the radiccio to the beans and stir gently to mix all the ingredients.

Tsatsiki

This Middle Eastern salad is a good accompaniment to cooked grain dishes. It also makes a refreshing starter, served on small plates and eaten with strips of warmed pitta bread.

SERVES 4–6 AS A SIDE SALAD, 6–8 AS A FIRST
COURSE

1 large cucumber, peeled and cut into small dice
salt
225 g/8 oz thick plain yogurt, preferably Greek, or vegan yogurt

4 tablespoons chopped fresh mint
2 garlic cloves, crushed
freshly ground black pepper
TO GARNISH
mild paprika pepper
mint leaves

1 Put the cucumber into a sieve or colander and sprinkle with salt. Set a weight on top and leave for 30 minutes, to draw out excess liquid which would dilute the dressing too much. Then squeeze and pat dry on kitchen paper.
2 Put the cucumber into a bowl and add the yogurt, mint, garlic and a grinding of pepper. Stir well, taste and add more salt and pepper if necessary. Put into a shallow serving dish, sprinkle with paprika and garnish with mint leaves.

Waldorf Salad

This classic salad goes well with cheese dishes and slices of cold nut or lentil loaf.

SERVES 4

3 red-skinned apples, cored and diced
2 tablespoons lemon juice
3 celery sticks, chopped
4 tablespoons Mayonnaise (p.231)

4 tablespoons plain yogurt
50 g/2 oz chopped walnuts
salt and freshly ground black pepper

1 Put the apple into a bowl, sprinkle with the lemon juice and mix well. Add the celery, mayonnaise, yogurt, walnuts and seasoning to taste.

2 Serve immediately; or, if the salad has to wait for any length of time, leave out the walnuts until just before serving.

Variation

GRAPE, CELERY, PEAR AND ALMOND SALAD

Replace the apples with 225 g/8 oz mixed black or red and white grapes, halved and seeded, and 2 ripe pears, peeled, cored and diced. Use 50 g/2 oz toasted flaked almonds instead of the walnuts.

Vegetarian Salade Niçoise

Served with crusty French bread, this makes an excellent light lunch, or, in smaller portions, a refreshing first course.

SERVES 4 AS A MAIN COURSE, 6–8 AS A STARTER

1 large lettuce, washed, torn into
  pieces and shaken dry
1 medium onion, peeled and sliced
  into rings
450 g/1 lb firm tomatoes, washed
  and sliced

5 hardboiled eggs, quartered
450 g/1 lb cooked French beans,
  cut into 2·5-cm/1-inch lengths
12 black olives
2 tablespoons chopped parsley
1 quantity Vinaigrette (p.229)

1 Line a large serving plate with the lettuce, then arrange all the ingredients, except the vinaigrette, on top, not too neatly.

2 Spoon a little of the vinaigrette over the salad just before serving. Serve the rest of the vinaigrette separately in a small jug.

Variation

VEGAN SALADE NIÇOISE

Use the drained contents of 1 × 425-g/15-oz can butter beans, or 100 g/4 oz butter beans, soaked, cooked and drained, instead of the hardboiled eggs cut into quarters.

Greek Salad

Instant nostalgia for anyone with happy
memories of Greece, this makes a substantial
salad for 4 people or a side salad for 8. A
generous portion of Greek salad, accompanied
by warm wholewheat pitta bread or rolls,
makes a delicious light lunch or supper.

SERVES 4 AS A MAIN COURSE, 8 AS A SIDE SALAD

1 large, mild onion, peeled and
  thinly sliced
1 quantity Vinaigrette (p.229)
450 g/1 lb tomatoes, skinned if
  necessary (p.108), and sliced
1 cucumber, diced

100 g/4 oz black olives (optional)
225 g/8 oz feta cheese or other
  white, crumbly cheese such as
  Wensleydale or Cheshire, diced
TO GARNISH (OPTIONAL)
chopped parsley

1 Put the onion into a bowl with the vinaigrette: mix well, then
leave to stand for 30–60 minutes, to allow the onion to soften in
the dressing. Stir occasionally. (If you find the raw onion too
strong, blanch it first by covering with boiling water, leaving for
2 minutes, then draining.)
2 Add the tomatoes, cucumber, olives, if used, and cheese,
stirring gently to distribute all the ingredients. Divide the salad
among the individual serving plates and sprinkle each portion
with chopped parsley, if wished.

Sauces

Sauces can add the final, delicious touch to a dish, often contributing colour as well as moisture; they also form an integral part of some vegetarian dishes such as Aubergine and Pasta Charlotte (p.381) and Stuffed Cabbage Rolls in Coconut Sauce (p.294). A good sauce, such as Fresh Tomato (below), Pesto (p.257) or Cheese Sauce (p.261) can turn plain freshly cooked pasta or vegetables into a quick and tasty meal. When making your favourite sauces, it's worth cooking extra portions which can be frozen. The sauces in this chapter are the ones which I consider the most useful both as components of recipes and for serving with other dishes.

Fresh Tomato Sauce

$\boxed{V}$

I find this fresh, lightly cooked tomato sauce one of the most useful. Its flavour and bright colour go well with many savoury dishes, and it's excellent with pasta and many cooked vegetables, especially pale ones like cauliflower. Another advantage is that, unlike many sauces, it is very low in calories. This sauce is definitely best when made with fresh tomatoes: canned tomatoes just don't give the same result. If you have to use these, make Italian Tomato Sauce (p.254) instead.

SERVES 6

1 onion, peeled and finely chopped
1 tablespoon olive oil
900 g/2 lb tomatoes, skinned
   (p.108) and roughly chopped

salt and freshly ground black
   pepper

1 Fry the onion in the oil in a large saucepan for 10 minutes, until softened but not browned.

2 Add the tomatoes and cook for a further 10 minutes, until the tomatoes are soft but still bright in colour and fresh in flavour.

3 Purée the tomato mixture in a blender or food processor. Season to taste with salt and pepper.

Variations

FRESH TOMATO AND BASIL SAUCE

For this summery version, make as described, adding 1 tablespoon chopped fresh basil just before serving.

FRESH TOMATO AND GARLIC SAUCE

Add 1–2 crushed garlic cloves to the onion with the tomatoes.

FRESH TOMATO AND MUSHROOM SAUCE

While the tomatoes are cooking, fry 100 g/4 oz finely chopped button mushrooms in 1 tablespoon olive oil in a pan, until tender. Stir into puréed sauce.

FRESH TOMATO AND CHILLI SAUCE

Add 1 green chilli, de-seeded and finely chopped, to the onion with the tomatoes.

Italian Tomato Sauce

A well-flavoured sauce which goes well with many vegetarian savoury dishes.

SERVES 4

1 onion, peeled and chopped
1 celery stick, finely chopped
1 carrot, scraped and finely chopped
2 tablespoons olive oil
2 garlic cloves, crushed
2 × 400-g/14-oz cans tomatoes

½ teaspoon each basil and oregano
1 bay leaf
150 ml/5 fl oz red wine, Dark Vegetable Stock (p.199) or water
salt and freshly ground black pepper

1 Fry the onion, celery and carrot in the oil in a medium saucepan for 10 minutes, until soft but not browned. Add the

garlic, tomatoes, basil, oregano, bay leaf, and the red wine, Dark Vegetable Stock or water.

2 Cook gently for 20 minutes, stirring from time to time, until the tomatoes have almost reduced to a purée.

3 Remove the bay leaf, then purée the sauce in a blender or food processor. Season to taste with salt and pepper. A little extra liquid can be added at this point for a thinner sauce, if wished. Add either more red wine, Dark Vegetable Stock or water.

KEEPING SAUCES WARM

It is often convenient to make sauces in advance, to avoid feeling pressured at the last minute. Both the Tomato Sauces (p.253 and 254), Vegetarian Gravy (below), Cranberry Sauce (p.260), Curry Sauce (p.265) and Savoury Coconut Sauce (p.266) can be reheated gently in a saucepan. Béchamel Sauce (p.261), and its variations, can also be reheated, but keep the heat low and stir, or use a double saucepan. A double saucepan is also best for Bread Sauce (p.262) and Sauce Soubise (p.258) and these can be kept warm in a bain marie (or a saucepan standing in a roasting tin half filled with boiling water, with foil over all). Hollandaise Sauce (p.262) can be kept warm in a bain-marie, too; take care that this sauce does not get too hot, or it may start to curdle. (If this happens, quickly add an ice cube – or start again, adding the curdled sauce gradually to a fresh egg yolk.)

Vegetarian Gravy $\boxed{V}$

This is a tasty gravy, quite like a conventional meat gravy. The soy sauce both flavours and colours it.

MAKES JUST OVER 450 ML/15 FL OZ

1 onion, peeled and chopped
2 tablespoons oil
2 tablespoons plain flour
1 garlic clove, crushed
450 ml/15 fl oz Dark Vegetable Stock (p.199) or water

1 teaspoon yeast extract
1-2 tablespoons soy sauce
salt and freshly ground black pepper

1 Fry the onion in the oil in a medium saucepan for 5 minutes, then add the flour, and cook for a further 5–10 minutes, until the

flour and the onion are nut-brown and the onion is soft and slightly pulpy.

2 Add the garlic, cook for 1–2 minutes, then gradually stir in the Dark Vegetable Stock. Bring to the boil, then simmer for 10 minutes.

3 Strain the gravy into a clean saucepan and add the yeast extract, soy sauce and salt and pepper to taste. Stir well to mix, then serve.

GRAVY TIP

Gravy freezes well, and it is very useful to have a supply in the freezer. Make a double batch and freeze in ice cube trays; when solid remove gravy cubes and store in a polythene bag to use as required. This is particularly useful if you only need small quantities of gravy at a time.

MAKING QUICK MEALS FROM SAUCES

It's useful to have some sauce in the fridge or freezer, because it can make the basis of good quick meals. Try:

☐ Fresh Tomato Sauce (p.253) – over hot cooked pasta or with lightly steamed root vegetables or winter squash, served with cooked brown rice and roasted sunflower seeds; or parboil halved and de-seeded green peppers, fill with a mixture of cooked brown rice, fried onion, mushrooms and nuts, place in a casserole, pour tomato sauce round the peppers and bake.

☐ Egg Sauce (p.261) – over any steamed vegetables; particularly good with fennel or courgettes.

☐ Vegetarian Gravy (p.255) – with fried onion and cubed left-over nut roast or bought canned nut savoury.

☐ Sauce Soubise (p.258), Béchamel (p.261) or Cheese Sauce (p.261) – over cooked leeks, cauliflower or diced mixed root vegetables, or over hardboiled eggs.

☐ Italian Tomato Sauce (above) – layered with lasagne, grated Mozzarella cheese and fried mushrooms or aubergines, or puréed spinach.

☐ Curry Sauce (p.265) or Savoury Coconut Sauce (p.266) – over hardboiled eggs, drained canned chick peas or butter beans, or lightly steamed cauliflower.

Pesto

This popular Italian sauce for pasta can also be
added to vegetable soups.

SERVES 4–6

2 garlic cloves, crushed
6 tablespoons finely chopped fresh
 basil
4 tablespoons chopped parsley

50 g/2 oz pine nuts or cashew nuts
50 g/2 oz grated Parmesan cheese
150 ml/5 fl oz olive oil
freshly ground black pepper

1 Put all the ingredients into a blender or food processor and
blend until smooth.

Variation

PARSLEY PESTO

Instead of fresh basil, use an extra 4–6 tablespoons chopped
parsley and 1 teaspoon dried basil.

Sweet Pepper Sauce

V

Like tomato sauce, this scarlet sauce is low in
calories and excellent with many savouries. For
non-vegans, it may be enriched by adding
15–25 g/½–1 oz butter just before serving.

SERVES 4

2 large red peppers
4 garlic cloves, peeled

salt and freshly ground black
 pepper

1 Put the peppers into a saucepan with enough water to almost
cover. Bring to the boil, then simmer until tender.
2 Remove the peppers from the water, discard the stems and
seeds. Chop and place in a blender or food processor.
3 Add the garlic to the peppers, together with 300 ml/10 fl oz of
the cooking water, and blend to a purée.
4 Transfer the sauce to a clean saucepan. Season to taste with
salt and pepper and reheat gently without boiling.

Sauce Soubise

V

One of my personal favourites, this delicately flavoured, thick onion sauce is excellent with crisp nut loaves, such as the one on p.351, and nut burgers. If there's any left it's excellent poured over hardboiled eggs, heated through in the oven and served with fingers of hot wholewheat toast. You do need to use white rice for this recipe because of its starchiness, which thickens the sauce.

SERVES 4

25 g/1 oz white long-grain rice
225 g/8 oz onions, peeled and coarsely chopped
15 g/½ oz butter or vegan margarine
75 ml/3 fl oz water
a few parsley sprigs
1 thyme sprig

1 small bay leaf
2 tablespoons double or non-dairy cream
salt and freshly ground black pepper
freshly grated nutmeg
a pinch of sugar

1 Parboil the rice in plenty of boiling water for about 5 minutes, then drain.
2 Meanwhile, fry the chopped onions in the butter or vegan margarine in a medium saucepan for 10 minutes. Add the drained rice, water and herbs.
3 Cover the pan and cook over a gentle heat for 20–25 minutes, or until the onions are very soft.
4 Remove from the heat and discard the parsley, thyme and bay leaf. Purée the onion mixture in a blender or food processor.
5 Reheat the sauce gently in a double saucepan or heatproof bowl set over a saucepan of simmering water.
6 Just before serving, add the cream, and season carefully with salt, pepper, nutmeg and sugar.

GRAVY ALTERNATIVES

Don't get stuck in a gravy rut! There are many other delicious sauces which go excellently with vegetarian savouries. Both the tomato sauces on pp. 253 and 254 make excellent alternatives to gravy and are delicious with many vegetarian dishes. Other good sauces to use in place of gravy are:

☐ Mushroom Sauce (below)
☐ Wine Sauce (p.260)
☐ Sweet Pepper Sauce (p.257)
☐ Sauce Soubise (opposite)

Mushroom Sauce

SERVES 4

100 g/4 oz button mushrooms, washed and chopped
15 g/½ oz butter or vegan margarine
1 teaspoon cornflour
150 ml/5 fl oz milk, soya milk or single cream

salt and freshly ground black pepper
a few drops of lemon juice
freshly grated nutmeg

1 Fry the mushrooms in the butter or vegan margarine in a small saucepan for 4–5 minutes, until just tender, then stir in the cornflour.

2 Cook for 1–2 minutes, then add the milk, soya milk or cream, stirring all the time. Boil for 1 minute, then remove from the heat.

3 Season the Mushroom Sauce to taste with salt and pepper, a little lemon juice and freshly grated nutmeg.

Variation

WILD MUSHROOM SAUCE

This is a good way of using just a few precious wild mushrooms, delicious with a special nut roast or as a filling for vol au vents. Replace all, or some, of the button mushrooms with wild mushrooms, well-washed and chopped.

Wine Sauce

Serve this rich sauce on individual plates, with
nut burgers or roasts.

SERVES 4

1 onion, peeled and finely chopped
50 g/2 oz mushrooms, finely
   chopped
2 tablespoons olive oil
300 ml/10 fl oz red or white wine

25 g/1 oz butter or vegan
   margarine
salt and freshly ground black
   pepper
a little sugar

1 Fry the onion and mushrooms in the oil in a small saucepan
for 10 minutes, until lightly browned.

2 Add the wine and let the mixture bubble away over the heat
for a few minutes, uncovered, until the liquid has reduced by
about half.

3 Cut the butter or vegan margarine into pieces, then add them
to the sauce. Stir gently. Season to taste with salt, pepper and a
little sugar. Serve the Wine Sauce immediately.

Cranberry Sauce

For me, cranberry sauce, made from fresh
cranberries, is an essential part of Christmas
dinner.

SERVES 8

175 g/6 oz cranberries, washed
4 tablespoons water
75 g/3 oz sugar

1 tablespoon port or fresh orange
   juice

1 Put the cranberries into a saucepan with the water. Bring to
the boil, then simmer for about 10 minutes, until the berries are
tender.

2 Add the sugar and cook gently until it has dissolved. Remove
the pan from the heat and add the port or fresh orange juice. Stir
well, then serve the Cranberry Sauce at once.

Béchamel Sauce

This sauce will keep, well covered, in the
fridge, for a few days.

MAKES 450 ML/15 FL OZ

25 g/1 oz butter or vegan
 margarine
25 g/1 oz plain flour
600 ml/1 pint milk or soya milk
a piece each of onion, celery and
 scraped carrot

1 bay leaf
6 black peppercorns
1 thyme sprig
1–2 mace blades
salt and freshly ground black
 pepper
freshly grated nutmeg

1 Melt the butter or vegan margarine in a medium saucepan.
Add the flour, stir over the heat for 1–2 minutes, then add the
milk, a quarter at a time, mixing well between each addition.
2 Add the onion, celery, carrot, bay leaf, peppercorns, thyme
and mace, then leave the sauce to simmer gently for 10-15
minutes.
3 Strain the sauce through a sieve into a clean saucepan. Season
to taste with salt, pepper and nutmeg.

Variations

PARSLEY SAUCE

Add 2–4 tablespoons chopped parsley and a few drops of lemon
juice to the sauce after straining.

MORNAY OR CHEESE SAUCE

For a non-vegan variation, make as described, then add 1
teaspoon Dijon mustard and 50–100 g/2–4 oz grated Cheddar or
Gruyère cheese to the sauce after straining. Reheat gently but do
not allow to boil after adding the cheese or it may become
stringy.

EGG SAUCE

Stir 2 finely chopped hardboiled eggs into the sauce after
straining (another non-vegan variation).

V

Bread Sauce

Serve with a nut roast such as White Nut Roast
(p.357) as part of a traditional vegetarian
Christmas dinner.

SERVES 4-6

3 cloves
1 onion, peeled
300 ml/10 fl oz milk or soya milk
1 bay leaf
50 g/2 oz white bread, crusts
   removed
15 g/½ oz butter or vegan
   margarine

2 tablespoons single or non-dairy
   cream
salt and freshly ground black
   pepper
freshly grated nutmeg

1 Stick the cloves into the onion, then put the onion into a
saucepan with the milk and bay leaf.
2 Bring to the boil, then remove from the heat, add the bread,
cover and set aside for 15–30 minutes, to allow the flavours to
infuse.
3 Remove the onion and the bay leaf. Beat the mixture to break
up the bread, and stir in the butter or vegan margarine, cream
and salt, pepper and nutmeg to taste. Sprinkle nutmeg on top.

Hollandaise Sauce

Wonderfully rich, horribly fattening, but great
for a special treat, such as with the first
asparagus of summer, or as a filling for globe
artichokes.

SERVES 6

2 egg yolks
1 tablespoon water
1–2 teaspoons lemon juice

100 g/4 oz unsalted butter
salt and freshly ground black
   pepper

1 Put the egg yolks, water and 1 teaspoon lemon juice into the top of a double saucepan, or into a heatproof bowl set over a saucepan of gently simmering water (with the base of the bowl above the level of the water).

2 Whisk the mixture until the egg yolks begin to thicken slightly.

3 Add the butter, about a teaspoon at a time, whisking well after each addition. The sauce will thicken and become creamy.

4 Add the rest of the lemon juice, and salt and pepper to taste. Serve warm.

Variations

LIGHT HOLLANDAISE SAUCE

For a lighter version, whisk 2 egg whites until stiff and fold into the sauce before serving.

SAUCE MOUSSELINE

For this richer variation, lightly whip 75 ml/3 fl oz whipping cream and gently fold into the sauce.

BLENDER HOLLANDAISE OR BÉARNAISE SAUCE

A blender or food processor can be used for no-fuss labour-saving versions of these sauces. Have the butter melted and cooled. Put the egg yolks into a blender or food processor with the lemon juice and water (for Hollandaise Sauce) or the strained reduced vinegar (for Béarnaise Sauce). Whizz until combined and thickened a little. Then add the melted butter through the top of the blender or food processor, a little at a time. The mixture will thicken. Add the lemon juice and seasoning to taste.

Béarnaise Sauce

Another rich sauce, though a little goes a long
way. It's wonderful with crisp nut or lentil
burgers. For a quick and easy blender version,
see above.

SERVES 6

½ small onion, peeled and chopped
1 bay leaf
6 black peppercorns
4 tablespoons white wine vinegar
1 tarragon sprig, or a pinch of
dried tarragon

2 egg yolks
100 g/4 oz unsalted butter
salt and freshly ground black
pepper

1 Simmer the onion, bay leaf, peppercorns, vinegar and tarragon in a small saucepan until the liquid has reduced to 1 tablespoon.

2 Put the egg yolks into the top of a double saucepan, or into a heatproof bowl set over a saucepan of gently simmering water (with the base of the bowl above the level of the water).

3 Strain the reduced vinegar liquid over the egg yolks, pressing against the sieve to extract as much as possible.

4 Whisk the mixture until the egg yolks begin to thicken slightly.

5 Add the butter, about a teaspoon at a time, whisking well after each addition. The sauce will thicken and become creamy. Season to taste with salt and pepper. Serve warm.

Curry Sauce

$\boxed{\text{V}}$

A useful sauce for turning a few vegetables into
a meal, or for serving with a spiced rice dish.
The quantities of the spices can be adjusted
according to taste.

SERVES 4

4 tablespoons olive oil
1 garlic clove, crushed
1 onion, peeled and chopped
1 teaspoon grated fresh ginger
2½ teaspoons ground coriander
2½ teaspoons ground cumin
½ teaspoon curry powder
½ teaspoon turmeric
½ teaspoon white mustard seed
  (optional)
1 bay leaf

1 × 225-g/8-oz can tomatoes
450 ml/15 fl oz Dark Vegetable
  Stock (p.199) or water
1 teaspoon garam masala
salt and freshly ground black
  pepper
TO GARNISH
1 lime slice
mustard seeds
1 bay leaf

1 Heat the oil in a medium saucepan and add the garlic, onion
and ginger. Fry gently for 10 minutes, until the onion is soft but
not brown.
2 Add all the spices except the garam masala, together with the
bay leaf, and cook for a further 2 minutes, then add the
tomatoes, Dark Vegetable Stock or water and simmer gently for
15 minutes, uncovered.
3 Stir in the garam masala and season to taste with salt and
pepper and mix well together.
4 Remove the bay leaf. Serve the sauce as it is, or blend in a
blender or food processor for a smoother texture. Transfer the
sauce to a small bowl and garnish with the lime slice, mustard
seeds and bay leaf.

Savoury Coconut Sauce

A delicately flavoured, golden sauce. Serve it
with steamed vegetables and brown rice, for a
simple meal, or heat halved hardboiled eggs
through in it for a delicious egg curry.

SERVES 4

100 g/4 oz desiccated coconut
600 ml/1 pint water
1 onion, peeled and chopped
25 g/1 oz butter or vegan
    margarine
1 teaspoon turmeric
1 teaspoon grated fresh ginger
1 garlic clove, crushed

½ cinnamon stick or a pinch of
    ground cinnamon
salt and freshly ground black
    pepper
a little sugar
a few drops of lemon juice
    (optional)

1 Put the coconut into a saucepan with the water. Bring to the
boil, then remove from the heat, cover and leave to stand in the
saucepan for 10 minutes.
2 Meanwhile, fry the onion in the butter or vegan margarine in
a medium saucepan for 5 minutes. Add the turmeric, ginger,
garlic and cinnamon, and fry gently for a further 5 minutes.
3 Strain the coconut mixture into the onion mixture, pressing as
much liquid through as you can. Discard the coconut in the
sieve.
4 Remove the cinnamon stick, then purée the mixture in a
blender or food processor. Return the sauce to the rinsed-out
pan, season to taste with salt, pepper and a little sugar, and add
the lemon juice to sharpen if necessary.

Accompanying Vegetables

These recipes for accompanying vegetable dishes are the ones which I find the most practical and useful. Some, such as Red Cabbage Casserole (below), are labour-saving because they can be cooked slowly and add moisture to a main dish, eliminating the need for a separate sauce. Many also add a bright splash of colour, enhancing the look of the meal. Sometimes a simply cooked accompanying vegetable is best, especially if the main course is vegetable-based; you will find some recipes for these in this section, and further ideas in the Ingredients section (p.49), under individual vegetables.

Steamed and Marinated Aubergine

A very simple yet delicious way of preparing aubergine without any oil. This is especially good with Chinese and Japanese dishes.

SERVES 4

2 medium aubergines, total weight about 450 g/1 lb
2 tablespoons soy sauce
1 teaspoon sugar
2 teaspoons vinegar
salt and freshly ground black pepper

1 Remove the stems from the aubergines and cut the flesh into large dice.
2 Steam the aubergine until tender – 5–10 minutes. Transfer to a shallow dish and sprinkle with the rest of the ingredients.
3 Serve hot, warm or cold.

Red Cabbage Casserole

V

A useful dish, because it can cook away gently,
and the result is moist enough to stand in for
both a vegetable and a sauce.

SERVES 4–6

1 red cabbage, about 1 kg/2¼ lb,
 cored and shredded
1 large onion, peeled and chopped
2 tablespoons oil

2 tablespoons lemon juice
salt and freshly ground black
 pepper
a little sugar

1 Put the cabbage into a large saucepan, cover with water and
bring to the boil, then drain thoroughly.
2 Meanwhile, fry the onion in the oil in a large saucepan for 5
minutes, then add the cabbage, cover and cook very gently for
45–60 minutes, until the cabbage is very tender, stirring occasionally.
3 Add the lemon juice and salt, pepper and sugar to taste.

Stir-fried Carrots with Watercress and Sesame Seeds

V

A quick vegetable dish, excellent with Japanese
or Chinese meals.

SERVES 2–4

2 teaspoons oil
4 spring onions, trimmed and
 sliced
350 g/12 oz carrots, scraped and
 cut into matchsticks
1 bunch watercress, tough stems
 removed

1 tablespoon soy sauce
salt
TO GARNISH
1–2 tablespoons sesame seeds

1 Heat the oil in a wok or saucepan, then add the onions and
carrots and stir-fry for 2 minutes.
2 Add the watercress, stir-fry for 1–2 minutes, then cook gently

for a further 3–4 minutes, stirring from time to time.
3 Stir in the soy sauce and a little salt, then sprinkle the vegetables with sesame seeds and serve immediately.

QUANTITIES FOR VEGETABLES

It's difficult to give exact quantities, because these depend on what else you're serving at the meal – whether there's another vegetable, for instance, and the type of main dish – and how much you like vegetables!

As a general rule, allow 175–225 g/6–8 oz per person. I'm quite greedy with vegetables, because my favourite way of staying slim is to have lots of vegetables and just a small amount of the main course.

Spring Vegetable Braise   [V]

This is a particularly good way to cook a
colourful selection of tender young vegetables,
but this method can be used throughout the
year for different mixtures, according to what is
in season.

SERVES 4

6 tablespoons olive oil
6 tablespoons water
pared rind of ½ lemon
a good sprig each of parsley and
  thyme
450 g/1 lb tender young carrots,
  scraped and halved or quartered
  if large
450 g/1 lb tender young turnips,
  scrubbed and halved or
  quartered if necessary

225 g/8 oz mangetouts, topped and
  tailed
225 g/8 oz broad beans (shelled
  weight)
salt and freshly ground black
  pepper
2–3 tablespoons chopped parsley

1 Put the oil into a large saucepan with the water, lemon rind, parsley and thyme and bring to the boil.
2 Add the carrots and turnips; cover and simmer gently for 5–10 minutes, until just tender.

3 Meanwhile, blanch the mangetouts by plunging them into a saucepan of boiling water, bringing back to the boil and boiling for 1 minute. Drain and refresh under the cold tap, to preserve the colour.

4 Add the beans and mangetouts to the carrot mixture and cook for a further 2–3 minutes, until heated through.

5 Season with salt and pepper. Serve sprinkled with parsley.

[V] *Braised Celery Hearts*

Braised vegetables are cooked slowly with a
little liquid and flavouring ingredients.
Sometimes the vegetables are lightly browned
in fat before the liquid is added. Braising suits
bulb vegetables such as celery, leeks and fennel
particularly well.

SERVES 4

4 celery hearts, trimmed to about
   12–15 cm/5–6 inches
1 onion, peeled and chopped
2 carrots, scraped and diced
1 bouquet garni, including a piece
   of lemon peel

salt and freshly ground black
   pepper
TO GARNISH
chopped parsley

1 Wash the celery thoroughly, using a bottle brush, if necessary, to clean the inside.

2 Put the celery into a large saucepan, cover with water, bring to the boil, then boil for 10 minutes. Drain well, saving the water.

3 Cover the base of a large, heavy saucepan with the onion and carrot, then place the celery on top. Add the bouquet garni, season to taste with salt and pepper, then pour in enough of the reserved cooking water to cover.

4 Bring to the boil, then simmer, with a lid on the pan, until the celery is very tender – 45–60 minutes.

5 Remove the celery from the saucepan with a slotted spoon and put it into a warmed shallow serving dish.

6 If the liquid has reduced to a sauce-like consistency, strain this over the celery. If not, boil it vigorously for a minute or two to reduce it, then strain it over the celery.

7 Sprinkle the celery with parsley and serve immediately.

Variation

BRAISED FENNEL

Make this in the same way, but cut the bulbs in half and instead of par-boiling the fennel, fry it in a little olive oil, for about 10 minutes, in a covered pan. Turn the fennel pieces from time to time during the cooking, allowing them to brown evenly on all sides.

Glazed Carrots

For a special effect and a professional finish, the carrots can be 'turned' (cut into 5-cm/2-inch lengths, then rounded by slicing down the corners to form a barrel shape). I do this sometimes when I feel like being impressive, but normally I cut them into rings or sticks. They are particularly delicious with nut savouries.

SERVES 4

900 g/2 lb carrots, peeled or scraped and sliced into sticks or rings
25 g/1 oz butter or vegan margarine
salt and freshly ground black pepper

2 tablespoons caster or soft light brown sugar

TO GARNISH
2 tablespoons chopped parsley

1 Put the prepared carrots into a large saucepan, cover them with cold water and bring the water to the boil.
2 Half cover the saucepan, and leave the carrots to simmer gently until just tender – 8–15 minutes.
3 Drain the carrots, then return them to the pan with the butter or vegan margarine, salt and pepper. Cook over a gentle heat until the butter or vegan margarine has melted, shaking the pan to coat all the carrots in butter or margarine.
4 Sprinkle on the sugar, mixing gently over the heat until all the sugar has melted and the carrots are shining with glaze. Sprinkle the chopped parsley over the top and serve immediately.

Variation

GLAZED TURNIPS

Cook as described, using whole baby turnips if you can get them, otherwise use sliced or 'turned' turnips.

V

Peas Cooked in the French Style

This is a wonderful way to make frozen peas (or fresh peas, when you can get young, tender ones) taste really good.

SERVES 4

1 small bunch spring onions, trimmed and chopped
25 g/1 oz butter or vegan margarine
outer leaves from 1 lettuce, washed and roughly shredded

450 g/1 lb frozen peas or shelled fresh peas
½ teaspoon sugar
salt and freshly ground black pepper
2-3 mint sprigs when available.

1 Fry the spring onions in half the butter or vegan margarine in a medium saucepan for 2–3 minutes on medium heat.
2 Add the lettuce and peas. Sprinkle with the sugar and salt and pepper to taste.
3 Dot with the remaining butter or vegan margarine, pop the sprigs of mint, if used, on top, then cover.
4 Cook over a gentle heat for 10–15 minutes, until the peas are tender.
5 Check the seasoning and remove the mint. Serve the cooked peas immediately, with (my preference) or without the shredded lettuce.

V

Julienne of Root Vegetables

This mixture of orange carrots, yellow swede and white turnip works well, but you could use just two of these vegetables, or different vegetables. Some kohlrabi makes a pleasant addition.

SERVES 4

300 g/10 oz carrots, scraped
300 g/10 oz turnips, peeled
300 g/10 oz swede, peeled
15 g/½ oz butter or vegan
  margarine

salt and freshly ground black
  pepper

TO GARNISH
1–2 tablespoons chopped parsley

1 Cut the vegetables into julienne strips (matchsticks), then put them into a saucepan, cover with cold water and bring to the boil.

2 Half cover the pan and cook gently until the vegetables are just tender – about 10 minutes, depending on how thinly you cut them.

3 Drain, saving the water which makes particularly good stock, then return the vegetables to the pan and add the butter or vegan margarine. Season to taste with the salt and pepper, sprinkle with the chopped parsley and serve.

Variations

JULIENNE BUNDLES

Keep the vegetables separate during cooking. Soften a chive or thin strip of leek by dipping in boiling water for 1-2 minutes. Serve the vegetables in bundles tied with the blanched chive or leek strip.

JULIENNE OF CARROTS

This is very good made with carrots alone, especially when you want to bring a splash of bright colour to a meal. A pinch or two of aniseed, caraway or dill gives a pleasant, unusual flavour to this vegetable dish.

Chinese-style Mushrooms $\boxed{V}$

This simple dish is pleasant with Chinese
dishes such as Chinese-Style Fried Rice (p.363).

SERVES 4

225 g/8 oz small button
  mushrooms, wiped
1 tablespoon olive oil
1 teaspoon cornflour

3 tablespoons soy sauce

TO GARNISH (OPTIONAL)
spring onion curls

1 Fry the mushrooms quickly in the olive oil in a small saucepan for 2–3 minutes, over high heat, until just tender.

2 Blend the cornflour and soy sauce. Add to the mushrooms, and stir for 1–2 minutes, until thickened. Garnish with the spring onion curls, if using, and serve immediately.

$\boxed{V}$ ## Golden Spiced Cauliflower

A beautiful golden dish, one of my favourite
ways of preparing cauliflower. Some chopped
fresh coriander (or parsley) is the perfect
finishing touch, but it's also very good without.

SERVES 4

1 onion, peeled and chopped
2 tablespoons oil
1 garlic clove, crushed
½ teaspoon turmeric
1 teaspoon ground coriander
2 cardamom pods
1 small cauliflower, divided into
   florets

150 ml/5 fl oz water
salt and freshly ground black
   pepper
TO GARNISH
sprig of mint

1 Fry the onion in the oil in a medium saucepan for 8 minutes, then add the garlic, turmeric, coriander and cardamom. Stir over the heat for a further 2–3 minutes.

2 Add the cauliflower, turning it gently with a spoon to coat with the onion and spice mixture, then add the water and some salt and pepper. Bring the mixture to the boil.

3 Cover and leave to cook gently for about 5 minutes, or until the cauliflower is just tender. Shake the pan from time to time to prevent sticking and ensure even cooking.

4 Check the seasoning, then garnish with a sprig of mint and serve the cauliflower immediately.

Variations

SPICED POTATOES

For this excellent variation, use 900 g/2 lb peeled potatoes, cut into 1-cm/½-inch dice. Make exactly as described, but do cook it gently and keep an eye on the pan, to prevent sticking. Most of the liquid should have been absorbed by the time the potatoes are cooked – 8–10 minutes – leaving them bathed in just a little golden, spicy sauce. The chopped fresh coriander is particularly good with potatoes cooked this way but parsley can be used if coriander is unavailable.

SPICED ROOT VEGETABLES

A delicious winter variation. Use 900 g/2 lb peeled root vegetables cut into 1-cm/½-inch dice. A mixture of root vegetables can be used: swedes, carrots, turnips, parsnips as well as sliced onions and celery, as available. Make as described for the Spiced Potatoes variation. This makes a good accompaniment to a mild-flavoured dish and goes well with nut or lentil burgers.

REHEATING VEGETABLES IN THE MICROWAVE

Cook the vegetables in the usual way until they are slightly underdone. Then drain, refresh under cold water and drain again well. Place in a shallow serving dish, dot with butter if you like, cover with a plate and keep in a cool place until needed. Then microwave on full power for a few minutes (the time will depend on the quantity of vegetables) until piping hot. Serve at once. It can be convenient to reheat vegetables in the microwave in this way when you're cooking for a dinner party and want to keep last minute preparations to the minimum.

Peperonata

For this delicious Italian pepper stew, you can use all red peppers, or a mixture of red, yellow and green peppers, which gives a particularly attractive result.

SERVES 4

1 large onion, peeled and chopped
15 g/½ oz butter or vegan margarine
1 tablespoon olive oil
2 large red peppers
2 large yellow peppers
2 large green peppers

1 large garlic clove, crushed
450 g/1 lb tomatoes, skinned (p.108) and chopped
salt and freshly ground black pepper

TO GARNISH
1–2 tablespoons chopped parsley

1 Fry the onion in the butter or vegan margarine and the oil in a large saucepan for 10 minutes, allowing the onion to brown lightly.

2 Meanwhile, de-seed the peppers and cut them into strips, then add them to the onion. Cover and cook gently for 10–15 minutes.

3 Add the garlic and tomatoes, then cover and cook for a further 40 minutes or so, until the peppers are very tender and soft.

4 Season to taste with salt and pepper, sprinkle with chopped parsley and serve. Peperonata reheats well, or is excellent served cold.

Okra with Cumin and Coriander

This lightly spiced dish can be made in advance
and then reheated.

SERVES 2, OR 4, WITH OTHER DISHES, AS PART OF
A CURRY MEAL

1 onion, peeled and chopped
2 tablespoons oil
225 g/8 oz okra, washed and
   trimmed
1 teaspoon salt
1 teaspoon whole cumin seeds
1 tablespoon ground coriander

200 ml/7 fl oz water
2 tomatoes, chopped
salt and freshly ground black
   pepper

TO GARNISH
1–2 tablespoons chopped coriander

1 Fry the onion in the oil in a medium saucepan for 5 minutes,
then add the okra, salt, cumin and coriander. Mix well, then
cook gently, uncovered, for 5 minutes.

2 Add the water, then simmer, uncovered, for 20 minutes, until
the okra is tender and most of the water has been absorbed.
Shake the pan, or stir, from time to time to prevent sticking.

3 Add the tomatoes, check the seasoning, and sprinkle with the
chopped coriander. Serve hot or warm. (It's also pleasant cold,
garnished with a slice of lemon and chopped parsley.)

Variations

SPICED RUNNER BEANS

This is also a good way to serve runner beans, especially if you
grow them and are getting tired of them while they're still
producing prolifically! Top, tail and slice the beans in the usual
way (p.89), then cook as described.

SPICED AUBERGINE

Another variation which works well and makes a useful side-
dish for serving with curries. Dice and degorge (p.106) a
medium-sized aubergine and fry with the onion for 10 minutes
before adding the tomatoes.

Ratatouille

This delicious Provençale vegetable mixture is
good with cooked brown rice or crusty bread
and a crisp salad. If you're serving it with rice,
put this on to cook before you start making the
Ratatouille.

SERVES 4

3 tablespoons olive oil
2 large onions, peeled and chopped
3 large red peppers, de-seeded and
 sliced
3 garlic cloves, crushed
450 g/1 lb courgettes, cut into
 even-sized pieces
450 g/1 lb aubergines, diced)

700 g/1½ lb tomatoes, skinned
 (p.108) and chopped
salt and freshly ground black
 pepper

TO GARNISH
chopped parsley

1 Heat the oil in a large saucepan and fry the onions and
peppers gently for 5 minutes.
2 Add the garlic, courgettes and the aubergines. Stir gently,
then cover and cook over a low heat for about 25 minutes, until
all the vegetables are tender.
3 Add the tomatoes, stir gently and cook, uncovered, for about 5
minutes, to heat through. Season to taste with salt and pepper
and sprinkle with parsley. Serve hot or cold.

FLAVOURING VEGETARIAN DISHES

You can introduce strong, almost
'meaty' flavours by using yeast
extracts and soy preparations
such as miso and soy sauces. Or
– and I must admit that this is my
own preference – you can
concentrate on the assets of the
vegetarian diet, which are the
fresh flavours of the vegetables,
nuts and grains, and accent these
by joyous use of fresh herbs,
chopped and in bouquets garnis;
citrus rinds and juices; good-
quality salt and freshly ground
black pepper; the judicious – and
sometimes generous – use of
spices; the use of wine.

Leek and Pear Purée

This is particularly good with pulse and nut
savouries.

SERVES 4-6

*450 g/1 lb leeks, trimmed, cleaned
 and sliced*
*450 g/1 lb pears, peeled, cored and
 sliced*
300 ml/10 fl oz water

4 garlic cloves
*25 g/1 oz soft butter or vegan
 margarine*
*salt and freshly ground black
 pepper*

1 Put the leeks and pears into a large saucepan with the water
and whole garlic cloves. Boil for about 15 minutes, until tender.
2 Remove the garlic cloves and pop them out of their skins; put
them into a blender or food processor with the leeks, pears and
cooking liquid, and blend until smooth.
3 Reheat the mixture gently and stir in the butter or vegan
margarine. Season to taste with salt and pepper.

Variations

CARROT, APPLE AND CORIANDER PURÉE

Make as described, using carrots instead of leeks and dessert
apples instead of pears, and a medium onion, peeled and sliced.
Add 1 tablespoon crushed coriander seeds, tied in a small piece
of muslin, to the mixture. Remove this, squeezing it well to
extract all the flavour, before puréeing. Garnish with fresh
chopped coriander, if available, or chopped parsley.

PUMPKIN AND GINGER PURÉE

Replace the leeks and pears with 900 g/2 lb pumpkin or winter
squash (weighed without skin and pips). Cook the squash with
the water as described and a walnut-sized piece of ginger,
grated.

CARROT AND SWEDE PURÉE

Replace the apples with swede, peeled and cut into even-sized
pieces. Some freshly grated nutmeg and a pinch of a warm spice
such as cinnamon, allspice or ground cloves are good with this,
or 2–3 tablespoons chopped parsley.

Potato and Almond Croquettes

These croquettes make a good vegetarian
cooked breakfast, served with grilled tomatoes
and mushrooms. For a light meal, serve them
with Sweet Carrot and Fennel Salad (p.242); or
with Mushrooms in Cream (p.115) and a green
vegetable.

SERVES 4

4 large potatoes, peeled and cut
  into even-sized pieces
15 g/½ oz butter or vegan
  margarine
2–3 tablespoons milk or soya milk
100 g/4 oz flaked or chopped
  almonds
3 tablespoons chopped parsley

salt and freshly ground black
  pepper
wholewheat flour or ground
  almonds for coating
oil for shallow-frying

TO GARNISH
lovage sprig

1 Boil the potatoes in water to cover until they are tender –
about 20 minutes.
2 Drain the potatoes, then dry them in the pan over a low heat
for 1–2 minutes.
3 Mash the potatoes with the butter or vegan margarine and
enough milk or soya milk to give a creamy consistency.
4 Stir in the chopped almonds and parsley, and season with salt
and pepper.
5 Form into 8 croquettes, then coat in wholewheat flour or
ground almonds.
6 Shallow-fry in a little hot oil in a frying pan until the
undersides are crisp, then turn the croquettes and fry on the
other side until crisp.
7 Drain on kitchen paper. Serve immediately, garnished with
lovage.

Potato Purée

This is really a way of saying very light,
smooth, mashed potatoes, perhaps made a bit
moister than you normally would. It's one of
my favourite ways of serving potatoes, very
useful because not only is it delicious, but it
adds some moisture to the meal, often
eliminating the need for extra sauces.

SERVES 4

*700 g/1½ lb potatoes, peeled and
    cut into even-sized pieces*
150 ml/5 fl oz milk or soya milk
*salt and freshly ground black
    pepper*

TO GARNISH
chopped parsley

1 Put the potatoes into a large saucepan, cover with cold water
and bring to the boil. Boil, half-covered, for about 15 minutes,
until just tender.

2 Drain the potatoes, and either return to the pan and mash very
thoroughly with a potato masher, or, for best results, pass the
potatoes through a vegetable mill.

3 Put the puréed potato back into the saucepan. Heat the milk
or soya milk in another saucepan and, when it comes to the boil,
add it gradually to the potatoes, beating all the time. The
potatoes will become fluffy and whiter and should be the
consistency of whipped cream.

4 Season to taste with salt and pepper. If you are serving the
potatoes straightaway, beat in the butter or vegan margarine; if
not, keep the potatoes warm by standing the saucepan in an
outer pan of boiling water; or transfer the potatoes to another
container standing in a saucepan of water. Then beat in the
butter or vegan margarine just before serving. Sprinkle with
chopped parsley, to serve.

Variations

POTATO PURÉE WITH GARLIC

Add 1–2 crushed garlic cloves to the mixture after puréeing the potatoes.

POTATO AND CELERIAC PURÉE WITH PISTACHIOS

Replace 225 g/8 oz of the potatoes with celeriac, peeled, cut into even-sized pieces and cooked with the potatoes. Garnish with a scattering of chopped shelled pistachio nuts.

CARROT PURÉE

Replace the potatoes with the same amount of carrots. Cook until tender, then drain. Use some of the cooking water instead of some of the milk, if wished. Garnish with chopped parsley.

Rösti

This delicious crisp golden potato cake from
Switzerland is quick and easy to make.

SERVES 4

4 tablespoons oil
salt

450 g/1 lb potatoes, scrubbed or
peeled, then coarsely grated

1 Heat the oil in a large frying pan with a lid, add the potatoes and salt. Press down.
2 Cook the potatoes gently, covered, until they are browned on the bottom.
3 Turn the rösti over, either with a fish slice, or by turning it out on to a plate then sliding it back into the frying pan.
4 Cook until the second side is browned and crisp. Serve immediately.

Baked Potatoes

V

Baked potatoes make one of the easiest and
most economical dishes. Simply scrub one or
two large potatoes per person, prick and bake at
230C/450F/Gas Mark 8 for 1–1½ hours, until the
potatoes feel soft when squeezed and the skins
are crisp. Then split open and serve with butter
and grated cheese, or some cottage cheese or
soured cream or plain yogurt, or with one of the
following toppings:

Toppings for Baked Potatoes

CREAMY MUSHROOMS

Top the potatoes with Mushroom Sauce (p.259).

CREAMY SWEETCORN

Heat 100 g/4 oz frozen sweetcorn kernels in 4 tablespoons cream,
dairy or vegan, stirring, until the sweetcorn is hot, then season
to taste with salt and pepper.

CHILLI-TOMATO-CHEESE

For a non-vegan topping, fry a small, finely chopped onion in
15 g/½ oz butter for about 10 minutes, until soft but not
browned. Then add a 225-g/8-oz can tomatoes, mashing them a
bit as you put them in, and a pinch of chilli powder and 100 g/
4 oz grated cheese. Stir gently over the heat until the cheese has
melted and the mixture is hot.

GUACAMOLE

Spoon Guacamole (p.218) over the hot potatoes.

SOURED CREAM AND CHIVES

Add 2 tablespoons snipped chives to 150 ml/5 fl oz soured cream
for this excellent non-vegan topping. Mix the chives and cream
together gently, season to taste with salt and pepper, and spoon
over the hot potatoes.

ACCOMPANYING VEGETABLES AS MAIN COURSES

Some accompanying vegetables make excellent main courses if served with extras such as cooked brown rice, warm rolls, garlic bread, hot cooked pasta or a potato dish. Some suggestions are:

☐ Spring Vegetable Braise (p.269) with wedges of hardboiled egg and new potatoes, or with warm crusty bread

☐ Red Cabbage Casserole (p.268) with Baked Potatoes (p.283) and soured cream, or with Gratin Dauphinois (below)

☐ Braised Celery Hearts (p.270) with Cheese Sauce (p.261) and crusty bread.

☐ Ratatouille (p.278) with hot cooked brown rice and a lettuce and fresh herb salad.

☐ Stir-Fried Carrots with Watercress and Sesame Seeds (p.268) with Chinese-Style Mushrooms (p.273) and Sweet Vinegared Rice (p.361).

☐ Baked Potatoes (p.283) with Technicolour Cabbage Salad (p.245).

☐ Stuffed Jacket Potatoes (p.286) with Favourite Coleslaw (p.242).

☐ Rösti (p.282) or Hashed Brown Potatoes (opposite) with Apple Sauce (p.122) and Carrot, Fennel and Red Pepper Salad (p.243).

Gratin Dauphinois

A delectable dish for a special occasion. Keep the other vegetables in the meal fairly simple.

SERVES 6

40 g/1½ oz butter
700 g/1½ lb potatoes, peeled and sliced as thinly as possible
salt and freshly ground black pepper

freshly grated nutmeg (optional)
1 large garlic clove, crushed
150 ml/5 fl oz double cream

1 Preheat the oven to 170c/325F/Gas Mark 3. Use half the butter to grease a shallow ovenproof dish generously.
2 Put the potato slices into a colander and rinse well under the cold tap; drain and dry on kitchen paper.

3 Layer the potato slices in the prepared dish, seasoning with salt, pepper and nutmeg, if using, and a smear of crushed garlic between each layer.

4 Pour the cream evenly over the top of the potatoes and dot with the rest of the butter.

5 Bake, uncovered, for 1½–2 hours, until the potatoes feel tender when pierced with the point of a knife.

Hashed Brown Potatoes

This American way with fried potatoes gives a
particularly savoury result.

SERVES 2–4

4 tablespoons oil
450 g/1 lb potatoes, scrubbed or
 peeled and diced, cooked or
 uncooked

1 small onion, finely chopped
 (optional)
salt and freshly ground black
 pepper

1 Heat the oil in a large frying pan with a lid, then add the potatoes with the onion, if used, and press down with a spatula.

2 If the potatoes are raw, cook them over a gentle heat, covered, until they are tender, then turn up the heat to brown them.

3 Fry cooked potatoes over a moderate heat until golden-brown underneath. Press them down into the oil several times with a spatula.

4 Divide the potatoes in the middle and turn each half over. When they are golden brown and crisp, drain on kitchen paper. Season and serve immediately.

Stuffed Jacket Potatoes

Serve these with some salad, such as
Technicolour Cabbage Salad (p.245) or Sweet
Carrot and Fennel Salad (p.243).

1–2 large potatoes per person
a little butter and milk per person
25–50 g/1–2 oz grated cheese per
person

salt and freshly ground black
pepper
2–3 tablespoons chopped fresh
herbs

1 Scrub and prick the potatoes, then bake them at 230c/450f/
Gas Mark 8 for 1–1½ hours until the skins are crisp and the
potatoes feel tender inside when squeezed.

2 Halve the potatoes and scoop out the insides. Place the skins
on a baking sheet. Mash the scooped-out potato with a little
butter and milk and half the cheese. Season to taste with salt and
pepper.

3 Pile the mixture back into the potato skins, sprinkle with the
remaining cheese and return the potatoes to the oven for about
20 minutes, until golden-brown and crisp.

Vegan Variation

HERBY STUFFED JACKET POTATOES

Omit the cheese, replace the butter with vegan margarine and
use plenty of herbs. Season well with salt and pepper.

Main Vegetable Dishes

Vegetables can be made into some filling and tempting main courses, ranging from simple homely dishes like Vegetable Hotpot (p.301), to exquisite stuffed vegetables, one of my favourite main courses for a special meal. Other particularly popular dishes include vegetable kebabs and vegetable tempura which, served with rice, make main courses that appeal – especially to non-vegetarians. Although some of the stuffed vegetables are a little fiddly to make, other recipes in this section, such as the Sweet and Sour Vegetable Stir-Fry (p.299) and the Potato and Cheese Layer (p.300), are particularly easy, good for mid-week and family cooking, when time is short.

Stuffed Aubergines à la Provençale

Served on a bed of cooked rice, potato purée or cooked noodles, and accompanied by a green salad, these stuffed aubergines make a delicious main course.

SERVES 4

2 aubergines, total weight about
    450 g/1 lb
salt
olive oil
1 large onion, peeled and chopped
4 tomatoes, skinned (p.108) and
    chopped

2 garlic cloves, crushed
2 tablespoons chopped parsley
freshly ground black pepper
4 tablespoons fresh wholewheat
    breadcrumbs
a little butter or vegan margarine

1 Remove the stalks from the aubergines and cut them in half lengthways. Cut around the edge and make criss-cross cuts

across the flesh, without piercing the skin, then salt and rinse as described on p.106.

2 Scoop the flesh out of the skins, and chop the flesh.

3 Preheat the oven to 200c/400f/Gas Mark 6.

4 Heat a little oil in a large saucepan and fry the aubergine skins for about 3 minutes on both sides. Remove from the pan, place in a shallow ovenproof dish and set aside.

5 Next, fry the onion and aubergine flesh for 7 minutes, adding a little more oil if necessary. Add the tomatoes and garlic and fry for a further 3 minutes, then mix in the parsley and season to taste with salt and pepper.

6 Spoon the mixture into the aubergine skins, sprinkle with the crumbs, dot with butter or vegan margarine and bake for 20–30 minutes, until the aubergine skins are tender and the filling mixture is browned on top.

Courgettes with Carrot, Ginger and Almond Stuffing

Light and delicately spiced, these courgettes are good with a green salad and a Vegan Yogurt and Herb Dressing (p.233).

SERVES 4

1 large onion, peeled and chopped
2 tablespoons olive oil
4 medium courgettes, total weight about 750 g/1½ lb
1 garlic clove, crushed
350 g/12 oz carrots, scraped and finely diced
¾ teaspoon grated fresh ginger
75 g/3 oz flaked almonds
salt and freshly ground black pepper

1 Preheat the oven to 190c/375f/Gas Mark 5.

2 Fry the onion in the oil in a medium saucepan for 5 minutes.

3 Meanwhile, halve the courgettes lengthways and use a tea-spoon to scoop out as much of the seeds and pulp as you can, to make a good cavity for stuffing.

4 Chop the scooped-out courgette and add it to the onion along with the garlic, carrot and ginger. Cover and fry gently for about 10 minutes, until the vegetables are soft.

5 Remove from the heat and add the almonds and salt and pepper to taste.

6 Place the courgette skins in a greased shallow casserole and fill them with the carrot mixture. (If the courgettes are long, they can be cut in halves or thirds.)

7 Cover with foil and bake for about 40 minutes, until the courgettes are tender. Serve immediately.

Variation

COURGETTES WITH CURD CHEESE AND ALMOND STUFFING

For this variation, which is good served on a base of stir-fried shredded Chinese leaves, replace the carrots with 350 g/12 oz curd cheese. Flavour with fresh ginger as suggested, or with 1–2 teaspoons grated lemon rind and a few drops of lemon juice. 1–2 tablespoons chopped parsley or chives can also be added.

Marrow with Hazelnut Stuffing and Apple Sauce

This is a pleasant blend of flavours. Serve as a
main course with crisp roast potatoes and one
or two cooked vegetables, such as French beans
and carrots. A Vegetarian Gravy (p.255) can be
served with it as well as the apple sauce.

SERVES 4–6

1 medium marrow, weighing about
  1 kg/2¼ lb
2 large onions, peeled and chopped
50 g/2 oz butter or vegan
  margarine
100 g/4 oz hazelnuts, roasted,
  skinned and grated
100 g/4 oz fresh wholewheat
  breadcrumbs

2–3 tablespoons chopped fresh
  sage
salt and freshly ground black
  pepper
a little extra butter or vegan
  margarine for greasing
1 quantity Apple Sauce (p.122)

1 Preheat the oven to 200c/400f/Gas Mark 6.

2 Cut the stalk off the marrow, then peel the marrow, keeping it whole. Cut a slice off one end and reserve. Then, using a spoon,

scoop out the seeds, to leave a cavity for stuffing.

3 Fry the onions in the butter or vegan margarine for 10 minutes, until soft, then add the hazelnuts, breadcrumbs, sage and salt and pepper to taste. Push the mixture into the marrow, and replace the sliced-off end.

4 Grease a large piece of greaseproof paper with butter or vegan margarine and wrap the marrow completely in this. Place in a baking tin.

5 Bake for about 1 hour, until the marrow is tender when pierced with a skewer. Remove the greaseproof paper and serve cut into slices with Apple Sauce.

[V]

Stuffed Peppers

Red, green or yellow peppers can be used for
this, either 6 of one type, or a mixture, for a
multicoloured dish. I think a puréed vegetable,
particularly potatoes, or buttered noodles with
poppy seeds, and a simple green salad of
cucumber or lettuce goes well with this dish.

SERVES 6

1 large onion, peeled and finely
  chopped
4 tablespoons olive oil
2 garlic cloves, crushed
2 large tomatoes, skinned (p.108)
  and chopped
225 g/8 oz long-grain brown rice
1 teaspoon dried oregano

600 ml/1 pint water
salt
6 peppers with a good, squarish
  shape
freshly ground black pepper
2 tablespoons chopped parsley
a little extra oil, for greasing

1 Fry the onion in the oil in a medium heavy-based saucepan, then add the garlic, tomato and rice, and cook gently, stirring often, for a further 3–4 minutes until the onion is soft.

2 Add the oregano, water and a teaspoon of salt. Bring up to the boil, then cover tightly and leave to cook very gently for 45 minutes.

3 Meanwhile, slice the peppers in half lengthways, cut out the white membranes, then rinse away the seeds. Parboil the

peppers in 2·5 cm/1 inch water for 5 minutes, then drain and dry on kitchen paper.

4 Preheat the oven to 180c/350f/Gas Mark 4. Season the rice mixture with pepper and more salt if necessary, and stir in the parsley, then spoon this mixture into the peppers.

5 Stand the peppers in a lightly oiled casserole. Bake for 25–30 minutes, until the peppers feel tender when pierced with a skewer.

Variations

The stuffing mixture can be varied in many ways. Try adding small quantities of tasty vegetables such as finely chopped mushrooms or celery; add grated cheese for non-vegan versions. For a Middle Eastern flavour, replace the oregano with 1 teaspoon ground cinnamon or allspice and add 50 g/2 oz each of chopped dried apricots, currants and pine nuts or cashew nuts to the mixture.

Tomatoes with Spicy Stuffing $\boxed{V}$

Beefsteak tomatoes lend themselves to many different stuffings. One of my favourites is this spicy potato mixture. Serve these tomatoes with plain or spiced brown rice, and, if you've time, Curry Sauce (p.265) or a moist side-dish, such as Okra with Cumin and Coriander (p.277).

SERVES 4

4 large beefsteak tomatoes
salt and freshly ground black
  pepper
1 large onion, peeled and chopped
4 tablespoons oil
450 g/1 lb potatoes, peeled and cut
  into 5-mm/¼-inch dice
2 garlic cloves, crushed
2 teaspoons cumin seeds

½ teaspoon turmeric
2 tablespoons roughly chopped
  coriander
salt and freshly ground black
  pepper
butter for greasing

TO GARNISH
coriander sprigs

1 Cut off and reserve the tops of the tomatoes, then use a teaspoon to scoop out the pulp. Chop the pulp, season with salt

and pepper, and put it in the base of a lightly greased shallow ovenproof dish large enough to hold all the tomatoes.

2 Sprinkle the inside of each tomato with salt, then turn them upside down to drain. Preheat the oven to 200c/400f/Gas Mark 6.

3 Next, make the stuffing. Fry the onion in the oil in a frying pan for 5 minutes, then add the potato and garlic.

4 Cook gently for 10 minutes, then add the spices and coriander. Cook for a further 4–5 minutes, until the potato is just tender. Season to taste with salt and pepper.

5 Spoon the potato mixture into the tomatoes. Stand the tomatoes in the dish on top of the tomato pulp, replace their sliced-off tops, and bake for 15–20 minutes, until the tomatoes are just tender. Garnish with the coriander sprigs and serve immediately.

Variation

TOMATOES WITH HERB STUFFING

This variation has a Provençal flavour. Prepare the tomatoes as described. For the filling, use the Herb Stuffing mixture on p.357. Bake as described. These tomatoes are good served on a

---

STUFFED VEGETABLE PLATTER

A selection of 3 or 4 different types of stuffed vegetables arranged on a base of saffron rice makes a stunning centre-piece for a special meal. Choose small vegetables, so that everyone can have several types, and arrange them attractively on a base of saffron rice on two large, flat serving dishes. This is a slightly fiddly meal to make, but the work can be done well in advance, and a cold sauce or dip, such as Guacamole (p.218), or Yogurt and Herb Dressing (p.233), and a green salad, are all the accompaniments needed.

This selection would serve 6:
☐ 3 small Stuffed Aubergines à la Provençale (p.287), using ½ stuffing ingredients
☐ 2 Courgettes with Carrot, Ginger and Almond Stuffing (p.288), using ½ stuffing ingredients, and halved to give 8 portions
☐ 6 large (but not 'beefsteak') tomatoes filled with 1 quantity Herb Stuffing (p.357)
☐ 6 flat mushrooms stuffed with Broad Bean Dip as described on p.88
☐ Double quantity Saffron Rice (p.361)

base of potato purée, accompanied by a lightly cooked vegetable, such as French beans, or a green salad.

TOMATOES WITH COURGETTE AND SWEETCORN STUFFING

Replace the potatoes with 225 g/8 oz courgettes, cut into 6-mm/¼-inch dice, and 225 g/8 oz frozen sweetcorn. Omit spices and add 2 tablespoons roughly chopped parsley and a pinch of chilli powder, if wished.

Baked Stuffed Avocado

A hot stuffed avocado makes an easy and luxurious meal. Serve with Sauce Soubise (p.258) and lemony carrots, or on a base of cooked rice or puréed carrot or potato.

SERVES 4

1 onion, peeled and chopped
15 g/½ oz butter or vegan margarine
2 large ripe avocado pears, halved and stones removed (p.223)
100 g/4 oz brazil nuts, chopped
100 g/4 oz Gruyère cheese, diced
4 tablespoons grated Parmesan cheese
2 tablespoons chopped parsley
2 tablespoons sherry
salt and freshly ground black pepper

1 Preheat the oven to 200c/400f/Gas Mark 6.
2 Fry the onion in the butter or vegan margarine for 10 minutes, until soft but not browned.
3 Meanwhile, scoop the flesh out of the avocado skins with a teaspoon, taking care not to damage the skins. Dice the flesh.
4 Add the fried onion to the avocado flesh, together with the brazil nuts, cheeses, parsley and sherry. Season to taste with salt and pepper.
5 Pile the mixture back into the avocado skins, place them in a shallow ovenproof dish and bake for 10–15 minutes. Serve immediately.

V   *Stuffed Cabbage Rolls in Coconut Sauce*

In this recipe cabbage leaves are rolled around a
simple rice stuffing and baked in a lightly
spiced Savoury Coconut Sauce (p.266). I think a
crunchy salad, such as Sweet Carrot and Fennel
(p.242), or Chicory, Watercress and Walnut
Salad (p.241), goes well with it, or lightly
cooked French beans (p.88).

SERVES 4

1 onion, peeled and chopped
1 tablespoon oil
175 g/6 oz long-grain brown rice
450 ml/15 fl oz water
salt
8 outer cabbage leaves

50 g/2 oz cashew nuts, chopped
50 g/2 oz raisins
freshly ground black pepper
double quantity Savoury Coconut
    Sauce (p.266)

1 Fry the onion in the oil in a large saucepan for 10 minutes.
Add the rice, stir for a moment or two over the heat, then add the
water and a teaspoon of salt.
2 Bring to the boil, then reduce the heat, cover and cook for 45
minutes.
3 Meanwhile, blanch the cabbage leaves by adding them to half
a pan of boiling water and simmering for 2 minutes. Drain and
refresh under the cold tap, then drain again.
4 Preheat the oven to 190c/375f/Gas Mark 5.
5 Add the nuts and raisins to the rice and check the seasoning.
6 Divide the rice mixture between the cabbage leaves, rolling
each one around the filling to make a fat parcel.
7 Place the rolls in a shallow ovenproof dish and pour the sauce
on top of them.
8 Bake, uncovered, for about 40 minutes, until heated through.

Crepes Stuffed with Asparagus and Cream Cheese

Serve this summery main course with baby carrots and new potatoes. Begin the meal with a chilled soup.

SERVES 4–6

750 g/1½ lb fresh asparagus, trimmed, washed and cooked as described on p.91, or 450 g/1 lb frozen asparagus, cooked
450 g/1 lb curd cheese
finely grated rind of 1 lemon
salt and freshly ground black pepper

FOR THE BATTER
100 g/4 oz plain flour
½ teaspoon salt
2 eggs

1 tablespoon olive oil or melted butter
150 ml/5 fl oz milk
150 ml/5 fl oz water

TO FINISH
300 ml/10 fl oz single cream

TO GARNISH
lemon twists
asparagus spears

1 First make the filling: cut the asparagus into 2·5-cm/1-inch lengths, then mix with the curd cheese and lemon rind and season to taste with salt and pepper.
2 Next make the pancake batter: either put all the ingredients into a blender or food processor and whizz until smooth, or put the flour into a bowl with the salt, make a well in the centre and add the eggs, oil and a little of the liquid. Beat until smooth, then gradually add the rest of the liquid.
3 Preheat the oven to 180c/350f/Gas Mark 4.
4 Use the pancake batter to make about 12 thin pancakes as described on p. 447.
5 Roll each pancake around a little of the asparagus mixture, dividing it between them. Place them side by side in a shallow casserole.
6 Pour the cream over the top of the pancakes. Cover with foil and bake for 20–30 minutes, until heated through. Remove the foil and garnish the pancakes with lemon twists and asparagus spears.

Variations

VEGAN CREPES

For vegan pancakes, mix 100 g/4 oz chick pea flour (p.60) with 350 ml/12 fl oz cold water and ½ teaspoon salt. Fry as described, using enough oil to prevent the pancakes from sticking; these pancakes need more fat than egg-based pancakes, but are excellent. Use Sauce Soubise (p.258) instead of the curd cheese, and non-dairy cream instead of the single cream.

CREPES WITH CREAM CHEESE AND MUSHROOMS

Use 450 g/1 lb sliced button mushrooms instead of the asparagus. Fry in 25 g/1 oz butter for 2-3 minutes, until just tender. Mix the mushrooms with the curd cheese, omitting the lemon rind.

COLOURED CREPES

The basic crepe batter can be coloured with saffron, turmeric, or vegetable purées, and, served with contrasting fillings, some attractive colour effects can be created:

☐ To make pale yellow crepes, soak a few strands of saffron in the milk before making the batter, or add ½–1 teaspoon turmeric. The turmeric version is good with a spicy vegetable filling such as Okra with Cumin and Coriander (p.277).

☐ For pale green crepes, add 2 tablespoons spinach purée to the batter; try this with a vivid red filling such as Ratatouille (p.278) or Peperonata (p.276).

FILLINGS FOR CREPES

☐ Golden Spiced Cauliflower (p.274)
☐ Red Cabbage Casserole (p.268)
☐ Ratatouille (p.278)
☐ Peperonata (p.276)
☐ Multicolour Butter Beans (p.307)
☐ Brown Lentil Bake mixture (p.315)

☐ Mushrooms — or Wild Mushrooms — in Cream (p.115)
☐ Glazed Carrots (p.271)
☐ Okra with Cumin and Coriander (p.277)
☐ Spring Vegetable Braise (p.269)

Vegetable Tempura with Dipping Sauce

SERVES 4

225 g/8 oz aubergine, cut into 1-cm/½-inch cubes
2 large carrots, scraped and cut into strips
8 medium flat mushrooms, wiped
1 green pepper, de-seeded and cut into strips
½ cauliflower, broken into florets, larger ones halved or quartered
FOR THE DIPPING SAUCE
4 tablespoons mirin (p.185)
150 ml/5 fl oz soy sauce
1 teaspoon grated fresh ginger

FOR THE BATTER
2 large eggs
300 ml/10 fl oz water
225 g/8 oz plain flour
1 teaspoon salt
oil for deep-frying
TO GARNISH
julienne strips of carrot, fresh ginger and pepper

1 First make the dipping sauce. Bring the mirin to the boil in a small saucepan.
2 Remove from the heat and add the soy sauce and ginger. Pour the dipping sauce into 4 small bowls.
3 Make the batter: break the eggs into a bowl and beat gently until just broken up but not foamy.
4 Mix in the water, then sift in the flour and salt; mix lightly until combined. Don't worry if there are one or two lumps.

5 Have all the vegetables prepared and in separate piles ready for coating in batter.

6 Heat a deep-fryer, half-filled with vegetable oil, to 180c/350F, or when bubbles form on a chopstick dipped into the hot oil.

7 Dip the aubergine into the batter, then put into the hot oil. Do not put in more than a single layer at a time.

8 After about 2 minutes turn the pieces over and fry the other side for a further 2 minutes, until light golden-brown.

9 Remove from the oil on to kitchen paper. Keep the aubergine fritters warm while you fry the rest of the vegetables in the same way.

10 As soon as all the vegetables are done, serve them on 4 heated plates or in baskets lined with paper napkins, garnished with strips of carrot, ginger and pepper. Serve with the bowls of sauce.

SERVING IDEAS FOR VEGETABLE TEMPURA

A basket of these crisp mixed vegetable fritters looks appetizing and makes a delicious meal. Serve them with Sweet Vinegared Rice (p.361), and follow with fresh lychees, for a meal with a Japanese flavour. All the main preparation can be done in advance, leaving only the frying to be completed just before eating.

 ## *Aubergine Fritters in Chick Pea Batter*

Serve these fritters with potatoes and a green
vegetable, and follow with a substantial
pudding, such as Rose Cheesecake (p.431).

SERVES 4

2 medium-sized aubergines	350 ml/12 fl oz cold water
oil for shallow frying	TO SERVE
FOR THE BATTER	lemon slices
100 g/4 oz chick pea flour	Soured Cream or Yogurt and Herb
½ teaspoon salt	Dressing (p.215)

1 Cut the aubergines lengthways into 5-mm/¼-inch slices, place in a colander, and degorge, as described on p.106.

2 Rinse the aubergine slices under cold water; pat dry on kitchen paper.

3 To make the batter, mix the chick pea flour and salt with the water until the mixture is completely smooth and thick.

4 Dip the aubergine slices in the batter, then fry on both sides in hot shallow oil.

5 Drain on kitchen paper. Keep the first batch warm while you fry the rest, then serve at once, garnished with lemon slices and accompanied by Soured Cream and Herb Dressing.

Sweet and Sour Vegetable Stir-fry with Almonds

A delicious mixture of sweet and sour flavours
with the crunch and nourishment of almonds.
If you are planning to serve this with cooked
brown rice (which goes very well with it), put
the rice on to cook well in advance, as the
stir-fry is very quick to make, and the rice takes
45 minutes. It's also very good cold, as a salad
or first course.

SERVES 4

225 g/8 oz red pepper, de-seeded
225 g/8 oz green pepper, de-seeded
225 g/8 oz courgettes
225 g/8 oz celery
225 g/8 oz spring onions
225 g/8 oz button mushrooms, wiped
4 tablespoons olive oil
100 g/4 oz blanched almonds

FOR THE SWEET AND SOUR DRESSING
2 garlic cloves, crushed
15 g/½ oz fresh ginger, grated
4 tablespoons soy sauce
4 tablespoons lemon juice
1 tablespoon wine vinegar
2 tablespoons clear honey

1 Cut the peppers, courgettes and celery into 5-cm/2-inch matchsticks. Trim the spring onions so that there is about 2 cm/1 inch of the green part left. Slice the mushrooms.

2 Next make the sweet and sour dressing: blend all the ingredients in a blender or food processor, or mix them in a bowl.

3 Make the stir-fry just before you want to eat: it only takes a

few minutes to cook. Heat the oil in a wok or large saucepan, then put in the vegetables and stir-fry for 2 minutes, until they are beginning to soften.

4 Add the almonds and the sweet and sour mixture and stir-fry for a further 1–2 minutes, to heat through.

Potato and Cheese Layer

This is very quick and easy to make and popular with children; you need to allow time for it to cook slowly in a cool oven. It's nice with a plainly cooked green vegetable or some watercress.

SERVES 2–4 AS A MAIN COURSE

25 g/1 oz butter
2 large potatoes, peeled and thinly
  sliced
2 onions, peeled and thinly sliced
100 g/4 oz Cheddar cheese, grated
salt and freshly ground black
  pepper

4 tablespoons milk or soya milk

TO GARNISH
parsley sprigs
tomato slices

1 Preheat the oven to 170c/325f/Gas Mark 3. Grease a shallow casserole with half the butter.

2 Put a layer of potatoes in the bottom of the dish, then a thin layer of onion slices, a little grated cheese, then season with salt and pepper.

3 Continue in layers like this until all the ingredients are used, ending with a layer of potato slices. Pour the milk over the top and dot the remaining butter over the top.

4 Bake for about 1½ hours, until the potato feels tender when pierced with a sharp knife or skewer. Garnish with parsley and tomato slices.

QUICK MAIN COURSES

Multicolour Butter Beans (p.307) and Red Kidney Bean Stew (p.308) are both quick to make if you use canned beans; Lentil Dal (p.312) is also speedy and good served with Spiced Potatoes (p.275) or Golden Spiced Cauliflower (p.274). The Spicy Peanut Sauce, in the Ingredients section (p.54), makes an excellent quick meal if served over hot cooked potatoes. Many egg and cheese dishes are quick, especially Baked Eggs (p.321), Pipérade (p.322), Cheese Fondue (p.325) and any of the omelettes (p.329–332).

Quick Savoury Nut Roast (p.351), Peanut Burgers (p.346), Risotto (p.366), Rice Pilaf with Apricots, Raisins and Pine Nuts (p.362) and Millet Pilaf with Nuts and Raisins (p.367) are fast to make, too, as are many pasta dishes, especially Fusille Verde with Mushrooms and Cream (p.115), Tagliatelle with Gorgonzola and Walnuts (p.371), Tagliatelle Verde with Lentil Sauce (p.374) and Summer Linguine (p.378).

Quick Spring Onion and Fresh Herb Flan (p.394) is a speedy pastry dish, and Sweet and Sour Vegetable Stir-Fry with Almonds (above) is a particularly quick vegetable mixture.

Vegetable Hotpot [V]

Serve this family dish with lightly cooked
broccoli and perhaps Vegetarian Gravy (p.255).

SERVES 4

1 × 400-g/14-oz can chopped
 tomatoes
100 g/4 oz walnuts, chopped
1 tablespoon dried oregano
salt and freshly ground black
 pepper
4 large potatoes, peeled, cut into
 5-mm/¼-inch slices, parboiled
 for 4 minutes, then drained

2 green peppers, de-seeded and
 sliced
2 onions, peeled and sliced
1 tablespoon olive oil
butter for greasing

TO GARNISH
parsley sprigs

1 Preheat the oven to 200c/400f/Gas Mark 6. Grease a deep casserole with a little butter.
2 Mix together the tomatoes, walnuts and oregano. Season with salt and pepper.

3 Put a layer of potato slices in the casserole, followed by a layer of pepper, a layer of onion and then some of the tomato and walnut mixture.

4 Continue in this way until all the ingredients are used, ending with potato. Drizzle the olive oil on top.

5 Cover with foil and bake for 1 hour, removing the foil for the last 20 minutes, to brown the top. Garnish with parsley.

Variation

CHEESY VEGETABLE HOTPOT

For a richer, non-vegan version, add 225 g/8 oz grated cheese, layering it with the rest of the ingredients.

[V] Vegetable Kebabs with Rosemary

Marinating the vegetables for several hours
allows them to absorb the flavours. Serve with
Rice Pilaf with Apricots, Raisins and Pine Nuts (p.362).

SERVES 6

12 small button mushrooms, wiped
225 g/8 oz firm tofu, cut into
1 cm/½ inch cubes
1 small red pepper, de-seeded and
cut into strips about 2.5 cm/
1 inch long and 1 cm/½ inch
wide
12 miniature sweetcorn
3 small courgettes, total weight
about 350 g/12 oz, cut into slices
1 cm/½ inch thick
12 cherry tomatoes

6 × 20–25-cm/8–10-inch rosemary
sprigs, leaves scraped off the
lower part, or 6 kebab skewers

FOR THE MARINADE
1 teaspoon mustard powder
1 garlic clove, crushed
2 tablespoons clear honey
2 tablespoons soy sauce
2 tablespoons olive oil
1 teaspoon salt
freshly ground black pepper

1 Thread the vegetables and tofu on to the rosemary sprigs or skewers, putting on first a mushroom, then a piece of tofu followed by some red pepper, sweetcorn, courgette and a cherry tomato.

2 Continue in this way until all the rosemary sprigs or skewers are full.

3 To make the marinade, mix together the mustard, garlic and honey, then gradually stir in the other ingredients.

4 Lay the kebabs on a non-metal tray, polythene container, large plate or casserole big enough for them to lie flat.

5 Spoon the marinade over them, turning them to make sure that all the vegetables are coated.

6 Let the kebabs marinate for at least 1 hour, preferably for several hours, spooning the marinade over them occasionally.

7 Cook the kebabs under a hot grill or on the grid of a barbecue for 10–15 minutes, until the vegetables are tender, turning the skewers so that the vegetables cook evenly.

8 Pour the remaining marinade into a small jug and serve separately.

Variation

All kinds of vegetables, cut into suitably sized pieces, can be used for Vegetable Kebabs, and the tofu can be replaced by the same amount of seitan, or cubes of bought or home-made nut or lentil loaf.

Vegetable Curry $\boxed{V}$

This curry is easy to make and has a good
balance of spices. Serve it with plain or spiced
rice and whatever accompaniments you fancy.

SERVES 4

1 onion, peeled and chopped
40 g/1½ oz butter or vegan
  margarine
2 teaspoons each turmeric, ground
  cumin and ground coriander
¼ teaspoon chilli powder
2 bay leaves
100 g/4 oz cabbage, shredded
450 g/1 lb potatoes, peeled and
  quartered

600 ml/1 pint water
salt and freshly ground black
  pepper
100 g/4 oz frozen peas or green
  beans

TO GARNISH
coriander sprig
lemon twist

1 Fry the onion in the butter or vegan margarine in a large saucepan for 7 minutes, until beginning to soften.

2 Stir in the spices and bay leaves, and cook for a further 2–3 minutes.

3 Add the cabbage, potatoes, water and some salt and pepper. Bring to the boil, then simmer, uncovered, for 15–20 minutes, until the potatoes are nearly tender and the liquid well reduced.

4 Add the peas or beans and cook for a further 5 minutes. Check the seasoning and serve, garnished with a coriander sprig and a lemon twist.

SIDE DISHES FOR CURRIES

Any of these, served in small wooden bowls or ramekins, make attractive accompaniments to curries and spiced rice dishes:

- ☐ Nuts and raisins
- ☐ Macadamia nuts
- ☐ Sliced tomatoes
- ☐ Mango chutney or pickle
- ☐ Sweet Spiced Apricot Chutney (p.516)

- ☐ Lime pickle
- ☐ Sliced banana
- ☐ Desiccated coconut
- ☐ Sliced cucumber in plain yogurt
- ☐ Roasted peanuts or cashew nuts
- ☐ Chopped celery and red pepper
- ☐ Diced apple

Parmigiana

This makes an excellent supper, especially when washed down with some red wine. Serve it with a green salad and some crusty bread, and follow with fresh fruit or a basket of home-made biscuits.

SERVES 4

900 g/2 lb aubergines
salt
olive oil, for frying
2 large onions, peeled and finely chopped
2 garlic cloves, crushed
1 × 400-g/14-oz can chopped tomatoes

225 g/8 oz cheese, preferably Mozzarella, thinly sliced
6 tablespoons grated Parmesan cheese
freshly ground black pepper

1 Cut the aubergines into 5-mm/¼-inch circles. Salt, drain and rinse the aubergine slices as described on p.106.

2 Preheat the oven to 200c/400f/Gas Mark 6. Heat a little oil in a large saucepan and fry the onion and garlic for 10 minutes.

3 Remove the onion mixture with a draining spoon to a plate, add the aubergine circles to the pan and fry until crisp and lightly browned, adding more oil if necessary.

4 Layer the aubergines, onion, tomatoes and sliced cheese in an ovenproof dish, sprinkling some Parmesan cheese and salt and pepper between the layers and ending with a layer of aubergines.

5 Bake, uncovered, for 40–60 minutes, until the aubergines are tender.

Spinach Gnocchi

Serve the gnocchi with buttered pasta and a
colourful salad with an Italian flavour for a light
main course.

SERVES 4

700 g/1½ lb fresh spinach, cooked, drained and chopped, or 450 g/ 1 lb frozen chopped spinach, thawed

225 g/8 oz skimmed milk soft white cheese

175 g/6 oz curd cheese

50 g/2 oz Parmesan cheese, grated

2 egg yolks

salt and freshly ground black pepper

freshly grated nutmeg

wheatgerm or flour for coating

a little butter

TO SERVE

grated Parmesan cheese

1 Make sure the spinach is well drained, then purée it in a blender or food processor. Put the purée into a saucepan and dry off over the heat for a minute or two. Remove from the heat.

2 In a bowl, mix together the skimmed milk cheese, curd cheese, Parmesan cheese, egg yolks, and spinach. Season with salt, pepper and nutmeg. If the mixture is very soft, put it into the fridge to firm up for about 30 minutes.

3 Roll heaped teaspoons of the mixture in wheatgerm or flour. (All this can be done in advance.)

4 To cook the gnocchi, first heat the oven to low, to keep the gnocchi warm as they're ready. Half fill a large saucepan with lightly salted water and bring just to the boil.

5 Drop 6–8 gnocchi into the water and let them simmer very gently for about 4–5 minutes, until they float to the surface.

6 Make sure the water does not get beyond a bare simmer, and remove the gnocchi as soon as they are ready, or they may fall apart.

7 Drain the gnocchi well, then put them into a warmed serving dish, dot with a little butter and keep them warm while you cook another batch.

8 When all the gnocchi are done, sprinkle with grated Parmesan cheese and serve immediately.

Pulse Dishes

I know that some people are put off using pulses because of the need to soak and cook them in advance. All the recipes in this section can either be made from quick-cooking pulses which do not need soaking first, or from canned ones, which I find excellent. However, the most economical way is to buy dried pulses and soak and cook them yourself, and all the information about this is to be found in the Ingredients section of the book (p.49) along with more ideas for using the various types of pulse. Once cooked, pulses can be made into a variety of excellent main dishes, ranging from colourful casseroles to savoury bakes, loaves and burgers.

Multicolour Butter Beans $\boxed{V}$

SERVES 4

3 celery sticks, cut into 5-mm/
  ¼-inch dice
1 small red pepper, de-seeded and
  cut into 5-mm/¼-inch dice
1 tablespoon oil
2 teaspoons curry powder
225 g/8 oz frozen sweetcorn
  kernels

225 g/8 oz butter beans, soaked,
  cooked and drained, or 2 ×
  425-g/15-oz cans butter beans,
  drained
salt and freshly ground black
  pepper
TO GARNISH
chopped parsley

1 Fry the celery and red pepper in the oil in a large saucepan for 10 minutes, until soft but not browned.
2 Stir in the curry powder, then add the sweetcorn and butter beans. Cook over a gentle heat for 4–5 minutes, until heated through. Season to taste with salt and pepper, sprinkle with parsley and serve.

Red Kidney Bean Stew

V

SERVES 4

1 tablespoon olive oil
1 large onion, sliced
1 large red pepper, de-seeded and
   chopped
2 carrots, scraped and diced
2 leeks or medium courgettes,
   sliced
2 celery sticks, sliced
175 g/6 oz mushrooms, washed
   and sliced

4 tomatoes, skinned (p.108) and
   quartered
100 g/4 oz red kidney beans,
   soaked, cooked and drained
   (p.58), or 1 × 425-g/15-oz can,
   rinsed and drained
½ teaspoon paprika pepper
salt and freshly ground black
   pepper

1 Heat the oil in a large saucepan and add the onion, red pepper, carrots, leeks or courgettes and celery.
2 Cook gently for 10 minutes, covered, then add the mushrooms, tomatoes, kidney beans, paprika and salt and pepper to taste.
3 Continue to cook, covered, for a further 10–15 minutes. Check the seasoning and serve.

Lentils and Mushrooms au Gratin

In this recipe, lentils are made into a thick
sauce, poured over mushrooms, topped with
crumbs and cheese and baked until crisp and
browned. Serve with a lightly cooked green
vegetable such as cabbage or broccoli.

SERVES 4

175 g/6 oz split red lentils
600 ml/1 pint water
1 large onion, peeled and finely
   chopped
50 g/2 oz butter

finely grated rind and juice of ½
   lemon
1 teaspoon yeast extract

salt and freshly ground black
   pepper
100 g/4 oz mushrooms, washed
   and sliced

50 g/2 oz fresh wholewheat
   breadcrumbs
50 g/2 oz Cheddar cheese, grated

1 Put the lentils and water into a medium saucepan and simmer very gently, uncovered, until the lentils are tender and all the liquid absorbed – about 20 minutes.

2 Preheat the oven to 180c/350f/Gas Mark 4.

3 Fry the onion in half the butter for 10 minutes until soft and lightly browned.

4 Add the onion to the lentils, together with the lemon rind and juice, yeast extract and salt and pepper to taste. Purée in a blender or food processor, or beat well with a wooden spoon, to make a thick purée.

5 Fry the mushrooms in the remaining butter for 2–3 minutes, then put them into a shallow ovenproof dish and pour the lentil mixture on top. Sprinkle with the breadcrumbs and the grated cheese.

6 Bake for 40–45 minutes, until golden and crisp on top, and hot and bubbly underneath.

Variation

LEEKS AND LENTILS AU GRATIN

Make the lentil sauce exactly as described. Replace the mushrooms with 1 kg/2¼ lb leeks, cleaned, cut into 2·5-cm/ 1-inch lengths, boiled until tender, then drained.

Pease Pudding

This is traditionally served as an
accompaniment to meat.

SERVES 4

450 g/1 lb yellow split peas
2 large onions, peeled and chopped
50 g/2 oz butter
2 teaspoons fennel seeds

2 eggs (optional)
salt and freshly ground black
   pepper

1 Put the split peas into a saucepan, cover with water and cook gently until soft – this takes about 30 minutes or so. Drain.

2 Preheat oven to 180c/350f/Gas Mark 4. (Or, if you're roasting potatoes at a higher temperature, put the pease pudding on a low shelf – the temperature isn't crucial.)

3 Fry the onions in the butter for 8 minutes, then add the fennel seeds, stir for 1–2 minutes, then add the split peas and the eggs, if you're using these. Season with salt and pepper.

4 Spoon the mixture into a lightly greased fairly shallow oven-proof dish and bake for 50–60 minutes, until browned on top.

Chilli con Carne Vegetariana

A tasty, substantial dish which has been
responsible for more than one male convert to
vegetarianism. Serve with hot brown rice or
jacket potatoes with soured cream and chives,
and a green salad.

SERVES 4

1 tablespoon olive oil
1 onion, peeled and chopped
1 red pepper, de-seeded and
  chopped
1 garlic clove, crushed
1 × 400-g/14-oz can tomatoes
225 g/8 oz red kidney beans,
  soaked, cooked and drained
  (p.58), or 2 × 425-g/15-oz cans
  red kidney beans

100 g/4 oz whole green lentils,
  simmered in plenty of water for
  40–45 minutes, until tender
1 teaspoon mild paprika pepper
½–1 teaspoon chilli powder
salt and freshly ground black
  pepper
a little sugar
TO GARNISH
coriander sprig

1 Heat the oil in a large saucepan and fry the onion and pepper for 10 minutes, then add the garlic and tomatoes.

2 Drain the red kidney beans and lentils, reserving the liquid. Add the beans and lentils to the tomato mixture, together with the paprika and chilli powder.

3 Simmer for about 15 minutes, then season with salt, pepper and sugar, and serve, garnished with coriander.

Felafel in Pitta Pockets

SERVES 4

225 g/8 oz chick peas, soaked, ·
  cooked and drained, or 2 ×
425-g/15-oz cans, drained
1 egg, beaten
1 large onion, finely chopped
2 tablespoons chopped parsley
1 garlic clove, crushed
1 teaspoon ground coriander
1 teaspoon ground cumin
a pinch of chilli powder
salt and freshly ground black
  pepper
FOR COATING AND FRYING
plain flour for coating

1 egg, beaten
dry breadcrumbs
oil for shallow frying
TO SERVE
4 wholewheat pitta breads
2 tomatoes, sliced
½ cucumber, sliced
lemon wedges
fennel sprigs

1 Mash the chick peas thoroughly, then add the egg, onion, parsley, garlic and spices. Mix well; season to taste with salt and pepper.

2 Shape the mixture into balls about the size of chestnuts, then coat in flour, beaten egg and breadcrumbs.

3 Put the pitta bread to warm under the grill or in a moderate oven.

4 Pour enough oil into a frying pan to cover the base thinly, and when it is hot fry the felafel for about 3 minutes on each side, or until golden-brown. Drain well on kitchen paper.

5 Cut each pitta bread in half across the centre, then fill each with felafel, sliced tomato and cucumber and garnish with lemon and fennel.

Variation

VEGAN FELAFEL

Use 2 tablespoons chick pea flour to bind the felafel mixture instead of the beaten egg. Mix it in well. Dip the balls in the chick pea flour blended with cold water to make a coating consistency, then into dry breadcrumbs. Fry as described above.

SERVING IDEAS FOR FELAFEL

These crisp, tasty little savoury balls make a filling and delicious snack, served in a pocket of pitta bread with salads and any spicy relishes you fancy. Or the felafel is good served with a salad and a Yogurt and Herb Dressing (p.233). If you're using canned chick peas, which are usually softer than home-cooked ones, you may need to add a few fresh breadcrumbs to the mixture to make it firm enough to shape. The parsley is important for the flavour.

Lentil Dal

Dal is usually served as an accompaniment to curries or spiced rice dishes, spooned or poured over the top, adding extra flavour.

SERVES 4

225 g/8 oz split red lentils
1 onion, peeled and chopped
1 large garlic clove, crushed
1 bay leaf
1 whole fresh green chilli
2·5-cm/1-inch piece fresh ginger, peeled and grated
½ teaspoon turmeric

2 teaspoons each ground cumin and ground coriander
1–2 teaspoons salt
25 g/1 oz coconut cream
1 tablespoon lemon juice

TO GARNISH
bay leaves

1 Put the lentils into a saucepan with enough cold water to come 1 cm/½ inch above them, and add the chopped onion, garlic, bay leaf, whole chilli, ginger and turmeric.

2 Cook gently, half-covered, for about 20 minutes, until the lentils are soft, stirring occasionally and adding a little more water if necessary to prevent the lentils from sticking. The final mixture should be quite runny, like a purée, but not watery.

3 Stir in the cumin, coriander and salt to taste. If possible, leave to stand, covered, for 20–30 minutes, to allow the flavours to blend.

4 Discard the bay leaf and chilli, and stir in the coconut cream. Reheat gently, stirring, until the coconut has melted. Add the lemon juice, check the seasoning and serve the lentil dal, garnished with a few bay leaves.

SERVING IDEAS FOR LENTIL DAL

I also like dal as a main dish, poured over lightly cooked vegetables and served with mango chutney and lime pickle, or with some plain boiled rice and some wedges of hardboiled egg. It's also good served with the Spiced Potatoes on p. 275, with a side-dish of tomato and onion salad. It depends how hungry you're feeling!

Spicy Lentil Burgers

Lightly spiced, moist and delicious, these burgers can be served in soft wholewheat burger buns, with salad and a yogurt and herb sauce or mayonnaise, or with cooked vegetables and a savoury sauce. The burgers freeze well and can be cooked from frozen.

SERVES 4

2 large onions, peeled and finely chopped
2 carrots, scraped and finely chopped
1 celery stick, finely chopped
2 tablespoons olive oil
1 large garlic clove, crushed
225 g/8 oz green or brown lentils, cooked until tender and well drained (p.58)
½ teaspoon ground cumin

½ teaspoon ground coriander
6 tablespoons chopped parsley
1 tablespoon lemon juice
salt and freshly ground black pepper
plain flour for coating
oil for shallow frying

TO GARNISH
watercress
tomato slices

1 Fry the onion, carrot and celery in the oil in a large saucepan for 10 minutes until soft and lightly browned, stirring from time to time.

2 Add the garlic, lentils, cumin, coriander, parsley and lemon juice. Mash by hand, or purée roughly in a food processor or blender, until the mixture holds together. Season with salt and pepper.

3 With floured hands, shape the mixture into 10–12 flat burgers, using a palette knife. Coat the burgers with flour.

4 Fry the burgers in a little oil until crisp and browned, turning them over carefully to fry the second side.

5 Drain on kitchen paper and serve garnished with watercress and tomato.

Lentil Shepherd's Pie

This can be prepared in advance, ready for cooking, and only needs a quickly cooked vegetable, such as sprouts or carrots, to go with it.

SERVES 4

225 g/8 oz green or brown lentils
50 g/2 oz butter or vegan margarine
2 large onions, peeled and thinly sliced
1 garlic clove, crushed
1 teaspoon dried mixed herbs
1 × 425-g/15-oz can tomatoes, chopped

2 tablespoons soy sauce
2–3 tablespoons chopped parsley
salt and freshly ground black pepper
700 g/1½ lb potatoes, cooked and mashed
a little extra butter or vegan margarine

1 Put the lentils into a large saucepan, cover with water and boil gently until tender – about 45 minutes. Drain.

2 Preheat the oven to 200c/400f/Gas Mark 6. Use half the butter or vegan margarine to grease a shallow ovenproof dish.

3 Fry the onions in the remaining butter or vegan margarine in a large saucepan for 10 minutes.

4 Add the garlic, mixed herbs, tomatoes, soy sauce, lentils, parsley and salt and pepper to taste.

5 Spoon the mixture into the dish. Spread the mashed potatoes evenly over the top, draw the prongs of the fork over the surface to make ridges and dot with a little butter or vegan margarine.

6 Bake the pie for 45 minutes, until the potato is golden-brown.

Middle Eastern Chick Pea Stew [V]

SERVES 4

900 g/2 lb aubergines
salt
2 large onions, peeled and chopped
4 tablespoons olive oil
2 garlic cloves, crushed
1 × 425-g/15-oz can tomatoes

100 g/4 oz chick peas, soaked,
   cooked and drained, or 1 ×
   425-g/15-oz can chick peas,
   drained
freshly ground black pepper
TO GARNISH
bay leaves

1 Cut the aubergines into 1-cm/½-inch dice, sprinkle with salt, place in a colander, put a weight on top and leave for 30 minutes.
2 Rinse the aubergines and gently squeeze out as much liquid as you can.
3 Preheat the oven to 200c/400f/Gas Mark 6.
4 Fry the onion in half the oil in a large saucepan for 10 minutes. Remove with a slotted spoon, and fry the aubergine pieces in the remaining oil until crisp and lightly browned. Drain on kitchen paper.
5 Put the onion and aubergine into a casserole with the rest of the ingredients and bake in the oven for about 40 minutes, until all the vegetables are tender and the flavours have blended.

Brown Lentil Bake with Pineapple [V]

SERVES 4

2 large onions, peeled and finely
   chopped
2 tablespoons olive oil
1 large garlic clove, crushed
225 g/8 oz green or brown lentils,
   cooked until tender and well
   drained (p.58)
2 tablespoons chopped parsley

1 teaspoon mixed herbs
2 tablespoons soy sauce
salt and freshly ground black
   pepper
25–50 g/1–2 oz wholewheat
   breadcrumbs
1 × 225-g/8-oz can pineapple
   rings, drained

1 Preheat the oven to 180c/350f/Gas Mark 4.
2 Fry the onion in the oil in a large saucepan for 10 minutes until

soft and lightly browned, stirring occasionally.

3 Add the garlic, lentils, parsley, mixed herbs and soy sauce. Mash by hand, or purée roughly in a blender or food processor, until the mixture holds together. Season to taste with salt and pepper.

4 Transfer to a shallow ovenproof dish. Sprinkle with the crumbs.

5 Bake for 20 minutes, then remove from the oven, carefully place the pineapple rings on top and bake for a further 10–15 minutes, until the pineapple is hot.

FRUIT WITH PULSES

The flavour of fruit complements pulses well and a number of traditional recipes, especially in Germany, Scandinavia and Russia, feature this combination. Try the Brown Lentil Bake with Pineapple (p.315), the Savoury Lentil Loaf (p.318) with Cranberry or Apple Sauce, and the Spicy Lentil Burgers (p.313) with sliced pineapple or mango.

V | *Savoury Brown Lentil Stew*

SERVES 4

1 large onion, thinly sliced
4 tablespoons oil
900 g/2 lb potatoes, cut into even-sized chunks
450 g/1 lb carrots, scraped and diced
4 celery sticks, sliced
225 g/8 oz mushrooms, wiped and sliced
100 g/4 oz brown or green lentils, or split orange lentils

2 tablespoons plain flour
2 teaspoons dried mixed herbs
1·2 litres/2 pints Dark Vegetable Stock (p.155) or water
4 tablespoons soy sauce
salt and freshly ground black pepper

TO GARNISH
chopped parsley

1 Fry the onion in the oil in a large saucepan over a moderate heat for 3–4 minutes, stirring occasionally until soft, but not brown.

2 Add the potatoes, carrots, celery, mushrooms and lentils; stir, then sprinkle in the flour and the herbs and stir again.

3 Add the stock or water, soy sauce and salt and pepper to taste. Bring to the boil, stir well, then cover and simmer gently until the lentils are tender – 20–30 minutes for split lentils, 40–50 minutes for whole green or brown. Stir the stew occasionally.

4 Check the seasoning, then sprinkle a little chopped parsley over the top and serve immediately.

Savoury Lentil Loaf

Serve this loaf with roast potatoes, green
vegetables and Apple Sauce (p.122).

SERVES 6—8

350 g/12 oz split red lentils
475 ml/16 fl oz water
1 bay leaf
225 g/8 oz Cheddar cheese, grated
1 large onion, peeled and finely
  chopped
50 g/2 oz button mushrooms,
  washed and finely chopped
75 g/3 oz fresh wholewheat
  breadcrumbs

1 tablespoon chopped parsley
1 tablespoon lemon juice
2 eggs, lightly beaten
salt and freshly ground black
  pepper
butter and dried breadcrumbs for
  coating

1 Line a 900 g/2 lb loaf tin with a long, narrow strip of greased greaseproof or non-stick paper on the base and up the narrow sides. Grease well with butter and sprinkle generously with dried crumbs.

2 Put the lentils, water and bay leaf into a medium saucepan, cover and simmer very gently, until the lentils are tender and all the liquid absorbed – about 20 minutes. Remove the bay leaf.

3 Preheat the oven to 190c/375f/Gas Mark 5.

4 Add the cheese to the lentils, together with the onion, mushrooms, breadcrumbs, parsley, lemon juice and egg. Mix well and season to taste with salt and pepper, then spoon the mixture into the tin and level the top.

5 Bake, uncovered, for 1–1½ hours, until firm and golden-

brown on top. Slip a knife around the edges of the loaf to loosen, then carefully turn out.

Variation

VEGAN LENTIL LOAF

Omit the egg and cheese and beat in 75 g/3 oz vegan margarine. Form into a roll. Coat in crumbs and bake in a little oil on a baking sheet instead of in the loaf tin.

Vegetarian Moussaka

This is excellent with a crisp green salad and some full-bodied but inexpensive red wine. For a complete meal with a Greek flavour, start with Tsatsiki (p.250) and warm pitta bread and finish with an arranged fruit salad or dates with yogurt, cream and honey. The Moussaka freezes well, either fully cooked (for simply heating through when required) or uncooked, in which case the topping is best added just before baking.

SERVES 6

450 g/1 lb aubergines, thinly sliced
salt
2 large onions, peeled and chopped
4 tablespoons olive oil
1 garlic clove, crushed
225 g/8 oz black beans, soaked and cooked until tender, or 2 × 425-g/15-oz cans red kidney beans
1 × 225-g/8-oz can chopped tomatoes
¼ teaspoon ground allspice or cinnamon

freshly ground black pepper
a little sugar
150 ml/5 fl oz soured cream or plain yogurt
1 egg
freshly grated nutmeg
4 tablespoons grated Parmesan cheese
butter for greasing

1 Salt, drain and rinse the aubergine slices, as described on p.106.

2 Meanwhile, fry the onion in 2 tablespoons of the oil for 10 minutes. Add the garlic, drained beans, tomatoes and allspice or cinnamon.

3 Mix well, mashing the beans to make a rough purée. Season with salt, pepper and a pinch of sugar if necessary.

4 Preheat the oven to 180c/350f/Gas Mark 4. Grease a large shallow ovenproof dish.

5 Fry the aubergine slices in the rest of the olive oil for 2–3 minutes on each side, until tender. Drain on kitchen paper.

6 Put a layer of aubergine slices in the base of the ovenproof dish; cover with half the bean mixture. Repeat the layers, then finish with a final layer of aubergine.

7 Whisk the soured cream or yogurt with the egg. Season with salt, pepper and nutmeg. Pour over the moussaka.

8 Sprinkle with Parmesan cheese and bake for 40–45 minutes, until golden.

Egg and Cheese Dishes

Eggs and cheese are useful protein foods for lacto-vegetarians and can be made into some particularly pleasant dishes such as fondues (p.325), soufflés (p.334–335), roulades (p.337) and gnocchi (p.341). Served with lightly cooked vegetables or a fresh salad, there is no reason why cheese and egg dishes, although relatively high in fat, should not feature in the main meals of a healthy diet. Aim to achieve a good balance by serving pulse, pasta, cereal or nut dishes frequently on other days, and by keeping your other meals of the day low in fat. Then you can enjoy these tasty and time-saving dishes with a clear conscience! For simple, basic ways of cooking eggs, see the Ingredients section (p.49).

Eggs Florentine

SERVES 4

15 g/½ oz butter
900 g/2 lb fresh spinach, or 450 g/
1 lb frozen spinach, cooked,
    drained and chopped
salt and freshly ground black
    pepper

freshly grated nutmeg
4 eggs
300 ml/10 fl oz Cheese Sauce
    (p.261)
25 g/1 oz Gruyère or Cheddar
    cheese, grated

1 Add the butter to the spinach and mix well. Season to taste with salt, pepper and nutmeg and put it into a shallow oven-proof dish.
2 Heat the grill. Poach the eggs as described on p. 156.
3 Carefully place the eggs on top of the spinach, pour the Cheese Sauce on top and sprinkle with the grated Gruyère or Cheddar cheese.
4 Place the dish under the grill until the cheese is golden and melted. Serve immediately.

REDUCING THE CALORIES IN CHEESE

If you want to cut down on the calories in a cheese dish, try using small quantities of a strongly flavoured cheese such as a mature farmhouse Cheddar or Parmesan. Personally I prefer following this course of action to using the reduced-fat cheeses which are now available. I would rather have half or two-thirds the quantity of a traditionally produced cheese with a really good flavour and texture.

Baked Eggs

A quick and easy supper dish, baked eggs can be varied according to the ingredients available. Serve with hot wholewheat toast or warm rolls.

SERVES 1

1 egg
a little butter
2 tablespoons cooked vegetables
   (onion, sweet pepper, tomato,
   asparagus, ratatouille, etc.)

salt and freshly ground black
   pepper

1 Preheat the oven to 180c/350f/Gas Mark 4. Using a little butter, grease a small ramekin dish.
2 Have ready a roasting tin and a kettle of boiling water.
3 Put the cooked vegetables into the ramekin, making a well in the centre.
4 Break in an egg, season with salt and pepper and dot with a little butter.
5 Place the ramekin in the roasting tin and pour in boiling water to come halfway up the sides of the ramekin. Cover the top of the ramekin with foil.
6 Bake for 10–12 minutes, until the egg is lightly set. Serve immediately with toast or rolls.

Variation

BAKED EGGS IN TOMATO CUPS

Use a medium beefsteak tomato for each person. Cut off the top
and reserve this for a lid. Scoop out enough of the tomato pulp to
make room for the egg (keep this pulp for another use). Season
the inside of the tomato with salt and freshly ground black
pepper, and scatter with a little chopped fresh basil if available.
Break an egg into each tomato, season, dot with butter, replace
the tomato top, place in a lightly greased shallow casserole dish
and bake for about 20 minutes, until the egg is set and the
tomato tender. Serve with hot buttered toast or noodles for a
complete light meal.

Pipérade

This French version of scrambled eggs with
vegetables makes a delicious and economical
supper dish in the late summer when tomatoes
and peppers are cheap. It's an excellent dish for
one person: just halve the ingredients.

SERVES 2

1 large onion, peeled and chopped
25 g/1 oz butter
1 large green pepper, de-seeded
  and chopped
450 g/1 lb tomatoes, skinned
  (p.108) and chopped
1–2 garlic cloves, crushed
4 eggs, beaten
salt and freshly ground black
  pepper

TO GARNISH
lovage sprig

TO SERVE
hot, crusty rolls or fingers of hot
  wholewheat toast

1 Fry the onion in the butter for 10 minutes, until soft but not
browned.
2 Add the green pepper, tomatoes and garlic and cook gently,
uncovered, for a further 15–20 minutes, until the vegetables are
soft but not mushy, stirring from time to time.

3 Strain in the beaten eggs and stir gently until they begin to set. Remove from the heat (the eggs will continue to cook in their own heat).

4 Season with salt and pepper, garnish with lovage and serve with the crusty rolls or fingers of toast.

Stuffed Eggs

The best eggs for hardboiling are several days old. Newly laid eggs are difficult to peel because the white sticks so firmly to the shell. Lightly flavoured with curry, these make a tasty first course or snack. In my experience, they're particularly popular with children.

SERVES 4 AS A STARTER, 2 AS A LIGHT MEAL

4 hardboiled eggs, shelled
¼ teaspoon curry powder
50 g/2 oz Cheddar cheese, finely grated
4 tablespoons milk

salt and freshly ground black pepper

TO GARNISH
a few lettuce leaves
chopped chives

1 Cut the eggs in half lengthways and scoop the yolks into a bowl without breaking the whites.

2 Mash the yolks with the curry powder, cheese and milk and mix until smooth.

3 Season with salt and pepper.

4 Spoon the mixture back into the egg whites and place on a base of lettuce leaves on a serving plate. Sprinkle with chopped chives.

Variation

STUFFED EGGS WITH BLACK OLIVE PÂTÉ
Omit the curry powder and chives. Top each stuffed egg with ½ teaspoon Black Olive Pâté (p.383).

Scotch Eggs Vegetarian-Style

The colour of the eggs against the dark brown
lentils looks particularly attractive when these
eggs are cut, and the flavours combine
excellently. Serve with salad.

SERVES 4

4 hardboiled eggs, shelled
1 egg, beaten
½ quantity Brown Lentil Bake
    mixture (p.315)
salt and freshly ground black
    pepper

wholewheat flour and fresh
    wholewheat breadcrumbs for
    coating
vegetable oil for deep-frying

1 Dip each egg into beaten egg, then coat with a quarter of the
lentil mixture, pressing it round smoothly and firmly.
2 Coat the eggs first in the remaining beaten egg, then in
seasoned flour; then repeat egg and breadcrumbing.
3 Heat the oil in a deep-fryer to 160c/325F, or when a small cube
of stale bread browns in 1 minute. Put the Scotch eggs into the
oil and fry gently until golden.
4 Remove the Scotch eggs with a slotted spoon and drain on
kitchen paper. Cut the eggs in half and serve hot or cold.

COOKING CHEESE

Certain cheeses, mainly the hard
and semi-hard types, are best for
cooking, because they melt well
without becoming tough or
stringy. Sometimes a particular
type is best, in which case I have
suggested this in the recipe;
where no type is specified, use a
normal, reasonably priced
Cheddar or Cheddar-type
cheese.

Swiss Cheese Fondue

Cheese fondue makes an excellent, cosy supper
for 2–4 people. It's best made in a heavy-based
saucepan or casserole which can be brought to
the table and set on a fondue burner. It's also a
very good emergency meal. Keep a bag of
grated cheese and a couple of French sticks in
the freezer, and a bottle of dry cider or white
wine in the cupboard, and you can whizz up a
cheese fondue in minutes.

SERVES 4

1 garlic clove, halved
300 ml/10 fl oz dry white wine or
  cider
400 g/14 oz Gruyère or Edam
  cheese, grated
1 tablespoon cornflour
2 tablespoons Kirsch or gin
  (optional)

2 teaspoons lemon juice
salt and freshly ground black
  pepper
freshly grated nutmeg
TO SERVE
2 French sticks, 1 white and 1
  wholewheat, cut into bite-sized
  pieces and warmed in the oven

1 Rub the garlic around the inside of a medium saucepan, then
discard.
2 Put all but 4 tablespoons of the wine or cider into the
saucepan and bring just to the boil, then add the cheese and stir
over a gentle heat until melted.
3 Mix the cornflour with the remaining wine or cider and the
Kirsch or gin, if using. Pour this into the cheese mixture, stirring
until slightly thickened.
4 Remove from the heat and add the lemon juice. Season to taste
with salt, pepper and nutmeg. Put the warmed bread cubes into
2 baskets, mixing up the 2 types.
5 Place the pan of fondue in the centre of the table, and use long
forks to spear pieces of warm French bread and dip them into
the cheese fondue.

Cheese and Parsley Fritters

Children love these served with Parsley Sauce
(p.261), chips (if allowed!), and a lightly cooked
vegetable.

SERVES 4

600 ml/1 pint milk
1 small onion, peeled and stuck
　with 1 clove
1 bay leaf
100 g/4 oz semolina
100 g/4 oz Cheddar cheese, grated
1–2 tablespoons chopped parsley
good pinch cayenne pepper
salt and freshly ground black
　pepper

1 large egg, beaten with 1
　tablespoon water
dried breadcrumbs for coating
oil for shallow-frying
TO GARNISH
lemon slices
parsley sprigs

1 Bring the milk, onion and bay leaf to the boil in a large saucepan.
2 Remove from the heat, cover and leave to infuse for 10–15 minutes.
3 Remove and discard the onion and bay leaf. Return the milk to the boil, then gradually sprinkle the semolina over the top, stirring all the time.
4 Simmer for about 5 minutes, stirring often, to cook the semolina, then remove from the heat and beat in the cheese, parsley, cayenne pepper and salt and pepper.
5 Spread the mixture out to a depth of about 1 cm/½ inch on an oiled plate or baking sheet. Smooth the surface and allow to cool completely.
6 Cut the mixture into squares or triangles. Dip first into beaten egg, then dried breadcrumbs, to coat thoroughly. Shallow-fry in hot oil until crisp on both sides, then drain the fritters well on kitchen paper.
7 Garnish with lemon slices and parsley sprigs and serve immediately.

Yeast Pizza

SERVES 4

450 g/1 lb plain 85% wholewheat
  flour
1 sachet instant dried yeast
½ teaspoon salt
about 175 ml/6 fl oz warm water
2 tablespoons oil
FOR THE TOPPING
2 large onions, peeled and chopped
oil
4 tablespoons tomato purée

1 garlic clove, crushed
salt and freshly ground black
  pepper
100 g/4 oz mushrooms, washed
  and sliced or 1 green pepper,
  de-seeded and sliced
100 g/4 oz Mozzarella cheese,
  sliced
a few black olives
a little dried oregano

1 First make the dough. Put the flour, yeast, salt, water and oil
into a large mixing bowl and mix to a dough.
2 Turn the dough out on to a lightly floured work surface and
knead for 5 minutes until smooth and silky.
3 Put the dough into a large bowl, cover with a damp cloth and
leave until doubled in size.
4 Punch down the dough, divide it between two well-greased
20-cm/8-inch flan tins or one 30-cm/12-inch one, or press it into
a 30-cm/12-inch circle on a baking sheet. Leave in a warm place
while you make the filling.
5 To make the topping, fry the onion in 2 tablespoons oil for 10
minutes, until soft and lightly coloured, then stir in the tomato
purée and garlic and season to taste with salt and pepper.
6 Preheat the oven to 250c/500f/Gas Mark 9.
7 Flatten the dough with your hands, pressing it well into the
tins and up the sides a little, or raising the edge of the dough
circle slightly.
8 Spread the tomato mixture on top of the dough, then arrange
the mushrooms or green pepper, cheese slices and olives on top.
9 Drizzle a little oil over the top and sprinkle with oregano.
Leave in a warm place for 15–20 minutes, for the dough to prove,
then bake for 15–20 minutes, until the pizza is puffed up and
golden-brown on top.

Variations

QUICK SCONE PIZZA

Make the scone mixture (p.489), adding 40 g/1½ oz grated cheese before putting in the liquid. Use 150 ml/5 fl oz milk or soya milk and omit the egg. Roll out the dough and make the topping as described above. Bake the pizza immediately, at 220c/425f/Gas Mark 7, for 20–25 minutes until golden-brown.

KALEIDOSCOPE PIZZA

Using a knife, gently score the top of the pizza into six sections. Fill each section with a different coloured topping, for instance, cooked and drained sweetcorn kernels, sliced tomatoes, lightly fried onion rings, lightly fried green pepper, sliced and fried mushrooms, lightly steamed sliced courgettes. Sprinkle with a little grated cheese and oil, then bake as described.

PEPPER PIZZA

Divide the pizza as described above, making six or eight sections. Fill the sections with different coloured peppers, de-seeded, chopped and lightly fried. Use as many different colours as you can find: green, red, yellow and black, frying them separately to keep the colours clear. Sprinkle with cheese and bake as described.

FANCY PIZZA

For this pretty variation, arrange pepper slices in the centre, then a circle of sliced button mushrooms, a circle alternating sliced cooked baby sweetcorn and black olives and an outer circle of sliced Mozzarella cheese. Cover the pizza with foil. Bake for 10 minutes, then uncover for the remaining baking time. Garnish the pizza with bay leaves.

YEAST

Dried yeast, easy-blend yeast (which you add straight to the flour without mixing with water) and fresh yeast are all interchangeable.

Allow 25 g/1 oz fresh yeast or 15 g/½ oz (1 tablespoon) dried yeast to 1·5 kg/3½ lb flour. For easy-blend yeast, follow packet directions.

It is essential that the yeast, whether fresh or dried, is in good condition. Buy from a shop with a quick turnover and store carefully.

Fresh yeast will keep in a screwtop jar in a cool place for up to a week. It should be pale beige in colour with no dark specks and look moist but not damp; it should feel cool to the touch and break cleanly and easily when crumbled. It should have a sweet, fresh smell. Dried yeast does not last for ever. If it smells 'winey' and does not froth up vigorously when mixed with water and sugar, it is not working properly – throw it away; if you use it you will only waste your time and ingredients.

Although yeast likes warmth, too much heat kills it. So don't let it get too hot at any stage.

Omelette

SERVES 1

2-3 eggs
10 g/¼ oz butter

salt and freshly ground black pepper

1 Crack the eggs into a bowl, season with salt and pepper, and beat lightly, just to combine.

2 Put a 12–15-cm/5–6-inch non-stick frying pan over a moderate to high heat and add the butter. When it has melted and the froth has subsided, pour in the eggs.

3 Stir the eggs gently with a fork, and as the bottom begins to set draw it back with a spatula and tip the pan to allow the unset egg to run on to the hot pan.

4 When the omelette is almost set – remember it will go on cooking in its own heat – arrange your chosen filling on top of it.

5 To fold the omelette and turn it out of the frying pan in one movement, hold the frying pan up by its handle at right-angles to a warmed plate.

6 Using the spatula, roll the top third of the omelette down, and at the same time tip the frying pan over the plate, so that the omelette rolls over itself and comes out of the pan on to the plate, fold-side down, at the same time. Serve immediately.

FILLED OMELETTES

Allow about 2 heaped tablespoons filling for an omelette to serve 1 person. Have the filling warmed and ready when you start to make the omelette. Here are some ideas for fillings:

☐ Fines herbes: chopped fresh parsley, chives and chervil

☐ Skinned (p.108), de-seeded (if you like), chopped tomato, heated through – a little chopped fresh basil is good with this

☐ Cooked, chopped asparagus; reserve an asparagus tip to garnish

☐ Sliced button mushrooms fried in butter

☐ Black Olive Pâté, spooned thinly (p.383)

☐ Finely chopped spring onion, lightly fried in butter first, or used raw

☐ Watercress, lightly fried in butter to soften

☐ 4–6 tablespoons very finely grated cheese, half added to the eggs before cooking, then the remainder sprinkled on top before rolling the omelette

Filled omelette rolls also make a pleasant savoury nibble and look attractive as part of a canapés selection. Make a 1-egg omelette, keeping it flat. Spread thinly with a coloured filling such as spinach or tomato purée, Black Olive Pâté (p.383) or Mushroom and Herb Terrine (p.222), roll up like a Swiss roll, then cut into 6-mm/¼-inch slices.

Spanish Omelette

These quantities can be halved to serve one
person.

SERVES 2

2 tablespoons olive oil
1 onion, peeled and chopped
1 carrot, scraped and coarsely
   grated
1 small green pepper, de-seeded
   and chopped

225 g/8 oz courgettes, diced
1–2 garlic cloves, crushed
2 tablespoons chopped parsley
4 eggs, beaten
salt and freshly ground black
   pepper

1 Heat the oil in a large non-stick frying pan and fry the onion,
carrot and pepper, uncovered, for 5 minutes, then add the
courgette and cook for a further 5 minutes. Heat the grill.
2 Add the garlic, parsley and eggs to the vegetables and season
with salt and pepper. Stir gently until the omelette starts to set.
3 When the omelette is set underneath, put it under the grill to
set the top, but don't let it get too firm or it will be rubbery. Cut
the omelette in half and serve immediately.

Variation

KOOKOO

For this thick, Middle Eastern version of a Spanish omelette, fry
450 g/1 lb sliced courgettes or cauliflower florets, 3 garlic cloves
and a bunch of chopped spring onions in butter in a frying pan
with a lid for 2–3 minutes. Season with salt and pepper, then
pour in 6 beaten eggs. Cover and cook for about 20 minutes,
until browned on the underside, then turn the kookoo over and
cook the other side until set and flecked with brown. Cut into
thick wedges, like a cake, and serve with a tomato salad and
some crisp French bread.

SEPARATING EGGS

Crack the egg by tapping it smartly against the edge of a bowl or other hard surface, then, holding the egg over a bowl, carefully prise apart the two halves. Tip the white from the half of the shell which does not contain the yolk into a bowl, then tip the yolk into this empty half shell, allowing the white surrounding it to drip into the bowl. Transfer the egg yolk between the two shells until it is separated from as much of the egg white as possible.

Soufflé Omelette

A soufflé omelette can be savoury or sweet. Serve a savoury one with a simple salad, such as watercress, for a quick main course, and a sweet one with Apricot Jam Sauce, or one of the other suggestions below.

SERVES 1

2 eggs, separated (above)
2 tablespoons cold water
15 g/½ oz butter

salt and freshly ground black pepper, for a savoury omelette

1 Heat the grill.

2 Put the egg yolks into a fairly large bowl with the water. Season lightly with salt and pepper, for a savoury omelette.

3 In another bowl, whisk the egg whites until they form soft peaks.

4 Gently fold the egg whites into the egg yolk and water mixture.

5 Heat the butter in a small non-stick frying pan, swirling the pan so that the butter coats the sides as well as the base. Then pour in the egg mixture. Cook over a moderate heat until the omelette is golden-brown underneath.

6 Put the pan under the grill to cook and brown the top of the omelette, but don't let it get too firm.

7 Cut across the surface of the omelette at right angles to the frying pan handle and insert the filling, if using, then fold the omelette in half and lift it gently on to a serving plate.

SWEET FILLINGS FOR SOUFFLÉ OMELETTES

- ☐ Canned black cherries, heated through, with a little Kirsch added
- ☐ Apricot jam, warmed with a little water, a few flaked almonds and a dash of Grand Marnier
- ☐ 2 tablespoons raisins, soaked in rum for 30 minutes
- ☐ Any good reduced-sugar preserve, warmed through
- ☐ A little preserved ginger in syrup

Deep-fried Camembert

The crisp coating makes a delightful contrast
with the hot, runny cheese inside. Serve with a
fresh salad and mango or apricot chutney.

SERVES 2–3

1 box of Camembert, containing 6 individual triangles, chilled in the fridge
1 egg, beaten with 1 tablespoon water

dried breadcrumbs or wheatgerm for coating
oil for deep frying

1 Dip the Camembert triangles, with the rind, into the egg, then into the crumbs or wheatgerm, to coat well. Chill in the refrigerator while you heat the oil for deep-frying.

2 Pour oil into a deep-fryer so that it fills not more than one-third of the pan. Heat the oil to 190C/375F, or when a small

DEEP-FRYING

Use a deep, heavy pan, so that by the time the food has been put in the oil will not come further than halfway up the pan. The fat is hot enough if a small cube of bread sizzles and rises immediately it is dropped into it.

Make sure the food is dry before putting it into the oil, to avoid spluttering; after frying, drain well on crumpled kitchen paper.

cube of stale bread sizzles immediately it's dropped in and becomes golden-brown in 30 seconds.

3 Put in the pieces of Camembert and fry for 4–5 minutes, until crisp and golden-brown. Remove them with a slotted spoon and drain on kitchen paper. Serve immediately.

Cheese Soufflé

In spite of its reputation, a soufflé is very easy to make, and an excellent dish if you have to rustle up something good on the spur of the moment. This soufflé is light but filling and serves 4 people generously. Serve with a green salad and perhaps a tomato salad too.

SERVES 4

50 g/2 oz butter
50 g/2 oz plain flour
225 ml/8 fl oz milk
150 g/5 oz cheese, including some
  Gruyère if available, grated

4 eggs, separated (p.332)
salt and freshly ground black
  pepper
extra butter for greasing
buttered breadcrumbs for coating

1 Preheat the oven to 190c/375f/Gas Mark 5.

2 Grease a 1-litre/1¾-pint soufflé dish or straight-sided casserole generously with butter and press breadcrumbs into it, to give the finished soufflé a crisp coating.

3 Melt the butter in a medium saucepan and stir in the flour. Cook for 2–3 minutes, until frothy, then add the milk and stir over the heat until thickened.

4 Remove from the heat and beat in the cheese. Leave to cool until you can put your hand against the pan, then beat in the egg yolks and salt and pepper.

5 Whisk the whites until they form stiff peaks. Stir a couple of tablespoons of egg white into the cheese mixture to lighten it. Using a metal spoon, gently fold in the rest of the egg white, until none is visible.

6 Turn the mixture into the prepared dish. Bake for about 40 minutes, until the soufflé is puffed-up, doesn't wobble when shaken slightly, and a skewer inserted into the centre comes out clean. Serve immediately.

17. Vegetarian Barbecue (Special Menu p.553)

18. Autumn Dinner Party (Special Menu p.554)

19. Clockwise from top right: Lentil Dahl (p.312); Vegetable Curry (p.303); Sweet Spiced Apricot Chutney (p.516); sliced tomatoes and onions

20. Miso Soup with Bean Curd (p.201), Vegetable Tempura with Dipping Sauce (p.297) and Sweet Vinegared Rice (p.361)

21. Okra with Cumin and Coriander (p.277) and Golden Spiced Cauliflower (p.274)

22. Middle Eastern Chick Pea Stew (p.315)

23. (*Above top*) Summer Fruit Meringue (p.425) and Orange Parfait wi[th]
    Grand Marnier and Strawberries (p.421)

24. (*Above*) Passion Fruit, Pear and Blackcurrant Sorbets (pp.419-4[21])

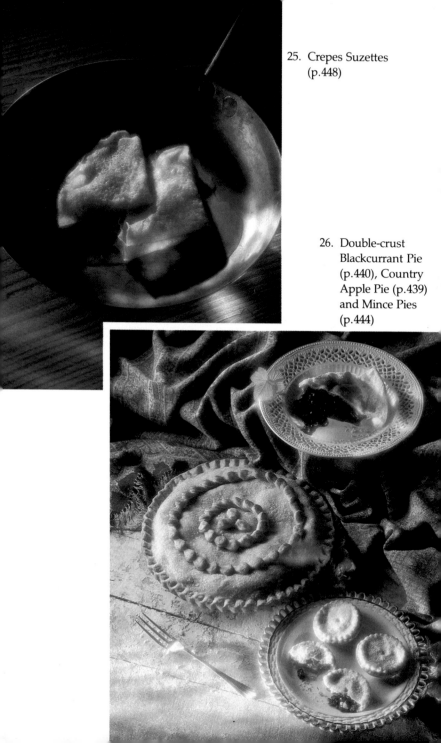

25. Crepes Suzettes
(p.448)

26. Double-crust
Blackcurrant Pie
(p.440), Country
Apple Pie (p.439)
and Mince Pies
(p.444)

27. Vegan Chocolate
Sponge (p.454) and
Vegan Lemon Cake
(p.455)

28. Madeira Cake
(p.461) and Carob
Brownies (p.463)

29. Vegan Fruitcake (p.470), Rock Cakes (p.462), Quick Buns (p.464)
and Parkin (p.462)

30. **Christmas Dinner** (Special Menu p.555)

31. **Children's Tea** (Special Menu p.556)

Variations

COURGETTE SOUFFLÉ

For this pretty, green-flecked version, stir 225 g/8 oz raw grated courgette into the soufflé mixture before beating in the egg yolks.

ASPARAGUS SOUFFLÉ

Mix 225 g/8 oz cooked asparagus, cut into 2·5-cm/1-inch lengths, into the mixture before adding the egg whites.

LEEK SOUFFLÉ

Use either 225 g/8 oz finely shredded raw leek (including some of the green), or 225 g/8 oz cooked thin leeks, cut into 2·5-cm/ 1-inch lengths. Add after the egg yolks.

MUSHROOM SOUFFLÉ

Add 225 g/8 oz mushrooms, sliced and fried until no liquid remains, to the mixture after adding the egg yolks.

SMALL SOUFFLÉS

You can make individual soufflés, an excellent first course or light lunch, by baking the mixture in 4 ramekins for 15–20 minutes.

For soufflé tomatoes, bake the mixture in 4 hollowed-out and seasoned 'beefsteak' tomatoes.

The basic quantities can be halved to make a soufflé for 2 people, and the soufflé will take about 30 minutes to cook.

To make a soufflé for 1 person, follow the method given, using a quarter of all the ingredients and baking for 15–20 minutes.

SOUFFLÉ TIPS

A soufflé can be completely prepared for baking, covered in clingfilm and kept in the refrigerator for several hours before cooking. Let it stand at room temperature for 30 minutes or so before putting it into the oven.

If the soufflé is ready before you are, leave it in the oven with the heat turned off: it will stay risen for several minutes, though it's best eaten immediately it's done.

Moulded Layered Soufflé

SERVES 4

50 g/2 oz butter
50 g/2 oz plain flour
225 ml/8 fl oz milk
150 g/5 oz cheese, including some
  Gruyère if available, grated
4 eggs, separated (p.332)
salt and freshly ground black
  pepper
150 g/5 oz cooked and puréed
  carrots

150 g/5 oz cooked and puréed peas
  or spinach
extra butter for greasing
TO GARNISH
pieces of cooked carrot, baby
  sweetcorn, mangetouts and
  sliced courgettes

1 Preheat the oven to 180c/350f/Gas Mark 4.
2 Grease a 1·4-litre/2½-pint pudding basin, mould or cake or bread tin generously with butter and line the base with well-greased non-stick paper.
3 Melt the butter in a medium saucepan and stir in the flour. Cook for 2–3 minutes, until frothy, then add the milk and stir over the heat until thickened.
4 Remove from the heat and beat in the cheese. Leave to cool until you can put your hand against the pan, then beat in the egg yolks and salt and pepper.
5 Remove half the mixture from the pan and put equal amounts of this into 2 bowls. Add the carrot purée to one bowl and the pea or spinach purée to the other. Mix each well.
6 Whisk the whites until they form stiff peaks. Divide this into 3 equal parts, adding one part to the mixture in the saucepan and one part to each of the bowls containing purée.
7 When adding the egg white, stir in one tablespoon first, to loosen the mixture, then gently but thoroughly fold in the rest until well mixed.
8 Spoon the carrot mixture into the base of the prepared basin, mould or tin, smoothing the surface level. Put the green mixture on top, then the plain mixture on top of that, and smooth the surface level.
9 Stand the container in a roasting tin and pour sufficient boiling water around it, to come halfway up the sides of the container.

10 Bake for 50 minutes, until browned and set.

11 Remove from the oven and leave the soufflé to stand for 4–5 minutes, to settle, then turn it out on to a warmed serving plate. Garnish the soufflé with pieces of cooked carrot, baby sweetcorn, mangetouts and sliced courgettes and serve immediately.

Variation

CREAMY LAYERED SOUFFLÉ

Turn the mould out on to an ovenproof plate, coat it all over, thinly, with lightly whipped cream, then sprinkle with grated Parmesan cheese. Return the mould to the oven and bake for 20 minutes, until slightly puffed up and golden-brown.

Gruyère Roulade

This is a soufflé baked flat, then spread with a filling and rolled up.

SERVES 6

1 quantity Cheese Soufflé mixture (p.334)

1 quantity Peperonata (p.276) or double quantity Mushroom Sauce (p.259)

butter for greasing

4–6 tablespoons grated Parmesan cheese for coating

TO GARNISH (OPTIONAL)
avocado slices
lime slices
fennel sprigs

1 Preheat the oven to 190c/375f/Gas Mark 5.

2 Line a 24 × 33-cm/9½ × 13-inch Swiss roll tin with non-stick paper, grease generously with butter and sprinkle with half the Parmesan cheese.

3 Spoon the soufflé mixture into the tin, easing it into the corners, and level gently with the back of the spoon.

4 Bake for 15–20 minutes, until puffed up, golden-brown and set in the middle.

5 Have ready a damp tea-cloth spread with a large piece of greaseproof paper sprinkled with the rest of the Parmesan.

6 Turn the roulade out on to the paper and carefully strip off the lining paper.

7 Trim the edges, then spread the roulade with your chosen filling. Gently roll up the roulade, from one of the long edges, like a Swiss roll, removing the paper as you do so.

8 Carefully lift the roulade on to a flat ovenproof dish and put into the oven for 5–10 minutes to heat through. Garnish, if wished, and serve immediately, cut into slices.

Variation

GRUYÈRE ROULADE WITH AVOCADO FILLING

For this cold version, turn the roulade out on to the greaseproof paper, strip off the lining paper and allow the roulade to get completely cold. Then spread it with Guacamole (p.218); carefully roll up. Salad fillings, such as mayonnaise and chopped lettuce, tomato and avocado can also be used.

Spinach Roulade with Curd Cheese and Pink Peppercorns

SERVES 4–6

900 g/2 lb fresh spinach, or 450 g/ 1 lb frozen spinach, cooked and drained
25 g/1 oz butter
4 eggs, separated (p.332)
salt and freshly ground black pepper
freshly grated nutmeg
225 g/8 oz curd cheese

1–2 tablespoons pink peppercorns
extra butter for greasing
4–6 tablespoons grated Parmesan cheese

TO GARNISH
radiccio
endive
pink peppercorns

1 Preheat the oven to 190c/375f/Gas Mark 5.

2 Line a 24 × 33-cm/9½ × 13-inch Swiss roll tin with non-stick paper, grease generously with butter and sprinkle with half the Parmesan cheese.

3 Using your hands, squeeze as much water as you can from the cooked and drained fresh or frozen spinach, then chop it.

4 Put the spinach in a saucepan with the butter and cook gently until heated through. Remove the saucepan from the heat and add the egg yolks, mixing them in thoroughly.

5 Whisk the egg whites until stiff but not dry and fold them into the spinach. Season with salt, pepper and nutmeg.

6 Spoon the soufflé mixture into the tin, easing it into the corners, and level gently with the back of the spoon.

7 Bake for about 15–20 minutes, until the roulade is puffed up, golden-brown and set in the middle.

8 Have ready a damp tea-cloth spread with a large piece of greaseproof paper sprinkled with the rest of the Parmesan cheese.

9 Turn the roulade out on to the paper and carefully strip off the lining paper. Allow the roulade to cool completely if you're serving it cold.

10 Beat the curd cheese to soften it, then spread it evenly over the roulade and sprinkle with the peppercorns.

11 Gently roll up the roulade, from one of the long edges, like a Swiss roll, removing the paper as you do so. Trim the ends with a sharp serrated knife.

12 If serving the roulade cold, put it on to a serving plate. If serving hot, lift the roulade on to a flat ovenproof dish and put into the oven for 5–10 minutes to heat through. Serve immediately, garnished with radiccio, endive and a few pink peppercorns.

Savoury Olive Mushroom Cake

This recipe was given to me by a French friend
and I love the combination of flavours. If you
haven't any left-over white wine, water will do,
but the wine gives a subtle, fruity flavour.
Serve cut into thick wedges, like a cake, with a
green salad dressed with walnut oil, and a glass
of full-bodied white wine, such as a Chablis or
robust Chardonnay.

SERVES 4

300 g/10 oz self-raising 85%
  wholewheat flour
a pinch of salt
4 eggs
150 ml/5 fl oz white wine
4 tablespoons olive oil
225 g/8 oz pitted green olives,
  sliced

175 g/6 oz mushrooms, sliced
175 g/6 oz cheese, grated
butter for greasing

TO GARNISH
chicory
watercress

1 Preheat the oven to 250C/500F/Gas Mark 9. Grease a 20-cm/8-inch cake tin or 900-g/2-lb loaf tin.

2 Put the flour and salt into a mixing bowl and break in the eggs. Add the wine and oil. Mix until smooth, then stir in the olives, mushrooms and cheese.

3 Spoon the mixture into the prepared tin. Bake for 10 minutes, then turn down the oven to 190C/375F/Gas Mark 5 and bake for a further 40–50 minutes, until firm, golden-brown and shrunk from the sides of the tin. Garnish with chicory and watercress and serve immediately.

Savoury Cheese Pudding

This cheese pudding is enlivened with green
pepper, tomatoes, onion, parsley and a dash of
Tabasco. Serve it for an economical supper,
with crisp celery, chicory or watercress.

SERVES 4

1 large onion, peeled and chopped
1 green pepper, de-seeded and
  chopped
25 g/1 oz butter
100 g/4 oz fresh wholewheat
  breadcrumbs
1 × 225-g/8-oz can tomatoes
2 tablespoons chopped parsley

100 g/4 oz Cheddar cheese, grated
1 egg
a few drops of Tabasco sauce
salt and freshly ground black
  pepper
a little milk (optional)
butter for greasing

1 Preheat the oven to 190c/375f/Gas Mark 5.
2 Fry the onion and pepper in the butter for 10 minutes, until
softened but not browned. Add the breadcrumbs, tomatoes with
their juice, parsley, cheese, egg and Tabasco. Season to taste
with salt and pepper.
3 Stir a little milk or water into the mixture if necessary to make
a soft consistency.
4 Spoon the mixture into a shallow greased dish and bake for 30
minutes until golden-brown. Serve the pudding cut into slices,
with crisp celery, chicory or watercress.

Gnocchi alla Romana

This is a little bit more trouble than some of the
dishes in this book, but it can be made in stages
and is cheap and delicious. Serve this with a
simple tomato and basil salad, or with Italian
Tomato Sauce (p.259) and Red Kidney Bean,
Haricot Bean and Black Olive Salad (p.235), or
Chicory, Watercress and Walnut Salad (p.241).

SERVES 4

600 ml/1 pint milk
100 g/4 oz semolina
1 small egg
75 g/3 oz Parmesan cheese, grated
salt and freshly ground black
*   pepper*

freshly grated nutmeg
15 g/½ oz butter
a little oil

TO GARNISH
dill sprig

1 Put the milk into a large saucepan and bring to the boil.
2 Gradually sprinkle the semolina over the top of the hot milk,
whisking well.
3 When all the semolina has been added, allow the mixture to
simmer gently for 5 minutes.
4 Remove from the heat and beat in the egg and two-thirds of
the Parmesan cheese. Season the mixture with salt, pepper and
nutmeg.
5 Spread the mixture out to a depth of about 8 mm/⅓ inch in a
lightly oiled shallow tin or on an oiled plate. Leave to get
completely cold.
6 Heat the grill to high. Lightly oil a shallow ovenproof dish or
pizza plate.
7 Cut the gnocchi into circles using a 6-cm/2½-inch pastry
cutter. First put the trimmings into the dish, then arrange the
circles on top.
8 Dot with the butter, sprinkle with the remaining Parmesan
and put under the grill until golden-brown and heated through.
Garnish with dill.

Nut Dishes

Nuts are one of the most nutritious ingredients and can also be one of the most tasty, forming the basis of some excellent recipes. I particularly like both a good nut roast and the 'dreaded nut cutlet', which can be moist, full of flavour and a real pleasure to eat. They are good served with some of the sauces and accompaniments generally reserved for meat: tasty Vegetarian Gravy (p.255), for instance, or Apple or Gooseberry Sauce (p.122), Horseradish Sauce (p.178) or, for that Christmas pièce de résistance, Bread Sauce (p.262) and Cranberry Sauce (p.260).

Brazil Nut Rings with Peperonata

Small ring moulds, measuring 11 cm/4½ inches in diameter, and holding about 75 ml/3 fl oz, or 10-cm/4-inch flan tins with a round pastry cutter in the centre, are used for these rings. They make an attractive main course, either served on a large dish, or arranged on individual plates with a selection of colourful vegetables.

SERVES 6

1 quantity Cashew Nut Roast mixture (p.345), using brazil nuts instead of cashew nuts
1 quantity Peperonata (p.343)

a little butter for greasing
dried breadcrumbs for coating
TO GARNISH
thyme sprigs

1 Preheat the oven to 190c/375f/Gas Mark 5.

2 Grease six individual ring moulds, or flan tins (see above), generously with butter and sprinkle with dried crumbs, tapping out the excess.

3 Spoon the nut mixture into the rings, smoothing the tops. Bake, uncovered, for 20 minutes, until firm.

4 While the rings are baking, make the Peperonata filling, as described on p. 276.

5 Slip a knife around the sides of the rings, then turn out the nut rings, tapping them firmly if necessary.

6 Put a heaped tablespoon of the Peperonata into the centre of each and garnish with a few thyme sprigs. Serve the rings at once.

Variations

VEGAN BRAZIL NUT RINGS

Use the Quick Savoury Nut Roast mixture (p.351) instead of the Cashew Nut Roast Mixture, and vegan margarine to grease the tins.

LITTLE BRAZIL NUT RINGS WITH ASPARAGUS HOLLANDAISE FILLING

Make the rings as described. For the filling, mix the stems of six chopped asparagus spears with 1 quantity Hollandaise Sauce (p.262), spoon into the centre of the rings, and top each with an asparagus tip.

LITTLE BRAZIL NUT RINGS WITH MUSHROOM AND CHESTNUT FILLING

Fill the centre of the rings with a mixture of 100 g/4 oz sliced fried button mushrooms and 100 g/4 oz hot cooked chestnuts. Sprinkle with chopped parsley.

SERVING NUT OR LENTIL ROAST

It's useful to make enough nut or lentil roast for one serving hot, and one cold. Sliced cold nut roast is delicious with salad and any of the following:

☐ Mayonnaise with Green Peppercorns (p.232)

☐ Mango Chutney Mayonnaise (p.232) or Cranberry Sauce (p.260)
☐ Sliced Fresh Mango
☐ Yogurt and Herb Dressing (p.233)

Cashew Nut Roast

This is a tasty nut roast which slices well both
hot and cold. It's excellent served hot, with a
tasty sauce and vegetables, or cold, when it
slices very thinly, and is good with chutney and
pickles, or a yogurt and fresh herb dressing,
and salad.

SERVES 6–8

1 medium onion, peeled and
  chopped
25 g/1 oz butter
1 large tomato, skinned (p.108)
  and chopped
2 medium mushrooms, washed and
  chopped
1½ teaspoons plain flour
150 ml/5 fl oz Light Vegetable
  Stock (p.194)
1½ teaspoons yeast extract
1 teaspoon dried mixed herbs
50 g/2 oz ground almonds
100 g/4 oz cashew nuts, finely
  ground

100 g/4 oz fresh wholewheat
  breadcrumbs
1 egg
salt and freshly ground black
  pepper
a little butter for greasing
2–3 tablespoons dried breadcrumbs
  for coating

TO GARNISH
2–3 mushrooms, sliced and lightly
  fried in butter
a few roasted cashew nuts
1 tomato, sliced (optional)

1 Preheat the oven to 190c/375f/Gas Mark 5. Grease a 450-g/1-lb
loaf tin with butter and line with a strip of buttered greaseproof
or non-stick paper to cover the base of the tin and extend up the
narrow sides. Sprinkle the base and sides with dried breadcrumbs.
2 Fry the onion in the butter for 10 minutes until soft, then add
the tomato and mushrooms and fry for 2–3 minutes.
3 Stir in the flour, cook for a minute or two, then add the stock
and stir until thickened. Remove from the heat and add the rest
of the ingredients. Season.
4 Spoon the mixture into the prepared tin, level the top and
cover with a piece of greased foil. Bake for 45 minutes, until firm
in the centre. (Remove the foil for the last 15 minutes' cooking
time to allow the top to brown.)

5 Let the loaf stand for 4–5 minutes, then slip a knife around the edges and invert it on to a warmed serving dish.

6 Decorate with the mushrooms, roasted nuts and tomato, if wished.

Variations

BROWN ALMOND NUT ROAST

Make as described, using whole almonds, ground, instead of the cashew nuts. For a darker, savoury nut roast, add 1–2 tablespoons soy sauce.

Peanut Burgers

These burgers freeze well and can be fried from frozen.

MAKES 6

50 g/2 oz butter or vegan margarine
1 onion, peeled and chopped
1 celery stick, finely chopped
1 teaspoon dried mixed herbs
1 tablespoon wholewheat flour
150 ml/5 fl oz Light Vegetable Stock (p.194)
1 tablespoon soy sauce
1 teaspoon yeast extract
175 g/6 oz roasted, unsalted peanuts, fairly finely ground

50 g/2 oz cashew nuts, fairly finely ground
100 g/4 oz fresh wholewheat breadcrumbs (opposite)
salt and freshly ground black pepper
dried breadcrumbs for coating
oil for shallow-frying
TO GARNISH
lettuce leaves
tomato slices
cucumber slices

1 Melt the butter or vegan margarine in a large saucepan and fry the onion and celery for 10 minutes. Stir in the herbs and flour and cook for a further 1–2 minutes.

2 Add the stock and stir until thickened, then add the soy sauce, yeast extract, nuts, breadcrumbs and salt and pepper.

3 Leave the mixture to cool, then form into 6 burgers about 1 cm/½ inch thick. To flatten the burgers and give them a professional look, tap them firmly on top and around the sides

with a palette knife. Then press together firmly, to help them remain intact when you fry them, and coat with dried breadcrumbs.

4 Fry the burgers in a very little oil – the frying pan should be 'greased' rather than oily – for about 3 minutes on each side, until browned and crisp. Drain on kitchen paper. Garnish and serve.

Variation

MACADAMIA BURGERS

Using macadamia nuts instead of the peanuts makes these burgers special. Serve with Béarnaise Sauce (p.264).

MAKING BREADCRUMBS

Bread which is a day or two old is best for these. Cut off the crusts and crumble the bread between your fingers, or pop chunks of bread into a food processor or blender and whizz for a moment or two. If you have a freezer, it's worth making any left-over pieces of bread into crumbs and freezing in a polythene bag. The breadcrumbs can be used straight from the freezer.

Alternatively, you can dry out slices of bread in the bottom of the oven while something else is cooking, or in a microwave (they only take about 5 minutes). Then crush them with a rolling pin. It's useful to have both fresh and dried breadcrumbs available.

PEELING CHESTNUTS

Place each chestnut flat-side down on a board and make a cut in the pointed end. Boil or bake the chestnuts in a hot oven for 10–20 minutes until the cuts open. Strip the skins off the chestnuts using a small, sharp, pointed knife.

Chestnut Roast

A pleasant roast for a chilly winter day, and a
traditional Christmas main course for many
vegetarians.

SERVES 4-6

25 g/1 oz butter
1 large onion, peeled and chopped
2 celery sticks, finely chopped
900 g/2 lb chestnuts, peeled
    (p.347) and cooked (yields about
    750 g/1½ lb), or 3 × 425-g/
    15-oz cans whole chestnuts, or
    about 250 g/8 oz dried
    chestnuts, soaked and cooked
2 tablespoons chopped parsley

2 tablespoons lemon juice
1 garlic clove, crushed
a few fresh wholewheat
    breadcrumbs (optional), p.347
salt and freshly ground black
    pepper
4 tablespoons oil
dried breadcrumbs for coating

1 Melt the butter and fry the onion and celery for 10 minutes
until soft but not brown. Transfer to a large bowl. Drain the
chestnuts and add to the bowl. Mix these ingredients together
well.

2 Mash the chestnuts, onion and celery, then mix into the bowl
the chopped parsley, lemon juice and garlic.

3 The mixture should be soft but firm enough to form into a roll,
so add a few wholewheat breadcrumbs, if necessary, especially
if you're using canned chestnuts. Season the mixture with salt
and pepper to taste.

4 Preheat the oven to 200c/400f/Gas Mark 6. Pour a little oil into
a roasting tin and put into the oven to heat.

5 Form the chestnut mixture into a roll about 20 cm/8 inches
long, pressing it together well, then coat with the dried crumbs.

6 Put the chestnut roll into the roasting tin and carefully turn it
so that it is coated with hot oil.

7 Bake for 45 minutes, until it is crisp on the outside, spooning a
little of the oil over the roll from time to time during the cooking.
Serve the Chestnut Roast cut into slices.

Croustade of Mushrooms

This is an updated version of my most popular
recipe, which I invented for one of my first
dinner parties, and which first appeared in my
second book, *Not Just a Load of Old Lentils*.

SERVES 4-6

75 g/3 oz flaked almonds, or other
  nuts, flaked in a food processor
75 g/3 oz fresh wholewheat
  breadcrumbs (p.347)
75 g/3 oz ground almonds or other
  finely ground nuts
1 small onion, peeled and grated
1 garlic clove, crushed

90 g/3½ oz softened butter
salt and freshly ground black
  pepper
450 g/1 lb mushrooms, washed and
  sliced
300 ml/10 fl oz soured cream
freshly grated nutmeg
paprika pepper

1 Preheat the oven to 180c/350f/Gas Mark 4.
2 Reserve a few of the flaked almonds for garnishing. Mix
together the breadcrumbs, ground and remaining flaked
almonds, or other nuts, onion, garlic and 75 g/3 oz of the butter.
Season well with salt and pepper. The mixture should hold
together like a crumbly pastry.
3 Press the mixture into the base of a 20-cm/8-inch loose-
bottomed flan tin. Bake for 20 minutes, until golden-brown and
crisp.
4 Meanwhile, fry the mushrooms in the remaining butter for
15–20 minutes, until all the liquid has evaporated. Season with
salt and pepper.
5 Spoon the mushrooms on top of the croustade. Stir the soured
cream with a fork, season with salt, pepper and nutmeg, then
swirl about half the soured cream on top of the mushrooms, so
that some show through the cream. Sprinkle with paprika.
6 Return the croustade to the oven for 10–15 minutes, to heat
through, then remove from the tin and serve on a warmed plate.
Scatter reserved flaked almonds over the top. Serve the rest of
the soured cream separately, in a small bowl or jug.

Variations

VEGAN CROUSTADE OF MUSHROOMS

Use vegan margarine instead of butter, and non-dairy cream or yogurt instead of soured cream.

CROUSTADE OF LEEKS

Replace the mushrooms with 450 g/1 lb cleaned and sliced leeks. Cook the leeks in a little fast-boiling lightly salted water for about 10 minutes, then drain well and add the soured cream and seasoning.

V *Hazelnut and Vegetable Crumble*

Simple and good, an excellent way of turning
vegetables into a main course. Serve with a
lightly cooked green vegetable, potato purée
and Vegetarian Gravy (p.355) for a family
winter meal.

SERVES 4

*900 g/2 lb peeled and diced
vegetables: carrots, swedes,
turnips, onions, celery*
*100 g/4 oz butter or vegan
margarine*
*salt and freshly ground black
pepper*
75 g/3 oz rolled oats

75 g/3 oz hazelnuts, finely ground
*75 g/3 oz hazelnuts, chopped or
flaked*
1 small onion, peeled and grated
1 garlic clove, crushed
*½ teaspoon dried thyme or mixed
herbs*

1 Preheat the oven to 180c/350f/Gas Mark 4.
2 Boil the vegetables in water to cover for 15–20 minutes, or until tender. Drain, reserving the water.
3 Blend about one-third of the vegetables with 25 g/1 oz of the butter or vegan margarine and enough of the reserved water to make a purée in a food processor or blender.
4 Add this purée to the rest of the vegetables. Season to taste with salt and pepper. Spoon the mixture into a shallow ovenproof casserole.

5 To make the crumble topping, put the oats into a bowl with all the nuts, the onion, garlic, herbs and salt and pepper. Add the rest of the butter or vegan margarine, and mix with a fork until the topping mixture resembles coarse breadcrumbs.

6 Sprinkle the crumble mixture evenly over the top of the vegetables. Bake for 30–40 minutes, until the topping is crisp and lightly browned.

Quick Savoury Nut Roast

This easy-to-make roast is good served hot or cold.

SERVES 4

50 g/2 oz butter or vegan
  margarine
2 large onions, peeled and finely
  chopped
1 teaspoon dried thyme
1 tablespoon wholewheat flour
150 ml/5 fl oz water
100 g/4 oz cashew nuts, fairly
  finely ground

100 g/4 oz hazelnuts, fairly finely
  ground
100 g/4 oz dried wholewheat
  breadcrumbs (p.347)
1 tablespoon lemon juice
salt and freshly ground black
  pepper
dried crumbs for coating
8 tablespoons oil for roasting

1 Preheat the oven to 200C/400F/Gas Mark 6.

2 Melt the butter or vegan margarine in a large saucepan and fry the onions gently for 10 minutes, until tender.

3 Add the thyme and flour; stir for 1–2 minutes, then add the water and stir until thickened.

4 Remove from the heat, add the nuts, breadcrumbs, lemon juice and salt and pepper to taste. Mix well. Form into a loaf shape and coat in dried crumbs. Heat the oil in a small roasting tin in the oven until smoking hot. Put the nut roast into the tin and baste with the oil.

5 Bake for 35–40 minutes.

6 Remove from the tin. Serve immediately, cut into thick slices or leave to cool if serving cold.

Brazil Nut Roast en Croûte

SERVES 8

1 quantity Flaky Pastry made with
  white flour (p.399) or 450 g/1 lb
  frozen puff pastry
beaten egg to glaze (optional)

FOR THE NUT ROAST
2 large onions, peeled and chopped
50 g/2 oz butter or vegan
  margarine
450 g/1 lb brazil nuts, finely
  ground
225 g/8 oz fresh fine breadcrumbs
½ teaspoon dried thyme
3 tablespoons lemon juice
2 eggs (optional)
a good pinch each of grated
  nutmeg, ground cloves and
  ground cinnamon
salt and freshly ground black
  pepper

FOR THE STUFFING
225 g/8 oz fresh fine white
  breadcrumbs
25 g/1 oz chopped parsley
grated rind of 1 lemon
1 tablespoon lemon juice
1 teaspoon each dried thyme and
  marjoram
1 tablespoon grated onion
75 g/3 oz butter or vegan
  margarine

TO GARNISH
8 clementine halves filled with
  cranberries
thyme sprigs

1 Preheat the oven to 200c/400f/Gas Mark 6.

2 To make the nut roast, fry the onion in the butter or vegan margarine for 10 minutes, until soft but not browned.

3 Remove from the heat and add the rest of the nut roast ingredients. Season.

4 Make the stuffing by mixing all the ingredients together to form a soft mixture which holds together. Season.

5 Roll out the pastry on a floured board to a 30 × 35-cm/12 × 14-inch rectangle.

6 Form the stuffing into a sausage about 25 cm/10 inches long and place down the middle of the pastry. Pile the nut roast mixture all over the stuffing, covering it.

7 Fold the ends of the pastry up to enclose the nut mixture completely. Tuck in the ends, then place on a damp baking sheet, join-side down. Mark a lattice design on the top.

8 Make one or two steam-holes, decorate with pastry trimmings and brush with beaten egg, if using. Bake for 30 minutes, until crisp. Garnish with clementine halves filled with cranberries and thyme sprigs.

Pine Nut Roulade with Asparagus Hollandaise Filling

This dish, which I've developed from a recipe
invented by Michael Smith, is very rich,
wonderful for a celebration summer meal. It can
be made a few hours in advance and reheated
just before serving. Serve with new potatoes,
mangetouts and baby carrots.

SERVES 6

4 large eggs
salt and freshly ground black
　pepper
175 g/6 oz pine nuts, lightly
　crushed
a little butter and oil for greasing

FOR THE FILLING
1 quantity Hollandaise Sauce,
　light version (p.263)
450 g/1 lb fresh young asparagus,
　lightly cooked, tips only
12 quail's eggs, hardboiled, shelled
　and halved
2 tablespoons snipped chives

1 Preheat the oven to 200c/400f/Gas Mark 6. Line a 33 ×
23-cm/13 × 9-inch Swiss roll tin with buttered greaseproof
paper, letting it extend 5 cm/2 inches above the edge of the tin
and snipping diagonally into the corners.
2 Whisk the eggs with salt and pepper until thick, fold in half
the pine nuts and pour into the tin, spreading the mixture
evenly into the corners.
3 Bake near the top of the oven for 6–8 minutes, until firm in the
middle.
4 Put a clean tea-towel, wrung out in cold water, on to a flat
surface. Cover with a piece of greaseproof paper spread evenly
with the remaining pine nuts. Invert the roulade on to the pine
nuts and remove the lining paper.
5 Spread the roulade with all but 2 tablespoons of the Hollandaise Sauce. Arrange the asparagus tips (reserving 6 for the
garnish), quail's eggs (reserving 3 halves) and chives on top.
6 Carefully roll up the roulade by folding one long side into the
centre and the other on top. Place a large oiled piece of foil on
top and turn the roulade upside down. Slide a baking sheet
underneath, and remove the cloth.

7 Reheat, either immediately, or when required, still wrapped in foil, at 190c/375f/Gas Mark 5, for 15–20 minutes.

8 Remove the foil and transfer the roulade to a heated oval or oblong serving plate. Spoon the reserved sauce down the centre and arrange the reserved asparagus tips and quail's eggs on top. Serve immediately.

Variations

ROASTED CASHEW NUT ROULADE WITH WILD MUSHROOM FILLING

Make as described, using roasted cashew nuts instead of pine nuts, and Wild Mushrooms in Cream (p.372) for the filling, instead of the asparagus and Hollandaise Sauce. Use the quail's eggs, or not, as you like, and garnish with fried mushrooms and roasted cashew nuts.

PECAN NUT ROULADE WITH RATATOUILLE FILLING

A less rich, but still very tasty version. Use pecan nuts instead of pine nuts, and replace the asparagus and Hollandaise Sauce with Ratatouille (p.278). Use the quail's eggs, or not, as you like, and garnish with parsley and pepper rings.

HAZELNUT ROULADE WITH LEEK FILLING

Use roasted hazelnuts instead of the pine nuts, 450 g/1 lb cleaned and sliced leeks, cooked in a little fast-boiling water until tender, and well-drained, instead of the asparagus, and 300 ml/10 fl oz soured cream instead of the Hollandaise Sauce.

Nut Balls in Tomato Sauce

Serve these with buttered spaghetti and a crisp
green salad.

SERVES 4

1 onion
1 tablespoon oil
100 g/4 oz brown nuts, such as
  unblanched almonds or roasted
  hazelnuts, finely ground
50 g/2 oz fresh wholewheat
  breadcrumbs
50 g/2 oz Cheddar cheese, finely
  grated
2 teaspoons tomato purée

1 egg yolk
½ teaspoon dried thyme
salt and freshly ground black
  pepper
butter for greasing
1 quantity Italian Tomato Sauce
  (p.254)

TO GARNISH
thyme sprigs

1 Preheat the oven to 180c/350f/Gas Mark 4.
2 Fry the onion in the oil for 10 minutes, until softened, then
remove from the heat and mix in all the rest of the ingredients
except the Italian Tomato Sauce.
3 Form the mixture into 8 balls. Place in a shallow ovenproof
dish.
4 Pour the tomato sauce over the nut balls. Bake for 25–30
minutes. Garnish with thyme and serve hot.

Variations

NUT BALLS BAKED IN RATATOUILLE

Make as described, but instead of baking the nut balls in tomato
sauce, add them to a shallow casserole of Ratatouille (p.278).

VEGAN NUT BALLS

Use 2 tablespoons peanut butter instead of the cheese and egg.
You may find you need less salt.

Sweetcorn Fritters

These fritters make a good light breakfast or
supper dish, perhaps accompanied by some
grilled tomatoes and lightly fried mushrooms.
Or they can be served as an accompaniment to
a nut roast with Potato Purée (p.281) and
Cranberry Sauce (p.260).

SERVES 2–3 AS A MAIN COURSE,
4–6 AS AN ACCOMPANIMENT

*225 g/8 oz frozen sweetcorn
kernels, or fresh ones scraped
from the cob, lightly cooked and
drained
50 g/2 oz chopped almonds*

*1 egg, separated
25 g/1 oz wholewheat flour
salt and freshly ground black
pepper
oil for shallow frying*

1 Put the cooked sweetcorn into a bowl with the chopped
almonds, egg yolk and flour. Mix well and season to taste with
salt and pepper.
2 Whisk the egg white until it stands in stiff peaks, then gently
fold into the sweetcorn mixture.
3 Heat a little oil in a frying pan, then drop tablespoons of the
sweetcorn mixture into the oil and fry them on both sides until
crisp.
4 Drain the fritters on kitchen paper. Keep the first batch warm
in a low oven while you fry the rest, then serve them immediately.

Variation

VEGAN FRITTERS

Make the batter using 225 g/8 oz chick pea flour, ½ teaspoon salt
and 200–250 ml/7–8 fl oz water. Put the flour and salt into a bowl
and mix in water to make a coating batter. Stir in the sweetcorn.

White Nut Roast with Herb Stuffing

I like to serve this at Christmas with all the
traditional accompaniments including Bread
Sauce (p.262), Cranberry Sauce (p.260) and
Vegetarian Gravy (p.255).

SERVES 8-10

1 large onion, peeled and chopped
50 g/2 oz butter
1 teaspoon dried thyme
1 tablespoon plain flour
300 ml/10 fl oz milk
225 g/8 oz mixed white nuts, finely
    ground: use cashew nuts,
    blanched almonds and pine nuts
100 g/4 oz fresh white
    breadcrumbs
salt and freshly ground black
    pepper
freshly grated nutmeg
2 egg whites
a little extra butter for greasing
3–4 tablespoons dried breadcrumbs
    for coating

FOR THE HERB STUFFING
175 g/6 oz fresh white
    breadcrumbs
100 g/4 oz butter
4 tablespoons chopped parsley
grated rind of ½ lemon
2 tablespoons grated onion
1 teaspoon each dried marjoram
    and thyme
2 egg yolks

TO GARNISH
lemon slices
parsley sprigs

1 Preheat the oven to 190c/375f/Gas Mark 5.
2 Grease a 900-g/2-lb loaf tin with butter and line with a strip of
buttered greaseproof paper to cover the base of the tin and
extend up the narrow sides. Sprinkle with dried breadcrumbs.
3 Fry the onion in the butter for 10 minutes until soft. Add the
thyme and flour and cook for a minute or two, then add the milk
and stir until thickened.
4 Remove from the heat and add the nuts and breadcrumbs.
Season generously with salt, pepper and nutmeg.
5 Whisk the egg whites until stiff but not dry, then fold in.
6 Make the stuffing by thoroughly mixing all the ingredients
together and seasoning to taste with salt and pepper.
7 Spoon half the nut mixture into the prepared tin in an even
layer.

8 With your hands, form the stuffing into a flat layer which will fit over the top of the nut mixture; put into the tin on top of the layer of nut mixture.

9 Cover the stuffing with the rest of the nut mixture.

10 Level the top, cover with buttered foil, and bake for 1–1¼ hours, until firm in the centre. (Remove the foil for the last 15 minutes of cooking time to allow the top to brown.)

11 Let the loaf stand for 4–5 minutes, then slip a knife around the edges and invert it on to a warmed serving dish. Garnish with the parsley sprigs and lemon slices.

Grain Dishes

*Nutritious, high-fibre protein food, grains can
be made into some particularly healthy dishes,
excellent for alternating with richer ones,
perhaps those based on cheese and eggs, to
create a balanced diet. Most grain dishes are also
quick and easy to make, thus being excellent
mid-week standbys; in addition, left-overs can
often be made into croquettes or used to stuff
peppers or large tomatoes, saving time another
day. It's worth experimenting with some of the
more unusual grains; you'll find full details of
basic cooking in the Ingredients section (p.49).*

Crunchy Granola

MAKES 1·25 KG/2¾ LB

300 ml/10 fl oz boiling water
200 ml/7 fl oz sunflower or corn oil
300 ml/10 fl oz clear honey
1 teaspoon vanilla extract
450 g/1 lb rolled oats
75 g/3 oz sesame seeds

50 g/2 oz wheatgerm
100 g/4 oz shredded coconut
100 g/4 oz sunflower seeds
175 g/6 oz raisins
100 g/4 oz hazelnuts

1 Preheat the oven to 180c/350f/Gas Mark 4.
2 In a large jug mix together the boiling water, oil, honey and
vanilla.
3 Put the oats, sesame seeds, wheatgerm and coconut into a
large baking tin.
4 Gradually add the honey mixture, stirring all the time, so that
all the dry ingredients get coated. (I find it easiest to use my
hands for this, rather like rubbing fat into flour.)

5 Bake for 15 minutes, stirring the mixture a couple of times. Then reduce the oven setting to 140c/275F/Gas Mark 1 and bake for 1½–2 hours, stirring every 15 minutes or so, until the granola is crisp and golden-brown.

6 Cool, then mix in the sunflower seeds, raisins and nuts. Store the granola in an airtight container.

Bircher Muesli

This muesli makes a nourishing snack at any time of day. It is the original muesli invented by Dr Bircher-Benner for the patients in his famous natural health clinic in Zurich. He used condensed milk because that was the only kind which was safe when he was practising at the end of the last century. You can replace this with ordinary milk or plain yogurt if you like, though the condensed milk gives a pleasant, almost jellied texture which ordinary milk and yogurt do not. Dr Bircher-Benner served his muesli to his patients for their evening meal, with thinly sliced wholemeal bread, honey and herb tea.

SERVES 1

2 tablespoons rolled oats
1 tablespoon sweetened condensed milk
3 tablespoons cold water
a little grated lemon rind

1 tablespoon lemon juice
100 g/4 oz grated apple or 200 g/ 7 oz soft fruit in season
1 tablespoon grated hazelnuts

1 Put the oats, condensed milk, water, lemon rind and juice into a bowl and mix to a creamy consistency.

2 Add the fruit. According to Dr Bircher-Benner, the whole apple should be used, skin, core and pips!

3 Spoon the mixture into a serving bowl. Sprinkle with the grated nuts.

Saffron Rice

SERVES 4

225 g/8 oz long-grain brown rice
600 ml/1 pint water

1 teaspoon salt
good pinch of saffron strands

1 Wash the rice, drain and dry on kitchen paper.
2 Put the rice into a heavy-based saucepan with the water, salt and saffron.
3 Bring to the boil, then cover and turn the heat down as low as possible.
4 Cook the rice for 40–45 minutes, until it is tender and all the water absorbed.
5 The rice will improve if you can allow it to stand off the heat, but still covered, for a further 15 minutes. Fluff the rice by stirring gently with a fork.

Variations

SWEET VINEGARED RICE

Sweet Vinegared Rice is used to make Sushi (p.213) and I like to serve it with Japanese vegetable dishes too. Make rice as described, above, using short-grain rice. Put a piece of kombu (wiped with a damp cloth), if available, in the saucepan with the rice and water. When the water comes to the boil, remove the kombu. This flavours the rice delicately. When the rice is cooked, add 2 teaspoons sugar which have been dissolved in 4 tablespoons rice vinegar. Mix gently.

RICE WITH WILD RICE

Wild rice is very expensive, but the addition of a little to brown rice makes it extra special. The dark brown grains of wild rice look attractive against the paler brown rice. Make as described, adding 50 g/2 oz wild rice and increasing the amount of water to 750 ml/1¼ pints.

Spiced Rice

[V]

This delicately flavoured golden rice is a good
accompaniment for curries, spiced vegetable
mixtures and stuffed vegetables.

SERVES 4

225 g/8 oz brown rice
1½ tablespoons oil
¾ teaspoon turmeric powder
3 cloves

1 bay leaf
600 ml/1 pint water
salt and freshly ground black
   pepper

1 Wash the rice, drain and dry on kitchen paper. Heat the oil in
a medium-sized saucepan, then add the rice, and fry without
browning, stirring, for 3–4 minutes.
2 Stir in the turmeric, cloves and bay leaf. Cook for a few
seconds longer, then pour in the water and add some salt and
pepper.
3 Bring to the boil, then put a lid on the saucepan and turn the
heat down as low as possible. Cook the rice undisturbed for
about 40–45 minutes, until the grains are tender and all the
water has been absorbed.
4 Fluff the rice by stirring gently with a fork to separate the
grains.

Rice Pilaf with Apricots, Raisins and Pine Nuts

[V]

SERVES 6

4 tablespoons olive oil
300 g/10 oz long-grain brown rice
good pinch of saffron strands
   (optional)
50 g/2 oz dried apricots, snipped
   into slivers

½ cinnamon stick
8 cloves
4 black peppercorns
4 cardamom pods, lightly crushed
salt and freshly ground black
   pepper

750 ml/1¼ pints water
2 onions, peeled and sliced
50 g/2 oz raisins
50 g/2 oz pine nuts or slivered
  almonds

TO GARNISH
mint sprig

1 Heat half the oil in a heavy-based saucepan. Add the rice and fry for 5 minutes, stirring gently.

2 Add the saffron, if using, the apricots, spices, 1 teaspoon salt and the water.

3 Bring to the boil, then cover tightly and leave to cook over a very gentle heat for 45 minutes. Then turn off the heat and leave covered.

4 Fry the onion in the remaining oil for 10 minutes, until softened and lightly browned. Add to the rice, together with the raisins and nuts. Check the seasoning and stir lightly with a fork. Garnish with a mint sprig to serve.

Chinese-style Fried Rice   V

SERVES 4

300 g/10 oz long-grain brown rice
2 tablespoons olive oil
100 g/4 oz mushrooms, chopped
100 g/4 oz frozen sweetcorn
  kernels

8 spring onions, trimmed and
  chopped
1–2 tablespoons soy sauce

1 Fill a large saucepan two-thirds full of lightly salted water, and bring to the boil, then put in the rice and return to the boil. Cover the pan and leave to boil for about 20 minutes until the rice is tender, then drain.

2 Heat the olive oil in another saucepan. Fry the mushrooms for 1–2 minutes, and add the rice, sweetcorn and spring onions. Stir-fry for 3–4 minutes, until heated through.

3 Add soy sauce to taste and check the seasoning.

V | *Paella Vegetariana*

In this vegetarian version of Spanish paella, the traditional fish is replaced by leeks and black olives, with red pepper, peas and chopped parsley, and a good flavouring of saffron, onion and garlic. It's one of my favourite vegetarian dishes. Nuts – blanched almonds, flaked brazil nuts or whole cashew nuts – can be served with this, separately, in a bowl, for people to help themselves if liked. I prefer it without. A wide shallow pan, such as a wok, large frying pan or, best of all, a special paella pan, if you have one, is ideal for this, as it is roomy enough to show off the pattern of the vegetables.

SERVES 4

4 tablespoons olive oil
225 g/8 oz long-grain brown rice
1 large onion, peeled and sliced
2 large garlic cloves, crushed
good pinch of saffron strands
750 ml/1¼ pints Light Vegetable
  Stock (p.194) or water
thinly pared rind of ½ lemon, cut
  into thin shreds

salt and freshly ground black
  pepper
450 g/1 lb washed and trimmed
  leeks, cut into 2·5-cm/1-inch
  lengths
100 g/4 oz frozen peas
50–100 g/2–4 oz black olives
TO GARNISH
chopped parsley

1 Heat the oil in a large, deep pan. Add the long-grain brown rice and onion slices and stir until the rice is coated and begins to turn opaque.

2 Add the garlic, saffron, stock or water, lemon rind and salt and pepper. Mix well, then bring up to the boil. Mix again, to distribute the saffron colouring.

3 Arrange the vegetables and olives attractively on top of the rice.

4 Bring to the boil. Cover with a lid or foil and simmer for 45 minutes.

5 Sprinkle with parsley and serve straight from the pan.

Variation

PAELLA VEGETARIANA WITH ARTICHOKES

Use 4–6 globe artichokes instead of the leeks. Very tender baby artichokes can simply be quartered; otherwise cut the leaves and choke from the artichokes as described on p.92, then halve or quarter the artichoke bottoms. Garnish with bay leaves and artichoke leaves.

Biriani

Serve this tasty dish with a Curry Sauce (p.265)
and some Indian breads, such as chapatti or
poppadums. I like to serve several side dishes
as well, such as cucumber a salad, tomato and
onion salad and some chutneys and pickles.

SERVES 6

1 large aubergine, cut into 1-cm/
  ½-inch dice
salt
350 g/12 oz long-grain brown rice
900 ml/1½ pints water
2½ teaspoons turmeric
50 g/2 oz butter or vegetable ghee
1 teaspoon poppy seeds
1½ teaspoons white mustard seeds

1 teaspoon garam masala
½ teaspoon ground coriander
pinch of cayenne pepper
freshly ground black pepper
1 red pepper, de-seeded and sliced
1 onion, peeled and sliced
2 garlic cloves, crushed
butter for greasing

1 Sprinkle the aubergine with salt and leave for 30 minutes, to draw out any bitter juices. Rinse and pat dry.

2 Put the rice into a heavy-based saucepan with the water, 1 teaspoon salt and 2 teaspoons of the turmeric. Bring to the boil, then cover and cook very gently for 45 minutes.

3 Preheat the oven to 180c/350f/Gas Mark 4. Grease a deep casserole.

4 Heat the butter or ghee in a saucepan, then add the poppy seeds and mustard seeds.

5 Stir for 1–2 minutes, then add the rest of the turmeric, the garam masala, coriander, cayenne and a generous grinding of black pepper. Cook for 1–2 minutes, stirring.

6 Add the aubergine, red pepper and onion. Cook gently, covered, for 7–8 minutes, then add the garlic and cook for a further 2 minutes. Taste the mixture and add more seasoning, if necessary.

7 Put one-third of the rice in a layer in the casserole. Top with half the vegetable mixture. Repeat the layers, ending with a final layer of rice.

8 Cover and bake for 30 minutes. Serve straight from the casserole.

Classic Risotto

SERVES 6

100 g/4 oz butter
1 onion, peeled and chopped
1 whole garlic clove
2 tablespoons finely chopped parsley
650 g/1¼ lb Italian arborio rice
2 litres/3½ pints boiling Light Vegetable Stock (p.194)

salt and freshly ground black pepper
4–6 tablespoons grated Parmesan cheese

TO SERVE
extra grated Parmesan cheese

1 Melt half the butter in a large, heavy-based saucepan and sauté the onion and garlic. When the onion is soft and golden, add the parsley.

2 Cook over a moderate heat for a few minutes, then discard the garlic and add the rice.

3 Fry the rice for a few minutes, stirring constantly, then add 250 ml/8 fl oz of the boiling stock and cook gently until absorbed.

4 Continue cooking gently, adding stock 250 ml/8 fl oz at a time, and stirring occasionally, for 20–30 minutes, or until the rice is tender and all the liquid absorbed.

5 Season to taste with salt and pepper, stir in the remaining butter and the Parmesan cheese, and leave the risotto over a low heat for a few minutes before serving.

6 Serve with plenty of extra grated Parmesan cheese handed separately.

Variations

ARTICHOKE RISOTTO

Cut the leaves and hairy choke from 3 globe artichokes. Slice the bases and fry them with the onion and garlic, then discard the garlic, add the rice and continue as described.

MUSHROOM RISOTTO

Make as described, frying 225 g/8 oz sliced button mushrooms with the parsley.

COURGETTE RISOTTO

Add 225 g/8 oz sliced courgettes with the parsley.

Millet Pilaf with Nuts and Raisins $\boxed{V}$

Millet cooks quickly and makes a good pilaf which is a pleasant change from rice. It is the richest grain in both protein and iron. Serve this pilaf as a main course accompanied by a juicy tomato salad, Sweet Carrot and Fennel Salad (p.242) or Green-bean Salad with Radiccio (p.249).

SERVES 4

300 g/10 oz millet
2 tablespoons oil
1 large onion, peeled and chopped
2 carrots, scraped and diced
1 garlic clove, crushed
1 walnut-sized piece of fresh
    ginger, grated

2·5 cm/1 inch cinnamon stick
750 ml/1¼ pints water
salt and freshly ground black
    pepper
50 g/2 oz raisins (optional)
50 g/2 oz flaked almonds (optional)

1 First toast the millet by putting it into a large saucepan and stirring over a moderate heat for 3–4 minutes, until it begins to smell roasted and some of the grains start to 'pop'. Remove from the heat and tip the millet on to a plate.

2 Heat the oil in the saucepan and fry the onion for 5 minutes, then add the carrots, garlic, ginger and cinnamon, and cook for a further 5 minutes.

3 Add the toasted millet to the onion and carrot mixture. Pour in the water and season to taste with salt and pepper.

4 Bring to the boil, then cover, turn down the heat and cook very gently for 15–20 minutes, until all the water has been absorbed and the millet is tender.

5 Check the seasoning, then add the raisins and flaked almonds, if using, mixing them in lightly with a fork.

Barley Casserole

Barley makes a pleasant change from rice and is
just as easy to cook. Other vegetables can be
used in Barley Casserole; try making it with
green and red peppers, plenty of onions and
garlic, tomatoes and button mushrooms. This
casserole is a simple, wholesome dish, good for
a family meal on a chilly autumn or winter day.
Serve it on its own, followed by a warming,
homely pudding like Treacle Tart (p.438), baked
apples or, for real indulgence and nostalgia,
steamed jam sponge.

SERVES 4

2 onions, peeled and chopped
50 g/2 oz butter or vegan
    margarine
900 g/2 lb leeks, cleaned, trimmed
    and sliced into 2·5-cm/1-inch
    lengths
225 g/8 oz carrots, scraped and
    diced
2 celery sticks, chopped

300 g/10 oz pearl barley
750 ml/1¼ pints Light Vegetable
    Stock (p.194)
salt and freshly ground black
    pepper
700 g/1½ lb potatoes, peeled and
    cut into even-sized chunks

TO GARNISH
4 tablespoons chopped parsley

1 Fry the onion in the butter or vegan margarine for 5 minutes in a large, heavy-based saucepan. Add the leeks, carrots and celery, mixing gently to coat with the butter.

2 Cover the pan and cook gently for 5 minutes.

3 Add the barley, mix well, then add the stock together with a good teaspoon salt and plenty of freshly ground black pepper.

4 Cover and cook over a gentle heat for 40 minutes, then add the potatoes, putting them into the top of the casserole.

5 Cook for a further 20 minutes, covered, or until the potatoes and barley are tender and all the water has been absorbed.

6 Check the seasoning: more salt will probably be needed. Sprinkle with the parsley and serve.

Couscous with Spicy Chick Pea Stew

Couscous is quick and easy to prepare because, being pre-cooked, it only needs soaking briefly before being heated through. The best way to do this is to put the couscous into a steamer saucepan, metal colander or sieve on top of the saucepan in which the stew is cooking; it can then absorb the flavour of the stew.

SERVES 4-5

450 g/1 lb couscous
½ teaspoon salt dissolved in
   600 ml/1 pint warm water
4 tablespoons olive oil
2 onions, peeled and chopped
225 g/8 oz carrots, scraped and
   sliced
2 teaspoons each ground
   cinnamon, ground cumin and
   ground coriander
100 g/4 oz sweetcorn
225 g/8 oz courgettes, diced

225 g/8 oz dried chick peas,
   soaked, cooked until tender,
   then drained, or 2 × 400-g/
   14-oz cans chick peas, drained,
   or 450 g/1 lb frozen broad beans
900 ml/1½ pints water
4 tablespoons tomato purée
salt and freshly ground black
   pepper

TO GARNISH
coriander sprig

1 Spread the couscous out on a large deep plate and pour the salt water evenly over it, then rub the couscous lightly with fingers to separate the grains. Set the plate of couscous aside.

2 Heat half the oil in a large saucepan or saucepan part of a steamer, add the onion and carrots and fry gently for 10 minutes. Stir in the spices and cook for a further 2–3 minutes, stirring.

3 Stir in the sweetcorn, courgettes and the chick peas or broad beans, then add the water and tomato purée. Bring to the boil, then turn the heat down so that the chick pea stew simmers.

4 By now the couscous will have absorbed the water. Put it into the steamer saucepan, metal colander or sieve, breaking it up a bit with your fingers again as you do so. (If your container has large holes, you may like to line it with a piece of cloth, to prevent the grains falling through, but I've never found this necessary.)

5 Put the steamer, colander or sieve over the vegetable stew, cover with a lid or plate, and cook gently for 25–30 minutes.

6 Season to taste with salt and pepper. Stir the remaining olive oil into the couscous, then put the couscous and the chick pea stew on to a large, warmed serving dish, garnish with the coriander and serve immediately.

Pasta Dishes

Another really healthy food, pasta is popular with most people and is quick, economical and very filling. It is interesting to try different types of pasta, as I have suggested in the recipes, although you can always substitute your personal favourite or fall back on good old spaghetti if the more unusual ones are not available. A number of different pastas are identified in the Ingredients section (pp.73–75), along with basic cooking instructions. Most of the pasta recipes in this section also make excellent first courses, if served in smaller portions, perhaps before a vegetable main course.

Tagliatelle with Gorgonzola and Walnuts

Serve this quickly made, rich and delicious dish with a green salad. If you can't get Gorgonzola, other blue cheeses such as Roquefort can be used.

SERVES 4

450 g/1 lb tagliatelle
½ oz butter
salt and freshly ground black
   pepper
100 g/4 oz walnuts, roughly
   chopped

300 ml/10 fl oz double cream
1 garlic clove, crushed
100 g/4 oz Gorgonzola cheese,
   crumbled

1 Cook the tagliatelle in a large saucepan as described on p.72, until *al dente*.
2 Drain immediately, then return to the still-warm pan with the butter, salt, pepper and walnuts.

3 While the tagliatelle is cooking, make the sauce. Put the cream into a small, heavy-based saucepan; add the garlic and Gorgonzola and heat gently, stirring occasionally, until the cheese has melted. Season with salt and pepper.

4 Turn the pasta on to a large warmed serving dish, or individual plates, and pour the sauce into the centre. Serve immediately.

[V]   *Fusilli Verde with Mushrooms and Cream*

SERVES 4

450 g/1 lb fusilli verde
FOR THE SAUCE
1 onion, peeled and chopped
40 g/1½ oz butter or vegan margarine
1 garlic clove, crushed

450 g/1 lb button mushrooms, wiped and sliced
150 ml/5 fl oz double or non-dairy cream
salt and freshly ground black pepper
freshly grated nutmeg

1 To make the sauce, fry the onion gently in 25 g/1 oz of the butter or vegan margarine for 10 minutes, until softened.

2 Add the garlic and mushrooms and cook for 15–20 minutes, until all the liquid has evaporated.

3 Add the cream. Season with salt, pepper and nutmeg. Remove from the heat.

4 Cook the fusilli in a large saucepan as described on p.72, until *al dente*.

5 Drain the pasta immediately, then return to the still-warm pan with the remaining butter, salt and pepper.

6 Quickly reheat the sauce, then tip the fusilli into a warmed serving dish, pour the sauce over the top and serve.

[V]   *Pasta Primavera*

SERVES 4

25 g/1 oz butter or vegan margarine
1 onion, peeled and finely chopped

salt and freshly ground black pepper

225 g/8 oz young carrots, scraped
   and diced
225 g/8 oz courgettes, sliced
225 g/8 oz fresh shelled peas or
   mangetouts

350 g/12 oz vermicelli
2 tablespoons chopped mint

TO GARNISH
mint sprig

1 Melt the butter or vegan margarine in a large saucepan, then cover and fry the onion without browning for 5 minutes.
2 Add the carrots and cook for 10 minutes, then put in the courgettes and cook for a further 5 minutes. Add the peas or mangetouts and cook for 2–3 minutes.
3 Just before the vegetables are ready, cook the vermicelli in a large saucepan as described on p. 72, until *al dente*. Drain immediately, then return to the pan.
4 Add the vegetables to the vermicelli, together with the mint, salt and pepper. Mix, then serve garnished with mint.

Wholewheat Pasta and Mushroom Bake

This is another tasty, homely dish, and like
many pasta bakes, freezes well. Frozen peas go
well with it, or fresh watercress.

SERVES 4

100 g/4 oz small wholewheat pasta
   shapes such as leaves or rings
2 onions, peeled and chopped
1 tablespoon oil
100 g/4 oz mushrooms, washed
   and chopped
225 g/8 oz tomatoes, skinned
   (p.108) and chopped

1 egg, beaten
100 g/4 oz grated Cheddar cheese
freshly ground black pepper
butter for greasing
a few wholewheat breadcrumbs
   mixed with chopped parsley for
   topping

1 Preheat the oven to 190c/375f/Gas Mark 5. Grease an oven-proof dish.
2 Cook the pasta in a large saucepan as described on p.72, until *al dente*. Drain.
3 While the pasta is cooking, fry the onions in the oil for 7 minutes, then add the mushrooms and tomatoes and cook for a further 3 minutes.

4 Stir in the egg and stir over the heat for a moment or two longer until the egg begins to set. Remove from the heat and add the drained pasta, two-thirds of the cheese and salt and pepper to taste.

5 Spoon the mixture into the dish and sprinkle crumbs and remaining cheese over the top. Bake for 25–30 minutes, until crisp and golden-brown.

V *Tagliatelle Verde with Lentil Sauce*

This is a useful dish to make when you have to
rustle up a meal for a crowd unexpectedly,
because it uses store cupboard ingredients.

SERVES 4

225–350 g/8–12 oz tagliatelle
  verde
15 g/½ oz butter or vegan
  margarine
FOR THE SAUCE
2 tablespoons olive oil
2 onions, peeled and chopped
2 garlic cloves, crushed
½ teaspoon ground cinnamon

225 g/8 oz red lentils, washed
1 × 425-g/15-oz can tomatoes
450 ml/15 fl oz water
salt and freshly ground black
  pepper
TO SERVE (OPTIONAL)
coriander sprig
grated Parmesan cheese

1 To make the sauce, heat the olive oil in a large pan and fry the onion for 10 minutes, then add the garlic, cinnamon, lentils, tomatoes and water. Bring to the boil.

2 Reduce the heat and let the mixture simmer gently for about 20 minutes, until the lentils are tender; season to taste with salt and pepper.

3 Meanwhile, cook the tagliatelle in a large saucepan as described on p.72, until *al dente*.

4 Drain immediately, then return to the still-warm pan with the butter or vegan margarine. Season with salt and pepper.

5 Turn the tagliatelle on to a large warmed serving dish, or individual plates, and pour the sauce into the centre. Garnish with coriander and serve immediately, with grated Parmesan cheese handed separately, if liked.

Variation

TAGLIATELLE VERDE WITH LENTIL AND RED WINE SAUCE

Make as described, replacing a little of the water with red wine, say 75–150 ml/3–5 fl oz – as much as you can spare! This makes an excellent supper, accompanied by a good green salad and the rest of the wine used to make the sauce.

Spaghetti Bolognese Vegetariana

This is popular with my student daughter and her friends, because it's quick to make, cheap, filling and tasty. The sauce freezes well.

SERVES 4

350 g/12 oz spaghetti
½ oz butter or vegan margarine
FOR THE SAUCE
175 g/6 oz whole green lentils
   cooked in plenty of water for
   45–50 minutes, until tender, or
   2 × 400-g/14-oz cans lentils
1 large onion, peeled and sliced
2 tablespoons oil

1 garlic clove, crushed
100 g/4 oz carrot, diced
2 tablespoons tomato purée
2 tablespoons chopped parsley
salt and freshly ground black
   pepper
TO SERVE (OPTIONAL)
grated Parmesan or Cheddar
   cheese

1 To make the sauce, drain the lentils, reserving the liquid.
2 Fry the onion in the oil in a medium saucepan for 5 minutes, allowing it to brown lightly, then add the garlic and carrot.
3 Cover the pan and cook gently for about 15 minutes, until the vegetables are tender.
4 Stir in the lentils, tomato purée, parsley, salt and pepper and a little of the reserved lentil liquid, to give a thick but moist consistency.
5 About 10 minutes before the lentil sauce is ready, cook the spaghetti in a large saucepan as described on p.75, until *al dente*.
6 Drain well, then return the spaghetti to the still-warm pan with the butter or vegan margarine and black pepper.
7 Check that the spaghetti and the sauce are really hot, then turn the spaghetti into a large warmed serving dish and pour the sauce on top. Offer grated cheese separately, if liked.

⟨V⟩ *Taglioni Verde with Tomato Sauce and Aubergines*

The green of the taglioni against the orange-red
tomato sauce and the purple tones of the
aubergine give this dish a warming, appetizing
look, ideal for a quick supper on a chilly
autumn day. I like to serve it on its own,
followed by a leafy salad, then a cheeseboard,
and, finally, perhaps a refreshing sorbet, such
as pear or blackberry.

SERVES 4

2 medium aubergines, total weight
  about 450 g/1 lb
salt
8 tablespoons olive oil
1 onion, peeled and chopped
750 g/1½ lb tomatoes, skinned
  (p.108) and chopped

freshly ground black pepper
350 g/12 oz taglioni verde

TO SERVE (OPTIONAL)
basil sprig
grated Parmesan cheese

1 Slice the aubergines thinly lengthways, then cut into strips
about 5 cm/2 inches long and 2·5 cm/1 inch wide. Salt, rinse and
drain the aubergine strips as described on p.106.

2 Fry the aubergine strips in 6 tablespoons of the olive oil in a
medium saucepan until crisp and brown on both sides. Remove
from the pan and drain on kitchen paper. Then fry the onion in
the olive oil left in the pan for 10 minutes, without browning.
Add the tomatoes and cook gently for 5 minutes.

3 Purée in a blender or food processor, return to the pan and
season with salt and pepper.

4 Cook the taglioni in a large saucepan as described on p.72,
until *al dente*.

5 Drain the pasta immediately, then return to the pan and add
the remaining olive oil and salt and pepper to taste.

6 Turn the taglioni on to a warmed shallow serving dish. Pour
the sauce on top, then put the aubergine strips on top of that.
Garnish with the basil sprig. Serve the pasta immediately, with
some grated Parmesan cheese handed separately, if liked.

Fusille Colbuco with Aubergine and Wine Sauce

Fusille colbuco, a long spiral pasta, is
particularly attractive in this dish, but any
other long type of pasta, including spaghetti,
would be good.

SERVES 4

350 g/12 oz fusille colbuco
FOR THE SAUCE
2 medium aubergines, total weight
   about 450 g/1 lb
salt
1 onion, peeled and chopped
4 tablespoons olive oil
1 garlic clove, crushed
1 green pepper, de-seeded and
   chopped

225 g/8 oz tomatoes, skinned
   (p.108) and chopped
1 tablespoon chopped fresh basil or
   1 teaspoon dried basil
4 tablespoons red or white wine
freshly ground black pepper
TO GARNISH
basil sprigs
TO SERVE (OPTIONAL)
grated Parmesan cheese

1 Dice the aubergines, then salt, drain and rinse as described on
p.106.
2 Fry the onion in half the olive oil in a medium saucepan for 5
minutes, without browning, then add the aubergine, garlic,
green pepper, tomatoes, basil and wine and cook gently for 25
minutes, until the vegetables are soft. Season with salt and
pepper.
3 Just before the sauce is ready, cook the fusille colbuco in a
large saucepan as described on p.72, until *al dente*.
4 Drain immediately, then return to the still-warm pan with the
remaining olive oil, salt and pepper.
5 Turn the pasta on to a warmed large serving dish, or individual plates, and pour the wine sauce on top. Garnish with the
basil sprigs and serve immediately, with some grated Parmesan
cheese handed separately, if liked.

Summer Linguine

A perfect dish for a lazy summer's lunch in the
garden, hot linguine (or any other long slim
pasta) is served here with summer vegetables
and soft melting cheese.

SERVES 4

450 g/1 lb tomatoes, skinned
  (p.108) and sliced
1 bunch spring onions, trimmed
  and chopped
2 garlic cloves, crushed
225 g/8 oz Mozzarella or Brie
  cheese, cubed

2–3 tablespoons fresh basil leaves
salt and freshly ground black
  pepper
450 g/1 lb linguine or other long,
  thin pasta
2 tablespoons olive oil

1 Put the tomatoes, onions, garlic, basil and cheese into a
serving bowl which is large enough to hold the cooked pasta as
well. Season with salt and pepper.
2 Cook the linguine in a large saucepan as described on p.72,
until *al dente*. Drain immediately, then return to the still-warm
pan with the olive oil, salt and pepper.
3 Mix well, then add the linguine to the vegetables in the bowl
and stir to distribute all the ingredients. Serve immediately.

Spinach Lasagne

This makes a big dish of particularly tasty
lasagne, great for feeding a crowd, especially if
accompanied by some robust red wine. A crisp
green salad with fresh herbs goes well with it.

SERVES 6

1 large onion, peeled and chopped
2 tablespoons olive oil
2 garlic cloves, crushed

900 g/2 lb cooked, fresh spinach,
  chopped, or frozen chopped
  spinach, thawed

900 g/2 lb skimmed milk soft
  cheese
salt and freshly ground black
  pepper
1 quantity Italian Tomato Sauce
  (p.254)

225 g/8 oz oven-ready lasagne or
  350 g/12 oz fresh lasagne
225 g/8 oz Mozzarella cheese
butter for greasing

1 Preheat the oven to 200c/400f/Gas Mark 6. Grease a large, shallow ovenproof dish.

2 Fry the onion in the olive oil in a large saucepan for 10 minutes, until soft but not browned. Add the garlic, cook for a minute or two longer, then remove from the heat.

3 Squeeze any excess liquid out of the spinach, then add to the onion mixture, together with the skimmed milk soft cheese, salt and plenty of pepper.

4 Cover the base of the dish with a thin layer of the tomato sauce, then put a layer of lasagne on top, followed by a layer of the spinach mixture. Thinly slice 175 g/6 oz of the Mozzarella cheese. Next, make a layer of Mozzarella cheese slices, then of tomato sauce.

5 Continue like this until all the ingredients are used up, ending with a layer of sauce. Grate the remaining cheese and arrange in 3 diagonal stripes on the top.

6 Bake for 1 hour, covering the dish with foil after 40–45 minutes if the top begins to get too brown.

Variations

MIXED VEGETABLE LASAGNE

Make as described, but instead of the spinach and cheese filling use a vegetable mixture. To make this, fry the onion in oil as described, then add the garlic and 700 g/1½ lb each of diced carrots and sliced leeks, 450 g/1 lb of diced courgettes and 1 chopped and de-seeded green pepper. Cover and fry for about 15 minutes until tender. Layer this mixture with the lasagne, Mozzarella cheese and tomato sauce.

LENTIL LASAGNE

Use a double quantity lentil Bolognese mixture (p.375), layered with Italian Tomato Sauce.

Macaroni Cheese

An ever-popular old favourite, with a tangy
sauce. My young daughter always asks for this
when she has a friend to a meal, and they
certainly eat it up enthusiastically. But I
sometimes wonder what their parents think
when they hear that their daughters have had
such an apparently uninspired vegetarian dish
in the home of someone who is supposed to be
an expert!

SERVES 4

225 g/8 oz quick-cook macaroni
50 g/2 oz butter or vegan
  margarine
2 rounded tablespoons plain flour
600 ml/1 pint milk
2 teaspoons Dijon mustard
175 g/6 oz cheese, grated
salt and freshly ground black
  pepper

100 g/4 oz fresh wholewheat
  breadcrumbs
a little extra butter or vegan
  margarine for greasing

1 Heat the grill, or preheat the oven to 200c/400f/Gas Mark 6.
Grease a shallow flameproof dish which will fit under the grill, if
using this method for browning the macaroni cheese.
2 Cook the macaroni in a large saucepan as described on p. 72,
until *al dente*. Drain well.
3 Meanwhile, make the sauce. Melt the butter or vegan margarine in a saucepan, then add the flour; stir for 1–2 minutes over
the heat, then stir in the milk, a quarter at a time, stirring well
and allowing the sauce to thicken between each addition.
4 Leave the sauce to simmer gently over the heat for 5 minutes,
then remove from the heat and add the mustard, two-thirds of
the grated cheese and salt and pepper to taste.
5 Mix together the cooked macaroni and the cheese sauce.
Check the seasoning, then spoon the mixture into the dish and
level the surface. Sprinkle the breadcrumbs and the remaining
cheese over the top.
6 Place the dish under the preheated grill for 5–10 minutes, or

heat through in the oven for about 20 minutes, until the macaroni cheese is hot inside and golden-brown and crisp on top.

Aubergine and Pasta Charlotte

Here is pasta dressed up for a special occasion, a tasty mixture of rigatoni with tomato sauce and cheese, encased in slices of aubergine in a round mould and turned out like a cake. It's easy to do, yet always impresses. Eat as a main course, with one or two simply cooked vegetables, like French beans and baby carrots.

SERVES 6 AS A MAIN COURSE, 8 AS A STARTER

2 medium aubergines, total weight about 450 g/1 lb
salt
olive oil
400 g/14 oz rigatoni
1 quantity Italian Tomato Sauce (p.254)
75 g/3 oz butter
225 g/8 oz Mozzarella cheese, grated

4 tablespoons grated Parmesan cheese
4 tablespoons grated mature Cheddar cheese
1 tablespoon dried oregano
freshly ground black pepper
2 tablespoons dried breadcrumbs

1 Slice the aubergines diagonally into 5-mm/¼-inch slices. Salt, rinse and drain the aubergine slices as described on p.72. Pat dry on kitchen paper.
2 Fry the aubergine slices in a little olive oil for 2–3 minutes on each side, until soft and lightly browned. Drain well on kitchen paper.
3 Preheat the oven to 190c/375f/Gas Mark 5. Brush a 20-cm/8-inch round springform tin with olive oil.
4 Cook the rigatoni in a large saucepan as described on p.72 until almost done: it should be a bit undercooked. Drain well, then return to the pan with 2 tablespoons of the tomato sauce. Mix well.

5 Melt the butter in the remaining tomato sauce; pour over the rigatoni and mix, together with the Mozzarella, Parmesan and Cheddar cheeses. Add the oregano, and season with plenty of salt and pepper.

6 Arrange the aubergine slices over the base and sides of the prepared tin. Make sure that the slices in the base of the tin radiate attractively from the centre, and that all gaps are filled.

7 Spoon the pasta mixture into the tin, press down lightly and sprinkle with the breadcrumbs. Bake for 20 minutes.

8 Allow the charlotte to stand for 15 minutes to settle, and for the flavours to develop, then slip a knife round the edges of the tin and turn the charlotte out on to a warmed serving dish.

9 Press any fallen aubergine slices back in place, and serve immediately.

Pasta with Black Olives

SERVES 4

350 g/12 oz rigatoni	1 quantity Sweet Pepper Sauce
2 tablespoons olive oil	(p.257)
salt and freshly ground black	50 g/2 oz black olives, stoned and
pepper	roughly chopped

1 Cook the rigatoni in a large saucepan as described on p.72, until *al dente*.

2 Drain immediately and return the rigatoni to the still-warm pan with the olive oil; season the pasta to taste with salt and black pepper.

3 While the pasta is cooking make the sauce.

4 Serve the pasta on warmed plates, pour the sauce on top and sprinkle with the chopped olives.

OLIVES

The fruit of a tree native to the Mediterranean, olives are gathered and preserved in oil or brine at various stages of development. The ones which are picked and pickled early become green olives, while the later, more mature olives become black olives. Green and black olives differ in flavour and both have their uses; green olives are also available stoned and stuffed with pimento. They make a delicious nibble, garnish and addition to salads and savoury dishes. The best way to buy olives is loose at a good delicatessen. They will keep for a couple of weeks or so in the fridge.

A delicious Olive Pâté can be bought in a jar or made by stoning and puréeing black olives in a blender or food processor. I think of this as the vegetarian answer to caviar and find it an attractive and piquant garnish for canapés, salads, hardboiled and scrambled eggs; it's also excellent thinly spread on Melba Toast (p.221) or with crusty bread.

Pastry Dishes

*Favourites with most people, pastry dishes are
useful for many occasions ranging from picnics
and hearty family meals to dinner parties and
celebrations. I use wholewheat flour for all
pastry-making except puff, for which I use
unbleached white flour, when I make it,
although for this pastry I do often take a short
cut and use a good quality frozen pastry, made
without animal fat (check the label). Keep the
high-fat pastries, such as puff, rough-puff and
flaky, for specials, and serve any pastry dish
with low-fat accompaniments such as steamed
vegetables or a lightly dressed salad, for healthy,
well-balanced eating.*

Basic Shortcrust Pastry

MAKES 225 G/8 OZ

225 g/8 oz plain 100% or 85%
    wholewheat flour
½ teaspoon salt

100 g/4 oz butter or vegan
    margarine, diced
3 tablespoons ice-cold water

1 Put the flour into a mixing bowl with the salt and butter or
vegan margarine.
2 Using your fingertips, rub the fat into the flour until the
mixture resembles fine breadcrumbs.
3 Add the water and gently press the mixture together to form a
dough.
4 Turn the dough on to a lightly floured board and knead
gently, pressing it into a round, square or oblong, as required,
then roll it out, using a floured rolling pin and short strokes, and
making sure that the pastry does not stick to the board. Use as
required.
5 If you do not need the pastry immediately, wrap it in clingfilm
and leave it in the fridge for up to 24 hours.

Variations

CHEESE SHORTCRUST

Add 50–100 g/2–4 oz finely grated Cheddar cheese before you add the water for this non-vegan variation.

NUT SHORTCRUST

Mix in 25 g/1 oz grated or finely chopped nuts – almonds, walnuts, brazil nuts or hazelnuts – before adding the water.

RICH SHORTCRUST

For this light, melt-in-the-mouth pastry, use self-raising flour and increase the fat to 150 g/5 oz. You won't need any water because the extra fat will bind the dough.

FATS FOR PASTRY

Traditional fats for pastries are butter and lard. Vegetarians can use a vegetable lard, or solid white fat. I use this for some pastries, such as flaky. Otherwise I use butter which I prefer to manufactured fats such as margarine and solid vegetable fat.

Polyunsaturated vegan margarine can be used in place of butter to make pastry. Some people use vegetable oil for shortcrust pastry, but I have never, myself, been able to make a really good, light pastry with this.

A QUICHE BY ANY OTHER NAME . . .

Strictly speaking, 'quiche' refers to a light, creamy French flan, and in particular, Quiche Lorraine (which contains cream, bacon, onion and Gruyère cheese). 'Flan' is the English term (which I prefer) and 'tart' generally refers to a pastry case with a sweet filling.

When you're handling wholewheat pastry, which tends to be more crumbly than pastry made with white flour, it helps to roll the pastry out on a lightly floured board, then you can tip it straight from the board into your tin or dish, avoiding any breakages.

French Onion Flan

Flans are adaptable, can be light and elegant,
with thin, crisp pastry, or hearty and rustic,
with thick pastry and a deep filling. They can
be party-sized or individual. Eminently
portable and ideal for picnics or lunch boxes, a
flan can also be eaten with pleasure at any meal
from brunch to late-night supper, as a starter or
main course. This rich and delicious classic
French flan makes a wonderful main course
with a tomato and basil salad or a crisp green
salad; or it can be served cut into thin slices, as
a first course.

SERVES 4–6 AS A MAIN COURSE, 6–8 AS A STARTER

½ quantity Basic Shortcrust
  Pastry (p.384)
FOR THE FILLING
450 g/1 lb onions, peeled and sliced
25 g/1 oz butter
150 ml/5 fl oz single cream
1 whole egg or 2 egg yolks

salt and freshly ground black
  pepper
freshly grated nutmeg
butter for greasing
TO GARNISH
chopped parsley

1 Preheat the oven to 200c/400f/Gas Mark 6. Heat a baking
sheet. Lightly grease a 20-cm/8-inch flan tin or ring.
2 Roll out the pastry as thinly as possible and use to line the tin
or ring. To do this, hold the pastry board tilted downwards at
the far edge of the flan tin. Then gently slide the pastry off the
board and on to the tin, moving the pastry board back towards
you as you do so. Bake blind as described on p.396. Turn down
the oven to 180c/350f/Gas Mark 4.
3 Meanwhile, make the filling. Fry the onions gently in the
butter for 25–30 minutes, until very soft. Remove from the heat
and add the cream, and egg or egg yolks, with salt, pepper and
nutmeg to taste.
4 Pour the onion mixture into the flan case, then return the flan
to the oven on the baking sheet and bake for 30–35 minutes,
until the filling is set.
5 Serve warm or cold, sprinkled with a little parsley.

Variations

RATATOUILLE FLAN

Make as described, using a good, thick, tasty Ratatouille mixture (p.278) instead of the onions.

SPINACH, CHEESE AND ALMOND FLAN

Use 450 g/1 lb fresh spinach, cooked (225 g/8 oz frozen spinach), 75 g/3 oz grated cheese and 100 g/4 oz toasted flaked almonds; mix with 1 egg and omit the cream or milk.

MUSTARD, TOMATO AND MOZZARELLA FLAN

Spread the base of the flan case with 2 tablespoons Dijon mustard, cover with 450 g/1 lb skinned and sliced tomatoes. Arrange 100 g/4 oz sliced Mozzarella cheese on top, season, then carefully pour in the egg and cream mixture.

CAULIFLOWER, CHEDDAR CHEESE AND WALNUT FLAN

Use cooked florets from a small cauliflower, 100 g/4 oz grated Cheddar cheese and 100 g/4 oz chopped walnuts, instead of the onion.

WATERCRESS AND STILTON CHEESE FLAN

For this tangy version, use 2 eggs, 300 ml/10 fl oz cream or milk, a bunch of watercress, chopped, and 100 g/4 oz grated Stilton cheese.

MUSHROOM FLAN

Fry just 1 small chopped onion for 7 minutes, then add 350 g/ 12 oz sliced mushrooms and a crushed garlic clove and fry for about 15 minutes until all the liquid has disappeared. Add 1 tablespoon chopped parsley to the egg mixture.

LEEK AND BLACK OLIVE FLAN

Use 700 g/1½ lb leeks, cooked, 2 tablespoons chopped parsley and 50–100 g/2–4 oz black olives.

VEGAN FLAN FILLINGS

Many combinations of cooked vegetables, vegetable purées and dips can be used to make colourful and delicious non-dairy fillings. Here are some possibilities:

☐ Ratatouille (p.278), made fairly thick
☐ Mushroom and Herb Terrine (p.222) topped with thin slices of mushroom brushed with oil
☐ Golden Spiced Cauliflower (p.274)

☐ Cooked leeks topped with Hummus (p.217), thin circles of red pepper and black olives
☐ A thick, well-flavoured purée of carrots or celeriac (p.282), topped with lightly fried circles of courgette

[V] *Broccoli, Red Pepper and Almond Flan*

In this flan, bright green broccoli is covered with a light-textured sauce of red peppers and almonds and finished with a topping of roasted flaked almonds.

SERVES 4–6 AS A MAIN COURSE, 6–8 AS A STARTER

½ quantity Basic Shortcrust Pastry (p.384)
450 g/1 lb broccoli, divided into even-sized florets, stalks removed
1 tablespoon oil

salt and freshly ground black pepper
1 quantity Red Pepper and Almond Dip (p.220)
25 g/1 oz flaked almonds
butter for greasing

1 Preheat the oven to 200cC/400f/Gas Mark 6. Put a baking sheet into the centre of the oven, to heat up. Lightly grease a 20-cm/8-inch flan tin or ring.
2 Roll out the pastry as thinly as possible and use to line the tin or ring; trim the edges. Bake blind as described on p.396.
3 Meanwhile, cook the broccoli in 2·5 cm/1 inch boiling water for 4–5 minutes, or until just tender. Drain and return to the pan with the oil and salt and pepper.
4 Half-fill the flan case with the Red Pepper and Almond Dip,

then arrange the broccoli on top, pressing the florets into the dip to secure them.

5 Spoon the remaining Red Pepper and Almond Dip evenly over the top, making sure that it runs down between the broccoli florets. Leave a few florets peeping out, for colour contrast. Sprinkle with the flaked almonds.

6 Return the flan to the oven on the baking sheet and bake for 25–30 minutes, until the almonds are lightly browned and the filling heated through and 'set'-looking. Serve hot, warm or cold.

Variations

MUSHROOM, RED PEPPER AND ALMOND FLAN

For this tasty variation, replace the broccoli with 450 g/1 lb button mushrooms, sliced and fried until all the liquid has evaporated.

SPICY VEGETABLE AND LENTIL FLAN

Use 225 g/8 oz cooked mixed vegetables such as carrots, potatoes and peas, and 1 quantity Lentil Dal (p.312). Top with flaked or desiccated coconut.

PASTRY QUANTITIES FOR FLANS

Flan size	Weight of flour for pastry
10 cm/4 inch	50 g/2 oz
15 cm/6 inch	100 g/4 oz
18 cm/7 inch	150 g/5 oz
20 cm/8 inch	175 g/6 oz
23 cm/9 inch	200 g/7 oz
25 cm/10 inch	225 g/8 oz
30 cm/12 inch (shallow)	300 g/10 oz

By convention, the weight of pastry needed for a recipe is always given as the weight of the flour used to make it. So 225 g/8 oz pastry means pastry made from 225 g/8 oz flour. However, the weight stated on a packet of frozen pastry is the weight of the whole amount.

Asparagus Tartlets

These tartlets – made in 10-cm/4-inch flan tins –
are perfect for a summer garden lunch. The
little Asparagus Boats are ideal for a buffet
party.

MAKES 6

1½ quantity Basic Shortcrust
   Pastry (p.384)
1 bunch asparagus, trimmed and
   cooked as described on p. 91, or
   450 g/1 lb frozen asparagus,
   cooked and drained

300 ml/10 fl oz single cream
2 egg yolks
salt and freshly ground black
   pepper
freshly grated nutmeg

1 Preheat the oven to 200C/400F/Gas Mark 6. Put a baking sheet
into the centre of the oven, to heat up. Lightly grease 6 ×
10-cm/4-inch flan tins.
2 Divide the pastry into 6 equal pieces. Roll out each piece as
thinly as possible and use to line the tins; trim the edges. Bake
blind as described on p.396.
3 Turn the oven down to 180C/350F/Gas Mark 4.
4 Remove the tips from the asparagus and chop the tender part
of the stalks. Divide the chopped asparagus and the tips among
the tartlets.
5 Whisk the cream and egg yolks together; season to taste with
salt, pepper and grated nutmeg. Divide this mixture between
the tartlets, then put them back into the oven on the baking
sheet and bake for about 15 minutes, until the filling is set. Serve
hot or warm.

Variations

INDIVIDUAL AVOCADO FLANS

Use the diced flesh from 3 small ripe avocado pears, skinned, a
crushed garlic clove and 2 tablespoons lemon juice instead of the
asparagus. Make as described. These need to be cooked just
before eating, and it's important not to over-heat the avocado as
this gives it a bitter taste.

ASPARAGUS BOATS

The ingredients given above make 30 boats. Roll out the pastry, line boat-shaped tins and bake as above. Cut the asparagus spears into lengths to fit each boat shape; divide amongst the boats, pour in the egg mixture and bake for 8–10 minutes. Garnish each serving with a slice of lemon and parsley sprig.

PREPARING FLANS IN ADVANCE

Filled flans do not freeze well – they emerge with soggy bottoms. It's best to make the flan cases (and be sure to give them the hot-oil treatment (p.396) for superb results), then freeze. Pack carefully. Ideally, fill and bake just before eating, though if you've a lot to do, they can be cooked the night before, then kept in a cool, airy place until required.

Potato and Mushroom Pasties   V

These pasties are good either hot or cold and are popular for picnics and lunch boxes. Serve with a mixed salad.

MAKES 4

1 quantity Basic Shortcrust
   Pastry, Plain or Cheese (p.385)
beaten egg to glaze (optional)
FOR THE FILLING
1 onion, peeled and chopped
2 tablespoons oil
225 g/8 oz potato, peeled and cut
   into 5-mm/¼-inch dice

1 garlic clove, crushed
225 g/8 oz mushrooms, washed
   and chopped
1 tablespoon chopped parsley
salt and freshly ground black
   pepper

1 First make the filling. Fry the onion in the oil for 5 minutes, then add the potato and garlic.
2 Cook gently for 10 minutes. Add the mushrooms and cook for a further 4–5 minutes, until the vegetables are just tender. Add the parsley and season with salt and pepper. Cool.

3 Preheat the oven to 200c/400F/Gas Mark 6. Divide the pastry into 4 equal pieces; roll each into a circle 15 cm/6 inches in diameter.

4 Spoon a quarter of the potato mixture on to each circle. Fold over the pastry and press the edges together, pinching them to form a 'frill' along the seam.

5 Make a couple of small steam-holes in each pasty, brush the pasties with beaten egg, if used, then place them on a baking sheet and bake for 20–25 minutes, until golden-brown.

Variations

SPICED CHICK PEA AND POTATO PASTIES

Make these in the same way, adding 1 tablespoon ground coriander and 1 teaspoon ground cumin to the onion, and replacing the mushrooms with 100 g/4 oz chick peas, soaked, cooked and drained, or 1 × 425-g/15-oz can chick peas, drained.

VEGETABLE PASTIES

Replace the mushrooms with 100 g/4 oz scraped and diced carrots and 100 g/4 oz shredded leeks and a chopped skinned tomato, added to the pan with the potatoes and fried until tender. Flavour with ½ teaspoon each dried oregano and basil. Other combinations of cooked vegetables can be used and different flavourings such as rosemary or thyme. Drained cooked chick peas, red kidney beans or cannellini beans can be added to the mixture, or some chopped nuts, such as hazelnuts or almonds.

Savoury Cheshire Cheese and Onion Pie

Simple and good, a vegetarian family favourite.

SERVES 4

1 quantity Basic Shortcrust Pastry (p.384)
FOR THE FILLING
700 g/1½ lb onions, peeled and sliced

175 g/6 oz Cheshire cheese, grated
salt and freshly ground black pepper
freshly grated nutmeg

1 Preheat the oven to 220c/425f/Gas Mark 7. Put a baking sheet into the centre of the oven, to heat up.
2 Parboil the onions in 2·5 cm/1 inch lightly salted water for 5 minutes, then drain and cool.
3 Roll out just under half the pastry to fit a 20–23-cm/8–9-inch pie plate.
4 Add the cheese to the onions; mix together and season with salt, pepper and nutmeg, then spoon on top of the pastry.
5 Roll out the remaining pastry to fit the top; press the edges together and trim. Bake for 30 minutes, until golden-brown. Serve hot.

Variations

BUTTER BEAN, CHEESE AND PICKLE PIE

Make this in the same way, using 100 g/4 oz butter beans, soaked, cooked and drained, or 1 × 425-g/15-oz can butter beans, drained, in place of one of the onions, and reducing the amount of cheese to 50 g/2 oz. Add 3 tablespoons pickle or chutney to the mixture before spooning on top of the pastry.

LEEK PIE

Wash 900 g/2 lb leeks and cut them into pieces about 2·5 cm/1 inch long. Cook them in 2·5 cm/1 inch boiling water for about 10 minutes, until just tender. Drain them very well, then mix them with 300 ml/10 fl oz soured cream or Béchamel Sauce (p.261). Season.

MUSHROOM AND CHESTNUT PIE

Fry 1 large chopped onion and 2 chopped celery sticks in 25 g/1 oz butter for 10 minutes, then add 225 g/8 oz washed and sliced mushrooms and cook for a further 2–3 minutes, or until the mushrooms are tender. Remove from the heat and add 350–450 g/12 oz–1 lb cooked chestnuts (you can use fresh cooked chestnuts, or canned whole chestnuts, or dried ones which have been soaked and cooked as described on p.52). Add 1 tablespoon soy sauce and salt and pepper to taste.

Mushroom Flan

SERVES 6 AS A MAIN COURSE

double quantity Basic Shortcrust
    Pastry (p.384)
double quantity Mushrooms in
    Cream (p.115)

butter for greasing

TO GARNISH
chopped parsley

1 Preheat the oven to 200c/400f/Gas Mark 6. Put a baking sheet into the centre of the oven, to heat up. Lightly grease a 30-cm/12-inch flan tin.
2 Roll out the pastry and use to line the tin; trim the edges. Bake blind as described on p.396.
3 Spoon the Mushrooms in Cream into the flan case and smooth the top. Return the flan to the oven on a baking sheet for 10–15 minutes to heat through. Sprinkle with parsley. Serve hot or cold.

Quick Spring Onion and Fresh Herb Flan

This is a light and melting flan, rather than a
crisp one. It is quick and makes a delicious
lunch or supper, with a crisp, leafy salad, such
as radiccio, watercress and walnut.

SERVES 4

½ quantity Rich Shortcrust Pastry
    (p.385)
butter for greasing
FOR THE FILLING
150 ml/5 fl oz milk or single cream
2 eggs

3 tablespoons chopped fresh herbs
salt and freshly ground black
    pepper
freshly grated nutmeg
1 bunch spring onions, washed,
    trimmed and chopped

1 Preheat the oven to 190c/375f/Gas Mark 5. Put a baking sheet into the centre of the oven, to heat up. Lightly grease a 20-cm/8-inch flan tin or ring.

2 Roll out the pastry and use to line the tin or ring; trim the edges. Chill in the fridge for a few minutes while you make the filling.

3 Whisk together the milk or cream and the eggs. Add the herbs and salt, pepper and nutmeg to taste. Put the spring onion into the base of the flan, then pour the egg mixture on top.

4 Place the flan case on the baking sheet and bake for 35–40 minutes, until the filling is set and lightly browned. Serve hot or warm.

Variations

QUICK MUSHROOM FLAN

Use 100 g/4 oz button mushrooms, thinly sliced, instead of the onions, and a crushed garlic clove instead of the chopped fresh herbs.

QUICK SWEETCORN FLAN

Use 100 g/4 oz frozen sweetcorn kernels instead of the onions and parsley.

QUICK CHEESE AND TOMATO FLAN

Add 50–100 g/2–4 oz grated Gruyère cheese and 1 thinly sliced tomato.

QUICK MINT AND PEA FLAN

Use 2 tablespoons finely chopped mint and 100 g/4 oz frozen peas. This mixture is good with or without the onion.

QUICK BEAN FLAN

Add ½ teaspoon made mustard to the egg mixture and put the well-drained contents of ½ × 425-g/15-oz can butter beans, chick peas or cannellini beans on the flan base before pouring on the milk and egg mixture. Omit the onion and parsley, or keep them as liked. A crushed garlic clove mixed in with the eggs is also nice in this, and so are a few juicy black olives.

MAKING A REALLY CRISP FLAN CASE

I find this method of 'baking blind' better than the conventional one, where the flan base is weighed down with greaseproof paper and dried beans, because it's less trouble and gives a crisper result. Have a look at the flan after 5 minutes to see if the base is rising up; if so, simply press it down gently with the back of a fork.

1 Heat the oven to 200c/400f/ Gas Mark 6. Put a baking sheet into the centre of the oven, to heat up. Lightly grease a flan tin or flan ring set on baking sheet.
2 Roll out the pastry and ease it into the tin or ring. Press down, trim edges.
3 Prick the pastry base all over. Bake for 12–20 minutes, depending on the size and thickness of the pastry, until firm to a light touch and lightly browned.

4 When the flan comes out of the oven, have ready 2–3 tablespoons sizzling hot oil and pour this into the pastry case. This will ensure that the base of your flan will be wonderfully crisp.
5 Next brush a little beaten egg over the base of the flan to seal any holes and return the flan to the oven for 3–4 minutes, until the beaten egg glaze is thoroughly set.

Steamed Vegetable Pudding

This is a vegetarian version of a steamed steak and kidney pudding, with vegetable suet or butter used for the pastry and vegetables in a savoury sauce instead of the steak and kidney.

SERVES 4

FOR THE FILLING
1 onion, peeled and chopped
1 potato, peeled and cut into 1-cm/ ½-inch dice
2 carrots, scraped and thinly sliced
225 g/8 oz mushrooms
2 tablespoons flour

2 tablespoons water
2 tablespoons soy sauce
salt and freshly ground black pepper
350 g/12 oz self-raising wholewheat flour
½ teaspoon salt

175 g/6 oz vegetable suet, coarsely
   grated
cold water to mix

TO GARNISH
parsley sprigs

1 Grease a 1·5-litre/2½-pint pudding basin thoroughly with butter or vegan margarine.

2 To make the filling, mix all the vegetables together with the flour, water, soy sauce and seasoning.

3 To make the pastry, put the flour into a bowl with the salt and suet. Mix the suet with the flour – don't rub it in like you do for ordinary pastry. Then add enough cold water to make a smooth dough which leaves the edges of the bowl clean. Leave the pastry to rest for 5 minutes.

4 Turn the dough on to a floured board and knead lightly, then roll out three-quarters of it to fit the pudding basin. Use to line the basin and press down well.

5 Spoon the vegetable mixture into the pastry-lined basin.

6 Roll out the rest of the dough to fit the top of the pudding. Press down firmly and trim the edges.

7 Prick the top of the pudding several times with a fork, then cover with a piece of pleated greased greaseproof paper and a piece of foil and tie down.

8 Stand the basin in a large saucepan and pour in boiling water to come halfway up the sides of the basin. Return to the boil, then simmer gently for 3 hours. Keep the water level topped up with boiling water as necessary.

9 To serve the pudding, remove the paper coverings, slip a palette knife around the sides of the basin to loosen the pudding, then turn it out on to a warmed serving plate. Serve immediately, garnished with parsley sprigs.

LIFTING A STEAMED PUDDING OUT OF THE PAN

Before cooking your pudding, fold a long piece of foil over several times to make a strip about 10 cm/4 inches wide. Place this strip under the pudding basin, leaving enough on either side to stick up over the sides of the pan. Holding the foil strip firmly at either end, you can then lift the pudding into the pan, and out again when it is cooked. When using this method, take care to hold the pudding level and have the serving plate close at hand.

FLAKY PASTRY

There are three types of flaky pastry:

Rough puff pastry
The quickest and easiest of the flaky pastries to make, this rises in flaky layers but does not get as high and light as puff pastry.

Flaky pastry
Almost as quick to make as rough puff, this rises higher and looks better. It is also possible to get a good result using 100% wholewheat flour.

Puff pastry
This is the richest pastry of all, rising in glorious golden flaky layers. It's wonderful for special occasion cookery, feuilletés, fleurons, bouchées and vol au vents. Making your own puff pastry is satisfying and rewarding, though you can also buy excellent frozen puff pastry: look for a brand which does not contain animal fat. Puff pastry made with 100% wholewheat flour is not very successful; it does not rise any higher than flaky pastry made with 100% wholewheat flour.

Rough Puff Pastry

MAKES 225 G/8 OZ

225 g/8 oz fine wholewheat flour
1 teaspoon salt
175 g/6 oz chilled butter or block
  vegan margarine
4 teaspoons lemon juice
about 8 tablespoons ice-cold water

1 Put the flour and salt into a mixing bowl and grate in the butter or vegan margarine. Add the lemon juice and water, then mix quickly to a fairly soft dough.

2 Gather the dough into a ball, wrap in clingfilm and chill in the fridge for at least 1 hour.

3 Take the dough out of the fridge. If it's very cold, leave it for 10 minutes to soften a bit, then roll it into a rectangle on a lightly floured board.

4 Mark the oblong lightly into 3 equal sections, then fold the bottom third up and the top third down, to make 3 layers.

5 Seal the edges by pressing them lightly with your rolling pin (to keep the air in), then give the pastry a quarter turn.

6 Repeat the rolling, folding and turning 4 times. The pastry is then ready to be used, or can be wrapped in clingfilm and put back into the fridge until needed.

7 Roll the pastry out about 5 mm/¼ inch thick and bake at 220c/425f/Gas Mark 7.

MAKING PALMIERS

These crunchy biscuits are an excellent way to use up left-over pieces of puff pastry. Push the pieces of pastry roughly together, and roll out into a rectangle about 3 mm/⅛ inch thick. Sprinkle thickly with demerara sugar.

Fold each of the 2 long sides to the centre, so they meet. Then fold the long edges to the middle again. Finally fold one of these rolled edges on top of the other and press down gently.

Cut into slices about 3 mm/⅛ inch thick and place on a baking sheet. Bake at 230c/450f/Gas Mark 8 for 7–8 minutes, until golden-brown. Cool on a wire rack.

Flaky Pastry

MAKES 225 G/8 OZ

225 g/8 oz unbleached white flour
pinch of salt
75 g/3 oz butter

150 ml/5 fl oz ice-cold water
75 g/3 oz white vegetable fat

1 Sift the flour and salt into a mixing bowl. Rub in half the butter. Add enough water to make a dough.

2 Turn the dough on to a lightly floured board and knead until smooth. Shape the dough into a rectangle.

3 Roll the dough into a 12 × 25-cm/5 × 10-inch rectangle. Make sure you have the edges of the pastry straight and the ends square.

4 Cut half the vegetable fat into small pieces and place them in rows over the top two-thirds of the pastry, well clear of the edges of the pastry rectangle.

5 Fold the bottom of the dough (without the fat on it) up, and the top third down. Seal the edges by pressing them lightly with a rolling pin. Give the dough a quarter turn, so that the folds are at the sides.

6 Roll and fold the pastry once more, without adding any fat.

7 Repeat steps 4, 5 and 6, using the rest of the butter.

8 Repeat steps 4 and 5, using the rest of the vegetable fat.

9 Wrap the dough in clingfilm and chill in the fridge for 15–30 minutes, then roll and fold again without adding any fat. The pastry is now ready for use. Roll out as required and bake at 230c/450f/Gas Mark 8.

Puff Pastry

Puff pastry is quite time-consuming but not difficult to make and is very rewarding. Most of the time the dough is resting in the fridge between rollings.

MAKES A 250 G/9OZ QUANTITY, WEIGHING 450 G/
1 LB (EQUIVALENT TO A 450 G/1 LB PACKET OF
FROZEN PUFF PASTRY)

225 g/8 oz strong unbleached plain
white flour
225 g/8 oz chilled butter or block
vegan margarine

½ teaspoon salt
150 ml/5 fl oz ice-cold water
1½ teaspoons lemon juice

1 Put the flour into a mixing bowl with 25 g/1 oz of the fat, and rub it into the flour until the mixture looks like coarse breadcrumbs.

2 Dissolve the salt in the water and add to the flour mixture, with the lemon juice. Mix to a dough.

3 Place the dough on a lightly floured surface, knead lightly and shape into a square. Wrap in clingfilm and chill in the fridge for 1 hour. (Have the remaining butter or vegan margarine chilling at the same time.)

4 Put the chilled butter or vegan margarine into a roomy polythene bag and beat with a rolling pin to soften it slightly. Then put it on to a floured board and roll it into a square about 15 cm/6 inches.

5 Next, roll out the dough on a lightly floured work surface, to make a 25-cm/10-inch square.

6 Put the square of butter or vegan margarine diagonally on the square of dough and fold the corners of the dough over,

overlapping them a little, to make a package which completely encloses the fat.

7 Put this package of dough on a lightly floured work surface and roll it out, using short, sharp, firm forwards and backwards strokes, to a rectangle 1 cm/½ inch thick.

8 Mark the dough into thirds. Fold the bottom third up and the top third down. Seal the edges by pressing them lightly with the rolling pin.

9 Now give the dough a quarter turn so that the folds are at the sides, and roll it out again so that it is about 5 mm/¼ inch thick and three times as long as it is wide. Fold the dough in 3 again.

10 The dough has now had 2 foldings, so mark it by pressing 2 fingers into the dough, then put it into a polythene bag and chill it in the fridge for 1 hour (or longer, if this is more convenient).

11 Remove the dough from the fridge and unwrap it. If it is very cold, let it rest for 10 minutes before you roll it. Then roll and fold the dough twice as before, and mark it with 4 fingers. Wrap and chill the dough for 1 hour or more as before.

12 Repeat step 11. The dough is then ready for use, or it can be kept in the fridge for several days, or frozen for several weeks. When you have rolled out the pastry, chill it again for about 30 minutes before baking at 230c/450f/Gas Mark 8.

Mushroom Pâté en Croûte $\boxed{\text{V}}$

A favourite recipe, this makes a delicious main
course served with a Soured Cream and Herb
Dressing (p.233) with cooked vegetables to
accompany.

SERVES 6

1 quantity Flaky Pastry (p.399), or
    450 g/1 lb frozen puff pastry,
    thawed
a little raw egg yolk
FOR THE FILLING
1 onion, peeled and chopped
25 g/1 oz butter
900 g/2 lb mushrooms, washed and
    finely chopped

2 garlic cloves, crushed
2 tablespoons chopped parsley
100 g/4 oz dried wholewheat
    breadcrumbs
2 tablespoons lemon juice
salt and freshly ground black
    pepper

1 Preheat the oven to 220c/425f/Gas Mark 7.

2 Fry the onion in the butter in a large saucepan for 10 minutes. Add the mushrooms and fry for 20–30 minutes, until all the liquid has evaporated.

3 Remove from the heat and add the garlic, parsley, breadcrumbs, lemon juice and salt and pepper to taste. Allow the mixture to cool.

4 Roll one third of the pastry into a 15 × 30-cm/6 × 12-inch rectangle. Place on a baking sheet and spoon the mushroom mixture on top, heaping it up well. Brush the edges of the pastry with water.

5 Roll out the remaining pastry to a 23 × 30-cm/9 × 12-inch rectangle.

6 Fold the pastry in half lengthways and make diagonal cuts with scissors to give a fancy finish, if you like. Open out and carefully place over the mushroom mixture, being careful to maintain the shape of the mushroom mixture.

7 Press the edges together and trim. Make a few steam-holes, decorate with pastry trimmings and brush with egg yolk. Bake for 30 minutes, until golden-brown. Serve hot or warm.

 ## Flaky Vegetable Pie

SERVES 4–6

½ quantity Rough Puff (p.397) or Flaky Pastry (p.399), or 225 g/8 oz frozen puff pastry, thawed

beaten egg to glaze

FOR THE FILLING

1 onion, peeled and chopped

2 tablespoons oil

2 garlic cloves, crushed

350 g/12 oz carrots, scraped and diced

350 g/12 oz courgettes, trimmed and diced

450 g/1 lb leeks, trimmed, washed and sliced

2 tomatoes, skinned (p.108) and chopped

2 tablespoons dried breadcrumbs

2 tablespoons chopped parsley

½ teaspoon each dried basil and oregano

salt

100 g/4 oz haricot beans, soaked, cooked and drained, or 1 × 425-g/15-oz can cannellini beans, drained

freshly ground black pepper

1 Preheat the oven to 220c/425f/Gas Mark 7.

2 First make the filling. Fry the onion in the oil in a large saucepan for 5 minutes, then add the garlic, carrot, courgette, leek, tomato, breadcrumbs and herbs.

3 Season with a little salt, then cook for 10–15 minutes, covered, until the vegetables are tender, stirring occasionally. Add the beans and check the seasoning.

4 Put the vegetable mixture in a 1·1-litre/2-pint pie dish and leave to cool.

5 Roll the pastry out 2·5 cm/1 inch larger all round than the pie dish. Cut off a strip from all round the pastry. Place the strip round the rim of the pie dish and brush with cold water, then place the rest of the pastry on top.

6 Trim the edges of the pastry and press together firmly to seal, then knock up and flute. Make a steam-hole in the centre. Decorate with pastry trimmings, sticking them on with cold water.

7 Brush the pie with beaten egg, if used, then bake for 30 minutes, until puffed up and golden-brown. Serve hot.

Choux Pastry

Choux pastry works well with either unbleached white or wholewheat flour, but sometimes with wholewheat flour the mixture will only take about ¾ of the egg; more and it would become sloppy, so stop adding it at this point.

MAKES ENOUGH FOR 8 ÉCLAIRS OR 12
PROFITEROLES

50 g/2 oz butter or block margarine *65 g/2½ oz plain or strong flour*
150 ml/5 fl oz water *2 eggs, lightly beaten*

1 Preheat the oven to 200c/400f/Gas Mark 6.

2 Put the fat and water into a saucepan and heat gently until the fat has melted, then bring to the boil.

3 Remove from the heat and add the flour all at once, beating well with a wooden spoon.

4 Return the pan to the heat and stir with the wooden spoon for 1 minute until the dough leaves the sides of the pan. Tip the dough into a clean bowl.

5 Add about a quarter of the egg, beating vigorously until the dough has absorbed it and become glossy again, then add another quarter of the egg in exactly the same way.

6 Repeat until all the egg has been used and the mixture is glossy and soft, but not sloppy. Cover with a plate until needed.

Wild Mushrooms in Cream with Pastry Leaves

As the puff pastry is such an important part of this dish, it is best when made with home-made puff pastry, which has a buttery flavour lacking in most bought puff pastry. It makes a beautiful autumn main course, served with Potato Purée (p.281) and followed by a Chicory, Watercress and Walnut Salad (p.241).

SERVES 6

1 quantity Puff Pastry (p.399) or
   450 g/1 lb frozen puff pastry,
   thawed
beaten egg to glaze
double quantity Wild Mushrooms
   in Cream (p.115)

TO GARNISH
fennel sprigs
thyme sprigs

1 Roll out the pastry 5 mm/¼ inch thick and cut into 6 leaf-shaped ovals about 10 × 5 cm/4 × 2 inches. Chill for 1 hour.

2 Preheat the oven to 230c/450f/Gas Mark 8.

3 Moisten the surface of a baking sheet and place the pastry leaves on it. Make leaf markings on the top. Brush the pastry leaves with beaten egg.

4 Bake the leaves for 10 minutes, then turn down the oven to 190c/375f/Gas Mark 5 and bake for a further 10–15 minutes, until the pastry is baked crisply through.

5 Gently reheat the wild mushroom mixture. Slit the pastry

leaves in half horizontally, using a sharp knife. Place the bases on a warmed serving dish, or individual dishes.

6 Spoon the mushroom mixture on top of the bases, letting it flow over the edges of the pastry. Then cover with the tops of the pastry leaves. Garnish with fennel and thyme sprigs and serve immediately.

Vol au Vents with Artichoke Heart Filling

Light, crisp vol au vent cases are filled with a
creamy mixture of artichoke hearts. They make
a good main course, with Potato Purée (p.281)
and green beans. It's best to make the vol au
vent cases in advance, then reheat and fill them
just before serving.

MAKES 12, SERVES 4–6

1 quantity Puff Pastry (p.399), or
450 g/1 lb frozen puff pastry,
thawed, or 12 frozen uncooked
vol au vent cases

FOR THE FILLING

100 g/4 oz spring onions, peeled
and finely chopped

15 g/½ oz butter or vegan
margarine

300 ml/10 fl oz single or non-dairy
cream

2 teaspoons cornflour

1 × 400-g/14-oz can artichoke
hearts

salt and freshly ground black
pepper

paprika

TO GARNISH

fennel sprigs

onion tassels

artichoke heart slices

1 Preheat the oven to 230c C/450f/Gas Mark 8.

2 Roll out home-made pastry 5 mm/¼ inch thick, bought puff pastry a little thinner.

3 Cut into circles or ovals using a 7·5-cm/3-inch cutter, then cut into the centre of each one, but not right through, with a 5-cm/2-inch cutter. (This will form the lid when the vol au vent has risen.)

4 Put the vol au vents on to a baking sheet and bake for about 5 minutes, until risen and golden-brown. Cool on a wire rack,

then remove the lids and some of the pastry from inside the vol au vents.

5 To make the filling, fry the onions gently in the butter or vegan margarine in a saucepan for 10 minutes, until soft but not browned. Stir in the cornflour, cook for a minute or two, then add the cream. Stir over the heat until thickened. Remove from heat.

6 Drain the artichoke hearts and chop roughly. Add to the onion mixture and season with salt, pepper and paprika.

7 Before serving, reheat the vol au vent cases at 180C/350F/Gas Mark 4 for 15 minutes. Have the filling hot and spoon this into the vol au vents as soon as they come out of the oven. Replace the lids, garnish and serve immediately.

Variation

MUSHROOM VOL AU VENTS

Replace the artichoke hearts with 350 g/12 oz sliced mushrooms, fried in 15 g/½ oz butter or vegan margarine for 15 minutes, until the liquid has evaporated. Fill the vol au vents as above.

Vegetable Gougère

An impressive and delicious dish, a big puffed-up ring of golden choux pastry, the centre filled with colourful vegetables.

SERVES 6

double quantity Choux Pastry (p.403)
a good pinch of cayenne pepper
175 g/6 oz Cheddar cheese, finely grated

1 quantity Peperonata (p.276), or Spring Vegetable Braise (p.269), or 1 quantity Mushrooms in Cream (p.115)

1 Preheat the oven to 220C/425F/Gas Mark 7.
2 Make the choux pastry as described on p.403. Add the cayenne and 100 g/4 oz of the grated cheese.

3 Spoon or pipe the choux pastry round the edge of a 30-cm/ 12-inch pizza plate or large shallow ovenproof dish.

4 Sprinkle with the rest of the cheese and bake for about 40 minutes, until the gougère is puffed up and golden-brown.

5 Reheat the Peperonata or other chosen filling and spoon this into the centre of the gougère when you remove it from the oven. (If there is any filling over, serve this separately.)

Samosas

These crisp, spicy little savouries are delicious
as an accompaniment to curries, or as a snack,
with some mango chutney or thick plain yogurt
to dip them into.

MAKES 32

FOR THE FILLING

1 large onion, peeled and chopped
2 tablespoons olive oil
1 large garlic clove, crushed
2 teaspoons each mustard seed, grated fresh ginger, ground cumin and ground coriander
700 g/1½ lb potatoes, cooked and diced
225 g/8 oz frozen peas, thawed
salt and freshly ground black pepper

FOR THE PASTRY

300 g/10 oz plain wholewheat flour
1 teaspoon salt
2 teaspoons baking powder
4 tablespoons oil
150–200 ml/5–7 fl oz ice-cold water
oil for deep-frying

1 First make the filling. Fry the onion in the oil for 8 minutes, until soft but not browned, then add the garlic, mustard seed, ginger, cumin and coriander and cook for a further 2 minutes.

2 Remove from the heat and add the potato and peas, mix well. Season with salt and pepper, then cool.

3 Meanwhile, make the pastry. Put the flour, salt and baking powder into a bowl, then add the oil and water. Mix to a soft but not sticky dough.

4 Knead the dough for 5 minutes, then divide into 16 equal pieces. Roll each into a circle about 15 cm/6 inches in diameter,

then cut each circle in half, using a sharp knife, to make 32 half-circles.

5 Take one of the half-circles of pastry and brush the cut edges with water, then fold it in half and press the moistened cut edges firmly together to form a cone.

6 Fill the cone with about 2 heaped teaspoons of the filling, then moisten the top edges and fold them over to enclose the filling. Fill the rest of the samosas.

7 Heat the oil in a deep-fryer to 180C/350F, then fry the samosas in batches until golden-brown and crispy. Drain on kitchen paper and keep the samosas warm in a low oven until all are ready.

Spanikopita

This Greek pie is equally good as a starter or main course. It's good served with a Yogurt and Mint Dressing (p.233),

**SERVES 6 AS A MAIN COURSE,
8 AS A FIRST COURSE**

10 sheets phyllo pastry
150–175 g/5–6 oz butter, melted
900 g/2 lb fresh spinach or 450 g/
  1 lb frozen spinach, cooked,
  drained and cooled
butter for greasing

1 bunch spring onions, trimmed
  and chopped
100 g/4 oz feta cheese, crumbled
salt and freshly ground black
  pepper

1 Preheat the oven to 200C/400F/Gas Mark 6.

2 Grease a deep pie dish, then place a sheet of phyllo pastry in it, allowing the edges to hang over the sides of the dish.

3 Brush with melted butter, then place another sheet of phyllo pastry on top. Continue in this way, using 5 sheets of phyllo pastry. (Keep the rest covered with a damp cloth, see p. 227)

4 Chop the spinach and mix with the spring onions, cheese and salt and pepper to taste. Spoon on top of the pastry.

5 Cover with the rest of the phyllo pastry sheets, brushing each one with melted butter as before, and finishing with melted

butter. Neaten the sides; prick and decorate the top with leaves cut from pastry trimmings.

6 Bake for 40–45 minutes. Serve hot or warm.

Variation

VEGAN SPANIKOPITA

Make in the same way, but replace the cheese with mashed tofu or 100 g/4 oz pine nuts or flaked almonds. Use vegan margarine or olive oil for brushing the pastry instead of butter.

Asparagus Strudel

SERVES 6

2 large onions, peeled and finely
  chopped
175 g/6 oz butter or vegan
  margarine
100 g/4 oz fine fresh breadcrumbs
8 sheets phyllo pastry (p.226)
700 g/1½ lb trimmed asparagus,
  washed, chopped and cooked
  until tender (p.91)
4 tablespoons finely chopped
  parsley

TO GARNISH
chervil sprigs
lemon slices
asparagus tips

TO SERVE
1 quantity vegan Yogurt and Herb
  Dressing (p.233)

1 Preheat the oven to 200c/400f/Gas Mark 6.

2 Fry the onions in 25 g/1 oz of the butter or vegan margarine for 10 minutes, until soft but not browned.

3 In another pan, heat 50 g/2 oz of the butter or vegan margarine and fry the crumbs until crisp. Melt the remaining butter or vegan margarine in a small saucepan.

4 Spread one phyllo pastry sheet out on a large board and brush with melted butter or vegan margarine. Put another pastry sheet on top, and brush with more butter or vegan margarine. Repeat until all the sheets have been used.

5 Spread the onion evenly on top of the pastry, keeping the edges clear.

6 Put the asparagus over the top of the onion and sprinkle with three-quarters of the crumbs and the parsley.

7 Fold over 5 cm/2 inches all round the pastry, then fold the long edges over, to make a roll.

8 Place the roll, seam-side down, on a baking sheet and bend it round into a horseshoe shape.

9 Brush with the remaining melted butter or vegan margarine and sprinkle with the remaining crumbs.

10 Bake for 40 minutes, until golden and crisp. Garnish with chervil sprigs, lemon slices and asparagus tips. Serve with the Yogurt and Herb dressing.

Puddings

*A pudding rounds off a meal perfectly, and even
if, like me, you eat them rarely, it is good to have
the occasional indulgence. This chapter opens
with cold desserts, including cheesecake and
sorbets, and progresses to hot puddings, amongst
which you will find pies, tarts, a hot soufflé, and
Christmas pudding. Finally, there are some
sweet sauces to serve with fresh and poached
fruit, ice cream, pancakes and other puddings.
Lots more pudding ideas feature on the fruit
pages in the Ingredients section (pp.49–189),
and you will also find a number of cakes, in the
next chapter, to finish a meal in style.*

Little Baked Custards

These smooth, velvety custards can be served
warm or chilled; I like them best chilled.

SERVES 6

3 eggs
3 egg yolks
50 g/2 oz caster sugar
450 ml/15 fl oz milk or single
   cream

1 vanilla pod or 1 teaspoon vanilla
   extract

TO DECORATE (OPTIONAL)
   whipped cream

1 Preheat the oven to 170c/325f/Gas Mark 3.
2 Put the eggs, egg yolks and sugar into a bowl and whisk until
well combined.
3 Heat the milk or cream with the vanilla pod or extract to just
below boiling point. Remove the vanilla pod if used (rinse, dry
and keep for future use).
4 Add the hot milk or cream to the eggs, whisking gently.

5 Strain the custard mixture into a jug, then pour into 6 ramekins.

6 Put the ramekins into a baking tin and pour boiling water around them to come about two-thirds of the way up the sides of the ramekins.

7 Bake the custards for 40–45 minutes, until set. Remove from the oven, leave to cool, then chill before serving. Decorate the custards with piped whipped cream if liked.

Variation

LITTLE COFFEE CUSTARDS

For this delicious variation add 2–3 teaspoons continental or espresso instant coffee, dissolved in a little boiling water, to the milk or cream.

COFFEE

A cup of coffee goes particularly well with the richness of puddings such as the Little Baked Custards and Chocolate Pots. There are many varieties to choose from; it is interesting to experiment with different ones, and to blend two or more. Some of the best are:

Blue Mountain
Very rare and expensive; the best, full-bodied, with a fine, sweet flavour

Brazilian
Smooth and mild

Colombian
Strong, rich flavour

Continental
Dark roasted with a strong flavour

Java
A good after-dinner coffee with a mellow flavour

Kenya
Mild. Has a slightly sharp flavour: another good after-dinner one

Mocha
Strong but with a subtle flavour
Mysore
Rich and flavoursome, one of my favourites
Vienna
Smooth and strong

The traditional way to make coffee is to put coarse grounds into a pot, pour on almost boiling water, cover, leave to infuse for 4 minutes, then strain into cups. Allow 50 g/2 oz coffee to 600 ml/1 pint water.

My favourite ways of making coffee are: the filter method, pouring almost boiling water on to finely ground coffee in a filter and letting it drip through into a jug; and in a cafetière, where you put medium-ground coffee into the cafetière, pour on the water, leave to infuse for 4 minutes, then push the plunger down into the coffee, pushing the coffee grounds to the bottom of the pot.

Chocolate Mould

This pudding is easy to make, healthy and, in
my experience, always popular with children. If
preferred, it can be made in one large bowl.

SERVES 4–5

2 tablespoons cocoa or carob
  powder
50 g/2 oz soft light brown or caster
  sugar
600 ml/1 pint milk or soya milk
2 teaspoons agar agar
1 teaspoon vanilla extract

TO DECORATE
2 tablespoons flaked almonds, or
  grated chocolate or carob bar

TO SERVE (OPTIONAL)
single or non-dairy cream

1 Put the cocoa or carob powder into a medium saucepan with
the sugar.
2 Gradually add the milk, stirring all the time. Heat to boiling
point.
3 Over a low heat, gradually sprinkle the agar agar over the
surface of the milk, whisking all the time. Boil the mixture for 1
minute.
4 Remove from the heat and add the vanilla.
5 Pour into 4 serving glasses. Cool, then chill.
6 Decorate with the flaked almonds or grated chocolate or carob.
Serve with the cream, if liked.

Vanilla Ice Cream

3 egg yolks
75 g/3 oz caster sugar
100 ml/4 fl oz water

450 ml/15 fl oz whipping cream
1 teaspoon vanilla extract

1 Whisk the egg yolks until thick and pale.
2 Put the sugar into a heavy-based saucepan with the water.
Heat gently until the sugar has dissolved, then bring to the boil
and boil for 5 minutes.
3 Add the hot sugar syrup to the egg yolks in a steady stream,

whisking all the time. (Keep the syrup away from the whisk or it may solidify on this.)

4 Whisk until the mixture is thick, pale and mousse-like. Allow the mixture to cool completely.

5 Whip the cream with the vanilla until thick, then fold into the egg yolk mixture. Pour into a polythene container.

6 Freeze until half solid, then beat again and return to the freezer until firm.

Chocolate Pots

This is a versatile recipe, because it can be
served chilled or the mixture can be baked, to
make Little Chocolate Soufflés (see variation).
Both versions are equally good.

SERVES 6

75 g/3 oz plain chocolate
150 ml/5 fl oz double cream
3 egg yolks
1 teaspoon continental or espresso
  instant coffee
4 egg whites

pinch of cream of tartar
25 g/1 oz caster sugar

TO DECORATE
whipped cream
chocolate coffee beans

1 Break the chocolate into pieces and put into a heavy-based saucepan with the cream. Heat over a gentle heat until melted.

2 Remove from the heat and beat in the egg yolks and coffee.

3 Whisk the egg whites with the cream of tartar until stiff, then whisk in the sugar.

4 Lightly but thoroughly fold the egg white mixture into the chocolate mixture until all the egg white is distributed.

5 Pour the mixture into 6 ramekins. Chill until set. Decorate each pot with a whirl of cream and a chocolate coffee bean.

Variation

LITTLE CHOCOLATE SOUFFLÉS

Fill ramekins to within 1 cm/½ inch of the tops and place on baking sheets. (This can be done several hours in advance and the mixture covered and refrigerated if convenient. Remove from the fridge at least 30 minutes before baking.) Bake at 220c/425f/Gas Mark 7 for 10 minutes, until risen. Sift icing sugar on top. Serve immediately, with whipped cream handed separately if liked.

CHOCOLATE FOR COOKING

As with most ingredients, you get what you pay for with cooking chocolate. The large bars of chocolate sold as 'cooking chocolate' are not a good buy because they have a synthetic flavour and fatty consistency. The chocolate which gives the best results is a good quality plain or dessert chocolate or *chocolat menier*.

CHOCOLATE CURLS, SHAPES AND LEAVES

Chocolate curls make an attractive garnish for chocolate puddings and cakes and are easy to make. Pour 100 g/4 oz melted chocolate in a thin layer on to a baking tray and leave until it is firm enough not to stick to your hand when you touch it lightly. Then, holding a knife in both hands so that the blade is straight, draw it across the chocolate, like a comb, to draw off the chocolate in long curls. Another way to make curls, is to 'shave' a block of chocolate with a potato peeler.

Chocolate shapes can be made by cutting a sheet of chocolate, made as described above, with tiny pastry cutters.

For chocolate leaves, dip one side of clean, dry, non-poisonous leaves, such as rose leaves or small fresh bay leaves, in chocolate. Leave until the chocolate has set, then gently peel away the leaf.

Quick Vanilla Ice Cream

A simple ice cream, but always popular, especially with children. Serve with Almond Tuiles (p.486).

SERVES 8

600 ml/1 pint whipping cream
1 teaspoon vanilla extract

1 × 400-g/14-oz can condensed skimmed milk

1 Whip the cream until thick, then add the condensed milk and vanilla and whip again until thoroughly blended.
2 Pour the mixture into a polythene container and freeze until firm.

MAKING SOYA MILK

The soya milk used in the vegan version of ice cream is widely available. However, it is also possible to make a delicious soya milk at home. This is a bit fiddly, but it works out cheaper than bought soya milk, and tastes delicious.

To make soya milk, soak 225 g/8 oz soya beans in plenty of water for 2 days, changing the water twice a day. Then liquidize the beans with 1·4 litres/2½ pints fresh water. Line a sieve with a piece of clean muslin, then scald it by pouring boiling water through. Put the sieve over a large saucepan and pour the soya mixture through the sieve, squeezing through as much liquid as possible. Add a vanilla pod, or 1–2 teaspoons vanilla extract. Heat the milk to boiling point, then remove the vanilla pod (wash, dry and re-use). Then put the milk into a blender or food processor with 1 tablespoon cold-pressed sunflower oil and a little sugar or honey to taste, and whizz. Strain through muslin again, and it's ready.

Chocolate Ice Cream

SERVES 6—8

900 ml/1½ pints milk
100 g/4 oz plain chocolate or carob bar, broken into pieces
40 g/1½ oz sugar
1 tablespoon custard powder

1 × 410-g/14½-oz can evaporated milk or 300 ml/10 fl oz single cream

TO DECORATE
grated chocolate

1 Put all but 4 tablespoons of the milk into a saucepan with the chocolate or carob pieces and sugar and bring gently to the boil.
2 Mix the custard powder to a paste with the rest of the milk in a bowl.
3 Add a little of the boiling milk mixture to the custard mixture, blend, then pour the custard mixture into the saucepan of hot milk.

4 Stir over a moderate heat for 2–3 minutes, until the mixture has thickened a little. Remove from the heat and cool slightly, then add the evaporated milk or single cream and whizz in a blender or food processor, to give a smooth consistency.

5 Pour into a polythene container and allow to cool completely. Freeze until half solid, then beat again and return to the freezer until firm. This ice cream freezes hard; remove from the freezer to room temperature 30–40 minutes before eating. Decorate with grated chocolate.

VEGAN ICE CREAM

To make a vegan version of Chocolate Ice Cream, use soya milk (opposite) instead of dairy milk and replace the evaporated milk or single cream with concentrated soya milk or a non-dairy cream such as parev.

Raspberry Ice Cream

$\boxed{V}$

Fruit ice creams are among the simplest to make, because all you do is fold a sweetened fruit purée into whipped cream, then freeze. Many different types of fruit are suitable; soft fruits only need puréeing (and sieving if necessary to remove pips), other types should be stewed gently with the sugar first.

SERVES 8–10

450 g/1 lb fresh raspberries, washed, or frozen raspberries, thawed
225 g/8 oz caster sugar

600 ml/1 pint whipping or non-dairy cream
TO SERVE (OPTIONAL)
raspberry leaves
1 quantity Raspberry Coulis (p.448)

1 Reserve 16 raspberries for decoration. Purée the remainder in a blender or food processor, then sieve to remove the pips. Stir in the sugar.

2 Whip the cream until thick, then gently fold in the raspberry purée.

3 Pour the mixture into a polythene container. Freeze until half solid, then beat well and return to the freezer until firm.

4 Transfer the ice cream from the freezer to the fridge 30–40 minutes before you want to serve it. Serve in individual bowls decorated with the reserved raspberries and raspberry leaves, if available. Hand the Raspberry Coulis separately in a jug, if liked.

Variations

APPLE ICE CREAM WITH BLACKBERRY SAUCE

Use 450 g/1 lb cooking or dessert apples, peeled, cored and stewed with the sugar and 2 tablespoons water. Drain if necessary, then purée and cool before folding into the cream. Taste and add more sugar if liked. I like to colour this ice cream pale green with a little vegetable colouring. Serve with a Blackberry Coulis (p.448) or Sorbet (p.420) for a pleasant blend of autumn flavours.

MANGO ICE CREAM

Remove the stones and peel from 2 large mangoes. Purée the flesh in a blender or food processor, then fold into the cream.

Apricot and Orange Fool

SERVES 4

225 g/8 oz dried apricots, covered
    with boiling water, soaked
    overnight, then simmered in the
    soaking liquid for 20–30 minutes
    until tender.

240 g/8½ oz strained Greek yogurt
clear honey or sugar to taste
2 egg whites
grated rind of 1 orange

1 Purée the apricots in a blender or food processor, or mash them very well.

2 Mix the apricot purée with the yogurt to make a thick, creamy mixture. Add honey or sugar to taste.

3 Whisk the egg whites until they form stiff peaks. Fold a tablespoon of egg white into the apricot mixture, to loosen, then gently fold in the rest, together with half the orange rind.
4 Spoon the apricot mixture into individual glasses and chill. Sprinkle with the remaining rind before serving.

MAKING FRUIT FOOLS

Any soft, puréed fresh fruit, or firmer fruit, stewed, then mashed, or puréed, is suitable for making into a fool. Yogurt can be used, or chilled egg custard, or cream, or a mixture of these.

For a richer, special-occasion version of Apricot Fool fold in 150 ml/5 fl oz whipping cream, whipped, and 2–3 tablespoons apricot brandy or Cointreau before folding in the egg whites.

Try using 450 g/1 lb drained, stewed gooseberries. Purée, then sieve if you like, although puréed but unsieved gooseberries produce a fool with a pleasant texture.

Or use 450 g/1 lb drained, stewed rhubarb. Mash or purée. This is pleasant with a delicate flavouring of ginger (up to ½ teaspoon added to the rhubarb when stewing it).

Passion Fruit Sorbet   V

SERVES 6

175 g/6 oz caster sugar
300 ml/10 fl oz water
16–18 passion fruits

1 tablespoon lemon juice
2 egg whites (optional)

1 Dissolve the sugar in the water over a low heat, then bring to the boil and boil for 3–4 minutes to make a sugar syrup. Remove from the heat and cool.
2 Scoop all the pulp and seeds out of the passion fruits and add to the cooled sugar syrup, through a nylon sieve if you like.
3 Add the lemon juice. Pour the mixture into a polythene container and freeze, uncovered, until half solid.
4 Mash the mixture well to break up the icy particles and return to the freezer until solid. Or whisk the egg whites, if used, until they form stiff peaks, then gradually add the mashed frozen

mixture, whisking all the time. Return to the freezer until solid.

5 Remove the sorbet from the freezer to room temperature 10 minutes before you want to serve it.

6 Mash the sorbet well with a fork to break it up, then spoon it into serving glasses, or mould it as described on p.423 and serve on a flat plate.

Variations

BLACKCURRANT SORBET

Cook 750 g/1½ lb blackcurrants without water in a covered saucepan until soft – about 10 minutes. Purée in a blender or food processor, then sieve. Use in place of the passion fruit pulp. 1-2 tablespoons cassis is excellent in this: add before the first freezing. Decorate the sorbet with a few blackcurrants and blackcurrant leaves, if available.

BLACKBERRY SORBET

Make as described for Blackcurrant Sorbet, using blackberries instead of blackcurrants and adding 1–2 tablespoons orange liqueur, or port, instead of the cassis.

PEAR SORBET

Stew 750 g/1½ lb ripe dessert pears, peeled, in enough water just to cover. Remove the pears from the water; boil the water rapidly to reduce to 300 ml/10 fl oz, then add the sugar and proceed with the recipe, using the pear purée instead of the passion fruit pulp. 1–2 tablespoons Poire Williams liqueur stirred into the mixture makes a wonderful addition for a special occasion.

VEGAN SORBET

Egg whites give a sorbet a particularly light texture, but thorough beating can also achieve this, so they are not essential. Sorbets therefore make a delightful vegan dessert.

Orange Parfait with Grand Marnier and Strawberries

A parfait is an extra rich ice cream which is useful because it can be kept in the freezer until the beginning of the meal, then turned out and served with a flourish.

SERVES 8-10

6 egg yolks
175 g/6 oz caster sugar
finely grated rind of 1 large, well-scrubbed orange
600 ml/1 pint whipping cream
1 tablespoon lemon juice
3 tablespoons Grand Marnier

TO DECORATE
100 g/4 oz small sweet strawberries, plus leaves
thinly pared rind of 1 orange, cut into strips
orange segments

1 Whisk the egg yolks with the sugar and grated orange rind until thick and pale, then stand the bowl over a saucepan of steaming water off the heat (don't let the bowl touch the water) and continue to whisk until the mixture is tepid.

2 Remove the bowl from the heat and whisk until the mixture is cold.

3 Whisk the cream until it stands in soft peaks. Fold into the egg yolk mixture with the lemon juice and Grand Marnier.

4 Pour the mixture into a 1·1-litre/2-pint mould, pudding basin or cake tin. Freeze until solid.

5 Transfer the parfait from the freezer to the fridge 30–40 minutes before you want to serve it.

6 Loosen the sides of the parfait by slipping a knife round the edge.

7 Invert the mould over a serving plate; if it does not come out with a slight shake, hold the mould under the hot tap for a second or two; dry the edges of the plate with kitchen paper. The parfait should slide out easily.

8 Arrange the strawberries, strips of orange rind and orange segments on top of the parfait and serve at once.

Variations

CHOCOLATE AND ORANGE PARFAIT

Stir 100 g/4 oz coarsely grated plain chocolate into the parfait before freezing. Decorate with chocolate curls, pared orange rind – and strawberries, too, if liked.

CHRISTMAS PARFAIT

For this delectable alternative to Christmas pudding, omit the Grand Marnier and grated orange rind. Sprinkle 175 g/6 oz mixed crystallized fruits (including a little ginger, if you like) with 4–5 tablespoons brandy (or fruit juice or the syrup from the ginger, if children are sharing this). Make the parfait as described, folding the crystallized fruits (and any syrup) into the egg yolks before adding the cream; 50 g/2 oz toasted flaked almonds or hazelnuts can be added, too. Freeze in a pudding basin.

V | Champagne Sorbet with Wild Strawberries

Bringing the champagne to the boil removes
the alcohol which could otherwise prevent the
sorbet from freezing properly, but does not
spoil the flavour. This, however, is unnecessary
if you're making the sorbet in a sorbetière. Pink
champagne makes the sorbet especially pretty.

SERVES 6

600 ml/1 pint champagne
350 g/12 oz granulated sugar
450 ml/15 fl oz water
4 tablespoons lemon juice

4 tablespoons orange juice
100 g/4 oz wild strawberries or
  strawberry slices

1 Put three-quarters of the champagne into a saucepan and bring to the boil. Remove from the heat and cool.
2 Heat the sugar and water gently until all the sugar has dissolved, then boil the mixture hard for about 20 minutes, until it becomes syrupy and forms a short thread when you pull a little between your finger and thumb. Remove from the heat immediately.

3 Add the champagne and fruit juices to the sugar syrup and leave to cool.

4 Pour the mixture into a polythene container and freeze until icy. This will take several hours: I leave it overnight.

5 Turn the frozen mixture into a chilled bowl, or the bowl of an electric mixer, and whisk until smooth and creamy.

6 Return the mixture to the freezer until firm. When you are ready to serve the sorbet, scoop on to chilled plates or glasses and quickly decorate with the wild strawberries or strawberry slices. Serve immediately.

SHAPING SORBET FOR SERVING

Fill a dessert spoon with sorbet, heaping it up. Cup another dessert spoon on top of the sorbet and press down, to mould the sorbet, scraping off any excess. Repeat this once or twice, moving the sorbet between the two spoons, until you have a smooth oval shape, then place on a plate.

NOTES ON LIQUEURS

A dash of liqueur adds a delicious flavour to many sweet dishes. Some of the most popular and useful liqueurs are:

Amaretto Disaronno
Almond flavour
Anisette
Aniseed liqueur
Bailey's Irish Cream
Chocolate, double cream and whiskey liqueur
Calvados
An apple brandy
Chartreuse
Herb-flavoured liqueur
Cointreau
Orange curaçao

Eaux-de-Vie
Delicious fruit brandies, including Kirsch (cherry), framboise (raspberry), Poire Williams (pear) and fraise (strawberry)
Maraschino
Cherry liqueur
Tia Maria
Jamaican liqueur made from coffee, rum and spices

Traditional Trifle

Traditional English trifle, properly made, is a
delicious treat, and the preparation can be done
in stages, fitted in when convenient.

SERVES 6

½ quantity Whisked Sponge Cake
(p.453), unfilled, or 8 trifle
sponges
100–175 g/4–6 oz raspberry jam
100 g/4 oz macaroons, lightly
crushed

100 ml/4 fl oz medium sherry or
sweet white wine
double quantity Pouring Egg
Custard (p.450), cooled
150 ml/5 fl oz whipping cream
50 g/2 oz flaked almonds, toasted

1 Spread the cake or trifle sponges with the jam, cut into pieces
and place in a 2-litre/3½-pint glass serving bowl with the
macaroons.
2 Sprinkle the sherry or wine over the top and leave to soak for
about 2 hours.
3 Pour the custard on top of the cake mixture. Whip the cream,
then spread over the custard, and top with the flaked almonds.
Chill until needed.

Pineapple Jelly

A useful pudding for children. Skimmed Milk
Topping (p.451) or Nut Cream (p.51) go
particularly well with it. Other combinations of
fruits and juices can also be used; try orange
juice with orange segments or strawberries; or
halved and de-seeded grapes with non-
sparkling grape juice.

SERVES 6

1 × 425-g/15-oz can pineapple
pieces in pineapple juice
just under 600 ml/1 pint
unsweetened pineapple juice
1½ teaspoons agar agar (p.427)

a little caster sugar or clear honey
(optional)

TO DECORATE
mint sprigs

1 Drain the pineapple, reserving the juice.

2 Divide the pineapple between 6 individual serving dishes or glasses.

3 Measure the reserved juice and make up to 600 ml/1 pint with the extra pineapple juice.

4 Put the 600 ml/1 pint pineapple juice into a medium saucepan and bring to the boil. Sprinkle on the agar agar, a little at a time, whisking constantly.

5 When all the agar agar has been added, boil for 1 minute. Then remove from the heat. Taste and sweeten with sugar or honey if necessary. Cool slightly if using glass dishes.

6 Pour the mixture over the pineapple pieces. Cool, then chill until set. Decorate with mint sprigs.

Variation

RASPBERRY JELLY

Use 225 g/8 oz fresh or thawed frozen raspberries instead of the pineapple, and a red fruit juice, such as redcurrant, instead of the pineapple juice; sweeten to taste.

Summer Fruit Meringue

This version of the classic Pavlova makes a stunning centrepiece to any table, and when served with a selection of other puddings at a party, is always the first one to go.

SERVES 8

4 egg whites
a pinch of cream of tartar
225 g/8 oz caster or demerara sugar
2 teaspoons vinegar
4 teaspoons cornflour
½ teaspoon vanilla extract
FOR THE FILLING
300 ml/10 fl oz whipping cream, whipped

2 kiwi fruits, peeled and sliced into thin rounds plus leaves, or greengages, stoned and sliced
2 nectarines or peaches, skinned, halved and thinly sliced
100 g/4 oz strawberries, hulled and halved, or raspberries or blackberries

1 Preheat the oven to 140c/275f/Gas Mark 1. Line a baking sheet with non-stick baking parchment.

2 In a clean, grease-free bowl, whisk the egg whites and cream of tartar until the egg whites are so stiff that you can turn the bowl upside down without the egg whites falling out.

3 Add a quarter of the sugar to the whisked egg whites and whisk well. Then add another quarter. Continue in this way until all the sugar has been added.

4 Mix in the vinegar, cornflour and vanilla. Pipe or spoon the mixture into a large circle on the prepared baking sheet.

5 Bake the meringue in the coolest part of the oven for 1¼ hours, until crisp. Remove from oven and cool on a wire tray.

6 Just before you are ready to serve, place the meringue on a flat plate and spread most of the cream on top. Arrange circles of kiwi fruit and nectarines or peaches in the centre of the meringue. Pipe the remaining cream in rosettes around the edge and arrange the strawberry slices on top. Place a strawberry slice and leaves in the centre.

Fresh Fruit Salad

An attractive mixture of colours.

SERVES 4

2 large oranges, peeled and segmented

175 g/6 oz black grapes, halved and de-seeded

2 kiwi fruits, peeled and sliced into rounds

2 apples, cored and sliced, unpeeled if skin is good

150 ml/5 fl oz orange or apple juice

TO DECORATE
mint sprig

1 Put all the fruit into a large bowl. Add the orange or apple juice. Mix well.

2 Transfer to a large serving bowl or divide between 4 individual dishes. Chill before serving.

Variations

GREEN FRUIT SALAD

Replace the oranges with a small melon with green flesh: dice the flesh or use a melon baller to scoop it out of the skin. Use green grapes instead of black.

ORANGE AND KIWI FRUIT SALAD

Use 4 large oranges and 4 kiwi fruits and omit the apples and grapes. Either segment the oranges, or cut them into thin rings, arranging them alternately with the kiwi fruit in circles on a flat plate, on top of the orange juice.

TANGERINE AND LYCHEE FRUIT SALAD

A refreshing mixture to serve after a Chinese or Japanese style meal. Omit the apples, kiwi fruit and grapes. Use 6–8 tangerines, instead of the oranges, skinned and sliced into thin rounds, and the white flesh of 10–12 lychees. One star fruit, sliced, makes an attractive decoration to this salad.

MAKING FRUIT SALADS AND COMPOTES

For best effect aim either for a real multi-colour look, combining five or six colours, or keep it simple and bold, with just one or two colours. For the liquid, you can use a fruit juice such as orange or apricot, or a sugar syrup (p.124) made from water or wine. Soft fruits will produce their own juice if sprinkled with a little sugar, and treated this way make a delicious red fruit compote.

An Arranged Fruit Salad, of prepared pieces of fruit arranged attractively on a coulis of raspberries or blackberries, can look jewel-bright and stunning.

AGAR AGAR

Agar agar is a vegetarian gelatine made from a number of seaweeds and can be obtained in the form of powder, flakes, strips and strands, which are dissolved in boiling water (2 teaspoons powder, 1 tablespoon flakes, to 600 ml/1 pint liquid) to give a firm jelly.

Pashka

This traditional Russian Easter dish makes a
luscious dessert. Unless you have a special
wooden Russian Pashka mould, you'll need a
15-cm/6-inch clay flower-pot, scrubbed and
baked in a hot oven for 30 minutes or so, or a
1-kg/2 lb 2 oz-yogurt pot with some holes
pierced in the bottom.

SERVES 6

2 egg yolks
75 g/3 oz vanilla sugar, or caster
　sugar and a few drops of vanilla
　extract
4 tablespoons single cream or
　creamy milk
100 g/4 oz unsalted butter,
　softened

700 g/1½ lb curd cheese
50 g/2 oz whole candied peel,
　chopped
50 g/2 oz chopped blanched
　almonds

TO DECORATE
crystallized fruits

1 Beat the egg yolks in a bowl with the sugar until pale and
foamy. Heat the cream or milk in a saucepan to just below
boiling point, then add to the egg yolks. Stir well.
2 Return the mixture to the saucepan and stir until thickened.
This only takes a moment, so watch it carefully: the mixture
must not boil, or it will curdle. Remove from the heat and set
aside to cool.
3 Beat the butter until light and creamy, then gradually beat in
the egg yolk mixture.
4 Continuing to beat, add the curd cheese, a little at a time, then
add the chopped peel and almonds.
5 Line the flower-pot or yogurt carton with a double layer of
kitchen paper, to extend over the top.
6 Spoon the pashka mixture into the lined mould and smooth
the surface, then fold the ends of the kitchen paper over the top.
7 Put a small plate on top and weight down. Stand the pashka
on a plate to catch any moisture which seeps out of the base.
Refrigerate for 6–8 hours or overnight.
8 To serve, invert the container on to a serving dish, turn out the
pashka and remove the kitchen paper. Decorate with crystallized fruits.

FLOWER WATERS

A little orange or rose water makes a delectable flavouring for Pashka; add 1–2 tablespoons to the mixture.

When choosing flower waters, look for the 'triple distilled' type; you can buy these from specialist food shops, shops specializing in Middle Eastern foods, and some chemists.

Rose water is delicious in many creamy puddings, fillings, toppings and icings, and can be used to flavour a delectable jam (p.507). Orange flower water can be used similarly, but is particularly good, I think, as a flavouring for a fresh orange salad, together with a little orange blossom honey.

Quick Cherry and Lime Cheesecake

SERVES 6

175 g/6 oz semi-sweet wholewheat biscuits, crushed
75 g/3 oz butter, melted
225 g/8 oz curd cheese
150 ml/5 fl oz double cream
50 g/2 oz caster sugar
grated rind and juice of 2 limes or 1 lemon

284 g/9½ oz drained canned cherries, pitted
TO GLAZE
2–3 tablespoons strawberry jam or redcurrant jelly, melted
TO DECORATE
lime twists

1 Mix the biscuit crumbs with the butter. Press the mixture firmly into the base of a 20-cm/8-inch spring-form cake tin or other suitable shallow dish, using the base of a clean jam jar.
2 Put the curd cheese, cream, sugar and lime, or lemon, rind and juice into a bowl and whisk together until smooth and thick. Spoon the mixture on top of the biscuit mixture and level the surface.
3 Arrange the cherries on top. Pour the jam or jelly over the cherries. Chill well. Decorate with lime twists to serve.

Hot Black Cherry Soufflé

A hot soufflé makes an impressive and
delicious ending to a meal, yet is very easy to
make. The uncooked soufflé will keep perfectly
in the freezer, so you can do all the preparation
a day (or more) in advance, but use a container
which can withstand the extremes of
temperature.

SERVES 4

350 g/12 oz *drained canned black*
  cherries, pitted
3 tablespoons *Kirsch*
5 *egg whites*
50 g/2 oz *caster sugar*
a little oil

TO DECORATE (OPTIONAL)
icing sugar

TO SERVE
whipped cream

1 Prepare an 18-cm/7-inch soufflé dish by tying a double layer
of greaseproof paper round it, to extend its height by about
one-third. Brush the dish and paper with oil, then dust with
caster sugar. Secure the top of the paper with a paper clip.
2 Preheat the oven to 190c/375F/Gas Mark 5.
3 Purée the cherries in a blender or food processor and add the
Kirsch.
4 Whisk the egg whites until they form stiff peaks, then whisk
in the sugar until stiff and glossy.
5 Fold the cherry purée into the egg whites.
6 Pour the mixture into the soufflé dish, level the top, then draw
a teaspoon handle round about 1 cm/½ inch from the edge, to
make a deep groove, so that it cooks with a 'top hat' effect.
7 Bake for 30–35 minutes, until the soufflé is firm and doesn't
wobble when shaken.
8 Remove the greaseproof paper, sift a little icing sugar over the
soufflé, if liked, and serve with whipped cream.

Variations

RASPBERRY SOUFFLÉ

Make as described, using 350 g/12 oz puréed and sieved fresh or
thawed frozen raspberries. Flavour with a little Kirsch or framboise.

APRICOT SOUFFLÉ

Use 350 g/12 oz stewed and puréed apricots and 50 g/2 oz sugar. Use Cointreau or Grand Marnier instead of Kirsch.

BLACKCURRANT SOUFFLÉ

For this excellent variation, use 350 g/12 oz stewed, puréed and sieved blackcurrants and 100 g/4 oz sugar. Use kir instead of Kirsch.

Rose Cheesecake

This is an exquisite cheesecake. Rose Petal Jam (p.507) can be made from fragrant roses in the summer, or bought at a shop specializing in Middle Eastern produce.

SERVES 8–12

175 g/6 oz semi-sweet wholewheat
   biscuits, crushed
50 g/2 oz butter, melted
325 g/11 oz rose petal jam
225 g/8 oz curd cheese
150 ml/5 fl oz soured cream
75 g/3 oz vanilla sugar or caster
   sugar with a few drops of
   vanilla extract

1 tablespoon cornflour
1 tablespoon lemon juice
2 large eggs, separated
a pinch of cream of tartar
a little extra butter for greasing

TO DECORATE
crystallized rose petals
pistachio kernels

1 Preheat the oven to 170c/325f/Gas Mark 3. Grease a 20-cm/8-inch spring-form cake tin.
2 First make the crumb crust. Mix together the biscuit crumbs and melted butter. Spoon this mixture into the bottom of the tin. Press down firmly, using the base of a clean jam jar.
3 Spread the rose petal jam evenly on top of the crumbs. Chill.
4 Next make the filling. Put the curd cheese into a bowl with the soured cream, sugar, cornflour, lemon juice and egg yolks. Beat until smooth.
5 Whisk the egg whites in a clean bowl with the cream of tartar until stiff but not dry. Fold into the curd cheese mixture.

6 Pour the mixture into the tin on top of the crumb crust. Bake the cheesecake for 1–1½ hours, until firm in the centre.

7 Turn off the oven and leave the cheesecake to cool in the still-warm oven for 15–20 minutes. When cool, chill.

8 To serve, decorate with the crystallized rose petals and pistachios.

COOLING AND FREEZING BAKED CHEESECAKES

A cheesecake cracks if it is cooled too quickly; that is the reason for allowing it to cool gently in the turned-off oven.

To freeze, cool the cheesecake thoroughly as described, then remove from the tin. Place on a plate and freeze until solid, then remove from the plate, pack carefully, label and store in the freezer. (Baked cheesecakes freeze excellently.) To use, remove wrappings, place on a wire rack for about 3 hours to thaw, then transfer to a serving plate.

Lemon Surprise Pudding

Another old favourite, this mixture separates as it cooks, ending up as a light sponge on top of a lemon flavoured sauce.

SERVES 4

25 g/1 oz butter
100 g/4 oz caster sugar
grated rind and juice of 1 lemon
2 eggs, separated

150 ml/5 fl oz milk
25 g/1 oz plain flour
a little extra butter for greasing

1 Preheat the oven to 190c/375f/Gas Mark 5. Lightly grease a 600-ml/1-pint ovenproof dish. Have ready a roasting tin which is large enough to hold the ovenproof dish.

2 Cream the butter with 25 g/1 oz of the sugar, then beat in the lemon rind and juice, egg yolks, milk, flour and the remaining sugar.

3 Whisk the egg whites until stiff, then fold into the lemon mixture.

4 Pour the mixture into the prepared dish. Stand the dish in the roasting tin and pour 2·5 cm/1 inch boiling water into the tin.

5 Bake for about 40 minutes, until risen and golden-brown. Serve the pudding immediately.

Lemon Meringue Pie

A traditional family favourite.

SERVES 4

⅔ quantity Basic Shortcrust
   Pastry (p.384)
FOR THE FILLING
4 tablespoons cornflour
300 ml/10 fl oz water

175 g/6 oz sugar
grated rind and juice of 2 small
   lemons
25 g/1 oz butter
2 eggs, separated

1 Preheat the oven to 200c/400F/Gas Mark 6. Roll out the pastry and line a 20-cm/8-inch flan dish; prick the base and bake for 20 minutes (p.396).

2 Meanwhile, put the cornflour into a bowl and blend to a paste with a little of the water.

3 Bring the rest of the water to the boil with 50 g/2 oz of the sugar. Stir into the cornflour paste, then return the mixture to the pan, add the lemon juice and rind, and stir over the heat until the mixture has thickened.

4 Remove from the heat and stir in the butter and egg yolks. Pour into the flan case and allow to cool.

5 Turn down the oven to 170c/325F/Gas Mark 3. Whisk the egg whites until stiff and dry, then whisk in the remaining sugar.

6 Spread the meringue over the top of the lemon mixture, being sure to take it right to the edges, to prevent the meringue from going soggy.

7 Bake for 40–45 minutes, until lightly browned and crisp on the outside. Serve warm or cold.

THICKENING AGENTS

The lemon layer of the lemon meringue pie is thickened with cornflour, which is starch extracted from maize. This is just one of the thickening agents available; others are:

Arrowroot
A fine white powder originally made from the *aru* root of the Aruac Indians. Less refined than cornflour so preferred by wholefood cooks for small thickening jobs, but arrowroot loses its thickening powers if cooked for more than 1–2 minutes. Excellent for thickening fruit juice for a clear glaze for fruit flans. The proportions are 1 rounded teaspoon to 150 ml/5 fl oz liquid.

Potato flour
The gluten-free starch from potato; can be used in the same way as arrowroot and cornflour, but as it has a slight potato flavour it is best in savoury dishes.

Kuzu
Made from the roots of a mountain plant in Japan, and gluten-free, kuzu is used in similar ways to the above and in Japan is used to prevent colds and as a general digestive tonic.

Pumpkin Pie

SERVES 6

1 egg
75 g/3 oz soft light brown sugar
225 g/8 oz cooked and puréed pumpkin
1 teaspoon ground cinnamon
½ teaspoon each ground ginger, cloves and allspice
a pinch of ground cardamom (optional)

a pinch of salt
3 tablespoons double cream
⅔ quantity Basic Shortcrust Pastry (p.384)

TO DECORATE
50 g/2 oz pecan or walnut halves

1 Preheat the oven to 230c/450f/Gas Mark 8.
2 Whisk the egg with the sugar until pale and light, then stir in the pumpkin purée, cinnamon, ginger, cloves, allspice, cardamom, salt and cream.

3 Roll out the pastry and use to line a 20-cm/8-inch flan tin. Trim the edges. Pour in the filling.

4 Bake for 7 minutes, then turn down the oven to 170c/325f/ Gas Mark 3 and bake for a further 35–40 minutes, until a skewer inserted in the centre comes out clean.

5 Remove the flan from the oven and arrange pecan or walnut halves decoratively around the edge, pressing them lightly into the warm filling. Put 2 more pecans or walnuts in the centre. Allow the pie to cool completely before cutting into slices.

Glazed Red Fruit Tart [V]

A luscious, shiny red tart is one of the best
things to make from summer strawberries or
other red fruit, such as redcurrants, glazed with
a toning jam or jelly. I like to use a 30-cm/
12-inch diameter round flan tin; for a 20-cm/8-
inch tin, halve all the ingredients. This flan is
delicious served with some crème fraîche,
soured cream or plain (or vegan) yogurt.

SERVES 8

*1 quantity Basic Shortcrust Pastry
    (p.384) or Pâté Sucrée (p.437)
700–900 g/1½–2 lb strawberries or
    a mixture of strawberries,
    redcurrants and raspberries*

*450 g/1 lb redcurrant jelly
butter for greasing*
TO DECORATE
strawberry leaves

1 Preheat the oven to 190c/375f/Gas Mark 5. Lightly grease a 30-cm/12-inch flan tin.

2 Roll out the pastry to fit the flan tin. Place in the tin and trim the edges. Prick the base and bake blind for 20 minutes (p.396), until pale brown. Cool.

3 Prepare the fruit. Slice any large strawberries. Arrange in the pastry case.

4 Melt the jelly gently in a small saucepan and pour over the fruit. Allow to cool and set. Decorate with strawberry leaves before serving.

Variation

JEWELLED FRUIT FLAN

For this very pretty variation, a variety of ripe fruits replace the red fruits. Choose contrasting colours, such as 175 g/6 oz each of strawberries or raspberries, sliced peaches or oranges, kiwi fruit, black grapes, banana or pear. Arrange slices overlapping each other in circles; use sieved apricot jam to glaze instead of redcurrant jelly.

Linzertorte

I'm particularly fond of the combination of
flavours in this Austrian tart. It is especially
good after a vegetable main course.

SERVES 6

175 g/6 oz plain wholewheat flour
1 teaspoon ground cinnamon
a pinch of ground cloves
175 g/6 oz ground almonds
grated rind of 1 lemon
40 g/1½ oz soft light brown sugar
175 g/6 oz butter, softened

1 egg yolk (optional)
225 g/8 oz raspberry, black cherry
  or blackcurrant preserve
butter for greasing

TO FINISH
icing sugar

1 In a mixing bowl, combine the flour, cinnamon, cloves, ground almonds, lemon rind, sugar, butter and egg yolk, if used, to make a dough.
2 Knead lightly, then wrap in clingfilm and chill for 30 minutes.
3 Preheat the oven to 200c/400f/Gas Mark 6. Lightly grease a 20–23-cm/8–9-inch flan dish or loose-based flan tin.
4 Roll out three-quarters of the dough, fairly thickly, to fit the flan dish or tin. Ease into the dish or tin and trim the edges.
5 Spoon the jam evenly over the pastry.
6 Roll out the remaining pastry, again fairly thickly, and cut into long strips. Arrange these in a lattice pattern on top of the jam.
7 Bake for 25–30 minutes, until the tart is slightly risen and golden-brown. Dredge with sifted icing sugar. Serve hot, warm or cold.

Pâté Sucrée

MAKES 250 G/9 OZ

250 g/9 oz plain 85% wholewheat
   flour
150 g/5 oz caster sugar

150 g/5 oz butter, softened
4 egg yolks

1 Sift the flour on to a clean work surface.
2 Make a well in the centre and into this put the caster sugar, butter and egg yolks.
3 Work these ingredients together with one hand while you push the flour to the centre with the other hand, to make a dough.
4 Knead firmly until smooth, then wrap in clingfilm and chill for at least 1 hour before use.
5 Roll out as required, and bake at 190c/375f/Gas Mark 5.

Pithiviers

This delicious almond tart, which originated in the town of Pithivier, in northern France, is easy to make and delicious served with crème fraîche, whipped cream or thick Greek yogurt.

SERVES 6

25 g/1 oz butter
50 g/2 oz caster sugar
2 egg yolks
100 g/4 oz ground almonds
2 tablespoons rum

1 quantity Puff Pastry (p.399) or
   450 g/1 lb bought puff pastry
beaten egg
icing sugar

1 Preheat the oven to 230c/450f/Gas Mark 8.
2 Cream together the butter and sugar, then add the egg yolks and beat until creamy. Fold in the ground almonds and rum.
3 Divide the puff pastry into two pieces, one slightly larger than the other. Cut the smaller one into a 20-cm/8-inch circle. Place on a baking sheet.

4 Spread the almond filling on top of the pastry circle to within 1 cm/½ inch of the edges.

5 Roll out the second piece of pastry to go on top. Ease into place, trim and decorate the edges. Make a hole in the middle.

6 Brush with beaten egg and place in an oven which has been heated to 250c/500f/Gas Mark 9. Then lower immediately to 200c/400f/Gas Mark 6 and bake for 25 minutes until risen and golden.

7 Sprinkle with a little icing sugar and put back into the oven for a few minutes until the icing sugar has melted and formed a shiny glaze.

NOTE ON PITHIVIERS

This is a particularly useful pudding to serve when you're entertaining, because it can be completely prepared, except for cooking, the night before. You can then put it into the oven either when you start your main course, or, if you're serving cheese first, when you start the cheese course, and it will be ready, all puffed-up, flaky and golden, 25 minutes later. Serve it with single cream.

V

Old-fashioned Treacle Tart

Top favourite pudding with many of the men I know, treacle tart is easy to make if you follow the tip I learnt from Prue Leith and pour the syrup straight into the pastry case on top of the crumbs, without attempting to mix.

SERVES 4

⅔ quantity Basic Shortcrust Pastry (p.384)
100 g/4 oz fine wholewheat breadcrumbs

1 teaspoon lemon juice
350 g/12 oz golden syrup

1 Preheat the oven to 190c/375f/Gas Mark 5.
2 Roll out the pastry and use to line a 20-cm/8-inch flan dish.
Trim the edges.
3 Put the crumbs evenly into the pastry case without pressing
them down. Sprinkle with the lemon juice.
4 Pour the golden syrup on top of the crumbs (you can do this
straight from the jar or tin) so that they are all evenly covered.
Don't try to mix; the crumbs will soak up the syrup as the tart
cooks.
5 Roll out the pastry trimmings and cut into strips. Arrange the
pastry strips in a lattice pattern on top of the tart.
6 Bake for 25 minutes, until the pastry is crisp and lightly
browned. Serve warm.

Country Apple Pie

SERVES 4

⅔ quantity Basic Shortcrust
  Pastry (p.384)
700 g/1½ lb cooking apples,
  peeled, cored and sliced
75 g/3 oz soft light brown sugar

3–4 cloves (optional)

TO GLAZE
milk or soya milk
caster sugar

1 Preheat the oven to 220cC/425f/Gas Mark 7.
2 Roll out the pastry so that it is about 2·5 cm/1 inch bigger all
round than a 900-ml/1½-pint pie dish. Cut a 2·5-cm/1-inch wide
strip from the pastry.
3 Brush the rim of the pie dish with water and press the pastry
strip on to it. Put the apples into the pie dish, sprinkle with the
sugar and add the cloves if used.
4 Brush the pastry strip with water, then put the large piece of
pastry on top, pressing it down round the edges. Trim, knock up
and flute or fork the edges. Make a steam-hole in centre of
pastry.
5 Cut decorations from the pastry trimmings, if you like, and
stick these on to the pie with water.
6 Brush the pastry with milk or soya milk and sprinkle with a

little caster sugar. Bake for 10 minutes, then turn down the oven to 180c/350F/Gas Mark 4 and bake for a further 35–40 minutes.
7 Sprinkle with more caster sugar and serve hot or cold.

Variations

PLUM PIE

Make as described, using plums instead of apples, and omitting the cloves. Halve and stone large plums (small types, such as damsons, can be left whole). Unless the plums are very sweet, increase the amount of sugar to 100–150 g/4–5 oz.

GOOSEBERRY PIE

Make as described, using gooseberries instead of the apples and omitting the cloves. Increase the amount of sugar to 150–175 g/ 5–6 oz, depending on how sharp the gooseberries are.

V | *Double-crust Blackcurrant Pie*

SERVES 4

650–700 g/1¼–1½ lb fresh or thawed frozen blackcurrants, topped and tailed
150 g/5 oz soft light brown or caster sugar
1 quantity Basic Shortcrust Pastry (p.384)

butter or vegan margarine for greasing

TO GLAZE
milk or soya milk
caster sugar

1 Preheat the oven to 200c/400F/Gas Mark 6. Grease a 24-cm/ 9½-inch pie plate.
2 Put the blackcurrants into a heavy-based saucepan and cook gently for 4–5 minutes, until the juices run. Drain the fruit, to remove excess juice (which can be used for another pudding, such as a jelly).
3 Stir the sugar into the blackcurrants. Set aside to cool.
4 Roll out just over half the pastry to a round which will fit the pie plate. Transfer this to the pie plate by gently sliding it off the board.

5 Put the fruit into the pastry-lined plate to within 1 cm/½ inch of the edge. Dampen the edge with water.

6 Roll out the remaining pastry and place on top of the fruit. Press the edges together, trim, knock up and flute or fork the edges. Make a steam-hole in the centre of the pastry.

7 Cut decorations from the pastry trimmings, if you like, and stick these on to the pie with water.

8 Brush with milk or soya milk, sprinkle with caster sugar, and bake for 30 minutes. Serve hot or cold.

Variations

SUMMER FRUIT PIE

Make as described, but use a mixture of fresh or frozen raspberries, redcurrants and blackcurrants.

APPLE PIE

Use 700 g/1½ lb apples, stewed as described on p.123.

Rhubarb Crumble [V]

I use a shallow French glazed pottery ovenproof dish measuring 25 × 32 cm/10 × 12½ inches, which seems a large quantity for 4, but in my experience there's never any problem with leftovers!

SERVES 4-6

900 g/2 lb rhubarb cut into 2·5-cm/ 1-inch lengths
75 g/3 oz sugar
butter or vegan margarine for greasing

FOR THE CRUMBLE
250 g/9 oz self-raising 85% wholewheat flour
175 g/6 oz butter or vegan margarine
175 g/6 oz demerara sugar

1 Preheat the oven to 200c/400F/Gas Mark 6.

2 Put the fruit into a lightly greased large shallow ovenproof dish. Mix in the sugar; make sure the fruit is in an even layer.

3 Put the flour into a mixing bowl and rub in the butter or vegan margarine with your fingertips until the mixture looks like fine breadcrumbs and there are no lumps of fat showing.

4 Add the sugar and mix gently. Spoon the crumble topping over the fruit in an even layer, covering all the fruit.

5 Bake for 30–40 minutes, until the crumble is crisp and lightly browned and the fruit feels tender when pierced with a skewer. Serve hot.

Traditional Christmas Pudding

In this pudding, soft butter or margarine
replaces the traditional beef suet. The pudding
tastes just as good, and has a deliciously spicy
flavour. It can be made up to 2 months in
advance and will keep well (and mature) in a
cool, dry place.

SERVES 8

225 g/8 oz butter, softened, or vegan margarine
175 g/6 oz real barbados sugar
2 eggs, beaten
100 g/4 oz plain 85% or 100% wholewheat flour
½ teaspoon salt
½ teaspoon freshly grated nutmeg
½ teaspoon ground ginger
1½ teaspoons mixed spice
50 g/2 oz ground almonds
75 g/3 oz finely grated carrot
100 g/4 oz currants
100 g/4 oz raisins
100 g/4 oz sultanas
100 g/4 oz chopped candied peel
50 g/2 oz blanched almonds, chopped
100 g/4 oz fresh wholewheat breadcrumbs
grated rind and juice of 1 lemon
1 tablespoon treacle
about 4 tablespoons water or water and rum mixed
butter for greasing

TO FLAME
4 tablespoons brandy

TO SERVE
holly sprigs
Brandy Butter (p.443)

1 Grease a 1·2-litre/2-pint pudding basin and have ready a saucepan which is large enough to hold the pudding basin.

2 Cream together the butter or vegan margarine and the sugar, until light and fluffy, then whisk in the beaten egg, a little at a time.

3 Sift the flour, salt and spices into the bowl on top of the creamed mixture.

4 Add the remaining ingredients with just enough of the water or water and rum to make a soft mixture which will fall heavily from the spoon when you shake it. Mix well.

5 Spoon the mixture into the prepared pudding basin, cover with a piece of pleated greased greaseproof paper and then a piece of foil, and tie down securely with string. To lift your pudding in and out of the pan, see p.397.

6 Put the basin into the saucepan and pour in enough boiling water to come halfway up the sides of the basin.

7 Bring to the boil, then cover the pan and steam gently for 4 hours. Check the water level and top up with boiling water.

8 Remove the pudding from the pan and allow to cool, then store in a cool, dry place. Steam the pudding again for 3 hours before serving, then remove the paper and foil and turn the pudding out on to a warmed serving plate. Flame with brandy, decorate with holly and serve with brandy butter.

FLAMING A CHRISTMAS PUDDING

Flaming a Christmas pudding with brandy just before serving gives it a wonderful flavour. The important thing is to warm the brandy first. Put 4 tablespoons brandy into a metal ladle and warm by holding over a gas flame or electric ring, then quickly light the brandy and pour over and round the pudding.

Brandy Butter

SERVES 6

100 g/4 oz unsalted butter
100 g/4 oz soft light brown sugar
2 tablespoons brandy

TO DECORATE
holly leaves

1 Cream the butter and sugar together until light, pale and fluffy, then gradually beat in the brandy.

2 Transfer the mixture to a serving dish and chill until required. Decorate with holly to serve.

Mince Pies

V

This mincemeat is unusual in that it contains
no sugar or fat; the dried fruits provide the
sweetness. It tastes delicious, but doesn't store
in the same way as ordinary mincemeat
because of the lack of sugar. This recipe makes
12 mince pies, with enough mincemeat left over
for 2 further batches. The mincemeat will keep
for up to a week in a covered bowl in the fridge.
Uncooked mince pies freeze excellently; put
them into the tin, freeze, then carefully remove
them from the tin and store in a polythene
container until required. Replace the mince
pies in the tin for baking. (They can be baked
from frozen, allowing a few extra minutes.)

MAKES 12

1 quantity Basic Shortcrust Pastry
(p.384)
butter or vegan margarine for
greasing
TO FINISH
caster sugar
FOR THE MINCEMEAT
100 g/4 oz currants
100 g/4 oz raisins
100 g/4 oz sultanas

100 g/4 oz cooking dates, chopped
50 g/2 oz candied peel, chopped
50 g/2 oz glacé cherries, quartered
50 g/2 oz flaked almonds
4 tablespoons brandy or whisky
½ teaspoon each ground ginger,
mixed spice, freshly grated
nutmeg
1 ripe banana, peeled and mashed

1 To make the mincemeat, put the dried fruit, peel, cherries and
almonds into a bowl. Sprinkle with the brandy or whisky and
the spices. Stir, then leave to stand for 1–2 hours, stirring from
time to time. Add the banana and mix well.

2 Preheat the oven to 200c/400F/Gas Mark 6. Grease a 12-hole
bun tin.

3 Roll the pastry out thinly. Using 2 cutters, cut out 12 ×
8-cm/3-inch circles and 12 × 6-cm/2½-inch circles.

4 Press the larger circles gently into each section of the bun tin,
then put a heaped teaspoon of mincemeat into each and cover
with the smaller pastry circles.

5 Press down at the edges and make a steam-hole in the top of each pie. Bake for 10 minutes, until lightly browned.
6 Cool in the tin, then transfer to a wire rack. Serve the pies warm, sprinkled with a little sugar.

VEGETARIAN SUET

A vegetarian suet is available from health shops and can replace animal suet in recipes such as Christmas pudding, mincemeat and suet pudding.

Waffles

Waffles are nourishing and make an excellent breakfast, supper or snack at any time. They're particularly popular, in my experience, with children and teenagers. You need a waffle iron to make them.

MAKES 6

250 g/9 oz plain 85% or 100% wholewheat flour
3 teaspoons baking powder
½ teaspoon salt

3 eggs, separated
450 ml/15 fl oz milk
50 g/2 oz butter, melted
3 tablespoons caster sugar

1 Heat the waffle iron according to the manufacturer's instructions.
2 Put the flour, baking powder and salt into a mixing bowl. Add the egg yolks, milk and melted butter. Mix well to make a smooth batter.
3 Whisk the egg whites until stiff but not dry, then add the sugar and whisk again until glossy.
4 Fold the egg white mixture into the batter.
5 Spread ½ cup batter in the hot waffle iron. Bake for 2–3 minutes, until golden. (If it sticks, cook for a minute longer.)
6 Serve hot, with butter and honey or golden or maple syrup. Or serve the waffles with a jam sauce or cream or ice cream and fresh fruit.

WAFFLE IRONS

Most automatic waffle irons have a thermostat showing when they are hot enough to add the batter. If yours does not, put 1 teaspoon water into the iron: it is ready when the steaming stops. Since the batter contains fat, you do not need to grease a waffle iron. If the waffle sticks, simply cook for a minute longer. You shouldn't have any trouble with sticking after the first one.

Steamed Pudding

Everybody's favourite homely pudding, wonderful to keep out the chill on a winter's day.

SERVES 4

4 tablespoons jam or golden syrup
100 g/4 oz self-raising 85%
  wholewheat flour
1 teaspoon baking powder

100 g/4 oz butter, softened
100 g/4 oz sugar
2 eggs
extra butter for greasing

1 Grease a medium pudding basin with butter and put the jam or golden syrup into the base.
2 Put the flour, baking powder, butter, sugar and eggs into a large mixing bowl and beat together for 1–2 minutes until the mixture is thick, smooth and looks slightly glossy.
3 Spoon the mixture into the bowl on top of the jam or syrup. Cover the basin with a piece of pleated greased greaseproof paper and then with foil. Tie down securely. Stand the basin in a saucepan and pour in boiling water to come halfway up the sides of the basin.
4 Bring to the boil, then simmer for 1½ hours. Check the water level and top up with boiling water if necessary.
5 Remove the paper and foil, run a palette knife around the sides of the pudding and turn it out on to a warmed plate. Serve hot.

Pancakes

Pancakes can be thin and lacy, so that you can
almost see through them – these are the elegant
French crepes – or they can be thick and filling
– cheap and comforting homely food. The thick
variety were the favourite after-college snack of
one of my daughters and her friends who
seemed to arrive at our door on motor bikes in
droves. It was then that I really learnt to make
pancakes – fast!

MAKES 12-14

100 g/4 oz plain 85% wholewheat
    flour
½ teaspoon salt
2 eggs
150 ml/5 fl oz milk
150 ml/5 fl oz water

1–2 tablespoons melted butter or
    sunflower oil
oil or melted butter for frying
TO SERVE
caster sugar
4 lemons

1 Put all the ingredients into a blender or food processor and
whizz until smooth. Or put the flour and salt into a mixing bowl,
mix in the eggs, then gradually beat in the milk and water and
melted butter.
2 Using a bristle pastry brush (not a nylon one), brush the
inside of a small non-stick frying pan with oil or melted butter.
Set the frying pan over a high heat until a drop of water flicked
into it sizzles immediately.
3 Remove the pan from the heat, pour in 1½–2 tablespoons of
batter for thin pancakes, more for thick ones, tipping the frying
pan as you pour it in, so that the batter runs all over the bottom
of the frying pan.
4 Immediately return the pan to the heat and cook the pancake
for about 30 seconds, until it is set on top and golden-brown
underneath, then flip the pancake over, using your finger and a
small palette knife, and cook the other side until golden-brown.
5 Serve immediately, or stack the pancakes on a plate and keep
them warm until all are ready. Re-grease the frying pan as
necessary. Serve sprinkled with sugar, with the lemons cut in
half to squeeze over.

Variation

CREPES SUZETTES

This is my daughter Katy's favourite pudding. Make the pancakes as described. Heat 100 g/4 oz butter, 150 g/5 oz caster sugar, the grated rind and juice of 3 medium oranges and the grated rind and juice of 1 lemon in a shallow flameproof oven-to-table casserole or good-looking frying pan. When the mixture is melted, remove from the heat and dip in the pancakes on both sides, one by one, folding them in half and then in half again to make triangles. When each pancake is done push it to the side of the frying pan. When they're all done, leave them in the frying pan until you're ready to eat, then reheat gently. When all the pancakes are heated through, turn the heat up high for 1 minute to make the sauce really hot, then flame it in the pan with 4 tablespoons warmed brandy.

Raspberry Coulis

A delicious sauce for serving with fruit salads,
over ice cream or poached fruits.

SERVES 4

350 g/12 oz fresh raspberries,
washed, or frozen raspberries,
thawed

6 teaspoons water
6 teaspoons caster sugar

1 Blend the raspberries in a blender or food processor with the water and sugar. Sieve, then turn into a saucepan, bring to the boil and boil for 1 minute, to make the sauce clear and glossy.
2 Cool and refrigerate until needed.

Variation

BLACKBERRY COULIS

Make exactly as described, using blackberries instead of raspberries.

SWEET PANCAKES

Pancakes are delicious served simply with warmed maple syrup, honey or golden syrup. They are, however, marvellously adaptable, since both the batter and the fillings are infinitely variable.

For chocolate pancakes, replace 2 teaspoons of the flour with 2 teaspoons of cocoa powder and add a teaspoon of vanilla extract or 1 tablespoon rum; serve with warmed black cherry preserve and whipped cream.

For nutty-tasting buckwheat pancakes, replace 25–50 g/1–2 oz of the flour with buckwheat flour. These are good with strongly flavoured fillings, either sweet or savoury.

For orange pancakes, add grated orange rind and 1 tablespoon Cointreau or Grand Marnier to the batter; try these with pineapple, peaches or apricots.

Fill pancakes with sliced ripe peaches or nectarines.

For spicy pancakes, add ½ teaspoon cinnamon or ginger to the batter; try filling these with toning fruits, such as apples with cinnamon, pears with ginger.

Hot Chocolate Sauce

This sauce is delicious over meringues, profiteroles or ice cream.

SERVES 4

100 g/4 oz plain chocolate, broken into pieces

150 ml/5 fl oz single or non-dairy cream

1 Put the chocolate and cream into a small saucepan.
2 Heat gently until the chocolate has melted. Stir well, then serve.

CHOCOLATE FONDUE

Hot Chocolate Sauce makes a delicious sweet fondue, a special-occasion pudding that children and teenagers love. Serve surrounded by prepared fresh fruit for dipping; pieces of apple, apricot, pineapple, peach – whatever is available. Some marshmallows, soft peppermints and pieces of Turkish delight are also good for dipping (though not as healthy!).

Pouring Egg Custard

Delicate in flavour and texture, this sauce is
well worth making, although it does need a
little care, because it separates if it gets too hot.
Making it in a double saucepan – or a bowl set
over a pan of simmering water helps to avoid
this problem.

SERVES 4-6

300 ml/10 fl oz milk
1 tablespoon caster sugar

1 vanilla pod
2 egg yolks

1 Put the milk into a medium saucepan with the sugar and
vanilla pod and bring to the boil. Immediately remove the
saucepan from the heat. Remove the vanilla pod (which can be
thoroughly rinsed, then dried and kept for re-use).
2 Meanwhile mix the egg yolks together in a bowl. Pour on the
scalded milk, stirring, then return the mixture to the pan.
3 Stir over a gentle heat until the mixture thickens enough to
coat the back of the spoon. Do not let the custard get too hot or it
will curdle. Pour into a clean bowl until ready to use.

Sabayon Sauce

SERVES 4

50 g/2 oz caster sugar
4 tablespoons water
2 egg yolks
4 tablespoons sweet white wine or
  sherry

a little lemon juice (optional)
150 ml/5 fl oz whipping cream,
  whipped (optional)

1 Put the sugar and water into a small pan and heat until
syrupy.
2 Mix the egg yolks in a bowl. Add the hot syrup to the egg
yolks in a thin stream and whisk well until thick and pale, then
add the wine and a little lemon juice, if liked. Fold in the cream,
if used.

TIPS FOR MAKING EGG CUSTARD

To make life easier for yourself when making an egg custard, a teaspoon of cornflour can be mixed in with the egg yolks to stabilize the mixture and prevent it from curdling if it does get too hot.

To prevent a skin from forming on top of egg custard, sprinkle the top with a thin layer of caster sugar and whisk in just before serving.

USING SWEET SAUCES

A sweet sauce can add the finishing touch to a pudding, transforming a simple dish like home-made ice cream into something special.

Try Raspberry Coulis with Vanilla Ice Cream; Blackberry Coulis with Apple Ice Cream; or a coulis made from blackberries or blackcurrants with Chocolate Ice Cream.

For a pretty effect, pour a pool of coulis on to an individual serving plate, top with poached fruit or ice cream, then pour circles of cream on top of the coulis. Make a 'feather' pattern in the circles of cream by drawing a cocktail stick through them, in lines like spokes of a wheel, first towards the centre, then, with the next one, from the centre to the outside.

Sweet sauces are excellent with fresh or cooked fruit; try Chocolate Sauce, Raspberry Coulis or Sabayon Sauce with poached pears; or Pouring Egg Custard with thin circles of juicy tangerines or satsumas (and flavour the custard with some of the grated rind).

Skimmed Milk Topping

This is a whipped, low-calorie, low-fat topping. It's useful on top of fruit salads or as a filling for a cake you're going to eat the same day. You need an electric whisk to make this and you must use skimmed milk powder from the health shop, and not a milk-substitute powder nor granules.

SERVES 4-6

40 g/1½ oz skimmed milk powder
150 ml/5 fl oz ice-cold water
2 tablespoons lemon juice

½ teaspoon vanilla extract
1–2 tablespoons caster sugar

1 Put the skimmed milk powder and water into a bowl or the bowl of a food processor and whisk electrically for 4–5 minutes, until the mixture is thick and forms soft peaks.

2 Add the lemon juice and whisk again until the mixture forms stiff peaks.

3 Carefully fold in the vanilla extract and sugar. Use the topping within a few hours of making it.

Cakes

*This chapter contains a medley of favourite cakes,
ranging from homely Rock Cakes (p.462),
Parkin (p.462) and easy All-in-one Sponge (p.456) to
classics such as Carrot Cake (p.460), Madeira
Cake (p.461), Dundee Cake (p.466) and Rich Fruit
Cake (p.468), and some sheer indulgences like
Meringues (p.472), Éclairs (p.473) and the most
wonderful chocolate cake of all, Chocolate
Roulade (p.458). At the end of the chapter are some
favourite fillings and icings. Amongst the recipes are a
number which do not contain eggs or milk, for vegans
or people allergic to dairy produce.*

Whisked Sponge Cake

The lightest sponge of all and comparatively
low in calories, because it does not contain fat.

MAKES ONE 20-CM/8-INCH CAKE

4 eggs
100 g/4 oz caster sugar
100 g/4 oz plain unbleached white
   flour
a pinch of salt
butter for greasing

FOR THE FILLING
75 g/3 oz jam

TO FINISH
caster sugar

1 Grease two 20-cm/8-inch sandwich tins and line the base of
each with a circle of greased greaseproof paper.
2 Put the eggs and sugar into a mixing bowl and whisk
electrically for about 5 minutes until the mixture is very pale, has
doubled in bulk and leaves a ribbon trail on the surface when
the whisk is lifted.
3 Alternatively, put the eggs and sugar into a bowl fitted over a
saucepan of gently simmering water (make sure that the bowl

does not touch the water) and whisk until the same stage is reached. Allow to cool, whisking occasionally.

4 Preheat the oven to 180c/350f/Gas Mark 4.

5 Sift the flour with the salt gently on top of the egg mixture. Then, using a metal spoon, fold it in gently but thoroughly.

6 Pour into the cake tins. Bake for 30—35 minutes, or until the cakes are shrunk from the sides of the tins and spring back when touched lightly in the centre.

7 Cool in the tins for 2—3 minutes, then turn out on to a wire rack and carefully strip off the lining paper.

8 When the cakes are cool, sandwich with the jam and dredge with sugar.

Variations

SWISS ROLL

Use the same mixture, but bake it in a 33 × 23-cm/13 × 9-inch Swiss roll tin, lined with greased greaseproof paper, for 10—12 minutes, until golden-brown and firm to a light touch. Turn out on to a piece of greaseproof paper sprinkled with caster sugar. Spread with 100 g/4 oz warmed jam and roll up quickly, using the paper to help. Cool on a wire rack.

GENOESE SPONGE

This slightly richer whisked sponge is made in exactly the same way, except that 50 g/2 oz of very soft (but not melted) butter is added. Pour this around the edge of the bowl after folding in the flour, then carefully fold into mixture.

V | *Vegan Chocolate Sponge Cake*

MAKES ONE 20—22-CM/8—8½-INCH ROUND CAKE

300 g/10 oz self-raising 85%
   wholewheat flour
50 g/2 oz cocoa powder
3 teaspoons baking powder
250 g/9 oz vanilla sugar or caster
   sugar with 1½ teaspoons vanilla
   extract
9 tablespoons sunflower oil

350 ml/12 fl oz water
vegan margarine for greasing
TO DECORATE
1 quantity Chocolate Fudge Icing
   (p. 475) or Chocolate
   Buttercream (p. 476)
coarsely grated chocolate
icing sugar

1 Preheat the oven to 170c/325f/Gas Mark 3.

2 Grease two 20−22-cm/8−8½-inch sandwich tins and line the base of each with a circle of greased greaseproof paper.

3 Sift the flour, cocoa and baking powder into a bowl. Add the sugar, vanilla, if used, oil and water. Mix well to a batter-like consistency.

4 Pour the mixture into the prepared tins and bake for about 40 minutes, until the cakes spring back to a light touch in the centre.

5 Turn the cakes out on to a wire rack and strip off the lining paper. Leave to cool completely.

6 Sandwich the cakes together with half the fudge icing or buttercream and coat the top with the rest. Decorate with grated chocolate and icing sugar.

Variation

VEGAN LEMON CAKE

Use 350 g/12 oz flour and omit the cocoa. Replace 2 tablespoons of the water with 2 tablespoons lemon juice, and add the grated rind of 1 lemon. Sandwich and top with lemon buttercream or fudge icing and decorate with mimosa balls and leaves cut from angelica.

MAKING ASSORTED FANCY CAKES

Whisked sponge cake, baked in a Swiss roll tin as described under Swiss Roll, can be cut up to make 12−16 tiny cakes. You can either cover the top of the cake with glacé icing (p. 474) before cutting into pieces, or cut the cake into different shapes, using a sharp knife and pastry cutters, then ice and decorate the shapes individually. If you're doing the cakes individually, there is plenty of scope for different colours and flavours: coffee icing decorated with chocolate or walnuts; chocolate icing with chocolate curls; vanilla icing with crystallized rose or violet petals; lemon icing with angelica and mimosa balls; orange icing with small pieces of jellied orange segments. If the cake is very 'crumbly', before putting on the icing or butter icing, dip the pieces of cake in a glaze made by boiling 225 g/8 oz sieved apricot jam with 3 tablespoons water for a few minutes, until syrupy.

RAISING AGENTS

Baking Powder
Consists of a mixture of bicarbonate of soda and cream of tartar in a base of flour. Low-sodium gluten-free baking powder, made from potassium carbonate and potato flour, is also available.

Cream of Tartar
A white powder with a slightly sour flavour, cream of tartar is an ingredient in baking powder and can also be used in soft drinks. If you need to make up a baking powder, the proportions are three parts cream of tartar to one part bicarbonate of soda, and they should be added separately to the mixture.

Bicarbonate of Soda
This white powder is one of the ingredients of baking powder and, because of its effervescent qualities, can also be used as a raising agent on its own. It is usually dissolved in a little acid liquid, such as buttermilk or milk and vinegar, then mixed quickly with the dry ingredients just before baking.

All-in-one Sponge Cake

This is a sponge which you can whizz up in
no time at all.

MAKES ONE 20-CM/8-INCH CAKE

175 g/6 oz self-raising 85% brown
  flour
1½ teaspoons baking powder
175 g/6 oz soft light brown sugar
175 g/6 oz butter, softened
3 eggs
extra butter for greasing

FOR THE FILLING AND TOPPING
4 tablespoons warmed jam,
  preferably reduced-sugar type
a little caster sugar

1 Preheat the oven to 170c/325f/Gas Mark 3. Grease two 20-cm/8-inch sandwich tins and line the base of each with a circle of greased greaseproof paper.
2 Sift the flour with the baking powder into a mixing bowl and add the sugar, butter and eggs.
3 Beat with a wooden spoon for 2 minutes, or in an electric mixer for about 1 minute, until the mixture is smooth, thick and glossy.

4 Spoon the mixture into the prepared tins and level the tops.

5 Bake, without opening the oven door, for 30 minutes, until the cakes spring back to a light touch in the centre.

6 Leave the cakes in the tins to cool for 1 minute, then turn them out on to a wire rack and carefully remove the lining paper, then leave the cakes to cool completely.

7 Sandwich the cakes together with the warmed jam and sprinkle the top with caster sugar.

Variations

VICTORIA SANDWICH CAKE

For this traditional version, omit the baking powder. Cream the butter and sugar together until light and fluffy, then gradually add the beaten eggs, beating well after each addition. Fold in the flour in 2 batches. Bake at a slightly higher temperature, 190c/375f/Gas Mark 5, for about 30 minutes.

COFFEE AND WALNUT SPONGE CAKE

Dissolve 3 teaspoons strong good-quality instant coffee in a little boiling water. Add to the rest of the ingredients, together with 50 g/2 oz walnut pieces. Sandwich together and coat with a double quantity of Coffee Buttercream (p. 476) and coat the sides of the cake with 50 g/2 oz chopped walnuts.

CHOCOLATE SPONGE CAKE

Replace 25 g/1 oz of the flour with 25 g/1 oz cocoa powder; or, for a rich, gooey cake, add 225 g/8 oz melted plain chocolate to the ingredients and bake for a little longer. Sandwich together with redcurrant, cherry or raspberry jam. Coat the top and sides with 7-Minute Frosting (p. 478) or Chocolate Buttercream (p. 476), then coat the sides with chopped toasted hazelnuts, and the top with a generous amount of coarsely grated chocolate or chocolate curls. Dust with icing sugar.

LEMON SPONGE CAKE

Add the grated rind of 1 lemon to the mixture. Sandwich together with Lemon Curd (p. 514) and dust with icing sugar.

ICED SPONGE FINGERS

Use 100 g/4 oz each flour, sugar and butter. Bake for 30 minutes in a shallow 28 × 18-cm/11 × 7-inch tin, lined with greased greaseproof paper. Ice with Glacé Icing (p. 474) and cut into 16–20 fingers. Decorate with chopped nuts or glacé cherries.

FRUIT AND ALMOND FINGERS

Make up a half quantity of mixture. Add 100 g/4 oz mixed dried fruit or chopped dates and sprinkle 25–50 g/1–2 oz flaked almonds on top before baking. This does not need icing.

DECORATING A SPONGE CAKE

Sponge cakes can be decorated in many different ways using smooth or piped icing, flaked nuts, chocolate curls and glacé fruits, to name only some of the possibilities.

You may also like to try applying a coating of chopped nuts to the sides. To do this, sprinkle the chopped nuts on a clean board. Then, before icing the top, coat the sides of your cake with buttercream icing and roll it over the nuts, like a wheel, until the sides are completely coated.

To make a feather pattern, first cover the top of your cake with a light-coloured glacé icing. Then quickly pipe thin lines of darker-coloured glacé icing across at regular intervals. Now make a feather pattern by drawing the point of a knife across the lines of darker icing, first in one direction, then the other, forming delicate points all the way along each line of darker icing. Plain white glacé icing makes a good base, with chocolate icing for the feather pattern.

Chocolate Roulade

Chocolate roulade freezes excellently; make it completely, open-freeze, then, when solid, wrap carefully. To use, unwrap and place on a serving dish to thaw, allowing 2–3 hours. It needs to be eaten with a fork, and makes a very good dessert.

SERVES 6 — 8

5 eggs, separated
175 g/6 oz soft light brown sugar
3 tablespoons hot water
175 g/6 oz plain chocolate, melted
icing sugar, sifted
butter for greasing

FOR THE FILLING
200 g/7 oz can unsweetened
    chestnut purée
300 ml/10 fl oz whipping cream
sugar to taste
a few marrons glacés

1 Preheat the oven to 200c/400F/Gas Mark 6. Grease a 25 × 35-cm/10 × 14-inch Swiss roll tin and line with greased grease-proof paper.

2 Put the egg yolks into a bowl with the sugar and whisk until thick and pale.

3 Stir the hot water into the melted chocolate, then gently mix this into the egg yolk mixture. Whisk the egg whites until stiff, then fold into the mixture.

4 Pour the mixture into the tin, spreading it out to the edges. Bake for 15 minutes. Remove from the oven and leave to cool in the tin for 10 minutes, then cover with a damp tea-towel and leave for a further 10 minutes.

5 Have ready a piece of greaseproof paper sprinkled with icing sugar. Remove the cloth and turn the roulade out on to the piece of greaseproof paper. Carefully strip off the lining paper and leave to cool completely.

6 To prepare the filling, beat the chestnut purée until soft, then add half the cream and whisk until thick. Sweeten to taste.

7 Trim the edges of the roulade and spread with the chestnut cream. Then carefully roll the roulade up from one long end, using the paper to help.

8 Whip the remaining cream and spoon or pipe on top of the roulade. Decorate with the marrons glacés and sprinkle with icing sugar. This roulade will keep well in the fridge for several hours, and also freezes well.

Variation

CHOCOLATE ROULADE WITH ROSEBUDS

Make the chocolate mixture as described. Fill with 300 ml/10 fl oz whipping cream, and decorate the plate with fresh pink rosebuds. Lovely for a summer birthday!

Carrot Cake

This cake is easy to make, but is best done by hand, rather than in a food processor, which chops up the nuts and fruit too much, spoiling the texture. Properly made, it's delicious, with a moist texture and spicy flavour. Carrot cake is particularly good for serving at picnics and barbecues, but pack carefully and supply forks and paper napkins.

MAKES ONE 23-CM/9-INCH CAKE

175 ml/6 fl oz sunflower oil
250 g/9 oz soft light brown sugar
2 large eggs
1 teaspoon vanilla extract
175 g/6 oz cold puréed carrot
150 g/5 oz canned pineapple chunks, drained and roughly chopped
75 g/3 oz walnuts, roughly chopped
75 g/3 oz unsweetened desiccated coconut

200 g/7 oz plain 85% wholewheat flour
½ teaspoon salt
1 teaspoon ground cinnamon
1 teaspoon baking powder
butter for greasing
TO DECORATE
1 quantity Cream Cheese Frosting (p. 475)
a few walnuts

1 Preheat the oven to 180c/350f/Gas Mark 4. Grease two 23-cm/9-inch sandwich tins and line the base of each with greased greaseproof paper.
2 Put the oil into a large mixing bowl and add the sugar. Mix well, until there are no lumpy bits of sugar.
3 Beat in the eggs, then add the vanilla, carrot purée, pineapple, walnuts and coconut.
4 Mix lightly, then sift in the flour, salt, cinnamon and baking powder. Mix together quickly but gently.
5 Spoon the mixture into the prepared tins and level the tops. Bake for 30 minutes, or until a warmed skewer inserted into the centre comes out clean.
6 Turn out on to a wire rack, and leave to cool for 10 minutes, then strip off the lining papers.
7 When the cakes are completely cold, sandwich them together with half the cream cheese frosting. Spread the rest on top. Decorate with walnuts.

Madeira Cake

I like this best made with unbleached white flour, because this allows the flavours to come through, though I have made it successfully too with both brown and wholewheat flours.

MAKES ONE 20-CM/8-INCH CAKE

175 g/6 oz plain flour
175 g/6 oz self-raising flour
250 g/9 oz butter
250 g/9 oz caster sugar with 1½ teaspoons vanilla extract

4 large eggs, beaten
2−3 tablespoons milk (optional)
extra butter for greasing
TO DECORATE
2−3 thin slices citron peel

1 Preheat the oven to 180c/350f/Gas Mark 4. Grease a 20-cm/8-inch round cake tin, then cut a thick band of greaseproof paper to go round the sides, snipping one edge diagonally at 1-cm/½-inch intervals to make it fit snugly into the tin. Next, draw round the tin and cut a circular piece to cover the base. Now grease both pieces of greaseproof paper and use them to line the tin.

2 Sift the flours together on to a piece of greaseproof paper.

3 Cream the butter with the sugar until light, pale and fluffy, then add the eggs, a little at a time, beating well each time.

4 Add the vanilla extract, then fold in the flour, adding a little milk if necessary to make a soft, dropping consistency.

5 Spoon the mixture into the prepared cake tin. Bake for 20 minutes, then carefully lay the citron peel on top of the cake and bake for a further 1¼ hours, or until a warmed skewer inserted into the centre of the cake comes out clean.

6 Turn out on to a wire rack and cool.

SERVING MADEIRA CAKE

Madeira cake makes, I think, a very pleasant accompaniment to a fruit salad or creamy fool; it is particularly good with Pashka (p. 428). Serve in thin slices.

Or, for a quick and easy pudding, serve with some lightly stewed fruit, such as blackcurrants, and some cream or thick yogurt.

Parkin

This parkin keeps well and gets stickier the
longer it's kept. Wrap in foil to store.

MAKES 12 — 16 SLICES

*100 g/4 oz plain 100%
  wholewheat flour*
2 teaspoons baking powder
2 teaspoons ground ginger
100 g/4 oz medium oatmeal
4 tablespoons real barbados sugar
100 g/4 oz black treacle

100 g/4 oz golden syrup
*100 g/4 oz butter or vegan
  margarine*
175 ml/6 fl oz milk or soya milk
*extra butter or margarine for
  greasing*

1 Preheat the oven to 180c/350f/Gas Mark 4. Line a 20-cm/
8-inch square cake tin with greased greaseproof paper.
2 Sift the flour with the baking powder and ginger into a bowl.
Add the bran from the sieve and the oatmeal.
3 Heat the sugar, treacle, golden syrup and butter or vegan
margarine gently in a saucepan until melted. Cool until you can
comfortably put your hand against the pan, then stir in the milk
or soya milk.
4 Add the melted mixture to the dry ingredients. Mix
thoroughly, then pour the mixture into the prepared cake tin.
Bake for 50—60 minutes, until the parkin feels firm on top.
5 Remove the parkin from the tin and put on a wire tray to cool,
then cut into slices and carefully remove from the lining paper.

Rock Cakes

Easy to make, spicy and delicious eaten while
still warm.

MAKES 10

*225 g/8 oz self-raising 85% or
  100% wholewheat flour*
½ teaspoon mixed spice
100 g/4 oz butter

75 g/3 oz demerara sugar
100 g/4 oz mixed dried fruit
*1 egg, beaten with 1 tablespoon
  milk*
extra butter for greasing

1 Preheat the oven to 200c/400f/Gas Mark 6.

2 Sift the flour with the spice into a mixing bowl, add the bran from the sieve, if you're using 100% wholewheat flour, then rub in the butter with your fingertips until the mixture looks like fine breadcrumbs.

3 Add two-thirds of the sugar, the fruit and the egg and milk mixture, and mix lightly, so that the mixture just holds together.

4 Spoon heaps of the mixture on to a greased baking sheet, leaving a little room around each for spreading, then sprinkle with the rest of the sugar.

5 Bake for about 15 minutes, until lightly browned. Remove with a fish slice, as these rock cakes are fragile while still warm, and cool on a wire rack.

Variation

VEGAN ROCK CAKES

Use vegan margarine instead of butter, add 1 teaspoon baking powder to the flour and use 4 tablespoons soya milk instead of the milk and egg.

Carob Brownies

Sweet and gooey, these brownies have a crisp,
cracked top and a wonderful flavour. Definitely
my favourite recipe using carob.

MAKES 12 – 16

100 g/4 oz butter
50 g/2 oz carob bar (not the sugarless type), broken up
2 eggs
225 g/8 oz soft light brown sugar
50 g/2 oz plain 85% wholewheat flour, sifted

½ teaspoon vanilla extract
50 g/2 oz walnuts or pecans, chopped
extra butter for greasing
TO FINISH
icing sugar, sifted

1 Preheat the oven to 180c/350f/Gas Mark 4. Line a 20-cm/8-inch square shallow tin with greaseproof paper and grease the paper well with butter.

2 Heat the butter and carob bar together in a small saucepan until melted. Cool.

3 Whisk the eggs with the sugar until thick and pale – this takes 10 minutes with an electric whisk.

4 Fold the melted mixture into the whisked eggs, then the flour, vanilla and walnuts or pecans.

5 Pour the mixture into the prepared tin. Bake for 40–45 minutes, or until the centre is set. Don't over-bake – the inside should be gooey.

6 Cool in the tin, then dredge with icing sugar, cut into fingers and remove from the lining paper.

Quick Buns

These colourful buns make an excellent teatime
treat for children.

MAKES 18

175 g/6 oz self-raising 85% or
   100% wholewheat flour
100 g/4 oz soft butter
100 g/4 oz soft light brown or
   caster sugar
2 eggs

TO DECORATE
Glacé Icing (p.474), made with 100
   g/4 oz icing sugar
chopped nuts, or a few chocolate
   dots and sliced glacé cherries

1 Preheat the oven to 190c/375f/Gas Mark 5.

2 Sift the flour into a mixing bowl and add the bran from the sieve, if you're using 100% wholewheat flour.

3 Add the butter, sugar and eggs and beat well with a wooden spoon or with an electric mixer, until all the ingredients are well-blended and the mixture is thick and slightly glossy-looking.

4 Drop a heaped teaspoon of mixture into 18 paper cases. Stand the cases in a deep bun tin, or on a baking sheet.

5 Bake for 15–20 minutes until the cakes have risen and feel firm to a light touch.

6 Cool on a wire rack, then ice and decorate as you like.

TEA

The natural partner for a piece of cake is a good cup of tea. Many types are available; for instance:

Assam
Has a strong flavour and is often blended with other teas

Gunpowder
One of the Chinese green teas with a sharp flavour

Ceylon
Good quality tea with a delicate flavour

Jasmine
My favourite; China tea mixed with jasmine flowers, to be taken without milk

Darjeeling
Fine flavoured tea from the Himalayan foothills

Keemum
The best China tea, with a delicate flavour and fragrance. Can be taken with or without milk

Earl Grey
Tea flavoured with oil of bergamot, originally formulated by the second Earl Grey; best without milk

Lapsang Souchong
A black China tea with a large leaf and a distinctive smoked flavour

English Breakfast
Generally a blend of Ceylon and Assam teas

The method for making tea is the same, whether you are using herb or flower tea, or traditional tea leaves. Warm the pot and, if you like normally strong tea, put in a teaspoon of tea for each person and, if it's for more than three people, an extra spoon for the pot. If, like me, you like weak tea without milk, use less tea. I use just 1 teaspoon to the pot; it's a question of personal taste. Bring a kettle of fresh cold water to the boil, then pour this on to the tea. Leave to infuse for 2–3 minutes for China or herb tea, 4–5 minutes for Indian tea, then strain into cups. Add milk or slices of lemon as required. For herb teas, try adding a little cinnamon or a dash of fragrant honey.

Dundee Cake

This cake is good made with unbleached white
or 85% wholewheat flour.

MAKES ONE 20-CM/8-INCH ROUND CAKE

225 g/8 oz butter
225 g/8 oz soft light brown sugar
4 large eggs, beaten
350 g/12 oz plain flour
1–2 tablespoons milk
175 g/6 oz sultanas
175 g/6 oz currants

175 g/6 oz raisins
75 g/3 oz candied peel, chopped
75 g/3 oz glacé cherries, halved
50 g/2 oz ground almonds
grated rind of 1 orange or lemon
75 g/3 oz blanched almonds, split
extra butter for greasing

1 Preheat the oven to 170c/325f/Gas Mark 3. Grease a 20-cm/
8-inch round cake tin and line with a double thickness of
greased greaseproof paper.
2 Cream the butter and sugar in a bowl until light and fluffy,
then add the eggs, a tablespoon at a time, beating well after each
addition.
3 Sift the flour in on top of the butter mixture, then fold it in
gently.
4 If the mixture seems stiff, add a little milk; it should drop
heavily from the spoon when you bang it against the side of the
bowl.
5 Gently stir in all the other ingredients except the split
almonds.
6 Turn the mixture into the prepared cake tin. Arrange the split
almonds lightly on top.
7 Bake for about 2½ hours, or until a warmed skewer inserted
into the centre of the cake comes out clean. Cool the cake in the
tin, then turn out on to a wire rack, strip off the lining paper and
leave to cool completely.

Variation

SUGARLESS DUNDEE CAKE

Replace the sugar with 225 g/8 oz cooking dates, stewed in
150 ml/5 fl oz water for about 10 minutes until soft, then beaten
to a purée. Cool, then use in place of the sugar.

CAKE-MAKING TIPS

The most critical part of making cakes by the traditional creaming method is the creaming of the butter and sugar, which should be done really thoroughly, until they are light, pale and fluffy. The beaten egg, which needs to be at room temperature, should be added very gradually, a tablespoon at a time, with thorough beating after each addition, so that the mixture doesn't curdle.

If the worst happens and it does curdle, however, don't despair. Add a little flour, then continue to add the egg and flour alternately. The texture of the cake will not be so light and crumbly, but it will still taste good.

If the top of a cake seems to be browning too quickly, cover it with a folded piece of greaseproof paper, with a hole cut in it, as described for the Rich Fruit Cake (p. 468).

Don't open the oven door when a cake is cooking until nearly the end of the cooking time, or the cake will probably sink in the middle. There's a delicate chemical reaction taking place which is upset by a blast of cold air!

ALTERNATIVE CHRISTMAS CAKE DECORATIONS

Almond paste can be used on its own, attractively fluted around the top of the cake (as you'd flute a pie), and perhaps lightly scored in a criss-cross pattern with a knife. Arrange a candle and holly or marzipan fruit around the centre and tie a toning ribbon around the side, or try a jewel-bright topping of crystallized fruits and brazil nuts, halved pecans and whole cashew nuts or blanched almonds. Stick these to the top of the cake in an attractive pattern with warmed clear honey; brush over with more warmed honey to glaze. For a sparkling finish, brush the whole cake over with clear honey then sprinkle with preserving sugar or coloured coffee sugar crystals and little silver balls.

Sieved apricot jam is often used to stick the almond paste on a rich fruit cake, but redcurrant jelly is easier, as no sieving has to be done.

Rich Fruit Cake

This is a rich, moist fruit cake, and the 20-cm/
8-inch size is excellent for Christmas or special
birthdays or celebrations. It can also be made as
a wedding cake: for the quantities for different-
sized tins, see next page.

MAKES ONE 20-CM/8-INCH CAKE

250 g/9 oz currants
250 g/9 oz sultanas
175 g/6 oz raisins
50 g/2 oz cherries
100 g/4 oz whole candied peel
250 g/9 oz plain 85% or 100%
  wholewheat flour
1 teaspoon baking powder
½ teaspoon salt
½ teaspoon mixed spice
¼ teaspoon freshly grated nutmeg
250 g/9 oz butter
250 g/9 oz soft light brown sugar
4 eggs, lightly beaten

grated rind of 1 orange
grated rind of 1 lemon
75 g/3 oz ground almonds
75 g/3 oz chopped blanched
  almonds
3 tablespoons sherry
2 tablespoons brandy
extra butter for greasing

TO DECORATE
1 quantity Almond Paste (p. 477)
1 quantity Royal Icing (p. 478)
red ribbon, Christmas cake
  decorations

1 Make sure that the dried fruit is clean; wash it if necessary in
warm water, dry with kitchen paper and spread it out on trays
lined with kitchen paper, to dry.
2 Wash the cherries to remove the syrup, then dry and cut into
quarters. Chop the candied peel.
3 Sift the flour with the baking powder, salt, mixed spice and
nutmeg. Set aside.
4 Preheat the oven to 140 c/275 f/Gas Mark 1. Grease a 20-cm/
8-inch round cake tin and line with a double thickness of
greased greaseproof paper.
5 Cream the butter with the sugar thoroughly, until very light
and fluffy, then add the eggs, a tablespoon at a time, beating
well between each addition.
6 Fold in the sifted flour mixture, then stir in the fruit, orange
and lemon rinds, ground and chopped almonds and the sherry.
7 Spoon the mixture into the cake tin, hollowing out the centre
slightly.

8 Tie a band of brown paper around the outside of the tin and place a folded piece of greaseproof paper, with a 2·5-cm/1-inch diameter circle cut in the middle, over the top of the brown paper, to prevent the top and sides of the cake browning before the inside is done.

9 Bake on a low shelf for 4½–5 hours. Do not open the oven door until the cake has been baking for at least 4 hours.

10 The cake is done when a skewer inserted into the centre comes out clean. Allow it to cool in the tin, then prick the top all over with a skewer and pour 2 tablespoons brandy over it.

11 Wrap the cake in a double thickness of greaseproof paper and store in an airtight tin until needed. It will keep well for 2–3 months and mature; prick the top and sprinkle a little more brandy over it occasionally during this time if you wish.

12 A week before you want to ice the cake, trim it if necessary to level it, then brush with melted redcurrant jelly.

13 Roll out two-thirds of the almond paste and cut into 2 pieces to cover the sides of the cake; press them into position.

14 Roll the remaining almond paste into a circle to cover the top; press down and trim. Leave the cake in a dry, airy place for 3–7 days.

15 Put all the icing on top of the cake and roll it backwards and forwards a few times with a palette knife to remove any air bubbles.

16 Spread the icing over the top and sides of the cake. Finally use the blade of the palette knife to flick the icing up into peaks. Arrange decorations on the cake and leave for at least 24 hours to set, then tie a ribbon round the cake.

Variation

SIMNEL CAKE

For this traditional Easter cake, put half the rich fruit cake mixture into the tin, then top with a 5 mm–1-cm/¼–½-inch thick circle of almond paste the same size as the tin. Spoon the rest of the mixture on top and bake as usual. Cool, then stick another circle of almond paste on top of the cake and a circle of 11 balls of almond paste (representing the Apostles minus Judas) around the edge. Pop the cake under a moderate grill just to brown the almond paste. Decorate with ribbon, and flowers and Easter chicks, if you like.

Vegan Fruit Cake

V

This eggless cake is best fresh, but will keep for
7—10 days in a tin.

MAKES ONE 20-CM/8-INCH ROUND CAKE

350 g/12 oz plain 100%
   wholewheat flour
1 teaspoon mixed spice
175 g/6 oz vegan margarine
175 g/6 oz real barbados sugar
225 g/8 oz mixed dried fruit
50 g/2 oz mixed peel
50 g/2 oz glacé cherries, rinsed and
   halved

grated rind of 1 orange
2 tablespoons ground almonds
25 g/1 oz blanched almonds,
   chopped
125 ml/4 fl oz soya milk or water
2 tablespoons vinegar
¾ teaspoon bicarbonate of soda
extra vegan margarine for
   greasing

1 Preheat the oven to 150c/300f/Gas Mark 2. Grease a 20-cm/
8-inch cake tin and line with a double layer of greased greaseproof paper.
2 Sift the flour with the mixed spice into a mixing bowl, adding
the bran from the sieve, too.
3 Rub the margarine into the flour with your fingertips until the
mixture looks like fine breadcrumbs, then stir in the sugar, dried
fruit, mixed peel, cherries, orange rind, ground and blanched
almonds.
4 Warm half the soya milk or water in a small saucepan and add
the vinegar. Dissolve the bicarbonate of soda in the rest of the
soya milk or water, then combine the two mixtures.
5 Stir this mixture into the dry ingredients, blending well so
that everything is combined.
6 Spoon the mixture into the prepared tin. Bake for 2—2½
hours, or until a skewer inserted into the centre of the cake
comes out clean.
7 Leave the cake in the tin to cool, then remove and strip off the
lining paper. Transfer to a wire rack to allow the cake to cool
completely.

QUANTITIES FOR RICH FRUIT CAKES IN VARIOUS TIN SIZES

Round tin sizes	15 cm	6 in	18 cm	7 in	20 cm	8 in	23 cm	9 in	25 cm	10 in	30 cm	12 in
Square tin sizes	13 cm	5 in	15 cm	6 in	18 cm	7 in	20 cm	8 in	23 cm	9 in	28 cm	11 in
Depth of cake	6 cm	2½ in	8 cm	3 in	8 cm	3 in	8 cm	3 in	9 cm	3½ in	9 cm	3½ in
		oz		oz		oz		oz		oz		oz
currants	150	5	200	7	250	9	350	12	450	1 lb	750	1 lb 10 oz
sultanas	150	5	200	7	250	9	350	12	450	1 lb	750	1 lb 10 oz
raisins	150	5	150	5	175	6	225	8	350	12	500	1 lb 2 oz
cherries	25	1	25	1	50	2	50	2	75	3	100	4
whole candied peel	75	3	100	4	150	5	175	6	250	9	400	14
butter	150	5	200	7	250	9	350	12	450	1 lb	750	1 lb 10 oz
soft brown sugar	150	5	200	7	250	9	350	12	450	1 lb	750	1 lb 10 oz
plain flour	150	5	200	7	250	9	350	12	450	1 lb	750	1 lb 10 oz
baking powder	½ tsp		½ tsp		1 tsp		1 tsp		2 tsp		2 tsp	
salt	pinch		pinch		½ tsp		⅔ tsp		1 tsp		1 tsp	
spice	⅓ tsp		½ tsp		1 tsp		1 tsp		2 tsp		2 tsp	
freshly grated nutmeg	pinch		pinch		¼ tsp		½ tsp		1 tsp		1 tsp	
eggs, lightly beaten	2		3		4		5		7		10	
grated rind of lemon	¼		½		1		1 large		2-3		2 or 3	
grated rind of orange	¼		½		1		1 large		2-3		2 or 3	
ground almonds	25	1	50	2	75	3	75	3	150	5	175	6
chopped blanched almonds	25	1	50	2	75	3	75	3	150	5	175	6
sherry	1 tbs		2 tbs		3 tbs		3 tbs		5 tbs		6 tbs	
brandy	1 tbs		1½ tbs		2 tbs		2 tbs		3 to 4 tbs		4 tbs	
almonds to make paste	225	8	350	12	450	1 lb	500	1¼ lb	800	1¾ lb	1·1 kg	2½ lb
icing sugar for royal icing	450	1 lb	700	1½ lb	900	2 lb	1·1 kg	2½ lb	1·6 kg	3½ lb	2·25 kg	5 lb

HERB TEAS

Many different herb teas are available; buy in small quantities and experiment until you find the ones that you like. Try serving scones, muffins and teabreads with herb teas instead of ordinary tea. Individual herb teas have healing properties:

Peppermint
Helps digestive upsets

Comfrey
Has cleansing
properties

Lemon Verbena and
Lemon Grass
Perks you up, good as
a tonic

Camomile
Calming and sleep-
inducing

Golden Rod
A natural diuretic,
helps get rid of excess
fluid

Lime Blossom
Helps you relax

Meringues

MAKES 6 WHOLE MERINGUES

2 egg whites
a pinch of cream of tartar

100 g/4 oz caster sugar or real
demerara sugar
300 ml/10 fl oz double cream

1 Preheat the oven to 150c/300F/Gas Mark 2. Line a baking sheet with non-stick baking parchment.
2 Put the egg whites into a clean, grease-free bowl with the cream of tartar and whisk until stiff and dry. You should be able to turn the bowl upside down without the egg white falling out.
3 Next whisk in half the sugar. When this has been absorbed, whisk in the remaining sugar, until the meringue is very stiff and glossy.
4 Drop spoonfuls of the mixture on to the prepared baking sheet, making 12 meringues in all.

5 Put the meringues into the oven, then turn down to 110c/200f/Gas Mark ¼. Bake the meringues for 1½–2 hours, until dried out.

6 Turn the oven off and leave the meringues to cool in the oven. Remove the meringues from the lining paper with a palette knife.

7 Whip the cream and use this to sandwich the meringues together in pairs. Serve as soon as possible.

Variations

HAZELNUT MERINGUES

Fold 50 g/2 oz roasted, skinned and finely ground hazelnuts into the meringues after the sugar has been added. These are delicious sandwiched with cream, as described, and served as a dessert, with Hot Chocolate Sauce (p. 449).

MINIATURE MERINGUES

Make as described, but drop heaped teaspoons of mixture on to the baking sheet; or use a piping bag fitted with a 1-cm/½-inch shell nozzle to make tiny meringues. Bake for 1½–2 hours. Sandwich together in pairs as described.

Éclairs

MAKES 8

1 quantity Choux Pastry (p. 403)   100 g/4 oz chocolate, melted
300 ml/10 fl oz whipping cream,
   whipped

1 Preheat the oven to 200c/400f/Gas Mark 6.

2 Grease a baking sheet then moisten it under the cold tap.

3 Pipe or spoon the choux pastry mixture on to the baking sheet to make strips about 10 cm/4 inches long and 2·5 cm/1 inch wide.

4 Bake for about 35 minutes, until crisp and golden.

5 Make a slit in the side of each éclair, then cool on a wire rack.

6 Just before serving, fill the éclairs with whipped cream, piping it into the slit in the side of each éclair, then carefully dip each top into the melted chocolate and leave for a few minutes to set.

Variation

PROFITEROLES

Pipe or spoon the choux pastry into small balls, about the size of walnuts. Bake for 15–20 minutes, slit and cool. Fill each with cream, then pile up in a pyramid shape on a flat serving dish or cake stand and pour some Hot Chocolate Sauce (p. 449) over the top. Serve the rest of the sauce in a jug.

PIPING TIP

Many people feel nervous about using a piping bag because they hardly get any practice. The way to become an expert is to have to hand a plastic piping bag, fitted with a star nozzle, and every time you're serving cream or have some butter icing over, have some fun piping it (and let eager children try, too!). Or even make up a batch of butter icing and keep practising with it. It's surprising how quickly you can get the knack, and once you have, it's satisfying to be able to give a cake a professional look quickly and easily.

USING BROKEN MERINGUES

Crush the meringues even more, so that they are in bite-sized pieces, then fold them into whipped cream. Or, to make a wonderful pudding, crush a whole batch of meringues, fold into 300 ml/10 fl oz lightly whipped whipping cream, then gently mix in a purée made from 450 g/1 lb blackcurrants, cooked, sweetened and sieved, to give a ripple effect. Cover and keep in the freezer until required. A useful pudding to have in the freezer as it can be served without thawing.

Glacé Icing

TO TOP A 20–23-CM/8–9 INCH ROUND CAKE

175 g/6 oz icing sugar   *1–2 tablespoons water*

1 Sift the icing sugar into a mixing bowl and beat in the water a little at a time. Continue beating in until you have a thick mixture.
2 Use the icing immediately to ice one large cake or 18 small buns.

Cream Cheese Frosting

TO TOP AND FILL, OR COAT, A 23-CM/9-INCH ROUND CAKE

225 g/8 oz cream cheese
50 g/2 oz butter, softened

50 g/2 oz soft light brown sugar
a few drops of vanilla extract

1 Put all the ingredients into a mixing bowl.
2 Beat well until thoroughly blended, light and fluffy.

Fudge Icing

$\boxed{V}$

The flavouring of fudge icing can be varied as
suggested for Simple Buttercream (p. 476).

TO TOP AND FILL, OR COAT, A 20−23-CM/8−9-
INCH ROUND CAKE

50 g/2 oz butter or vegan
  margarine
3 tablespoons water

250 g/9 oz icing sugar
a few drops of vanilla extract

1 Heat the butter or vegan margarine and water in a saucepan
until melted. Remove from the heat and sift in the icing sugar.
2 Add the vanilla and beat well. The icing will thicken up as it
cools.

French Buttercream

This is light and delicately flavoured, worth the
extra effort involved, although it isn't difficult
to make.

TO TOP AND FILL, OR COAT, A 20-CM/8-INCH
ROUND CAKE

2 egg yolks
50 g/2 oz vanilla sugar, or caster
  sugar and a few drops of vanilla
  extract

120 ml/4 fl oz milk
250 g/9 oz unsalted butter

1 Whisk the egg yolks with half the vanilla sugar or caster sugar until the mixture is pale and light.

2 Heat the milk with the rest of the sugar in a heavy-based saucepan, then pour on to the egg yolks. Return to the pan and stir until the mixture coats the back of the spoon.

3 Remove from the heat and allow to cool, then strain.

4 Beat the butter until light and fluffy, then gradually beat in the custard mixture a little at a time, and the vanilla extract if used.

Variations

COFFEE BUTTERCREAM

Make as described, adding 2 teaspoons good-quality strong instant coffee (continental or espresso type) to the hot milk and stirring until dissolved. Omit the vanilla.

CHOCOLATE BUTTERCREAM

Melt 50 g/2 oz plain chocolate and add to the butter with the custard.

Simple Buttercream

TO TOP AND FILL, OR COAT, A 20-CM/8-INCH ROUND CAKE

100 g/4 oz butter or vegan margarine	*200 g/7 oz icing sugar*
	1—2 tablespoons hot water

1 Beat the butter or vegan margarine in a mixing bowl until creamy, then sift in the icing sugar and beat again until light.

2 Add enough hot water to loosen the mixture a little, beating well.

Variations

CHOCOLATE BUTTERCREAM

Melt 50 g/2 oz plain chocolate, or dissolve 1—2 tablespoons cocoa powder in hot water; beat into the mixture.

COFFEE BUTTERCREAM

Dissolve 2 teaspoons good-quality strong instant coffee (continental or espresso type) in a little hot water; beat into the mixture.

VANILLA BUTTERCREAM

Add a few drops of vanilla extract.

LEMON OR ORANGE BUTTERCREAM

Add 1 teaspoon grated orange or lemon rind to the mixture, and replace 1 tablespoon of the water with orange or lemon juice.

REDUCED SUGAR BUTTERCREAM

Replace 50 g/2 oz of the icing sugar with skim milk powder. Beat well.

Fondant Icing

Fondant icing is easy to use because you simply roll it out. Decorations can be cut out with pastry cutters; children's pastry-making sets have some interesting shapes.

TO COAT A 20—23-CM/8—9-INCH ROUND CAKE

450 g/1 lb icing sugar
¼ teaspoon cream of tartar

1 egg white

1 Sift the icing sugar with the cream of tartar into a mixing bowl.
2 Whisk the egg white lightly, just to break it up, then gradually stir it into the icing sugar mixture, to give a firm but pliable consistency.
3 Roll the icing out on a surface dusted with icing sugar.

Almond Paste

TO COAT A 20—23-CM/8—9-INCH ROUND CAKE

450 g/1 lb ground almonds
450 g/1 lb soft light brown or
  caster sugar

1 teaspoon lemon juice
a few drops of almond essence
2 eggs, beaten

1 Mix all the ingredients together in a mixing bowl to give a pliable consistency. Do not over-work the mixture or it may become oily.
2 Use immediately, or keep wrapped in clingfilm.

Royal Icing

TO COAT A 20-CM/8-INCH ROUND CAKE

4 egg whites
900 g/2 lb icing sugar, sifted

1 tablespoon lemon juice
2 tablespoons glycerine

1 Whisk the egg whites until frothy, then gradually whisk in all the other ingredients.
2 Whisk until the mixture thickens and stands in peaks. Use immediately.

7-Minute Frosting

This icing sets crisp on the outside with a soft, marshmallowy texture inside.

TO COAT A 23-CM/9-INCH ROUND CAKE

2 large egg whites
350 g/12 oz caster sugar
4 tablespoons water

¼ teaspoon salt
¼ teaspoon cream of tartar

1 Put all the ingredients into a mixing bowl and whisk until foamy.
2 Set the bowl over a saucepan of simmering water (making sure that the bowl does not touch the water) and whisk until the mixture stands in soft peaks — about 7 minutes. Use immediately.

CRYSTALLIZED VIOLETS AND ROSE PETALS

A pretty, fragrant garnish for ice cream, cheesecake, sorbet or a special cake. Wash the violets or rose petals gently and shake dry. Beat an egg white until frothy, then dip the rose petals or violets first into this, then into caster sugar, to coat thoroughly. Spread out on baking sheets lined with non-stick baking parchment and bake in a very cool oven (lowest setting) until dry and crisp. Cool completely on wire racks, then store in an airtight tin.

Biscuits

Biscuits are easy and rewarding to make and delightful for when you want to offer something light with a cup of tea or coffee, or for giving a crisp texture to a smooth pudding such as a fruit fool or ice cream. Biscuits also make appealing gifts, packed in pretty boxes or jars, decorated with coloured ribbons, fabric or paper flowers and tissue paper. There are many different types, ranging from the quick tray bakes, such as Flapjacks, Easy Shortbread and Date Fingers, in which the mixture goes straight into the tin and is cut up after it is cooked, to the more fiddly but delicious Brandysnaps (p. 488) and Almond Tuiles (p. 486).

FREEZING BISCUITS

Biscuits freeze excellently; cool them thoroughly, then spread them out on a tray and freeze until solid. Pack in a rigid container.

To thaw, put the biscuits in a single layer on a wire rack and leave at room temperature for 30–60 minutes.

Flapjacks

One of the quickest recipes ever, flapjacks keep well in an airtight tin.

MAKES 12–16

175 g/6 oz butter or vegan margarine
175 g/6 oz real barbados sugar

2 tablespoons golden syrup
225 g/8 oz rolled oats

1 Preheat the oven to 190C/375F/Gas Mark 5.
2 Grease an 18 × 28-cm/7 × 11-inch Swiss roll tin.
3 Melt the butter or vegan margarine, sugar and syrup gently in

a saucepan. Remove from the heat and mix in the oats.

4 Spread the mixture into the tin and press down evenly with the back of the spoon. Bake for 20–30 minutes, until brown all over.

5 Mark into fingers while still hot, then leave in the tin until cold. The flapjacks become firm as they cool.

Easy Shortbread

MAKES 12 PIECES

175 g/6 oz butter or vegan
  margarine
75 g/3 oz soft light brown sugar

250 g/9 oz plain 85% wholewheat
  flour

1 Preheat the oven to 150c/300f/Gas Mark 2.

2 Beat the butter or vegan margarine with the sugar until blended, then add the flour and mix together to form a dough.

3 Knead the dough on a floured surface, then press into a 20-cm/8-inch flan tin and prick the top all over with a fork. Bake for 1¼–1½ hours until set and just beginning to turn golden.

4 Mark the shortbread into sections with a sharp knife, then leave to cool completely in the tin.

Variation

SHORTBREAD BISCUITS

Make the mixture as described, then roll it out about 3 mm/ ⅛ inch thick. Cut into circles, place on a baking sheet and bake for about 30 minutes.

Date Fingers

MAKES 12–16

225 g/8 oz dates (not sugar-rolled),
  chopped
150 ml/5 fl oz water
225 g/8 oz self-raising 85% or
  100% wholewheat flour

½ teaspoon salt
100 g/4 oz butter or vegan
  margarine
3 tablespoons cold water, to mix

1 Preheat the oven to 200c/400f/Gas Mark 6.

2 Put the dates into a saucepan with the water and cook gently for 5 minutes until soft and the liquid is absorbed.

3 Mash the dates, carefully discarding any hard pieces of stem or stone. Cool.

4 Put the flour into a mixing bowl with the salt. Rub in the fat with your fingertips until the mixture looks like fine bread-crumbs.

5 Add the 3 tablespoons water, then press the mixture together to make a dough. Roll out half to fit an 18 × 28-cm/7 × 11-inch Swiss roll tin.

6 Spread the date mixture on top of the pastry. Roll out the rest of the pastry to fit the top, press into position and trim the edges.

7 Prick the pastry all over with a fork. Bake for 30 minutes, until firm and lightly browned.

8 Cool for 30 minutes in the tin, then cut into fingers, ease out of the tin and place on a wire rack to cool completely.

Icebox Cookies

This dough will keep in the icebox of the refrigerator for up to 2 weeks, ready for you to cut thin slices off it for baking whenever you want fresh biscuits.

MAKES ABOUT 80

100 g/4 oz butter
200 g/7 oz vanilla sugar, or caster sugar and ½ teaspoon vanilla extract
1 large egg

225 g/8 oz plain 85% wholewheat flour
2 teaspoons baking powder
a pinch of salt

1 Cream the butter with the sugar and vanilla extract if used.

2 Beat in the egg, then sift the flour with the baking powder and salt on top. Mix well, to make a dough.

3 Turn the dough on to a lightly floured surface and form into a sausage about 5 cm/2 inches in diameter. Wrap in clingfilm and chill for several hours.

4 When you're ready to bake the biscuits, preheat the oven to 190c/375f/Gas Mark 5.

5 Using a sharp knife, cut 3-mm/⅛-inch slices from the cookie roll and place on baking sheets, leaving room for spreading.

6 Bake for 8–10 minutes, until the cookies are just turning brown at the edges. Remove from the oven and transfer to a wire rack to cool completely.

[V]

Oatcakes

These are thin, crisp oatcakes, based on the
recipe given in one of my favourite books,
Don't Mix Foods That Fight, by Doris Grant and
Jean Joice. Make sure the oatmeal smells and
tastes really fresh.

MAKES 16

½ teaspoon salt
1 teaspoon unsalted butter or
  vegan margarine

120 ml/4 fl oz boiling water
150 g/5 oz medium oatmeal
flour for rolling out

1 Preheat the oven to 180c/350f/Gas Mark 4.

2 Stir the salt and butter or vegan margarine into the boiling water, then add to the oatmeal in a bowl. Mix well, then leave for 2–3 minutes to allow the oatmeal to swell.

3 Turn the oat mixture on to a floured board and knead lightly.

4 Divide into 2 pieces. Roll each piece into a circle about 10 cm/4 inches in diameter, then cut each circle into 8 triangles.

5 Roll each triangle as thinly as possible, rolling from cut edge to cut edge (not from the outer edge to the point) to make a good wedge shape.

6 Using a fish slice, transfer the oatcakes to a baking sheet and bake for 20–25 minutes, carefully turning them over halfway through the cooking time, until they are pale golden, crisp and curled at the edges.

7 Transfer to a wire rack and leave to cool completely.

CHOOSING PEANUT BUTTER

Look for a variety which does not contain emulsifiers and other additives. It may have a layer of oil on top (because of the lack of emulsifiers), but this is normal; just stir the peanut butter before using it.

Crunchy Peanut Cookies

These cookies are quick to make and very popular, especially with children. They freeze well and thaw rapidly.

MAKES ABOUT 36

65 g/2½ oz butter or vegan margarine
65 g/2½ oz soft light brown sugar
65 g/2½ oz vanilla sugar, or caster sugar and a few drops of vanilla extract
1 egg
50 g/2 oz crunchy peanut butter

100 g/4 oz plain 85% wholewheat flour
1 teaspoon baking powder
½ teaspoon salt
50 g/2 oz chopped roasted peanuts (if salted, omit the ½ teaspoon salt)

1 Preheat the oven to 180c/350f/Gas Mark 4.
2 Cream the butter or vegan margarine with the sugars and vanilla, if used, then add the egg and peanut butter, and beat again until light.
3 Sift in the flour with the baking powder and salt and mix in. Add the peanuts and mix again, until thoroughly combined.
4 Roll teaspoons of the mixture into small balls, then place on a greased baking sheet, allowing plenty of room for spreading, and flatten them slightly.
5 Bake for 12–15 minutes. Cool slightly, then transfer to a wire rack to cool completely.

Variation

CHOCOLATE OR CAROB CHIP COOKIES

For this delicious variation, leave out the peanut butter and peanuts. Stir in 100 g/4 oz chocolate or carob chips and 25 g/1 oz chopped skinned hazelnuts after adding the flour.

Crunchy Orange Biscuits

MAKES 20–24

100 g/4 oz butter
75 g/3 oz soft light brown sugar
1 egg
grated rind of 1 orange
100 g/4 oz self-raising 81% or
   85% wholewheat flour

crushed wheatflakes, cornflakes or
   flaked almonds for coating
extra butter for greasing

1 Preheat the oven to 180c/350f/Gas Mark 4.
2 Grease one or two large baking sheets.
3 Cream the butter with the sugar, then beat in the egg and grated orange rind. Add the flour and mix until the ingredients are combined.
4 Roll heaped teaspoons of the mixture in crushed wheatflakes, cornflakes or flaked almonds.
5 Place the little balls on the baking sheets, allowing a little space for spreading, and flatten them slightly.
6 Bake for 15 minutes, until golden brown. Transfer to a wire rack to cool completely.

SERVING IDEAS FOR BISCUITS

Brandysnaps, filled with cream, make a luxurious accompaniment to a simple fruit salad, for a special meal.

Serve fruit salad, ice cream, sorbet or fool in a thin, crisp 'cup' made from an almond tuile.

If you haven't time to make a pudding or just want to serve something light, arrange several types of home-made biscuits in a pretty basket and offer with coffee or with little bowls of chilled strained Greek yogurt.

Crumbly Almond Biscuits $\boxed{V}$

The best biscuits of all, in the opinion of my
daughter, Claire. They are excellent for serving
with tea or coffee, or with ice creams, fools and
fruit salads.

MAKES 40

125 g/4½ oz butter or vegan
 margarine
65 g/2½ oz vanilla sugar or caster
 sugar and a few drops of vanilla
 extract
125 g/4½ oz plain 85%
 wholewheat flour

¼ teaspoon salt
25 g/1 oz flaked almonds, crushed
15 g/½ oz flaked almonds
extra butter for greasing

1 Preheat the oven to 170C/325F/Gas Mark 3.
2 Cream the butter or vegan margarine with the sugar until
light and fluffy.
3 Sift the flour with the salt into the bowl, then stir this into the
creamed mixture, with the crushed almonds.
4 Roll teaspoonfuls into small balls, then place on a greased
baking sheet, allowing plenty of room for spreading. Flatten the
biscuits with the prongs of a fork. Decorate with flaked almonds.
5 Bake for 25 minutes, until golden. Cool slightly, then transfer
to a wire rack to cool completely.

Gingersnaps

These ever-popular ginger biscuits are easy to
make, crisp and delicious. They keep well
either in the freezer or in a tin.

MAKES 36

50 g/2 oz butter
100 g/4 oz caster sugar
40 g/1½ oz golden syrup
1 tablespoon beaten egg
175 g/6 oz self-raising 85%
 wholewheat flour

1 teaspoon bicarbonate of soda
1 teaspoon ground ginger
extra butter for greasing

1 Preheat the oven to 180c/350f/Gas Mark 4.
2 Cream the butter with the sugar and syrup, then add the egg and beat again until light.
3 Sift in the wholewheat flour, bicarbonate of soda and ground ginger, then mix to a dough.
4 Divide the dough into 36 small pieces, roll each into a ball and place well apart on greased baking sheets.
5 Bake for 12–15 minutes. Cool slightly, then transfer to a wire rack to cool completely.

Variation

GINGERSNAP DESSERT LOG

Gingersnaps can be made into a delicious dessert log. Make the biscuits as described, then sandwich together with whipped double cream, to make a log shape. Cover with more cream and decorate with chopped crystallized ginger. Chill for 3–4 hours to allow the biscuits to soften in the cream and for the flavours to blend.

Almond Tuiles

These thin, crisp biscuits make an ideal
accompaniment to ice creams and light, fruity
desserts. They can also be made larger, to make
edible petal cases for holding ice cream.

MAKES 16

2 egg whites
100 g/4 oz vanilla sugar, or caster
   sugar and ½ teaspoon vanilla
   extract

50 g/2 oz plain 85% wholewheat
   flour
50 g/2 oz butter, melted
50 g/2 oz flaked almonds

1 Preheat the oven to 190c/375f/Gas Mark 5.
2 Line a large baking sheet with non-stick baking parchment.
3 Whisk the egg whites until frothy, then whisk in the sugar. Gently mix in the flour, butter and almonds.
4 Spread the mixture on the prepared baking sheet, making circles about 10 cm/4 inches across. Bake for 7–8 minutes, until flecked with golden-brown.

5 Allow the biscuits to stand for a second or two, then immediately lift them off the baking sheet with a spatula and place over the rim of a large empty bowl or over a stick balanced over 2 cans, so that they harden into a curved tuile shape.

6 Make the rest of the tuiles in the same way, re-using the paper. When the biscuits are cool, put into an airtight tin.

Variations

CIGARETTES RUSSES

Make as described, but omit the almonds. As you take the biscuits off the baking tray, roll them tightly round a greased wooden spoon handle. Cool slightly, then ease the rolled biscuits off the handle and place on a wire rack.

FLOWER CUPS FOR HOLDING ICE CREAM

To make these, draw 15-cm/6-inch circles on non-stick baking parchment and spread the uncooked mixture into these. Bake for about 10–15 minutes. As you take the biscuits off the baking sheet, put them over a lightly oiled upturned tumbler, pressing them down with your hands to make a cup shape and pulling the edges out slightly to give a petal effect.

BISCUIT-MAKING TIPS

Make the biscuits the same size and thickness so that they take the same amount of time to cook.

Use a flat baking tin or sheet to enable the heat of the oven to reach the sides of the biscuits.

Cooking sticky biscuits like brandysnaps on a tin lined with non-stick paper makes it easy to lift them off when they are done.

Leave space around the biscuits to allow them to spread during cooking. Some biscuits, such as brandysnaps, spread considerably.

Let the biscuits cool for a few minutes on the tin before removing with a spatula and placing on a wire rack to cool.

Biscuits which are to be rolled or shaped after baking, such as brandysnaps and almond tuiles, need to cool on the baking sheet until they are firm enough to lift but still pliable. Once you've made the first batch, you soon recognize this stage. If the biscuits harden too much, they will soften again if you pop them back into the oven for a minute or two.

V

Brandysnaps

A delicious treat on their own, and also an
excellent accompaniment to a creamy pudding
or fruit salad, brandysnaps are easy to make if
you use non-stick baking parchment and don't
try to roll them up too soon.

MAKES 20

50 g/2 oz butter or vegan
  margarine
100 g/4 oz caster sugar
50 g/2 oz golden syrup
50 g/2 oz plain 85% wholewheat
  flour, sifted
½ teaspoon ground ginger

½ teaspoon grated lemon rind
a little oil

FOR THE FILLING (OPTIONAL)
150 ml/5 fl oz double or non-dairy
  cream, whipped, with 1–2
  tablespoons brandy (optional)

1 Preheat the oven to 180c/350f/Gas Mark 4.
2 Melt the butter or vegan margarine, sugar and syrup gently in
a small saucepan.
3 Remove from the heat and stir in the flour, ginger and lemon
rind. Cool.
4 Line a large baking sheet with non-stick baking parchment.
5 Drop 2 heaped teaspoons of the mixture on to the baking
sheet, placing them well apart, then flatten them slightly. Bake
for 7–8 minutes, until evenly browned.
6 Cool on the tray for 3–4 minutes, until you can comfortably
pick up the brandysnaps. Quickly roll them up, by wrapping
them round the oiled handle of a wooden spoon. Slide them off
on to a wire rack. If the brandysnaps harden before you manage
to roll them up, pop them back into the oven for a minute or two
to soften up.
7 Make the rest of the brandysnaps in the same way; the same
non-stick baking parchment can be used for the whole batch.
8 Serve the brandysnaps plain, or fill the ends with whipped
cream, with the brandy added if liked, using a teaspoon or a
piping bag fitted with a shell nozzle.

Bread and Scones

Nothing ensures your reputation as a good cook more quickly than making your own bread, and there is something particularly satisfying about being able to offer friends and family your own home-baked bread. Yet making bread from a simple recipe is no more difficult than making a cake. This chapter contains my favourite recipes for yeast breads together with a selection of non-yeasted breads and scones, which are also easy to bake and make a pleasant change. If you like bread, it's worth making a bigger batch of the Quick and Easy Wholewheat Bread (p. 491); simply double or treble all the ingredients.

Easy Wholewheat Scones

Serve with butter and clear honey, or with jam and cream.

MAKES 10

225 g/8 oz 100% brown flour
2 teaspoons baking powder
50 g/2 oz butter

25 g/1 oz sugar
1 egg, whisked and made up to
150 ml/5 fl oz with milk

1 Preheat the oven to 220c/425f/Gas Mark 7.
2 Sift the flour with the baking powder into a mixing bowl, then add the butter and rub in with your fingertips. Mix in the sugar. Add the egg and milk and mix to a soft but not sticky dough.
3 Turn the dough out on to a floured board and knead lightly, then press out to a depth of at least 1 cm/½ inch.
4 Cut the scones out with a 5-cm/2-inch round cutter and place them on a floured baking sheet.

5 Bake for 12–15 minutes, until the scones are golden-brown and the sides spring back when lightly pressed. Cool on a wire rack, or serve immediately.

Variations

VEGAN SCONES

Use 150 ml/5 fl oz soya milk instead of the egg and milk, and 75 g/3 oz vegan margarine instead of the butter, for extra richness.

CHEESE SCONES

These are delicious to eat warm from the oven, for a quick lunch or supper. They're good buttered, with a little salad, and some fresh, firm tomatoes and crisp celery sticks. Omit the sugar. Add ½ teaspoon mustard powder and 40 g/1½ oz grated cheese to the mixture. Sprinkle another 40 g/1½ oz grated cheese on top of the scones before baking.

RAISIN SCONES

Add 50–100 g/2–4 oz raisins to the mixture. ½ teaspoon mixed spice or cinnamon is also a pleasant addition.

LIGHT BROWN SCONES

Replace the flour with 85% flour, or half wholewheat and half plain unbleached flour.

CRANBERRY SCONES

For this Christmas version, add 100 g/4 oz cooked sweetened cranberries to the mixture and a good pinch of ground cloves. Cook as above.

GHEE

A cooking fat which is much used in Indian cookery. To make ghee, melt 100–225 g/4–8 oz unsalted butter slowly in a saucepan, then cook it very gently for 30–45 minutes, until the sediment at the bottom of the pan has become a golden-brown. Strain the butter through a sieve lined with surgical gauze. Ghee can also be bought from supermarkets and Indian shops, and vegetable oil ghee is available.

Bran, Honey and Sultana Muffins [V]

These healthy muffins are quick and easy to
make and are delicious served warm from the
oven. You can use raisins instead of sultanas or
a mixture of both, if preferred.

MAKES 12

75 g/3 oz plain 100% wholewheat
   flour
25 g/1 oz bran
3 teaspoons baking powder
a pinch of salt

75 g/3 oz sultanas
50 g/2 oz clear honey
4 tablespoons sunflower oil
100 ml/3–4 fl oz water
a little extra oil for greasing

1 Preheat the oven to 180c/350f/Gas Mark 4. Grease a 12-section
bun tin.
2 Put the flour and bran into a mixing bowl with the baking
powder, salt and sultanas. Add the honey, sunflower oil and
water.
3 Mix well to make a batter-like consistency.
4 Spoon the mixture into the bun tin, dividing the mixture
equally among the sections.
5 Bake for 15–20 minutes, until the muffins are risen and feel
firm to a light touch. Serve warm.

Quick and Easy Wholewheat Bread [V]

This bread can be made in a variety of shapes.

MAKES ONE 450-G/1-LB LOAF

325 ml/8–10 fl oz tepid water
1 teaspoon sugar
2 teaspoons dried yeast
450 g/1 lb 100% wholewheat flour
   or 350 g/12 oz wholewheat flour
   and 100 g/4 oz unbleached white
   flour
2 teaspoons salt
butter or oil for greasing

TOPPING
sesame seeds
rolled oats
poppy seeds
cracked wheat or wholewheat
   flour

1 Put half the water into a measuring jug with half the sugar and the yeast; mix, then leave for 5−10 minutes to froth.

2 Grease a 450-g/1-lb loaf tin generously.

3 Put the flour into a bowl with the remaining sugar and the salt and make a well in the centre.

4 Pour in the frothed-up yeast, add the rest of the water and mix to a dough.

5 Turn out on to a clean work surface and knead for 10 minutes, until the dough is smooth, supple and silky.

6 Flatten the dough into a rectangle and gently roll it up to fit the tin. Put the roll into the tin with the fold underneath. Push it down into the sides and corners to give a nice domed shape to the loaf.

7 Cover with a clean tea-towel wrung out in hot water and put in a warm place for about 30 minutes to rise.

8 Preheat the oven to 180c/350f/Gas Mark 4.

9 When the dough has doubled in size and come right up out of the tin, sprinkle with any of the topping ingredients and bake for 40−45 minutes.

10 Turn out of the tin. It should sound hollow when you bang it on the base. Cool on a wire rack.

Variations

HERB AND ONION BREAD

Add 1 small finely chopped onion and ½ teaspoon each of oregano (or dill) and rosemary. Serve this bread warm.

THE GRANT LOAF

For this extra speedy variation, increase the water to 350 ml/12 fl oz to make a soft mixture. Don't knead; divide the mixture into two, shape the pieces as described and put each into a greased 450-g/1-lb tin. Leave to rise until the sides of the loaves are about 5 mm/¼ inch from the top of the tins. Bake for 30 minutes at 200c/400f/Gas Mark 6.

QUICK WHOLEWHEAT ROLLS

Rub 50 g/2 oz butter or vegan margarine into the flour, then use 150 ml/5 fl oz each of milk (or soya milk) and water to make the dough. Knead for 5 minutes, then put the dough into a clean, lightly oiled bowl, cover and leave in a warm place for about 1 hour, until doubled in bulk. Shape into 8–10 rolls, or rounds, plaits, knots, tricorns or miniature cottage loaves, and place well apart on a floured baking sheet. Cover and leave in a warm place for 15–20 minutes, until well risen. Bake for 15–20 minutes at 220c/425f/Gas Mark 7.

HOT CROSS BUNS

Make the dough as described for quick rolls. After the first rising, knead into the dough ½ teaspoon each of mixed spice, cinnamon and grated nutmeg, 75 g/3 oz currants, 50 g/2 oz chopped mixed peel and 25 g/1 oz sugar. Form into rolls, cut crosses out of 75 g/3 oz shortcrust pastry and place on top. Bake for 20 minutes. Heat 25 g/1 oz caster sugar in 2 tablespoons milk until dissolved; brush over the buns.

Poppyseed Plait

This is an attractive bread with a delicate flavour and a golden crust coated with poppy seeds.

MAKES 1 LARGE PLAIT

25 g/1 oz fresh yeast or 15 g/½ oz dried yeast plus ½ teaspoon sugar
450 ml/15 fl oz warm milk
700 g/1½ lb strong plain unbleached white flour

1½ teaspoons salt
1½ teaspoons sugar
50 g/2 oz butter
TO GLAZE
1 small egg, beaten
poppy seeds

1 Blend the yeast into the milk; for dried yeast, add the sugar, too, and leave for 10–15 minutes until frothy.
2 Put the flour, salt and sugar into a large mixing bowl and rub in the butter with the fingertips. Add the frothed-up yeast liquid and mix to a dough.
3 Knead for 10 minutes, put into a bowl, cover with clingfilm and leave until doubled in bulk – 1 hour in a warm place.
4 Knock back the dough, knead briefly, then make a plait: divide the dough into 3 equal pieces, roll each into a sausage

about 30 cm/12 inches long, fat in the middle and tapering at the ends. Start plaiting from the centre, finishing the ends of the plait off in a neat point.

5 Place on a greased baking sheet, cover and leave to prove for 30 minutes, until puffy. Preheat the oven to 230C/450F/Gas Mark 8.

6 Brush the plait with beaten egg, sprinkle with poppy seeds and bake for about 35 minutes. Cool on a wire rack.

Variations

VEGAN POPPYSEED PLAIT

Use soya milk instead of dairy milk and vegan margarine instead of butter. Brush the loaf with soya milk instead of egg.

SWEDISH TEA RING

Make the dough as described and let it rise in the bowl. Instead of making a plait, roll out to a rectangle 23 × 30 cm/9 × 12 inches. Brush with melted butter, then roll up like a Swiss roll, and join the ends to make a ring. Place on a baking sheet and using kitchen scissors make diagonal slashes 2·5 cm/1 inch apart. Pull open the cut sections. Leave to prove for 30 minutes, then bake at 190C/375F/Gas Mark 5 for 30–35 minutes. Decorate with icing, glacé cherries and almonds.

GUIDE TO BREAD RISING TIMES

Place	First rising times	Second rising times	Place	First rising times	Second rising times
In a warm place, 23C/74F, e.g. an airing cupboard, by a pilot light, near a radiator	45–60 mins	30 mins	In a refrigerator (brush with oil and cover bowl with clingfilm to prevent hard crust forming; leave at room temperature for 30 minutes before baking)	up to 24 hrs	up to 12 hrs
At room temperature, 18–21C/65–70F	1½–2 hrs	40–50 mins			
In a cool room or larder	8–12 hrs	2–3 hrs			

Soda Bread

Soda bread needs to be eaten the day it is made,
although it makes good toast the next day. I like
it particularly with clear honey.

MAKES ONE 450-G/1-LB LOAF

450 g/1 lb plain wholewheat and
   unbleached white flour mixed,
   or plain wheatmeal or scofa
   flour
1 teaspoon salt

2 teaspoons bicarbonate of soda
25 g/1 oz butter, softened
300 ml/10 fl oz buttermilk, sour
   milk, or milk warmed with 1
   tablespoon vinegar to sour it

1 Preheat the oven to 220c/425f/Gas Mark 7. Flour a baking
sheet.
2 Sift the flour, salt and bicarbonate of soda into a mixing bowl.
Add the butter and rub in with the fingertips until the mixture
resembles fine breadcrumbs.
3 Make a well in the centre and pour in the milk, then gradually
mix together to make a dough.
4 Turn the dough on to a floured board and knead it lightly,
then form it into a round loaf.
5 Put the loaf on the prepared baking sheet and cut a cross
shape in the top, using a sharp knife.
6 Bake the loaf for 30–35 minutes until it has risen and is
golden-brown and crusty. Cool on a wire rack.

MEASURING GOLDEN SYRUP OR HONEY

If you can set your scales, place
your mixing bowl or saucepan
on the scale, set to zero, and pour
in the golden syrup or honey
until you have the right weight.

   Or put the jar of honey or tin of
golden syrup on the scales and
remove it from the jar until the

scales show you've taken out the
quantity you need. Use a heated
spoon to remove the honey or
syrup from the jar, and flour the
inside of your scale pan if you
wish to transfer the honey or
syrup to another container.

Chapattis

These round unleavened breads make an
excellent accompaniment to curry or a lentil
soup. Brush with a little melted butter or ghee
before serving, if you like.

MAKES 12

250 g/9 oz plain 100%
   wholewheat flour
1½ teaspoons vegetable oil or ghee

1 teaspoon salt
about 150 ml/5 fl oz cold water

1 Put the flour into a mixing bowl with the oil or ghee, salt and
water and mix to a soft dough.
2 Turn the dough out on to a floured surface and knead for 5
minutes. Cover the dough with a damp cloth and leave for 2−3
hours, then knead again for a few minutes.
3 Divide the dough into 12 equal pieces. Form each into a ball,
then roll out to a circle 15−20 cm/6−8 inches in diameter.
4 Fry the chapattis on both sides in an ungreased frying pan
until set and lightly flecked with brown.
5 Pile the chapattis up on a plate as they're cooked, covering
with a piece of foil to prevent them from drying out.

Wholewheat Banana Tea Bread

Serve this tea bread sliced and buttered.

MAKES ONE 450-G/1-LB LOAF

50 g/2 oz butter
50 g/2 oz real barbados sugar
75 g/3 oz golden syrup or clear
   honey
225 g/8 oz self-raising 100%
   wholewheat flour

50 g/2 oz walnuts, chopped
2 ripe bananas, peeled and mashed
1 egg, beaten
extra butter for greasing

1 Preheat the oven to 180c/350f/Gas Mark 4. Grease a 450-g/
1-lb loaf tin and line with a strip of greased greaseproof paper to
cover the base of the tin and extend up the narrow sides.

2 Heat the butter, sugar and golden syrup or honey gently in a small saucepan until melted. Set aside to cool until you can comfortably put your hand against the saucepan: stand the pan in a bowl of cold water if you're in a hurry.

3 Put the flour into a mixing bowl with the chopped walnuts and mashed bananas. Add the cooled melted mixture and the egg. Mix well.

4 Spoon the mixture into the prepared tin. Bake for 40 minutes, or until a warmed skewer inserted into the centre of the loaf comes out clean.

5 Turn out on to a wire rack to cool. Strip off the lining paper.

Variations

VEGAN BANANA TEA BREAD

Use vegan margarine and 1 extra teaspoon baking powder. Replace the egg with 2 tablespoons soya milk.

DATE AND WALNUT LOAF

Make as described, using 100 g/4 oz chopped cooking dates and 2–3 tablespoons milk, instead of the bananas.

Sandwiches and Quick Snacks

Popular with everyone and the most practical of foods, sandwiches are also infinitely variable. They can be wafer-thin and delicate, enclosing a small amount of piquant filling, or rolled around some delicacy such as an asparagus spear, or rolled and sliced to make pinwheels, for serving at a formal occasion, with drinks or elegant cups of tea. Or sandwiches can be filling and easy-going for eating with friends round the kitchen table.

Pinwheel Sandwiches

Easy to make and attractive for a children's party or as part of a canapés selection. Prepare them in advance as they need chilling in the fridge.

MAKES ABOUT 50

100 g/4 oz butter, softened, or
  vegan margarine
2 tablespoons finely chopped
  parsley
2 tablespoons very finely chopped
  sweet red pepper
½ large sliced wholewheat loaf

TO GARNISH
thyme sprigs

1 Blend half the butter or vegan margarine with the parsley; in a separate bowl, blend the remaining half of the butter or vegan margarine with the chopped red pepper.
2 Cut the crusts off the bread and flatten each slice with a rolling pin.
3 Spread half the slices quite generously with the parsley butter and half with the red pepper butter.
4 Roll up the slices like a Swiss roll, from a long end.

5 Chill for 30–60 minutes, then slice thinly into rounds with a sharp knife and arrange on a plate to reveal the pinwheel effect.
6 Garnish with thyme sprigs.

BREAD FOR SANDWICHES

The bread for sandwiches can be soft and light or crusty; any shade ranging from white to black, through various shades of brown, with or without added grains or flavourings. The bread can be a slicing loaf, cut either downwards or across; it can be a pitta pocket, French stick, slightly hollowed out and packed with filling, then cut into lengths for feeding a crowd; or it can be a soft or crusty roll, bap or scone.

Club Sandwich

V

A chunky club sandwich, with layers of toasted bread and different fillings, turns a sandwich into a complete meal.

SERVES 1

3 slices wholewheat bread, toasted
butter or vegan margarine
a little wholegrain mustard
2 lettuce leaves
1 small tomato, sliced
a little Mayonnaise (p. 231), (optional)

1 slice Cashew Nut Roast (p. 345)
1 tablespoon sweet chutney or pickle
TO FINISH
4 stuffed olives

1 Spread one piece of toast with a little butter or vegan margarine and mustard and arrange the lettuce leaves, tomato slices and mustard or mayonnaise on top.
2 Spread another piece of toast on both sides with butter or vegan margarine, then top with the nut roast and chutney. Place on top of the other toast.
3 Spread the remaining piece of toast with butter or vegan margarine and place, spread-side down, on top.
4 Press down. Cut the sandwich into quarters.
5 Spear each quarter with a cocktail stick and decorate with a stuffed olive.

TOASTED SANDWICH FILLINGS

Cheese, perhaps with tomato, pickle or thinly sliced onion is probably the best-known and most popular filling, but there are many other possibilities. The filling should be moist, but not so runny that it runs out. Aubergine Dip (p.219), Mushroom and Herb Terrine (p.222), Hummus (p. 217) or Guacamole (p. 218) are also good, as are red kidney beans, perhaps mashed with some tomato or tomato sauce. Cooked cauliflower florets mashed with mayonnaise and grated nutmeg, and creamy coleslaw also make good fillings, and, for perfection, cooked asparagus with lemony mayonnaise.

Toasted Avocado Sandwich

If you haven't got a sandwich toaster, toast two pieces of bread on one side, spread with the filling, grill until heated through, then sandwich them together.

SERVES 1

½ ripe avocado pear, peeled and stoned
1 spring onion, finely chopped
1–2 teaspoons lemon juice
salt and freshly ground black pepper

2 slices wholewheat bread
butter or vegan margarine for spreading

1 Heat a sandwich toaster.
2 Mash the avocado with the spring onion, lemon juice, salt and pepper.
3 Butter the bread on one side. Spread the unbuttered sides with the avocado mixture and sandwich together.
4 Toast for 4–5 minutes, until crisp and golden-brown. Serve immediately.

Open Sandwiches

8 slices wholewheat or rye bread
butter or vegan margarine for
  spreading
8 radiccio leaves
½ endive
½ quantity Pink Potato Salad (p.
  249)

1 × 425-g/15-oz can artichoke
  hearts, drained and sliced
8 radishes, sliced
8 dill sprigs, or a few chopped
  chives

1 Spread the bread lightly with butter or vegan margarine, then place on a flat serving dish.

2 Put one radiccio leaf and a sprig of endive on each piece of bread.

3 Top the radiccio with some Pink Potato Salad, artichoke heart slices, radish slices and dill or chives, making an attractive arrangement.

OPEN SANDWICH TOPPINGS

☐ Lettuce, curd cheese, sliced ripe pear, halved black grapes

☐ Lettuce, scrambled egg, asparagus spears, parsley

☐ Watercress, sliced Lentil Loaf (p.318), cranberry mayonnaise or mango chutney

☐ Lettuce, slices of cheese and tomato, chopped parsley, stuffed green olives

☐ Lettuce, Hummus (p.217), paprika, black olives and a drizzling of olive oil

☐ Radiccio, Guacamole (p.218) or mashed avocado, pink peppercorns

☐ Watercress, coarsely grated carrot, mayonnaise, sliced tomato, Black Olive Pâté (p. 383)

Filled Pitta Pocket

1 wholewheat pitta bread
2 lettuce leaves, shredded
1 tomato, sliced

¼ quantity Continental Lentil and
  Walnut Salad (p. 236)

1 Slit the pitta bread at the top and ease it open, to make a pocket for the filling.

2 Fill the pitta bread with the lettuce, tomato and lentil salad.

FRENCH BREAD, TACOS AND PITTA BREAD FILLINGS

Build these up into glorious colourful extravaganzas with your choice of:

☐ Juicy black olives, chopped fresh herbs, walnuts or pecans

☐ Cubes of cold nut or lentil loaf

☐ Sliced, grated or diced cheese

☐ Wedges of hardboiled egg

☐ Favourite Coleslaw (p. 242)

☐ Sliced red or green pepper, avocado pear, cooked asparagus tips or artichoke hearts

☐ Grated carrot, cauliflower, cooked or raw button mushrooms, sliced or whole

☐ Mayonnaise (p.231), Guacamole (p.218), Sweet Pepper Dressing (p.234)

☐ Shredded crisp lettuce, sliced tomato, spring onion, cucumber

---

Filled French Bread

SERVES 4

2 wholewheat French sticks
butter, vegan margarine, mustard
    or mayonnaise
1 lettuce, washed and shredded
225 g/8 oz tomatoes, sliced
100 g/4 oz beansprouts

1 onion, peeled and sliced
1 × 425-g/15-oz can red kidney
    beans, drained
salt and freshly ground black
    pepper

1 Make a slit down the side of each French stick and scoop out a little of the crumb.

2 Spread the inside of each French loaf thinly with butter, vegan margarine, mustard or mayonnaise.

3 Fill each loaf with the vegetables and beans, and season with salt and pepper.

4 Press the slits together, wrap the loaves tightly in foil and chill until required, then cut each in half.

SCHOOL LUNCH BOX SANDWICH FILLINGS

Children have their own definite ideas about these — one of my daughters would only ever eat plain yeast extract sandwiches — and they generally like their sandwiches to look as much like everyone else's as possible. Here are some ideas:

- ☐ Yeast extract, miso, salad cream, peanut butter, sesame spread, curd or cream cheese with cucumber, lettuce, beansprouts, tomato or grated carrot
- ☐ Grated carrot mixed with mayonnaise and chopped herbs or raisins

- ☐ Chopped hardboiled egg mixed with salad cream or milk, or scrambled egg, with cress
- ☐ Curd or cream cheese with finely chopped nuts or dates
- ☐ Mashed cooked red kidney beans with salad
- ☐ Sliced or grated cheese with lettuce, tomato or cucumber

- ☐ Sliced banana, with or without peanut butter or sesame spread
- ☐ Honey and finely ground nuts

Quick Bread Pizza   [V]

SERVES 4

1 round or oval wholewheat loaf,
  about 450 g/1 lb
olive oil
2 large onions, peeled and sliced
2 garlic cloves, crushed
1 × 425-g/15-oz can chopped
  tomatoes

oregano
salt and freshly ground black
  pepper
100 g/4 oz cheese, grated
8 black olives

1 Preheat the oven to 220c/425f/Gas Mark 7. Cut the loaf in half horizontally and scoop out some of the crumbs. Brush inside and outside the halved loaf with oil and place on a baking sheet.
2 Fry the onions in a tablespoon of oil for 10 minutes, then add

the garlic and fry for a further minute or two.

3 Remove from heat and add tomatoes and a little oregano, salt and pepper.

4 Spoon the mixture on to the bread halves and sprinkle with grated cheese.

5 Bake for 15 minutes, then put on the olives and bake for a further 5–10 minutes. Serve hot.

Asparagus Rolls

A pleasant teatime or drinks party nibble.

MAKES ABOUT 40

½ *sliced large wholewheat loaf*
butter or vegan margarine

1 × 225-g/8-oz *packet frozen asparagus spears, cooked and drained, or* 1 × 350-g/12-oz *can asparagus spears, drained*

1 Cut the crusts off the bread, then flatten each slice with a rolling pin.

2 Spread the slices thinly with butter or vegan margarine, then wrap each piece of bread round an asparagus spear, cutting off any spare bread, so that the edges meet but do not overlap.

3 Cut each roll into 2 or 3 pieces so that they are a manageable size for eating.

4 Cover with clingfilm and keep in a cool place until needed.

Cheese on Toast

SERVES 1

1–2 *slices wholewheat bread*
75–100 g/3–4 oz *cheese, grated*

1–2 *tablespoons milk*
freshly ground black pepper

1 Heat the grill to high. Toast the bread on one side.

2 Blend the cheese to a paste with the milk, and season with pepper.

3 Spread the cheese mixture on the untoasted side of the bread and grill until puffed up and golden-brown. Serve immediately.

Mozzarella in Carrozza

SERVES 2

1 Mozzarella cheese
4 slices bread, crusts removed

2 eggs
oil for shallow frying

1 Cut the cheese into thin slices and arrange on 2 of the slices of bread. Top with the remaining slices.
2 Beat the eggs, then strain them into a shallow dish.
3 Put the sandwiches in the egg, leaving them to soak it up, and turning them over once.
4 Shallow-fry the sandwiches on both sides in a little oil, until golden-brown and crisp. Drain on kitchen paper and serve immediately.

ELEGANT SANDWICH FILLINGS

- ☐ Scrambled egg with asparagus tips
- ☐ Duxelles or mushroom pâté
- ☐ Cream cheese or curd cheese with chopped herbs or chopped nuts
- ☐ Yeast extract or a thin spreading of light miso and wafer-thin cucumber slices
- ☐ Ripe avocado mashed with a little vinaigrette
- ☐ Finely grated cheese blended with cream, milk or curd cheese
- ☐ Herb butters (p.167)
- ☐ Hummus (p. 217) with a little Black Olive Pâté (p. 383)

ICED TEA AND COFFEE

Make the tea as described on p. 465, then strain and chill. Serve with crushed ice and a slice of lemon and a sprig of mint or lemon balm, if liked. Iced herb teas make a specially good summer drink. For a fruity flavour, try Leslie Kenton's tip of adding a sliced peach to the tea before chilling.

For iced coffee, use the filter method, then chill. Serve in tall glasses with ice. Top with a spoonful of whipped cream, if liked, and hand sugar separately.

Sandwich Gâteau

This savoury gâteau looks attractive on a party
table, when sliced to reveal the coloured layers.

SERVES 8

100 g/4 oz butter, softened
1 tablespoon finely chopped
  parsley
1 tablespoon finely chopped red
  pepper
2 hardboiled eggs, finely chopped
1–2 tablespoons Mayonnaise (p.
  231)
salt and freshly ground black
  pepper

10 slices wholewheat bread
¼ quantity Hummus (p. 217)
450 g/1 lb curd cheese
TO GARNISH
whole chives
thin radish slices
endive

1 Beat the butter and divide into equal portions. Beat the
parsley into one half and the pepper into the other half.
2 Mix the eggs with mayonnaise to bind; season with salt and
pepper.
3 Cut the crusts off the bread. Place 2 slices side by side on a
serving platter and spread with the parsley butter.
4 Put 2 more slices on top, spread with the red pepper butter.
Continue in this way with the rest of the bread, using the
hummus and egg mayonnaise, building up the layers to make a
gâteau shape. Finish with a layer of bread.
5 Spread the curd cheese over the top and sides of the gâteau.
Arrange whole chives in a lattice pattern over the top of the
gâteau. Halve the radish slices and arrange between the chives
and around the edge of the gâteau. Arrange endive around the
base of the gâteau. Chill for 1 hour in the fridge before serving.

Preserves and Chutneys

Home-made jams, jellies, preserves and
chutneys add a delightful touch of luxury to a
meal, yet are both easy and satisfying to make. If
you're lucky enough to have fruit trees and
bushes, a cheap source of fruit is readily
available; but even if you have to buy them, at
the peak of their seasons fruit and vegetables are
likely to be inexpensive. Delicious with home-
made bread and scones, jams and jellies also
make excellent fillings and toppings. Chutneys
and pickles, with their piquant, sweet and sour
flavour, are excellent with cold nut and lentil
roasts and burgers.

Rose Petal Jam

Use petals from unsprayed roses which have
not been growing near a busy road. Cut away
the white triangle at the base of each petal.

MAKES 900 G/2 LB

150 g/5 oz scented rose petals,
    washed and trimmed
750 ml/1¼ pints water
185 ml/6 fl oz lemon juice

600 g/1¼ lb sugar
5 tablespoons commercial pectin
3 tablespoons rose water

1 Put the petals, water, lemon juice and sugar into a large
saucepan and heat gently until the sugar has dissolved.
2 Bring to the boil, then cover and simmer gently for 30
minutes.
3 Add the pectin and rose water, stir well, then boil hard for 5
minutes.
4 Test for a set (p.510); if the jam is not ready, test again in 2
minutes, and keep testing until a set is reached.
5 Cool slightly, then pour into warmed sterilized jars (p.510).
Cover, seal and label when completely cold.

SUGAR FOR PRESERVES

Granulated sugar is the cheapest and just as good as the more expensive preserving sugars (which give a particularly clear jelly) for normal use. Real brown sugar can be used, and gives a dark colour and mellow flavour to chutney and marmalade, but is not successful in jam, in my opinion. Whatever kind of sugar you use, make sure it is completely dissolved before the jam is boiled, or it may not set properly.

Plum Jam

Do not use any bruised or over-ripe plums for making jam as they will not give a good set and could cause the jam to ferment.

MAKES 2·25 KG/5 LB

1·4 kg/3 lb plums
450 ml/15 fl oz water

1·4 kg/3 lb sugar
a knob of butter

1 Wash the plums, then put them into a preserving pan with the water and simmer for about 30 minutes, until the fruit is soft.
2 Remove the pan from the heat and stir in the sugar. Stir well until the sugar has completely dissolved.
3 Bring to the boil, then boil hard for 10–15 minutes, stirring often.
4 Test for a set (p.510), then, when this point is reached, stir in the butter.
5 Using a slotted spoon, remove the plum stones from the top of the jam.
6 Let the jam stand for 15 minutes to settle, then pour it into warmed, sterilized jars (p.510). Cover, seal and label when completely cold.

Variations

DAMSON JAM

Use the same recipe but you'll only need 1·1 kg/2½ lb of fruit. Test for a set after 7–10 minutes.

BLACKCURRANT JAM

Use 900 g/2 lb blackcurrants, 900 ml/1½ pints water and 1·4 kg/3 lb sugar. Simmer the blackcurrants for 45 minutes, until the skins are really tender, before adding the sugar.

GOOSEBERRY JAM

Use 1·4 kg/3 lb gooseberries, 600 ml/1 pint water and 1·4 kg/3 lb sugar. Cook the gooseberries in the water for 30 minutes, until soft.

Strawberry Jam

MAKES 2·25 KG/5 LB

1·8 kg/4 lb small, slightly under-ripe strawberries, hulled and wiped

1·6 kg/3½ lb sugar
3 tablespoons fresh lemon juice
a small knob of butter

1 Put the strawberries into an enamel or stainless steel preserving pan with the sugar and leave for an hour or so, or overnight if convenient.
2 Add the lemon juice and heat slowly, over a very low heat, until the sugar has dissolved.
3 Return to the heat, bring to the boil and boil rapidly for 7–8 minutes, then remove from the heat and test for a set (see below).
4 If the jam isn't ready, return to the heat and test again in 2–3 minutes' time. Keep on testing until a set is reached.
5 Remove from the heat and stir in the butter.
6 Let the jam stand for 30 minutes, for the fruit to settle, then stir gently and pour into warmed, sterilized jars (see below). Cover, seal and label when cold.

Variation

RASPBERRY JAM

Make this in the same way, omitting the lemon juice, and using 1·8 kg/4 lb raspberries and 1·8 kg/4 lb sugar. After adding the sugar, boil the jam for about 30 minutes. Test for a set, then add the butter. Cover, seal and label when cold.

MAKING JAMS AND JELLIES

Preserving Pan

You need a preserving pan, or an extra-large saucepan or saucepan part of a pressure-cooker, because the mixture needs plenty of room. Because of this, it's best not to make too much at a time. If you're using a microwave — which is a very clean way to make preserves — it's best to make in even smaller quantities (see recipe) and to use a large bowl.

Preparing the Jam Jars

Wash the jam jars thoroughly and sterilize them by drying them off in a cool oven, 140c/ 275F/Gas Mark 1. Fill the jars while they are still warm.

Testing for a Set

Setting point is reached when the jam or jelly reaches 104c/ 220F on a sugar thermometer, or when a teaspoon of the mixture put on to a chilled saucer, and chilled for a few minutes in the freezing compartment of the fridge, wrinkles at the edges and does not run together again when you run your finger through it. It's important to take the pan off the heat while you test for a set, to avoid overcooking.

De-scumming Jam

Stirring in a knob of butter after setting point is reached helps disperse the surface scum on jam.

Potting Jam

Put circles of waxed paper on top of the jam immediately you pour it into the jars, when it is still very hot, or wait until it is completely cold. Putting the circles on warm jam may cause condensation and encourage mould.

Covers for the Jam Jars

Use cellophane covers for jam and plastic clip-on or Porasan covers for chutney. Wipe the jars after filling while still warm, but stick on the labels when the jars have cooled.

Microwave Strawberry Jam

MAKES 700 G/1½ LB

450 g/1 lb strawberries, washed and hulled

4 tablespoons fresh lemon juice
350 g/12 oz caster sugar

1 Put the strawberries into a 2·4-litre/4-pint bowl with the lemon juice. Cook, uncovered, on full power for 5−6 minutes, until the strawberries are soft.

2 Add the sugar, stirring until dissolved.

3 Return the bowl to the oven and cook on full power for 20 minutes, stirring at the end of every 5 minutes.

4 Test for a set (see opposite); if the jam has not yet reached setting point, return the bowl to the overn for a further 1½ minutes, then test again. Continue this process until the jam sets.

5 Leave the jam to cool until tepid, then pour it into warmed, sterilized jars (see opposite).

6 Cover, seal and label when cold.

FRUIT–SUGAR PROPORTIONS

Jam
For fruits rich in pectin and acid, such as cooking apples, red and blackcurrants and gooseberries, the proportions are 600–700 g/ 1¼–1½ lb sugar to each 450 g/ 1 lb of fruit. For fruits with a moderate amount of pectin and acid, such as blackberries, loganberries and raspberries, allow 450 g/ 1 lb sugar to 450 g/1 lb fruit.

Jelly
Basic proportions are 450 g/1 lb sugar to each 600 ml/1 pint fruit juice.

Sugar-free Mixed Berry Jam [V]

Although this delicious, fruity jam should be made in small quantities and kept in the refrigerator, it can be made from frozen berries throughout the year. The apple juice concentrate can be bought at health shops. As well as its use in preserves, and, well diluted, as a drink, concentrated apple juice makes a healthy sugar replacement in cakes, puddings and other sweet treats.

MAKES 700 G/1½ LB

225 g/8 oz strawberries, hulled
225 g/8 oz blackberries
225 g/8 oz gooseberries, topped and tailed

225 g/8 oz apple juice concentrate, weighed in a polythene container

1 Wash the berries, then purée half of them in a blender or food processor and place in a large saucepan with the rest of the fruit.
2 Simmer gently until the fruit is cooked.
3 Add the apple juice concentrate and boil for 15 minutes, then test for a set (p.510). If this is not achieved, continue to boil, testing frequently, until setting point.
4 Remove from the heat and cool slightly, then pour into warmed, sterilized jars (p.510). Cover, seal and label when cold.
5 Store in a cool place for up to 4 weeks, or in the refrigerator.

SUGARLESS JAM AND JELLY

I'm indebted to Jackie Applebee, of the Wholefood Cookery School, for this information on making sugarless jams and jellies, and for the sugarless jam recipes included in this book. The basic proportions are 450–700 g/1–1½ lb fruit to 225 g/8 oz concentrated apple juice weighed in a polythene container. You cook the fruit in just enough water to prevent sticking (soft fruits such as raspberries and strawberries can be puréed in a blender or food processor and heated gently without water), then add the apple juice concentrate and boil until a set is reached. Make this jam in small quantities and store in the refrigerator.

 Crab Apple Jelly

A delightful, sharp-tasting jelly, good with nut roasts.

MAKES 900 G — 1·4 KG/2–3 LB

1·8 kg/4 lb crab apples
1·2 litres/2 pints water

1·8–2·25 kg/4–5 lb sugar

1 Wash the fruit, then cut away any damaged parts, and cut any large fruits into halves or quarters, so that they are all about the same size.
2 Put the crab apples into a saucepan with the water and boil gently until the fruit is soft and pulpy.
3 Have ready a large nylon sieve lined with some muslin or

chemist's gauze and set over a large bowl.

4 Tip the apple mixture into the sieve and leave overnight to drip through.

5 Measure the liquid and put it into a saucepan with 450 g/1 lb sugar for every 600 ml/1 pint.

6 Heat gently, stirring, until the sugar has dissolved, then bring to the boil.

7 Boil for 10–15 minutes. Test for a set (p.510) and when this point is reached, remove from the heat and pour into warmed, sterilized jars (p.510). Cover, seal and label when cold.

PECTIN CONTENT OF FRUITS AND VEGETABLES

Pectin is a carbohydrate found in the cell walls of plants. It is important for the setting of jams and jellies. The pectin content of fruits varies (see below). Pectin can be bought and is useful for making preserves from ingredients with a low pectin content, such as rose petals, in Rose Petal Jam (p.507). It is widely available in liquid form from supermarkets.

*high in acid

High	Medium	Low
*Cooking and crab apples	Under-ripe apricots	Cherries
*Cranberries	*Bilberries	Elderberries
*Currants, black, red and white	Blackberries	Japonica
*Damsons	*Greengages	Marrows
*Gooseberries (should be under-ripe)	*Loganberries	Medlars
*Grapefruit	*Mulberries	Peaches (dried ones are best)
*Lemons	Nectarines	
*Limes	Ripe plums	Rhubarb
*Oranges	*Under-ripe raspberries	Under-ripe strawberries
Plums, if under-ripe,* especially yellow ones	*Sloes	
Quinces		

MAKING REDUCED-SUGAR JAMS AND JELLIES

The sugar in standard recipes can be reduced by 20% without affecting the set. This jam will not keep for more than about a month in a cool place, or 6—8 weeks in a refrigerator.

A few sprigs of sweet cicely cooked with acid fruit counteracts the sharpness so that less sugar is needed.

Lemon Curd

Tangy and delicious, and very easy to make.

MAKES 450 G/1LB

75 g/3 oz butter
grated rind and juice of 2 large, well-scrubbed lemons

225 g/8 oz caster sugar
3 eggs, beaten

1 Put all the ingredients into the top of a double saucepan or a heatproof bowl set over a saucepan of boiling water, making sure the base of the bowl does not touch the water.
2 Stir until the sugar has dissolved, then continue to cook gently for about 20 minutes, stirring often, until the curd thickens.
3 Strain into jars. Cover, seal and label when cold, then store in a cool, dry place.

Mary's Marmalade

This recipe, which was given to me by a friend who is an expert marmalade-maker, makes a light marmalade with a tangy flavour. It's easy to make with a blender or food processor.

MAKES ABOUT 4·5 KG/10 LB

12 Seville oranges
1 sweet orange
2 small lemons

2 litres/3½ pints water
2·25 kg/5 lb sugar
a knob of butter

1 Scrub the oranges and lemons well, then quarter them and remove the pips.

2 Put the pips into a piece of muslin and tie loosely with string.

3 Purée the oranges and lemons with the water in a blender or food processor. Put into a bowl with the bag of pips; leave overnight.

4 Next day, transfer mixture to a pan and simmer, uncovered, for 2 hours.

5 Put the puréed orange and lemon mixture into a large saucepan or preserving pan, strain in the pip liquid and bring to the boil. Add the sugar and cook, stirring often, until setting point is reached (p.510).

6 Remove from the heat and stir in the butter. Cool slightly, then pour into warmed, sterilized jars (p.510). Cover, seal and label when cold.

Pressure Cooker Marmalade

Pressure cooking cuts out messy preparation.

MAKES 3·1 KG/7 LB

12 *Seville oranges*	2·7 *litres/4½ pints cold water*
2 *lemons*	2·7–3·1 *kg/6–7 lb sugar*
	a knob of butter

1 Scrub the oranges and lemons, then put them into a pressure cooker with 1·2 litres/2 pints of the water. Cook at 6·75 kg/15 lb pressure for 25 minutes, or until the oranges are completely soft.

2 Drain juice into a non-metal bowl.

3 When the fruit is cool enough to handle, scoop the insides of the fruit away from the skin, using a teaspoon.

4 Sieve the pulp and add the purée to the bowl of juice.

5 Cut the peel into shreds and add this to the bowl, with the remaining water. Cover and leave overnight.

6 Next day, measure the mixture into a preserving pan. Bring to boil, then add 450 g/1 lb sugar for every 600 ml/1 pint.

7 Heat gently until the sugar has dissolved, then bring to the boil and boil until setting point is reached (p.510).

8 Remove from heat and stir in butter. Leave to settle for 15 minutes, then pour into warmed, sterilized jars (p.510). Cover, seal and label when cold.

SUGAR-FREE MARMALADE

Use 450 ml/15 fl oz freshly squeezed orange juice (ready-squeezed orange juice is not suitable) and the thinly pared rind of 1 orange and 1 lemon, well scrubbed. Make as for Sugar-free Mixed Berry Jam (p.511), boiling the mixture until the rind is soft before adding the apple juice concentrate.

V

Sweet Spiced Apricot Chutney

This is a sweet, spicy chutney, rather like mango chutney. It can be made with peaches or plums instead of apricots.

MAKES 1·8–2 KG/4–4½ LBS

1·8 kg/4 lb fresh apricots or 700 g/ 1½ lb dried apricots, soaked in water overnight, then drained

2 small cooking apples, peeled, cored and chopped

100 g/4 oz raisins

600 ml/1 pint distilled vinegar

350 g/12 oz granulated or demerara sugar

1 tablespoon ground ginger

3 garlic cloves, crushed

1 teaspoon freshly grated nutmeg

¼ teaspoon cayenne pepper

1 teaspoon salt

1 Put all the ingredients into a large saucepan or preserving pan.
2 Bring to the boil, then cook gently, uncovered, stirring occasionally, for about 1½ hours, until the mixture is thick and no excess liquid appears when it is parted with the spoon.

3 Spoon the mixture into warmed, sterilized jars (p.510) and cover immediately with airtight, vinegar-proof tops. Label when cold. Store in a cool, dry place.

BASIC CHUTNEY-MAKING

To make chutney, you cook together a mixture of chopped fruits and vegetables, including onions and dried fruit such as raisins or chopped dates, with vinegar, sugar and spices. The chutney should be simmered gently, uncovered, for 1—3 hours, until nearly all the vinegar has disappeared and when you part the mixture with a spoon the channel does not immediately fill with liquid. The chutney will thicken up more as it cools.

The covers for chutney and pickles are important as the vinegar may corrode metal, and will evaporate through paper coverings. So use plastic caps or synthetic covering material, or line metal covers with vinegar-proof paper.

Pieces cut from a wide (10 cm/ 4-inch) bandage, or some surgical gauze, from the chemist, can be used for tying up the pickling spices. Secure with string, then loop this round the handle of the pan, for easy removal.

Chutneys vary a good deal in spiciness, fruitiness and the balance of sweet and sour. So it's a good idea to make up a new recipe in a small quantity, to try. But remember most chutneys, pickles and relishes need at least 6—8 weeks to mature before you can judge their true flavour.

Apple Chutney

V

An easy chutney to make, with a deliciously spicy flavour.

MAKES ABOUT 2·7 KG/6 LB

1·4 kg/3 lb cooking apples, peeled, cored and diced
1·4 kg/3 lb onions, peeled and chopped
450 g/1 lb sultanas
700 g/1½ lb soft dark brown sugar
600 ml/1 pint malt vinegar
25 g/1 oz ground ginger
25 g/1 oz salt
½ teaspoon cayenne pepper

1 Put all the ingredients into a preserving pan and bring to the boil.

2 Reduce the heat and simmer gently, uncovered, for about 1½–2 hours, stirring occasionally, until the mixture is very thick and no excess liquid appears when it is parted with a wooden spoon.

3 Spoon the mixture into warmed, sterilized jars (p.510) and cover immediately with airtight covers (snap-on plastic covers are ideal – avoid metal which the vinegar may corrode). Label when cold.

4 This chutney improves with keeping, stored in a cool, dry place.

 ## Bread and Butter Pickles

Delicious on bread and butter, and very easy to make.

MAKES ABOUT 1·8 KG/4 LB

900 g/2 lb cucumber, washed and
  sliced
2 large onions, peeled and sliced
1 large green pepper, de-seeded
  and chopped
50 g/2 oz salt
450 ml/15 fl oz white wine vinegar
  or cider vinegar

350 g/12 oz soft light brown sugar
½ teaspoon ground turmeric
½ teaspoon ground cloves
2 teaspoons mustard seed
½ teaspoon celery seed

1 Put the cucumber into a bowl with the onion and pepper. Sprinkle with the salt, mix well, and leave for at least 3 hours.

2 Rinse the vegetables thoroughly under the cold tap. Drain well and put into a large saucepan with the vinegar.

3 Bring to the boil and simmer for about 20 minutes until vegetables are tender.

4 Add the sugar and spices to the pan and heat gently until the sugar has dissolved.

5 Bring to the boil, then remove from the heat, pour into a bowl, cover and leave until cold.

6 Spoon the mixture into warmed, sterilized jars (p.510) and immediately cover with airtight, vinegar-proof tops. Label when cold and store in a cool, dry place.

Preserved Kumquats

This is an attractive way to use baby kumquat oranges. They are delicious spooned over ice cream, or served as they are, chilled, with some whipped cream and a scattering of almonds. Packed into pretty jars, they make good presents, and keep well for up to 6 months.

MAKES 2 × 600-ML/1-PINT JARS

700 g/1½ lb kumquats
450 g/1 lb granulated sugar

600 ml/1 pint water
6 tablespoons brandy

1 Scrub the kumquats, then prick them all over with a fine skewer.
2 Put the sugar and water into a saucepan and heat gently until the sugar has dissolved, then bring to the boil.
3 Add the kumquats, cover and cook gently for about 15 minutes, or until they are very tender and almost transparent.
4 Using a slotted spoon, take the kumquats out of the syrup and place in warmed, sterilized jars (p.510).
5 Add the brandy, then pour in enough of the cooking syrup to cover the kumquats. Cover, seal and label when cold, then store in a cool, dry place.

Spiced Orange Slices

These spicy orange slices are good with cold nut or lentil roasts.

MAKES ABOUT 4·5 KG/10 LB

12 thin-skinned oranges
1·1 kg/2½ lb soft light brown sugar
600 ml/1 pint white wine vinegar or cider vinegar

12 whole cloves
5 cm/4 inches cinnamon stick
½ teaspoon ground mace or 6–8 mace blades

1 Scrub and dry the oranges. Slice them about 3 mm/⅛ inch thick; remove the pips.

2 Put the orange slices into a large saucepan and cover with cold water. Bring to the boil and simmer gently, covered, until the orange skin is just tender — about 20—30 minutes.

3 Put the remaining ingredients into another large saucepan and heat gently until the sugar has dissolved, then boil for 3 minutes.

4 Using a slotted spoon, remove the orange slices from the pan and add to the vinegar mixture.

5 Add enough of the orange cooking liquid to cover the orange slices, then simmer them gently until tender but not disintegrated — 35—45 minutes.

6 Remove from the heat and leave the oranges in the syrup for 24 hours.

7 Remove the orange slices with a slotted spoon and place in warmed, sterilized jars (p.510), filling them no more than half full.

8 Bring the syrup to boiling point, then boil for a few minutes to reduce slightly.

9 Cool for 15 minutes, then pour the syrup into the jars, filling them to the top. Cover immediately with airtight, vinegar-proof tops. Label the jars when cold. Store them in a cool, dry place for 4 weeks before using.

Sweets

Making sweets is frivolous but fun, and, as with puddings, I'm all for the occasional indulgence. The sweets in this section are the ones I find most popular and easy to make, without the need for any special equipment. Home-made sweets make a delightful treat; they can be served as petits fours at the end of a meal and they also make attractive gifts and bazaar items. If you're giving them away, it's worth making them look extra good, in bonbon cases, jars and pretty boxes, small baskets lined with a doily, or in cones made of coloured lightweight card or twists of coloured cellophane, with decorations of hearts, flowers and ribbons . . .

Fruit Snack Bites [V]

A healthy sweet that contains no added sugar.
In my experience children like these as long as
they don't have them too often!

MAKES 64

350 g/12 oz mixed dried fruit, such
 as dates, apricots, peaches and
 raisins
100 g/4 oz brazil nuts
100 g/4 oz desiccated coconut
 (unsweetened)

grated rind of 1 orange or lemon
1–2 tablespoons fresh orange juice
a little extra desiccated coconut for
 coating

1 Put the dried fruit and brazil nuts into a food processor and whizz until finely chopped. Or chop the dried fruits very finely by hand, grind the nuts and mix together.
2 Add the 100 g/4 oz desiccated coconut, grated citrus rind and enough orange juice to make the mixture stick together, and

process again, or mix the ingredients very well by hand.

3 Put the desiccated coconut into a shallow bowl. Roll the dried fruit mixture into small balls and toss in the coconut until they are thoroughly coated.

4 Place on trays and chill the fruit snack bites in the fridge for 1–2 hours, until they have firmed up.

HEALTHY SWEET IDEAS FOR CHILDREN

Dried fruits make natural sweets; add a mixture of sun-dried raisins, dates and apricots in a twist of clingfilm to a child's lunch box. For children over 6, replace the stone in dates with a whole almond or small brazil nut. For younger children, replace the stone with a paste of ground almonds and honey.

Coat peeled banana chunks first in clear honey, then in carob powder and chopped nuts. Freeze until firm. Eat as frozen sweets, or insert sticks before freezing and eat as lollies.

V

Treacle Toffee

MAKES ABOUT 600 G/1¼ LB

175 g/6 oz demerara sugar
75 g/3 oz butter or vegan
  margarine
250 g/9 oz treacle

3 tablespoons water
¼ teaspoon cream of tartar
extra butter for greasing

1 Grease a 20-cm/8-inch square tin, then line with non-stick baking parchment.

2 Put the sugar, butter or vegan margarine, treacle and water into a heavy-based saucepan. Heat gently until the sugar has dissolved, then bring to the boil, remove from the heat and add the cream of tartar.

3 Return the pan to the heat and boil until the mixture reaches 119–122c/246–252f, the hard ball stage (p.525), stirring from time to time.

4 Pour the mixture into the prepared tin. Leave until nearly set, then mark into squares.

5 When the toffee is completely cold and set, turn it out of the tin and break into squares.

CLEANING A TOFFEE PAN

To clean a sticky toffee pan, fill the pan with water and bring to the boil. The toffee will melt and can be poured away with the water.

Chocolate Rum Truffles

MAKES 36

225 g/8 oz plain chocolate
300 ml/10 fl oz double cream

2 tablespoons rum
cocoa powder for coating

1 Break the chocolate into pieces and put into a heavy-based saucepan with the cream.
2 Heat very gently until the chocolate has melted, then remove from the heat, transfer to a bowl and cool.
3 Add the rum, then beat until pale and thick. Chill in the refrigerator until firm enough to handle.
4 Sprinkle some cocoa on a plate, then put heaped teaspoons of the mixture on to this and sprinkle with more cocoa.
5 Roll each piece of mixture in cocoa, to make a truffle, and place in a bonbon case or on a small serving dish.
6 Chill until ready to serve.

Creamy Fudge

I've tried many fudge recipes, and this one I always find the best.

MAKES ABOUT 1 KG/2¼ LB

100 g/4 oz butter
1 × 425-g/15-oz can condensed milk

450 g/1 lb caster sugar

1 Line a 20-cm/8-inch square tin with non-stick baking parchment.

2 Put the butter, milk and sugar into a large, heavy-based saucepan.

3 Heat gently, stirring, over a low heat, until the sugar has dissolved.

4 Raise the heat and boil for 15 minutes, stirring all the time, or until the mixture starts to come away from the sides of the pan.

5 Pour the mixture into the tin. Leave to cool at room temperature.

6 Just before the fudge is cold, mark the fudge into squares. Cut into squares with a sharp knife when it is completely cold.

V Carob, Cashew and Honey Sweets

Another healthy sweet that children like in moderation. These sweets are rich and nourishing: a little goes a long way.

MAKES 21 PIECES

100 g/4 oz cashew nuts
1 tablespoon carob powder

a few drops of vanilla extract
1 tablespoon thick honey

1 Put the cashew nuts, carob and vanilla into a food processor and whizz to a powder. Or grind the nuts finely, then put into a bowl with the carob and vanilla.

2 Add the honey and process the mixture again (or mix by hand) until it forms a stiff paste.

3 Put the mixture into a 20-cm/8-inch square tin and press it out so that it is 1 cm/½ inch thick (it will fill only about a third of the tin).

4 Chill in the refrigerator until firm, then cut into squares.

Variation

CAROB, BRAZIL NUT AND HONEY SWEETS

Use brazil nuts instead of the cashew nuts, if preferred, and make the sweets as described above.

SUGAR BOILING STAGES

A cooking thermometer is useful for sweet-making, but not essential, because the mixture behaves quite distinctively at different temperatures:

Thread
(120c/225f): a little of the mixture forms a short thread when placed between finger and thumb and pulled apart

Soft ball
(135c/240f): a little of the syrup put into a cup of cold water forms a small soft ball

Hard ball
(140c/255f): a little of the mixture forms a hard ball when dropped into a cup of cold water

Crack
(150c/280f): a drop of the syrup put into cold water becomes brittle

Caramel
(160c/312f): the syrup turns a dark brown colour

When testing the sugar syrup, remove it from the heat to prevent further cooking.

Menu Ideas

A Typical Day of Healthy Vegetarian Eating

Breakfast

Orange or grapefruit juice
Whole-grain muesli with milk and raisins
Wholewheat toast with honey or marmalade
or
Fresh fruits in season
Tea, coffee or herb tea

Lunch

Salad sandwiches
or
Baked Potato (p.283) with grated carrot and watercress
or
A vitality salad of shredded lettuce, chopped tomatoes, grated carrot
and beetroot, sprouted beans, chopped nuts
or
A bowl of Leek and Potato Soup (p.202) and wholewheat bread
or
Hummus (p.217) with Crudités (p.218) or pitta bread
Apple
Tea, coffee or herb tea

Evening meal

Tagliatelle Verde with Lentil Sauce (p.374)
Green salad with avocado and fresh herbs
Apricot and Orange Fool (p.418)
Tea, coffee or herb tea

Snacks

Wholewheat bread
Nuts
Fresh and dried fruit

Seasonal Meals

Early Summer Celebration

Asparagus Soup (p.197)

Moulded Layered Soufflé (p.336)

surrounded by baby carrots, cooked spinach, mangetouts, cherry tomatoes,
broad beans, young whole turnips

Chocolate Pots (p.414)

Macaroons

Summer Supper for Two

Asparagus with Hollandaise Sauce (p.262)

Summer Linguine (p.378)

Blackcurrant Sorbet (p.420)

Late Summer Supper for Friends

Chilled Lettuce Soup (p.196)

Brazil Nut Roast en Croûte (p.352)
Horseradish Sauce (p.178)
Potato Purée (p.281)
Carrot Purée (p.281)
French Beans

Little Coffee Custards (p.412)

Early Autumn Lunch for Four

Roasted Hazelnut Soup (p.204)
Quick Wholewheat Rolls (p.491)

Stuffed Aubergines à la Provençale (p.287)
Fresh Tomato Sauce (p.253)
Potato Purée (p.281)
Buttered Spinach (p.79)

Poached Pears with Sabayon Sauce (p.450) and Pear Sorbet (p.420)

Autumn Meal for Six

Pumpkin Soup (p.113)

Mushroom Flan (p.394)
Red Cabbage Casserole (p.268)
Potato Purée (p.281)

Poached Pears with Cinnamon Cream (p.124)

Celebration Autumn Meal

Pumpkin Soup (p.113)

Wild Mushrooms in Cream with Pastry Leaves (p.404)
Potato Purée (p.281)
Chicory, Watercress and Walnut Salad (p.241)

Blackberry Sorbet (p.420)

Winter Brunch for Four

Rösti (p.282)

Scrambled Eggs (p.156)
Warm Quick Wholewheat Rolls (p.491)
Grilled Tomatoes

Fresh Fruit Salad (p.426)

Winter Brunch for Six

Classic Risotto (p.366)

Scrambled Eggs (p.156)
Mushrooms in Cream (p.115)

Muffins (p.491)
or
Warm Croissants with Assorted Preserves
Black Grapes

Coffee and Tea

Winter Brunch for Eight

Millet Pilaf with Nuts and Raisins (p.367)
Rösti (p.282)
Scrambled Eggs (p.156)

Waffles with Clear Honey (p.445)

Dried Fruit Compote (p.149)

Warming Winter Supper

Leek and Potato Soup (p.202)

Chilli Con Carne Vegetariana (p.310)
Baked Potatoes with Soured Cream (p.283)
Green Salad

Crepes Suzettes (p.448)

A Simple Winter Supper

Carrot and Ginger Soup (p.193)

Savoury Brown Lentil Stew (p.316)
Baked Potatoes (p.283)
Technicolour Cabbage Salad (p.245)

Regional Meals

Italian Supper

Sweet Carrot and Fennel Salad, decorated with a few black olives
(p.242)

Gnocchi alla Romana (p.341)
Italian Tomato Sauce (p.254)
Chicory, Watercress and Walnut Salad (p.241)

Fresh Fruit Salad (p.426)
Almond Tuiles (p.486)

Meal with a Mexican Flavour

Guacamole with Tortilla Chips (p.218)

Tomatoes with Courgette and Sweetcorn Stuffing (p.293)
Boiled Potatoes with Butter and Parsley

Chocolate Pots (p.414)

Japanese Meal

Miso Soup with Bean Curd (p.201)

Vegetable Tempura with Dipping Sauce (p.297)
Sweet Vinegared Rice (p.361)
Stir-fried Carrots with Watercress and Sesame Seeds (p.268)

Tangerine and Lychee Fruit Salad (p.427)

Chinese-style Meal

Chinese-style Fried Rice (p.363)
Chinese-style Mushrooms (p.273)
Stir-fried Carrots (p.268)

Lychees and Mandarin Orange Segments

Russian Supper

Beetroot Soup, chilled or hot (p.209)

Mushroom Pâté en Croûte (p.401)
Soured Cream and Herb Dressing (p.233)
Buttered Cabbage with Caraway Seeds (p.85)
Boiled Potatoes (p.102)

Pashka (p.428)

Middle Eastern Meal

Hummus (p.217)
Warm Pitta Bread Strips

Rice Pilaf with Apricots, Raisins and Pine Nuts (p.362)
Vegetable Kebabs (p.302)
Avocado, Lettuce and Tomato Salad (p.244)

Arranged Fruit Salad (p.427)

Coffee

Middle Eastern Supper for Friends

Stuffed Vine Leaves (p.215)
Hummus (p.217) with Warm Pitta Bread
Aubergine Dip (p.219)
Felafel (p.311)

Middle Eastern Chick Pea Stew (p.315)

Rose Cheesecake (p.431)
or
Yogurt with Dates and Honey
or
Fresh Figs

Family Meals

Family Sunday Lunch

Pease Pudding (p.309)
Yorkshire Pudding
Vegetarian Gravy (p.255)
Mint Sauce (p.170)
Buttered Brussels Sprouts (p.83)
Roast Potatoes (p.103)

Country Apple Pie (p.439)
or
Rhubarb Crumble (p.441)

Late Summer Sunday Lunch

Chilled Cucumber and Yogurt Soup (p.210)

Marrow with Hazelnut Stuffing (p.289)
Apple Sauce (p.122)
Vegetarian Gravy (p.255)
Roast Potatoes (p.103)
Carrot Purée (p.282)
Green Beans

Country Apple Pie (p.439)

Winter Sunday Lunch

Chilled Two-colour Soup (p.211)

Chestnut Roast (p.348)
Sauce Soubise (p.258)
Red Cabbage Casserole (p.268)
Braised Celery Hearts (p.270)

Traditional Trifle (p.424)

Easy Summer Garden Brunch

Savoury Olive Mushroom Cake (p.339)
Green Salad (p.76) with Walnut Vinaigrette (p.229)
Tomato and Basil Salad (p.108)

Cheeseboard and Assorted Breads

Bowl of Fresh Summer Fruits: Peaches, Nectarines, Figs

A Special Picnic

Mushroom and Herb Terrine with Melba Toast (p.222)

French Onion Flan (p.386)
Green-bean Salad with Radiccio (p.249)
Pink Potato Salad (p.249)

Peaches

Warming Family Supper

Hazelnut and Vegetable Crumble (p.350)
Baked Potatoes (p.283)
Steamed Broccoli
Vegetarian Gravy (p.255)
or
Italian Tomato Sauce (p.254)

Fresh Fruit
or
Pancakes with Lemon and Honey (p.447)

Bonfire Party

Warming food to come back to!

Leek and Potato Soup (p.202)
Warm Quick Wholewheat Rolls (p.492)

Parmigiana (p.304)
Crisp Green Salad (p.76)

Linzertorte (p.436)

Vegetarian 'Traditional' Christmas Dinner

Celery and Stilton Soup (p.198)

White Nut Roast with Herb Stuffing (p.357)
Cranberry Sauce (p.260)
Vegetarian Gravy (p.255)
Bread Sauce (p.262)
Roast Potatoes (p.103)
Baby Brussels Sprouts (p.83)
Glazed Carrots (p.271)

Christmas Pudding (p.442)
or
Christmas Parfait (p.422)

Quick and Easy Meals

Easy Summer Meal

Avocado Vinaigrette (p.229)

Couscous with Spicy Chick Pea Stew (p.369)
Green Salad (p.76)
Tomato Salad (p.108)

Strawberries with Cream or thick Greek Yogurt

Quick Autumn Lunch

Salad of Feuille de Chêne, Chèvre Cheese and Walnuts with Walnut
Vinaigrette (p.226)

Taglioni Verde with Tomato Sauce and Aubergines (p.376)
Crusty Bread

Fresh Fruit Bowl

Coffee

Easy Autumn Meal for Six

Taglioni Verde with Tomato Sauce and Aubergines (p.376)
Chicorȳ, Watercress and Walnut Salad (p.241) *with* Walnut
Vinaigrette (p.229)

Selection of White Cheeses, (including a cream one and one or two
goat's cheeses)
Assorted Breads and Crackers

Pear or Blackberry Sorbet (p.420)

Espresso, Filter or Capuccino Coffee

Speedy Supper

Pasta with Pesto (p.257)

Quick Savoury Nut Roast (p.351)
Stir-fried Carrots with Watercress and Sesame Seeds (p.268)
Potato Purée (p.281)

Black and Green Grapes

Spur of the Moment Supper for Two

Avocado Vinaigrette (p.229)
or
Cannellini Bean Salad with Fresh Herbs, served with Warm
Wholewheat Rolls (p.492)

Tagliatelle with Gorgonzola and Walnuts (p.371)
Green Salad (p.76)

Fresh Figs
or
Honeyed Poached Pears with Poire Williams Liqueur

Coffee

Quick Easy Supper for Two

Charentais Melon Halves

Eggs Florentine (p.320)
Crusty Wholewheat Stick
Tomato Salad (p.108)

Assorted Yogurts

Quick Late-night Supper for Two

Guacamole (p.218)

Cheese Fondue with French Bread (p.325)
Japanese Flower Salad (p.246)

Passion Fruit Sorbet (p.420)

Easy Supper for Four

Pears with Piquant Cream Dressing (p.224)
Wholewheat Pasta and Mushroom Bake (p.373)
Stir-fried Carrots with Watercress and Sesame Seeds (p.268)
Fresh Fruit or Linzertorte (p.436)

Freezer Supper for Six

Flaky Roquefort or Spinach and Fennel Pastries (p.227)

Mixed Vegetable Lasagne (p.379)
Green Salad (p.76)

Orange Parfait (p.422)
or
Vanilla Ice Cream (p.413)
with Raspberry Coulis (p.448)

Quick Main Courses

Pistou (p.206), using canned beans, with warm rolls and a few Crudités (p.218)

Cheese and Fresh Herb Dip (p.214), Hummus (p.217) or Roquefort Dip (p.221) with Crudités (p.218), pitta bread and fruit

Greek Salad (p.252) with crusty bread and fresh fruit

Spring Vegetable Braise (p.269), Ratatouille (p.278) or Peperonata (p.276) with brown rice (p.67)

Stuffed Jacket Potatoes (p.286) with lettuce, tomato, cucumber and grated carrot

Sweet and Sour Vegetable Stir-fry with Almonds (p.299) with brown rice (p.67)

Multicolour Butter Beans (p.307), buttered noodles or granary bread

Red Kidney Bean Stew (p.308) with Baked Potatoes (p.283)

Felafel in Pitta Pockets (p.311)

Baked Eggs (p.321), Pipérade (p.322) or Omelette (p.329)

Cheese Soufflé (p.334) with French beans

Savoury Olive Mushroom Cake (p.339) with a green salad

Quick Savoury Nut Roast (p.351) with mashed potatoes and frozen peas

Paella Vegetariana (p.364) Classic Risotto (p.366)

Fusilli Verde with Mushrooms and Cream (p.372)

Tagliatelle with Gorgonzola (p.371)

Tagliatelle Verde with Lentil Sauce (p.374)

Macaroni Cheese (p.380)

Taglioni Verde with Tomato Sauce and Aubergines (p.376)

Summer Linguine (p.378)

Quick Bread Pizza (p.503)

Main Courses for Slimmers

These recipes are relatively low in calories. Served with a generous amount of lightly cooked vegetables or salad dressed with lemon juice, they can help you to lose weight:

Corn Chowder (p.205) made with half the amount of fat

Golden Lentil Soup (p.203)

Courgettes with Carrot, Ginger and Almond Stuffing (p.288)

Stuffed Tomatoes (p.291)

Stuffed Aubergines (p.287)

Sweet and Sour Vegetable Stir-fry with Almonds (p.299)

Vegetable Hotpot (p.301)

Vegetable Curry (p.303) with brown rice

Lentils and Mushrooms au Gratin (p.308)

Chilli con Carne Vegetariana (p.310)

Spicy Lentil Burgers (p.313)

Lentil Shepherd's Pie (p.314)

Savoury Lentil Loaf (p.318)

Pizza (p.327)

Spanish Omelette (p.331)

Spinach Roulade (p.338)

Savoury Cheese Pudding (p.340)

Cashew Nut Roast (p.345)

Rice Pilaf (p.362)

Paella Vegetariana (p.364)

Millet Pilaf with Nuts and Raisins (p.367)

Barley Casserole (p.368)

Couscous (p.66)

Spaghetti Bolognese Vegetariana (p.375)

Tagliatelle Verde with Lentil Sauce (p.374)

Fusille Colbuco with Aubergine and Wine Sauce (p.377)

Children's Favourites

Children have their own individual tastes, but these are the dishes which I've found to be generally popular:

Watercress Soup (p.195)

Golden Lentil Soup (p.203)

Leek and Potato Soup (p.202)

Cheese and Fresh Herb Dip (p.214)

Red Kidney Bean Salad (p.234)

Favourite Coleslaw (p.242)

Baked Potatoes (p.283)

Stuffed Jacket Potatoes (p.286) with Fresh Tomato Sauce (p.253)

Potato and Cheese Layer (p.300)

Savoury Lentil Loaf (p.318)

Cheese Fondue (p.325)

Cheese and Parsley Fritters (p.326)

Pizza (p.327)

Spaghetti Bolognese Vegetariana (p.375)

Tagliatelle Verde with Lentil Sauce (p.374)

Macaroni Cheese (p.380)

French Onion Flan (p.386)

Savoury Cheshire Cheese and Onion Pie (p.392)

Chocolate Mould (p.413)

Any of the ice creams, but the Chocolate Ice Cream (p.416) particularly (and it's healthy)

Fresh Fruit Salad (p.426)

Pineapple Jelly (p.424)

Treacle Tart (p.438)

Fruit Pie (p.441)

Steamed Pudding (p.446)

Pancakes (p.449)

Any spongy cakes, and particularly Quick Buns (p.464)

Parkin (p.462)

543

Special Menus

*All the Special Menus
can be found among the illustrations*

Sunday Brunch

SERVES 8

Gratin Dauphinois
p.284

Wild Mushrooms in Cream with Pastry Leaves
p.404

Pipérade
p.322

Dried Fruit Compote
p.149

The preparation for this brunch can mainly be done the night before so that you can have a lie-in on Sunday morning if you feel like it. Don't forget to put the Gratin Dauphinois into the oven in good time. Move it to the coolest part of the oven (or take it out and keep warm) when you want to bake the pastry leaves quickly for the Wild Mushrooms in Cream with Pastry Leaves; these can be cut out the night before and kept overnight in the fridge. The Dried Fruit Compote can also be kept in the fridge, chilling, until the last minute.

Make the vegetable part of the Pipérade the night before, too. Then all you have to do at the last minute is bake the pastry leaves, heat through the wild mushroom mixture, and finish making the Pipérade after your guests have arrived. To drink, you could serve good spicy Bloody Marys, made by flavouring tomato juice with salt, pepper, lemon juice and a good dash each of Worcester sauce (choose a vegetarian one, without anchovy extract) and Tabasco, then serve in tall wine glasses with ice and vodka. Or, better still, offer Bucks Fizz, made from equal parts of freshly squeezed orange juice and non-vintage champagne, or a fruit juice-based cup using apple or orange juice.

Spring Dinner Party

SERVES 6

Mushroom and Herb Terrine with Melba Toast
p.222

Paella Vegetariana with Artichokes
p.365

Mixed Leaf Salad with Guacamole Dressing
p.76 and p.218

Glazed Red Fruit Tart
p.435

This is a relaxed, informal dinner party with fresh flavours. It is also very easy to prepare. Both the Mushroom and Herb Terrine and the Glazed Red Fruit Tart can be made in advance. The Melba Toast can also be made the day before and wrapped in foil to keep it crisp, although it doesn't take long to do on the day. Serve Guacamole as a salad dressing and garnish it with chopped tomato, onion and chilli. The main course of Paella is informal but delicious, and looks attractive served from the pan in which it was cooked (if this is presentable!); otherwise, transfer it to a warmed, shallow dish just before serving.

Choose a wine to reflect the informal nature of the meal; I would be inclined to go Spanish and choose a Rioja, or maybe a medium-dry white wine, with enough power to cope with the flavours of the Paella — a Chenin Blanc or a young Riesling, perhaps.

Summer Celebration

SERVES 6

Iced Beetroot Soup with Dill
p.209

Warm Herb and Onion Bread
p.492

Pine Nut Roulade with Asparagus
Hollandaise Filling
p.353

Courgettes with Herbs
New Potatoes
Bitter Leaf Salad
p.76

Champagne Sorbet with Wild Strawberries
p.422

This is a delectable meal, but not too difficult to cope with, because the Iced Beetroot Soup with Dill and the Champagne Sorbet can both be made in advance. The Pine Nut Roulade does need some last-minute attention; get it all ready (except for garnishing) before you sit down to the meal so that it can be heating through in the oven while you eat your soup.

The wine served with the roulade needs to be strong enough to support the flavour of the asparagus; perhaps a mature Graves or a medium-dry wine with a honeyed flavour such as a Savennières or Chenin Blanc. Finish this off with a cheeseboard if you are serving one, then end the meal with a flourish by serving chilled champagne with the sorbet.

Quick and Easy Supper

SERVES 4

Fusille Colbuco with Aubergine and Wine Sauce
p.377

Parmesan Cheese
Chicory, Watercress and Walnut Salad
p.241

Quick Cherry and Lime Cheesecake
p.429

This is a meal which you can whizz up on the spur of the moment, assuming you have some fresh salad vegetables in the fridge and the ingredients for the Quick Cherry and Lime Cheesecake. Otherwise, serve the pasta with some frozen vegetables which, hopefully, you have in the freezer, and offer fresh fruit or biscuits and cheese instead of a pudding, if you have them available.

First make the cheesecake, then while that is chilling prepare the Aubergine and Wine Sauce. While that cooks, wash the salad, make a dressing and, when the sauce is almost done, cook the pasta. Serve with whatever drink you happen to have in the kitchen: a chilled lager, or a wine with some body, to support all the flavours of the sauce, perhaps an Italian red, a Chianti, Barolo or Barbaresco, or a good value Cabernet Sauvignon from anywhere.

Family Lunch

SERVES 4–6

Tomato Soup with Basil
p.195

Garlic Bread
p.200

Cheese and Parsley Fritters with Parsley Sauce
p.326 and p.261

Healthy Chips
p.103

Green Beans

Fresh Fruit Salad
p.426

This is a warming lunch for a chilly winter Saturday, when everyone needs cheering up! Most children, in my experience, like this home-made Tomato Soup and they usually adore Garlic Bread, too. (If some don't like garlic, leave this out when you butter one end of the loaf.) The Cheese and Parsley Fritters are another winner, but get organized in advance for this, as the mixture has to get completely cold, before cutting; make it the evening before, or first thing in the morning. Since this is a day for spoiling the family, I've suggested chips and green beans to go with the fritters, with Fresh Fruit Salad for dessert, to balance the richness.

To drink, I suggest a sparkling fruit cup made from mixed apple and orange juices and soda water; or, if you feel like something alcoholic for the grown ups, I'd go Italian, with either a chilled white Soave or a red wine, a Chianti, perhaps.

Midsummer Wedding

SERVES 30

Pink Potato Salad
p.249

Asparagus Boats
p.391

Gruyère Roulade with Avocado Filling
p.338

Green Salad
p.76

Technicolour Cabbage Salad
p.245

Profiteroles
p.474

All the main preparation for this wedding buffet, with its pink theme, can be done in advance. Make the pastry cases (as thin as you can!) for the Asparagus Boats up to 4 weeks in advance and freeze. Fill them the day before the wedding, then warm them in the oven before serving.

Fill the roulade, assemble the salads and finish the profiteroles on the morning of the wedding. If you are a member of the bridal party, you will need a reliable friend to take over from you on the day, and mastermind the operation, together with someone to see to all the drinks and others to 'waitress'.

Phone round local catering hire firms well in advance to hire linen, plates, flat serving dishes, cups and saucers, cutlery. Book glasses for wine and champagne from the shop where you order these. Drink champagne throughout the wedding if your budget can stand it, otherwise welcome guests with a medium-dry white wine, such as a Vouvray which you can then drink throughout the meal, then, for the toast, pink champagne!

Vegetarian Barbecue

Get the barbecue lit in good time, so that it is at the white ash stage by the time you want to cook. I suggest that you cook the Saffron Rice beforehand, then keep it warm. Both the kebabs and burgers can be made in advance.

Brush the barbecue grill with oil and cook the kebabs on this for about 10–15 minutes, until the vegetables are tender, basting with the marinade. Fry the burgers for 10–15 minutes on an oiled baking sheet placed on the barbecue grill; turn them over once during cooking.

Prepare the baked apples as described on p. 00, filling them with dried fruit sprinkled with a little sherry or brandy and left overnight to marinate. Sprinkle them with a little brown sugar, dot some butter over and wrap in a double layer of kitchen foil. Cook on the barbecue grill for about 50 minutes, until tender.

Serve soft drinks as well as chilled beer, lager, or a white or rosé vin ordinaire, well chilled. Alternatively, sangria would be pleasant. Make this by mixing together a bottle of Spanish red wine and a bottle of lemonade, then adding a glass each of brandy and port, plenty of ice and a thinly sliced orange and lemon.

Autumn Dinner Party

SERVES 6

Salade Tiède
p.226

Vegetable Gougère with Peperonata Filling
p.406 and p.276

Potato Purée
p.281

Buttered Spinach
p.79

Apple Ice Cream with Blackberry Sauce
p.418

This is a warming dinner party full of fruity, autumn flavours. The salad can be mainly prepared in advance, ready for the hot Chèvre or goat's cheese to be added to the plates at the last minute. Both the Apple Ice Cream and the Blackberry Sauce can be made well in advance. Make the Peperonata for the Vegetable Gougère the night before, ready for reheating in the saucepan just before serving. The Gougère mixture can be put on to a shallow ovenproof serving dish and chilled in the fridge ready for popping into the oven 40 minutes before you want to serve it. Then just spoon the Peperonata into the centre. The potatoes can be sieved before you start the meal; add butter, cream and seasoning, but don't mix; cover the pan or bowl in a bain-marie, and keep warm, then mix the potatoes just before serving.

A sharp, flinty wine would go well with the salad – a Sancerre or a Pouilly Fumé would be ideal – and you could follow this with a medium-dry wine which goes well with vegetables, such as a Savennières, Vouvray or Macon Blanc, or you could serve a red Burgundy.

Christmas Dinner

All the traditional Christmas flavours — apart from the turkey, of course — are present in this dinner, and the Brazil Nut Roast en Croûte makes a handsome centrepiece. This can be made well in advance and kept in the fridge for a day or two, or frozen for up to 4 weeks. The pudding, of course, can also be made several weeks beforehand and kept in a cool, dry place. The Cranberry Sauce and Vegetarian Gravy can be made the day before. The Raspberry Coulis for the first course can be made the day before, too, but the dish needs to be assembled not more than an hour before you want to eat it. Garnish it with holly berries, but remove them before serving.

The nut and herb flavours in the roast need a firm wine to stand up to them, such as a Châteauneuf-du-Pape; or, if you prefer a white, choose a sturdy medium-dry one.

Children's Tea

SERVES 4–6

Little Basket of Crudités
p.218

Yogurt and Herb Dressing
p.233

Potato and Cheese Layer
p.300

Fresh Tomato Sauce
p.253

Peas

Chocolate Ice Cream with Crumbly Almond Biscuits
p.416 and p.485

This is a substantial meal for children arriving home from school ravenous, and features dishes which in my experience are always popular. The Potato and Cheese Layer is easy to make but allow time for it to cook. It is served with Tomato Sauce, Crudités and Yogurt and Herb Dressing – many children will eat vegetables raw that they wouldn't eat cooked!

I've never quite been able to understand why children like the Chocolate Ice Cream so much, but they always do, and as it's a low-fat, low-sugar one, I'm not arguing! A Crumbly Almond Biscuit goes well with it, or you could serve some slices of fresh fruit. To drink, whatever is your child's favourite healthy drink of the moment; sparkling apple or grape juice is usually popular, or apple juice concentrate, diluted with water or soda water.

Index